ACID CHRIST

Ken Kesey, LSD, and the Politics of Ecstasy

Mark Christensen

schaffner
press

Cover design: Jake Kiehle
Cover and interior photographs: Clyde Keller
Author photo on back cover: Clyde Keller
Author photo inside back cover: Greg Steiger
Book layout and design; jacket layout: Darci Slaten

Sections of this book have been previously published in different form and
have appeared in *Rolling Stone, Penthouse, High Times* and *Oregon Times.*

For information regarding sources and copyrighted material used in this book, contact
Schaffner Press, Inc.

This is a First Edition
Printed in the United States
2010
Schaffner Press, Inc. PO Box 41567 Tucson, AZ 85717

Library of Congress Cataloging-in-Publication Data

Christensen, Mark.
  Acid Christ : Ken Kesey, LSD and the politics of ecstasy / Mark Christensen. — 1st ed.
    p. cm.
  Includes bibliographical references and index.
  ISBN-13: 978-1-936182-00-8
  ISBN-10: 1-936182-00-9
  1. Kesey, Ken. 2. Authors, American—20th century—Biography. I. Title.
  PS3561.E667Z64 2010
  813'.54—dc22
  [B]
                                    2009036336

This book is a work of independent commentary and criticism about the life, times and work of a noteworthy and influential American author. It is not an authorized or definitive biography of Ken Kesey, and it is not endorsed by or affiliated with the Kesey family or any of the author's sources. Rather, the author provides a narrative that draws on both primary and secondary sources but reflects his own critical judgments. Every attempt has been made to identify and cite the original source materials that are quoted in the book. All such sources are used either with permission or pursuant to the Fair Use Doctrine. For further information on sources, see the acknowledgments and endnotes at the back of the book.

For Deb, Katie and Matt,
and in memory of David Kelly

Contents

PROLOGUE:
NEON RENAISSANCE MAN

"When you've got something like we've got you can't just sit on it and possess it, you've got to move off it and give it to other people. It only works if you bring other people into it."

—Ken Kesey

Old enough to have bought weed when most of it probably was, I grew up around the Kesey Chautauqua, whose personnel were space lumberjack demi-gods of literature and chaos, less actual than imagined, and—not too cosmopolitan. I first met the corporeal Kesey when my heroes were pretty much limited to John Reed, Rick Griffin, Fred Exley, the Byrds, Herman Kahn, Erma Bombeck, Rabbit Angstrom and the Midnight Rambler. I was puzzled. Who was he? The Kesey I remembered was healthy, almost big, but stood out because of the neon glow of his celebrity more than anything else.

As a college kid circa 1970, I expected Kesey to produce, in a book as thick as the Bible or a brick, what I, like the rest of my generation could not come up with on our own: The Answer. The problem: Kesey stood for community, not plans. ("Since we don't know where we're going we have to stick together in case someone gets there.") One did not "freak freely" according to a plan. So what then I wondered was…the *gestalt?*

Later, at age 27 I'd seen partial early drafts of *Sometimes a Great Notion* at the University of Oregon library. Kesey'd written three versions of key sections of the book—each seeming better than the last—at a time when I'd've given anything but my life to write one great version of *anything*. But when I met him, he seemed about as literary as Bronco Nagurski—he had the unassuming hyper-gregarious, kick-ass style of a frat boy turned hippie farmer turned high school football coach turned psychedelic Chevie salesman (he was promoting his Poetic Hoo-Haw arts festival at the time), an aw-shucks demi-god who did day labor during the height of his fame, or at least claimed to. By then, living-in-the-NOW Kesey had abandoned the novel, tired of the novelist's chore as a stagehand, having to supply the sun, moon, stars, chairs, tables, sofas, guns, Kleenex, fried chicken and femme fatales essential to the paper illusion, deciding: why not just, with a movie camera, *be the story yourself?*

Kesey's personal dramatis personae, his famous posse The Merry Pranksters, were soon revealed to me as a cross between a cult and a twenty-year-long fraternity party, at the helm of which Kesey—psychedelic America's leading figure of freedom and fun—reigned kingly as a clockwork control freak, a man who was much enamored of occult theories of history and who was said to plot the dreams and fates of those around him as adroitly as any good novelist ever plotted an imaginary cast of characters.

I was impressed. Friendlier to fame than fortune, Kesey had existed for me as a sort of medieval rustic monarch of the counterculture whose castle just happened to be—given the utopian rural ideal he championed—a barn, essentially a kid's fun house—a home fit more for Captain Kangaroo than William Faulkner.

But weren't groundbreaking novelists Zen-placid stone Buddhas who created and controlled a divinely revelatory universe? And weren't genius control freaks supposed to be in control of not only others but, well, themselves? For despite his commanding presence, after being around him for a while, Kesey didn't actually appear to be in control of much of anything. In fact, in ways he seemed like a great big kid. Energetic, jokey, always moving. He looked more like he was just making himself up as he went along.

But, given his awesome boy wonder bonafides, could that possibly be true?

* * *

As an alumnus of the University of Paul Krassner, who lived by his texts when I was in college, I had first intended to write the tale of how Krassner's patriotically seditious broadsheet *The Realist* was the core of Vietnam era social protest and how, as a relentless fashion critic of the emperor's new clothes, he scripted the yellow brick road map for cultural change in the 1960s, saved the Republic from corporate techno-fascism and provided the pivot around which all news media changed.

My idea: almost everything you think, feel, know or believe comes not from the Bible, science, Socrates, Avicenna, Descartes, Kant, Rousseau,

Hegel, Marx, Nietzsche or Tony Robbins but from the woefully under-recognized (that is to say sadly under-worshipped) Krassner. An early writer for *Mad* and *Playboy* who took elements from both, combined them with a brilliant libertarian political sensibility and a love of conspiracy theories, Krassner inspired the playbook for the Love Generation's 1960s Street Fighting Men—which had more to do with returning to the ideals of the American Revolution than achieving satori or killing your parents or your TV set.

A visionary's visionary (Krassner published his friend Lenny Bruce's obituary two years *before* Bruce died), a guru to the gurus—he had the ear of both Bob Dylan and John Lennon (and, on occasion, Lennon's wallet as well—John there in a pinch to underwrite *The Realist's* printing bill). *The Realist* was among the most inclusive, scary and funny catalogues of a world going haywire ever published. Krassner's formula combined investigative reporting with satire to create the template for everything from *Politically Incorrect with Bill Maher* and Jon Stewart's *The Daily Show,* to *Fahrenheit 9/11*, setting the bar for anti-authoritarian dissent before the Rolling Stones, *Rolling Stone* or Michael Moore.

Target of a vicious and surreal anti-Semitic campaign orchestrated by the FBI, variously identified as the most dangerous and funniest man in America, Krassner was, as author of "The Parts Left Out of the Kennedy Book"—in which he reported a horny, grieving LBJ having sex with a bullet wound in JFK's corpse—the true inventor of gonzo journalism. Not incidentally, he was also a pioneer of shock radio (Howard Stern owes the very idea of himself to Paul Krassner) and a founder of the Yippies—who ran a 500-pound pig, Pigasus, for President in 1968 (if he won, the Yippies vowed to eat him), upstaged the Democrat National Convention in Chicago so explosively that their theatrics were pivotal in changing the American media against the Vietnam War—and whose goals, demands, hopes, dreams, tactics and strategy were congealed thusly:

 * *"We will burn Chicago to the ground!"*
 * *"We will fuck on the beaches!"*
 * *"We demand the Politics of Ecstasy!"*
 * *"Acid for all!"*
 * *"Mandatory unemployment, let the machines do the work,"*

Essayist Ed McClanahan knighted Krassner "a latter-day Twain, a priapic Mencken…the best satirical journalist in America."[1]

Krassner was also the rare 60s popular figure who never traded recognition for money, megalomania or the Maharishi. Unlike "gospels" written by various gurus of that era's metaphysical heaven-on-earth—who used fantasy as fact to ignite a radical shape shift in the budding thought worlds of 20,000,000 Baby Boomers—atheist Krassner's "gospels" were significant because:

a) Despite the belly laughs, his was a thorough political vision based on one-man, one vote Jeffersonian Democracy, not a hookah dream, and

b) He was right. Branded a commie symp by mainstream media, Krassner noted that the only Marx and Lenin he knew were Groucho and John, and was a radical only if Richard Nixon, Spiro Agnew and J. Edgar Hoover represented the red, white and blue centrist norm.

But when I suggested a Krassner book to Krassner, Krassner suggested, better idea: that I should write about his pal, neo-Jacobin, wild-west woodsman cowboy outlaw novelist, American favorite son, Ken Kesey, "the undisputed king of the counterculture."

That was a thought. After all, Kesey had taken the CIA-financed illusion LSD from a curiosity to an inspiration to a sacrament to a Holy Grail that changed American culture forever if not for better—the paisley Promethean who lit the firestorm, the "first hippie," template for—if not the New Man—at least the new man-child, prototype for the anti-authoritarian "suburban-urchins" who rejected the lockstep conformity of the Eisenhower years. And that was just the beginning.

I was awed by Kesey's talents, awed more by how he had abandoned many of them, and fascinated by the evolution of his legend. As "King of the Counterculture," Kesey became key to guiding if not creating one of the greatest mass movements in contemporary history, a cultural tsunami that pushed an incredibly rich young consumer society away from *I pay, I take* consumption to a more nonmaterial, reflective way of living off the system.

---

1 And man of the people, too. He once told me, "I've had a lot of odd jobs. But it's hard for a humorist to answer phones at a suicide hotline. 'I know you're at the end of your rope, sir, but try this one on for size: Two dyslexics walk into a bra.'"

As down-home as an outhouse, erudite as a cow college Nabokov, flamboyant as a redneck Liberace, Kesey had less a writer's than wrestler's personality. Not the stoic Greco-Roman variety, but the WWF Smackdown kind. A frustrated actor, not unlike many other WWF superstars, it was probably no accident that he entered the art world by way of the theater. Yet, you could argue that he was, at least early on, a much more technically adroit writer than James Jones or Jack Kerouac, and certainly much more self-consciously aware of where the buttons and levers were placed on the literary myth machine.

A renaissance maniac out to change everything, a nonmaterialist for whom too much was never enough, who thought beyond big to Biblical (whittling, for example, the Ten Commandments to a more manageable Seven or Eight) Kesey's greatest notions were all but lost in the shadow of his own hallucinogenic ministry. For, driven by divine revelation and/ or an ego as big as all outdoors—Kesey had tried to trade up his huge literary talents for those on a more celestial plain…one seeded with psychedelia.

Kesey had become a culture king—or at least a cultural Kingfish— during the heyday of the psychedelic supernatural, in which the chemical and the occult merged to evoke a conspiratorial alter world. A world designed in part by that trippy Frank Lloyd Wright of the greatest cultural castle-in-the-air in modern history, Tim Leary, a man whose brilliant misunderstanding of reality revolutionized the era.[2]

In retrospect, acid was a no-brainer. When LSD came of age in the 1960s, it invited a…higher purpose. And soon found one. As the savior of the Self. A perfect virgin arena for the New Magic. In the age of empowerment, the Self would become all that really mattered, and for Ken Kesey and Tim Leary and other 1960s neuronauts who began preaching the unlimited powers of the utopian New You, the mind-expanding metaphysical wonders of LSD soon proved an ultimate elixir, God's alchemy for the Cosmic Consciousness. Kesey was at the vanguard of this, a young man all about stealing fire from a terminal God, delivering divine omnipotence by way of a pill.

Toward that end, acid was the perfect catalyst. Genius revelation and/or, omnipotence au go-go. Mao had said revolution came from the barrel of a gun; here revolution could come from a barrel of Orange

---

2 Leary once announced, "I declare that the Beatles are mutants. Prototypes of evolutionary agents sent by God with mysterious power to create a new species—a young race of laughing free men…They are the wisest, holiest, most effective avatars the human race has ever produced."

Sunshine—a mere 100,000,000,000 micro-dots of which, if introduced into the water supply, might initiate the national dream state.

See or be Jesus depending, one tab or two, go to heaven or beyond. Take it from that great voice of his time Minister of Information for the White Panther Party, Ken Kelley: "It was like if Jesus Christ came for the Second Coming and said, 'follow me.' That's what LSD was like."

And the fame generated by Tom Wolfe's *Electric Kool-Aid Acid Test* led Kesey away from literature to a more populist calling: acid evangelist if not secular messiah, his gospels sang of the glories of drugs, hallucinogenic or otherwise. Drugs—at least some of them—that could turn you into a caterpillar, white rabbit or a corpse.

The Lords of the lysergic Word were masters of enough hope and hype to make Jesus, Buddha or Joe Goebbels blush. "Hard shell Baptist" (his own description) Kesey standing tall among them.

Could LSD, as Kesey believed, have truly unleashed his astonishing abilities? Or made him a savior? The only truly successful "Christian acid artist" I knew about was Rick Griffin, a self-described Jesus Freak, whose steely hallucinations—spaced aliens, Hebrew-spouting cowboy bugs, flying eyeballs and wildly precise abstracts—graced the dreamscape pages of *Zap Comix* and *Surfer Magazine*. This after Griffin had found himself illuminated at Kesey's Watts Acid Test in 1965. Still, Griffin wanted to *follow* Jesus, not *be* Him.

But, as Kesey's friend Hunter Thompson was fond of saying, "When the going gets weird, the weird turn pro." From "on high," Kesey's central premise was this: American Society had become a cultural straight jacket. We were all buttoned-down rats in a corporate cage, living in a my-house-is-like-your-house-is-like-their-house suburbia in a purgatory of rules. We'd become robots, frozen inside. The Rx? To get back to the Garden we had to eat from the Tree of Divine Psychosis. If that meant destroying the mind in order to save it—what did they say about omelets and eggs? (Kesey is reported to have once told the Hell's Angels: "We're in the same business. You break bones, I break heads.") Acid would free—or rather dissolve—the Inner Mannequin, liberate us from our psychic corporate captors. Nirvana for nothing and the chicks were free. The young pauper's key to the penthouse.

Better living through chemistry, in the biggest, bitchenist most Kosmic way.

Or such had been the hope if not the plan.

In our McRehab world of fast food heroin and public high schools as discount crack pharmacies, it may be hard to recall the innocent siren song: Tune in, turn on, drop out. A call to acid revolution, a revolution of the oppressors against the oppressed. Americans born before Elvis and after the Bomb were the freest people to fight for freedom ever— young members of the soon-to-be greatest consumer generation in history waiting to be rescued not long after the publication of *Sometimes a Great Notion* from corporate tyranny, flag-waving hypocrisy, nine to five meaninglessness and adulthood—to be led to heaven or, failing that, utopia.

Courtesy the lysergic enthusiasms of Aldous Huxley, Tim Leary, Carlos Castaneda and a young Oregonian soon to be known as "The Chief." With a little help from his friends Dr. Leary and the Beatles— whom sociologist Henry Sullivan gave credit for presiding over "an epochal shift comparable in scale to that bridging Classical Antiquity and the Middle Ages."At a time when whirl was about to be king, could it be that Kesey peered into the incipient hurricane swirling around him and, a man to inherit the wind, saw the makings of a perfect storm? Or was he a clay-booted, snake charming Reverend Feelgood—terminally ambitious, simply a genius at outsmarting himself? Or, on yet another hand, had he been totally, so to speak, misread—victim of his own success, a bizarrely underrated superstar made a god of art and rebellion before being dismissed unfairly as one of the greatest literary burnouts ever?

PART ONE:
THE SHEPHERDS

Ken Kesey takes the stage at the Hoo-Haw Arts Festival, June 6th, 1976

CHAPTER ONE: REQUIEM FOR A HEAVYWEIGHT

"Once upon a time a young man of American background thought he had discovered the great Secret, the Skeleton Key to the Cosmos, the Absolute Answer to the Age-Old Question asked by every Wizard and Alchemist and Mystic that ever peered curiously into the Perplexity heavens, by every Doctor and Scientist and Explorer that ever wondered about the Winding Ways of the world, by every Philosopher and Holy man and Politician that ever listened for the Mysterious Song beneath the beat of the Human Heart…the answer to 'What Makes It All Go?'"
—Ken Kesey

Portland, Oregon 2003.

Death's door. Here's what can happen if, after a breakfast beer or two or three, you're not careful at a cross walk: multiple concussions, two broken shoulders, a broken neck, several broken ribs, both legs shattered below the knees. This was just days after my ex-cousin, poet Marty Christensen, had taken part in a eulogy to Ken Kesey. Marty—small, handsome, grizzled, quick—evoking the riches to rags élan of a broke blueblood down on his luck—as author of the following tribute to the man he referred to simply as the Commander.

THE SHAMAN

There is a strange boom
when he explodes

we go up
& remain aloft

he gestures from below

we feel calm
& flap our arms

But do not dare to bend over.

Marty and his beloved, tall, pretty, sad-eyed Lorna, lived in East Portland in a little house that featured plants cut to animal shapes in front, all Marty's stuff inside—dunes of tapes and books all over the livingroom floor—and the "Hole to Nowhere" out back, a hole the blackest of black which appeared totally bottomless. You could drop a beer bottle down there, send it on its way straight to hell or China, and never hear it hit bottom. Marty was the kind of off-center voice Oregon grows or hosts best: in-through-the-out-door talents including Ursula K. Le Guin, Raymond Carver, Katherine Dunn, Kent Anderson, Mikal Gilmore, Susan Orlean, Gus Van Sant, Larry Colton, John Shirley, Pierre Ouellette, Todd Grimson, Charles D'Ambrosio, Rick Steber and Chuck Palahniuk, whose novel *Fight Club* made him—for Gen X, Y or Z—the kind of New Normal Noir freak beacon Kesey had been for Flower Children.

The state has played home or host to bohemian writers going back to John Reed, "the father of modern journalism," who was born in Portland before writing the story of the Russian revolution, *Ten Days That Shook the World*, and dying of typhus at 31. A pioneer Marxist all about free love and anarchy, Reed, not Kesey, was arguably the true First Hippie. Oregon also abides more linear types. Bill Keller, current Executive Editor of *The New York Times*, was a reporter here for years. Low on oligarchs and movie stars (a young Clark Gable lived in Portland, did dinner theater, and moved south), killers and writers have long found Oregon a comfy windowed womb, and Ken Kesey, blessed with brilliant parents, was very much a product of this environment.

A man of the West—"homeland of the rootless" as Kesey's editor Malcolm Cowley called it—a still somewhat unsettled land recalling wilderness and fantasy, both the wild and the imaginary, from Paul Bunyan to Bigfoot, home to free spirits like DB Cooper, Gary Gilmore, Tonya Harding, Courtney Love and maybe the most successfully subversive modern American of all, Matt Groening, creator of "The Simpsons." As perhaps the most culturally complex of the northwestern states (though whitebread whack Norman Rockwell Nazi Idaho certainly gives it a run for its money and the Tom McGuane borough of Montana is not chopped liver either), Oregon is a fractured fairy tale, not one state, but several, home to cops who drive Volvos, liberals who hate blacks and bikers who vote Republican. Where put enough lead in the air and you're bound to come home happy, any man could shoot a duck for dinner, and where local Ishmaels fish for thirty pound steelhead on ten-pound test.

Marty had first met Kesey at a poetry reading across town at "Fool's Paradise" in Portland in 1972. Kesey came into the tavern with Prankster second-in-command Ken Babbs. They set up an applause-o-meter in the back of the gloomy beer mill as Marty was reading from a portfolio of poems including:

LASTING HATE

When I was a lad I'd roam
sewers in search of animals
which I would kill then try
to sell for money.

I hated them then and I still
feel nothing but complete contempt.

Of all the poets performing that night, Marty got the highest score on the Prankster applause-o-meter. Kesey was so impressed he named Marty head of the Portland delegation to "Bend in the River," Kesey's national symposium designed to determine the hippie/utopian/Keseyian future of the Republic.

"Auxiliary" Prankster Marty was one of Kesey's favorites perhaps because nuthouse alum Marty had lived the zero gravity life Kesey had only dreamt about, and because Marty gave Kesey shit. Claiming, for example, "Ken, contrary to your own opinions, do you realize that most people locked up in insane asylums are actually out of their minds? It sounds crazy, but it's true." Kesey got a kick out of that and, after all, Marty should know. Locked up at twenty-two for expressing too many "opinions" in front of a judge after a drunk and disorderly charge, Marty—like Kesey's *Cuckoo's Nest* anti-hero Randle P. McMurphy—parlayed a soft spot for hospital food and Demerol into a "Ward Leader" position at the state mental institution in Salem. In 1976, when Norman Mailer dropped out of Kesey's "Poetic Hoo-Haw" arts festival in Eugene because of a perceived anti-Semitic slight to his (Mailer's) son, Kesey scratched out Mailer's name in the marquee and scrawled in Marty's, commenting with a shrug, "Same thing."

Pretty much, Marty had lived a charmed life. But, as Kesey had long been fond of saying, "nothing lasts." Two weeks after reading poems at the Bagdad Theater, he and Lorna got up, drank a beer, and drove to the "Mouse Trap" tavern, where Marty drank more beer until the afternoon when Lorna came to fetch him. Marty wanted cigarettes and Lorna crossed the street to go to a liquor store. Marty was following behind when he was struck by a car and knocked twenty feet through the air.

He lay bleeding on the street until the ambulance arrived, bones broken from head to toe, and then began to go into seizures.

* * *

A Christ figure who quit his day job as the new Norman Mailer to deliver millennial baby boomers the psychedelic New Jerusalem, Ken Kesey's super hero career began with the biggest bang ever. Not even Ernest Hemingway, Norman Mailer or John Updike had, by age 28, enjoyed the double-whammy of two literary and commercial smash hit novels—only to then ditch literature to rescue mankind, hoping to "stop the coming end of the world."

"The Chief" was an archetypical American Fair-haired Boy (sub-species Son of the West) madman for all seasons, as profoundly American as John Wayne, Hugh Hefner, Sonny Barger or Britney Spears. Writer, artist (Kesey's illustrated jailhouse journal reveals a master of caricature), Olympic class (almost) athlete, musician (his frog voiced "Jimmy Crack Corn" ranks with, if not "White Rabbit," at least "Double Shot of My Baby's Love"), lady's man, magician, thespian, friend to those who had no friends, social architect, jail bird, original hippie cum great white father, the Great Truth Teller as consummate bullshit artist, he was that rare soul who had a talent for everything.

And as representative of an all-American ideal, the dream of unlimited success and total lack of restraint, Kesey remains hard to beat, and through his "freak freely" ministry great ideas flew from his head like illuminated dandruff. A writer who declared the novel was yesterday's paper and abandoned literature to create "the Art of I," starring himself as Pied Piper on the Seeker's New Path, he was an actor looking beyond the footlights to his base: the flower-haired seekers in the cheap seats. In a stunning new take on the old Hollywood saw, "But what I really want to do is direct," Kesey abandoned "archaic" prose to spend nearly every dollar he'd earned from his best-selling, culture-changing novels *One Flew Over the Cuckoo's Nest* and *Sometimes a Great Notion,* by shooting thirty reels of 16 millimeter film, recording the bohemian pranking of pure, government-inspected Sandoz LSD-25 acid-blasted, ex-college kids.

His famously unfinished capital M Movie was an epic tale of levitating hipsters on the road—the Kesey-invented Merry Pranksters, proto-hippie/neo-beats who, in tattered preppie dress, recalled body doubles off a Kingston Trio album cover. The Movie documented Kesey's soon-to-be famous 1964 bus trip, which served as a sort of New Testament for his LSD ministry—a trip that would have likely been a lot less "famous" if not chronicled by Tom Wolfe, but a movie which could have been a smash.

Doubt it? Witness the early documentary sensation, *Endless Summer: In Search of the Perfect Wave* filmed by Bruce Brown at about the same time, that reflected similar utopian themes (substitute acid for surfing). Had Kesey and his band of Stanford grads possessed the ability to match the recorded sound to the recorded film they shot (the single technical glitch that tunneled the Movie), Kesey might have become a sort of 21st century psychedelic Socrates.

Yet, courtesy Tom Wolfe's book *The Electric Kool-Aid Acid Test*, Kesey became nevertheless a walking, talking, heaven-hawking, Technicolor catalyst who jumped from the page to change our culture. In Kesey's wake Paul Krassner, Tim Leary, Tom Wolfe and Hunter Thompson became the Matthew, Mark, Luke and John of the Love Generation, (with Charlie Manson later on taking a star turn as Satan Lite) whose sudden, huge young audience waited with baited breath for them to write the new social and psychedelic testament.

Kesey's Kesey trumped Mailer's Aquarius (for one thing, Ken had that posse. The Pranksters became Kesey's beloved Beta house fraternity on wheels, the fraternity became the tribe—if not the Apostles). A Boho Robin Hood whose clubby sensibilities were expressed by his watch words: "You're either on the bus or off the bus," Kesey resembled a leader of a political party whose platform was party, party, party. He lived to get higher than high, take his mind to karmic Everest. Why? Perhaps, to paraphrase Sir Edmund Hillary—because it was there.

In the pre-metro-sexual, pre-Masters of the Universe universe, farm-bred wrestler/magician (he was able, among many other fitting illusions, to make his wedding band levitate weightless above his dining room table) Kesey—shepherd to a Woodstock Nation of sheep—became an American icon, at least briefly, almost equal to the Marlboro Man. A master of product placement, a commercial for a more ethereal leaf.

A metaphysical monster of the midway, a man of near limitless abilities and startling limitations, Kesey was Pied Piper for a generation for whom the willing suspension of disbelief was key to the Holy Grail. Golden Boy writ writer, "wildly gregarious," Kesey, with the build, as Cowley said, "of a plunging fullback" and the hail-fellow-well-met bonhomie of a literary Mad Man Muntz, posed an appropriate and puzzling Messiah for a generation that went from saving the world to selling it; from bongs to BMWs, in far less time than it took to go from "All You Need is Love" to "Cheeseburger in Paradise."

Kesey was, among many other things, big on symbols, one of the first to take the American flag off its staff and really fuck with it. The new edicts and gospels and megalomanias were born not to stone tablets and mountaintops but TV screens and electric guitars. The acid prophets Kesey and Leary—preached not commandments as much as permission, the promise of Aquarius Now delivered by forces powerful, wise and, above all, unseen.

"I never knew anyone in my life," novelist Robert Stone marveled, "before or since, who was a dreamer on that scale, who really believed in Possibility, the great American bugbear Possibility, to the degree that Kesey did. I never knew anyone who had his ability to communicate that sense of possibility."

While first painted as a radical, the collective portrait of Kesey amounts to pastel idolatry. Though he dedicated a good part of his life to drugs, romanticized their use with terrible effectiveness, and ultimately died because of them, in most popular portraits of Kesey he appears as a gentle giant, and at worst the high priest of a failed religion.[3]

Many details of Kesey's past have been lost to legend or convenience.

And too, his books are often oddly misremembered. *Cuckoo*, whose surreal narrative is often credited as psychedelia's first great gift to art, has also been dubbed the primer for 1960s anti-authoritarianism, though its hero, roustabout R. P. McMurphy, is about as prototypically hippie-like as John McCain. *Sometimes a Great Notion* is similarly credited as a totem to free-thinking individualism, though its protagonists are as locked in their "never give an inch" beliefs as the Christian fundamentalist Ken Kesey himself often seemed to mirror.

So why did Kesey's life seem to go so far downhill after those two novels?

It was certainly not for want of energy or ambition. No tendril-armed bi-focalist laboring in a cobwebbed garret, burly Kesey was the big man on campus writ artiste, acidhead alpha dog and action figure, an aging high school jock in flower power drag—and he was not particularly a free thinker, taking his cues not from proto-hippies Rousseau, Heathcliff or Walt Whitman but from his childhood comic book heroes, Superman, Spiderman, Plasticman, Batman, and Captain Marvel. But, fly as they might, comic book super heroes aren't free spirits. They are cops.

Kesey's novels were often populated by errant hollering Paul Bunyan manques from a wild west Oregon that most buttoned-down Oregonians barely knew existed: a dystopic realm in which brilliant rural rubes, "bull goose loony" Ayn Rand types in cork boots, ruled a feral mythological roost. But cosmopolitan myth-master and university town homeboy Kesey, who owed as much to Joseph Campbell as he did to William Faulkner, was no Noble Savage. Nor—as a prophet and Great Truth teller rabble rouser—was Kesey a tub-thumping Commie Madonna kneeling at the altar of Karl Marx or Mother Bloor.

A man of many contradictions, Kesey was a walking talking proof that belief as well as beauty could be in the eye of the beholder. People tended to believe in Kesey as whatever they wanted to believe. The Republic's favorite hallucinogenic, generous and lackadaisically self-centered, Houdini of hip, Kesey could write prose as tight or preposterous as the

---

3 Kesey on Kesey: "I'm a power junkie, I love power. For one thing, I think it's not corrupting like some people think; it is purifying. People who think they have power, yet do not, are corrupted. People who really have power are humbled by it."

New Testament; yet he also banged out typed-by-the-yard speed rants you could edit with a blow torch. However, there was always vision in the visionary—Kesey's ideas for an interactive "video democracy" were decades before their time. Sadly, though he had a transformative vision that went beyond hippie socialism, as a tribal genius but a corporate naif, he was unable to implement it beyond his Oregon statewide "Bend in the River." As a manifestation of perhaps the greatest idea he ever had—a radical new "people's democracy" created by shifting political power away from politicians to statewide referendums whose merits and shortcomings would be broadcast and debated on television and then voted on by ballots published in statewide newspapers—"Bend in the River" was truly revolutionary. What had gone wrong?

* * *

When Kesey returned from Egypt in 1975, he took his two poet pals Walt Curtis and Marty Christensen for a long ride from Portland to his farm outside Pleasant Hill in his big long convertible. Along for the ride were Marty's wife Lorna and a circulating bottle of whiskey. On the way, Ken addressed big issues: "I went to Egypt with Krassner and we debated the Venusians versus the CIA."

From the back seat, Marty said, "Uh-huh" and Kesey continued, "Now he (Krassner) believes the CIA-military-industrial complex has a conspiracy—and I believe it's the Venusians."

Marty said, "Do you think the CIA is not that smart?" and Kesey replied, "I think the CIA is not that smart. I don't think they can put it together."

It was left to Marty, who was by then perhaps a little gassed, to do the job. "I think the common man is probably on your side. You know, it's ironic that over fifty percent of the American people believe in flying saucers. But I doubt ten percent of them believe the CIA is in control. But all of the rational evidence points out to me—" Marty suddenly spoke in headlines. "THAT THEY PROBABLY ARE."

As an irradiated gold standard of bohemia—an isotope whose hand was sure on the joy stick during key flights to the stratosphere—Kesey had here behind his balding fleecy head a luminated dollop of a man with whom he could confide, "I feel that the Venusians are real. And they are the bad guys. But—that people with more power than we have, have those forces covered. I felt like, after being there in Egypt and talking to certain people, that those guys—those arcane forces—have those otherworldly villains under their thumb."

Long before being resurrected as a progressive savior from a metaphysical time gone by, Kesey had, like Ernest Hemingway before him, promoted himself from literature to fame. Hemingway had hotrodded nihilism, understatement, "life style," and celebrity to achieve, with his safari suit iconography, brand name identification. By the 1950s Hemingway was as recognizable as a stop sign. Writer promoted to product. But unlike that legendary literary lion, Kesey saw a much larger life than Letters. For like his sometimes mentor Tim Leary, Kesey understood what America wanted in 1965 was a magic sacrament to enfranchise a new religion—acid had told him so, and all you had to do was take one look around the psychedelic never-neverland that was Kesey's Stanford digs at Perry Lane to see that young America was ready for a new divinity. A religion not of God, but of the self. An "acid Christian" crucified as under-achieving psychedelic superman—Kesey liked to recite:

"Of offering more than what I can deliver,
I have a bad habit, it's true.
But I have to offer more than what I can deliver,
To be able to deliver what I do."

Which would be, of course, the Holy Grail.

A job that—if not God—at least fate had created for him. Hippie he-man Kesey waxed poetic like a prophet from a nihilist Bible Belt, a perfect poster boy for flower-powered liberation and godless heavenly ideals. Opinions vary. "I have great love and affection for Ken Kesey," Tim Leary said, "I have a deep sense of brotherhood and companionship for Ken Kesey. I have always seen him as very Protestant and quite moralistic, and quite American in a puritanical way. And basically untrustworthy, since he is always going to end up with a Bible in his hand."

Fitting perhaps for a man who got shit on his shoes milking cows, and was a friend of rural remedies. "I've used cornstarch on my balls for years," Kesey told Krassner. "Y'know how it is when you're swarthy anyway and maybe nervous like on a long freeway drive or say you're in court where you can't unzip to air things out, and your clammy old nuts stick to your legs? Well, a little handful of plain old cornstarch in the morning will keep things dry and sliding the whole day long. Works better than talcum and don't smell like a nursery."

A wearer of the coat of many colors, like no writer, hippie or messiah I'd ever heard about—who nevertheless wrote almost frighteningly well—or just wrote, Kesey was a man so eclectic in ideas, passions, insights and blunders to suggest a Ginsu knife of psyches and whose aforementioned watchwords of liberation, "You're either on the bus or off the bus" were actually Kesey-speak for, "My way or the highway." Was that because of, or despite of, LSD?[4]

* * *

Almost fifteen years younger than Kesey, in his company I was Q, he was A. One beery afternoon in a Portland tavern I held him—by cheating—to a draw at arm wrestling. He was not a gracious tie-er. The Commander's take: "I oughta knock you back to the Ohio River."

Leading me to wonder: was the legendary "truth teller" largely a figment of his own imagination? Kesey was a man of kaleidoscopic extremes—wildly imaginative in the smallest details of his life but otherwise about as free-spirited as a speeding ticket. Fair-haired farm boy turned messianic jock Apollo, Kesey sold himself as Mister Sixties. Rousseau's Natural Man for a post-Machine Age. But like most evangelicals, what Ken liked most was god and girls, an ethos at odds with the unalloyed idolatry he inspired as author of the new utopia that became the starry heart of the young national imagination.

That said, it's likely most everything people think they know about Ken Kesey is wrong. His decision to ditch literature was (or at least could have been) as brilliant and misunderstood as the Japanese attack on Pearl Harbor, and he never burned out—at least not in the sense that he lost his talent. The talent remained, if in later years reserved more often for the paragraph than the page. It was his concentration that became

---

4 I am, at best, a C-list acidhead. I didn't see a lot of guys melt, never had access to Sandoz-25 and so far down the devolutionary hallucinogenic road that not only was the street acid I often got supercharged with strychnine, but dealers actually bragged it was supercharged with strychnine.

a problem. Kesey represented the Freest American Ever, a man who embraced Open Marriage in a way it rarely had been embraced before, and the soul of a lost civilization that flourished, however briefly in the time between the Summer of Love and *Deep Throat.*

As the Man Behind the Curtain, if not the Hero with a Thousand Faces, Kesey was a savant with failures more brilliant than a lesser savant's triumphs, but who as a man whose life ended mired in booze, drugs and litigation, had created his own moral Mars-scape and left a wake of those who felt both inspired and betrayed.

Not that many of us hadn't felt inspired and betrayed before. By our fathers—the Greatest Generation who'd sold their white collar souls to the executive chain gang, who felt like slaves to their own children and resented sons not thankful to be drowning in their largesse; by the church, whose Norman Rockwell Jesus did not speak to *Zap Comix* souls; and by the state, desperate for AK-47 fodder in Vietnam. By the time Ken Kesey gave up art for action, he was playing to a unique audience of privileged seekers, a generation estranged from the organization men in the gray flannel suits who raised them, removed from religion more about control than compassion, rules than redemption, shame than salvation; and a government whose face was no longer that of George Washington, Abe Lincoln or John F. Kennedy, but J. Edgar Hoover, General William Westmoreland and Richard Nixon.

So why had Kesey squandered his every ability one by one? To rescue the world, sure, but otherwise, how had it come to pass?

CHAPTER TWO: NATURAL MAN

"Though my mama came from Arkansas and my daddy came from Texas, and though we all came to Oregon from Colorado by way of my daddy being stationed at Mare Island Navy Base in California during WWII, I nevertheless admit that I think of myself as an Okie.

Let me tell you what being an Okie means: Being an Okie means being the first of your whole family to finish high school, let alone go on to college...Being an Okie means being rooted out of an area and having to hustle for a toehold in some new area...Being an Okie means running the risk of striving out from under layers of heartless sonsabitches only to discover you have become a redneck of bitterness worse than those you strove against...Being an Okie is a low-rent, aggravating drag, but it does learn you some essentials."

—Ken Kesey

Ken Kesey's grandparents had headed west from "the cedars" of southwest Colorado to Oregon in 1938, all their belongings piled in a 1936 Willies and a Teraplane pickup. While his father was in the Navy in World War II, Kesey's family drove over a thousand miles of patchwork asphalt over the Rocky Mountains to Oregon. Of the trip Kesey recalled, "All the long, sweltering August afternoon we rolled through land baked as bleak and whipped as raw as the poorest prairie spreads back home—failed farms and ribby cattle and rutty side roads angling off to weedy nowheres. Even the names of the places along our bleak route sounded bleak. Burns. Hines. Wagontire. And the pass we were passing through? It was called Stinkingwater.

"Daddy reassured us that things were different on the other side of the mountains ahead—all milk and honey. But you could tell he was having some misgivings himself."

The idyllic west. Land of tall trees and taller tales. Hunting and fishing and football country. Oregon's immigrant ethnic mix was largely

W.A.S.P. on rye bread: German, English, Scandinavian, and a smattering of Jews. The morning after his family rolled into Eugene satellite Coberg at the end of the long hot drive from Colorado, Ken, eight, found a new world: "At dawn I was awakened by the swelling of birdsong and bladder. In a grumpy blur I made my barefoot way down off the porch. I shuffled to the blue-black loom of bushes at the edge of the lawn. And, standing there, blinking and shivering and draining myself of warm sleep, I suddenly became aware of a wondrous thing. Those looming bushes were covered with berries, festoons of glistening, dew-beaded berries!—sweeter than soda pop and more numerous than the stars fading in the sky.

"As I stood filling my mouth with this wild bounty, I watched the light come up…Through rising mists I saw Grandma's vegetable garden, heavy with tomatoes and string beans…and Grandpa's sweet-corn patch with its long ear lifted…haphazard orchards drooping with plum and pear and fat Guernseys standing to their bags in clover…and farther away, forest after emerald forest of timber, hemlocks and firs and pines, their points lifted like hope itself to the new day."

Aside from expeditions to Stanford, Mexico, Egypt, and Mars, he would live here the rest of his life.

Round about 1950, Jim Kesey, Ken's younger cousin, recalled as a boy trekking with other Kesey brothers and cousins behind adolescent Ken. "Following as if in a parade being led by a drum major, knees a pumpin', arms a flailin'." Through a barley field, scrub oak, alder, wading Little Muddy Creek up to a local Everest, a hill where "Ken cut his initials KK into a struggling oak…much like a wolf marking its territory, he proclaimed it Kesey Hill." This before discovering an old tire perfect for rolling lesser Keseys down Kesey Hill until they threw up.

Jim Kesey recalled Ken being "into magic and blowing stuff up," and being also ultra-hypnotized by his younger brother Chuck in their bedroom. To prove the trance-state, Chuck stuck pins into Ken's legs before commanding his brother to turn into a dog who "licked our faces and barked." Then, when Ken became a gorilla, Kesey cousins exploded from the room. But too late for Jim. He could run but not hide. Ken was "in the process of breaking my neck when my brother, in a gallant effort to save my life, hit the gorilla over the head with a two-by-four."

As novelist William Gibson once said, the future is already here, it just hasn't been distributed yet. By the time Ken Kesey was a teenager at the end of the 1940s, spending weekends at his granddad's farm arm-wrestling his young cousins, Allen Ginsberg had already written much of his epic poem, *Howl*, that would inspire the revolt Kesey would later champion against the Eisenhower Era. From Stella! to tail fins and the sound of one hand clapping to the Grassy Knoll and *The Son of Flubber*[5] —a rep tie decade told by Captain Queeg, Joe McCarthy, Cash McCall, confirmed bachelors, and Brand X. Solution begat solution, Sputnik to Thalidomide, a Promethean age. Tunnel visionary Germans had written the bass notes—but (forget Hitler, remember the V2) clearly here was a matter of the singer not the song. While this was a time according to Tim Leary where "pleasure was against the law" and where "you were allowed to work five days a week, get drunk on the weekend and bump against your wife for procreative purposes," one could argue that such a definition does nothing if not damn the post-war years with faint praise.

Twirled powerfully by the failed promise of utopian techno-fascism, the 1950s were the axle of the 20th Century, heyday of abstract expressionism and experimental jazz and the birthplace of rock and roll. The Eisenhower and Kennedy era was also the zenith of corporate creativity. Cars were never designed more wildly, while architects like Philip Johnson created sleek, minimalist modernist skyscrapers to invent the mirrored face of the American city.

In the West, long, low homes, some of which looked like wood UFO's designed to break the sound barrier, carpeted new suburbs, radical inventions in their own right. And if the novel was about to die, it certainly didn't know it yet—the "conservative" pre-psychedelic era spawned the defining literature of the century—*Catcher in the Rye, The Heart is a Lonely Hunter, Naked Lunch, Catch-22*—hardly rubber stamps for the status quo. Then there was film, the new noir—*Breathless* (which took cigarette smoking to high art), the social commentary of *The Blackboard*

---

5 A seditious sequel to *The Absent Minded Professor,* of which *Variety* wrote: "Beneath the preposterous veneer lurks a comment on our time, a reflection of the plight of the average man helplessly confronted with the complexities of a jet age civilization burdened with fear, red-tape, official mumbo-jumbo and ambitious anxiety. Deeply rooted within the screenplay is a subtle protest against the detached, impersonal machinery of modern progress."

Jungle and *Rebel Without a Cause* and neo-horror classics like *Psycho* and *The Birds.*

Finally, TV—the invention of the sit-com—and TV advertising, the elixir of the hidden persuaders. No matter that kids grew up in rigid social cliques, forced to dress like miniature adults, salute the flag, remember that sex was dirty, and go to war when they were told to, they were part of a 1950s economic revolution that dwarfed the 1960s cultural revolution—Baby Boomer parents were the first yuppies (their brand new plastic credit cards good for brand new stereos and TV sets). And, while considerably older than most of his flock, Kesey came to manhood during an era in which progress was our most important product and the collective consciousness was in the hands of *Mad*, Madison Avenue, Disneyland, and the *Playboy* Advisor.

Brought up a "hard-shell Baptist," and diagnosed (according to his mother) as "genius" by the time he was in elementary school, Kesey was raised outside the university town of Eugene, home of the University of Oregon, on the outskirts of these two conflicting cultures—the academic and the boots-in-the-mud mercantile. He learned to go in through the out door early. His junior high school music teacher recalled, "I saw a lot of Ken whenever he got kicked out of another class, they'd give him a choice of going either to music or shop, and he always chose music. I remember hearing other teachers say that he was right on the fence, either crazy or a genius...he was so multi-faceted. People were always trying to put him in a box. But he was too big for any of them."

Kesey's rural neighborhood was the front of the backwoods—one step up from the kind of primitive place where you might see a blind boy playing a banjo on somebody's front porch—and Kesey has been portrayed (like his creation Randle McMurphy) as a genius rube. At Stanford he starred as an idiot savant young hayseed good old boy blessed with Faulkner's muse. But Kesey's family had founded Darigold Dairy (scarcely a sorority of Eugene milkmaids, their products were as common as dollar bills in Oregon grocery stores by the 1960s, and Darigold now sells 3.5 billion quarts of milk a year), and his father was a very successful businessman, part of a larger and far more cosmopolitan community.

Ken grew up as a member of an extended clan, athletic, outgoing, successful, loving and progressive, surrounded by strong-minded, literate women, whose story telling inspired him to become a story teller himself. His sense of mystery grew out of childhood wonder. Once, he and his brother set out to investigate a drained irrigation tunnel that looked as if it had been "burrowed by a 700 pound mole." At the tunnel's bottom, the boys discovered an old accordion. They took it apart and found, inside, a note that read: "What the hell you looking here for, Daisy Mae?" Which inspired Kesey to admit: "I achieved some kind of *satori* (sic) right there—knowing that *somebody* had *somehow* a very *long* while ago *gone* in there and put that sign in that accordion, and he's betting all the time that *someday* somebody's going to come along and *find* it. A mystery for people to wonder about. Well, that's what I want for my books."

His idea of story came from his bootlegger grandma. "It was over 50 years ago before there was television," Kesey recalled, "she would sit us down around the table lamp bringing her hands up in a position to count on each finger the following: 'William, William trimble toes, he's a good fisherman, catch his hands put 'em in the pans, some lay eggs some not, wire, briar, limber lock three geese in a flock, a one flew east, a one flew west, a one flew over the cuckoo's nest; O U T spells out you dirty dish rag you go out!' Then she'd bend her finger after counting out the last line. Once you heard that as a five year old you can't get it out of your brain! I owe Grandma Smith a great deal."

Grandma Smith was a white lady Uncle Remus who infected young Ken with her love of language—once describing someone to him as "independent as a pig on ice," she inspired Kesey's novel *Seven Prayers for Grandma Whittier*. On his father's side, the Keseys came originally from Ireland, where they were Caseys, before migrating to Germany where they became Quiesie—which meant cheese, before becoming "Keseys" in America. The Kesey family were—in Kesey's words, "west walkers," wending from Tennessee and Arkansas to Texas and New Mexico, then on to Colorado, where he was born on September 17, 1935 in La Junta. His mother was sixteen. As a small boy, Ken told her that he had heard wild horses storming the Colorado sky, "with teeth like rows of barbwire and eyes like polished steel balls an' breath that peeled paint."

His mother had told him not to be frightened, it was just thunder, only the weather. This was an explanation of reality that did not please the boy meta-physician. As a writer, Kesey vowed his devotion to discovering what was hidden in plain sight. "The vein lies under the topsoil of external reality; it is not hidden. We've known of it for ages, this vein, but it has been put down so long by 'just,' disparaged so long by 'only,' that we have neglected its development.

"It can mean that as much emphasis can be placed on hyperbole, metaphor, simile, or fantasy as on actual events," he concluded, "In the vast seas between red and white corpuscles, Captain Nemo still secretly pilots his Nautilus, this white-haired scourge of Oppression and Warfare. Why not give him his head? Or through the dense growth of neurons, Lou Wetzel stalks the Zane Grey Indians, silent as moss until he strikes with a chilling war whoop. Why not let him stalk?"

Asked what provided his foundational abilities as a writer, Kesey's reply was quick: magic.

You might argue that the mystery of Ken Kesey was solved right there. For his abiding idea was that writing, no matter how good was a mere lieutenant to the general theater of literary magic.

Whether in literature, as a sacrament, in a pill, or by sleight of hand, Kesey loved illusion. While in high school he performed magic tricks and ventriloquism at the McDonald Theater in Eugene, traveled the state with his father and younger brother doing magic shows. "I...even had a show on television and (went) from ventriloquism into hypnotism. And from hypnotism into dope. But it's always been the same trip, the same kind of search."

He also, less magically, forged across the Siuslaw River in a barge carrying dairy goods and was fond of taking high-speed floats down the nearby McKenzie River on inner tubes, and if nobody drowned, so much the better. Too, there were sports. Kesey recalled, "My dad was a mighty (University of) Oregon fan, and every fall was full of Duck talk. I can remember long, drizzly, cold Saturday afternoons, shivering in the car with my father and my brother, parked somewhere along the river with our shotguns between our knees, watching for ducks as we listened to the Ducks game on the radio. 'Yep, we're rootin' for 'em and we're shootin' for 'em,' Dad used to say."

On his way to becoming alive in the public imagination as a cross between Paul Bunyan and a literary Big Foot, Kesey played high school football. Known for blocking kicks, he played right guard four years in high school. Single wing. "My senior year we got a new coach and a new system: The T formation. I seemed to be the only one able to remember the complicated new plays, so I was the play caller, as well as the right guard, offense and defense—a star!

"Later that year I took third in State High School Wrestling Championships. Shoulda taken first. Got caught in a roll and pinned. Fine with me. I was ready for college, and for college football."

* * *

That would take place a few miles down the street. Trees, college professors, and more trees. Eugene was mostly just a Mecca for loggers and Betty Coed types until the early 1960s. Then came the hippies, the famous football coaches, Nike, the anarchists (today the local "anarchists' bar" operates successfully right across from the city jail representing, thus, a near perfect closed loop system) and post-bourgeoisie New Age food. Originally tagged "Skinner's Mudhole," Eugene later became known variously as "The World's Greatest City of the Arts and Outdoors," "The Emerald Empire," "The Athens of the West," and finally "The People's Republic of Eugene."

But when Kesey grew up, Eugene was simply a Siamese twin of a burg whose civic consciousness was defined by the low-down interests of the logging industry and the highblown sensibility of the University of Oregon, whose campus was the city's flagship cultural monument and oasis of high-minded literacy.

Here in the leaden-skied rainy Willamette Valley often the easiest thing to do was stay inside and read or drink or even write, and by the time Kesey was named "Most Likely to Succeed" by Springfield High School's class of 1953, up the road in Corvallis, Bernard Malamud was dreaming up *The Fixer* and over in Estacada another Oregon boy, Raymond Carver, was discovering plot and the all American writer's elixir he'd use to fuel it: booze.

By the rigid early 1950s, the elastic 1960s future had already begun to colonize the straighten-up-and-fly-right postwar present. In 1953, Aldous Huxley wrote about listening to Bach while on mescaline: "The mescaline experience is without any question the most extraordinary and significant available to human beings this side of the Beatific Vision. To be shaken out of the rut of ordinary perception, to be shown for the first few timeless hours the outer and inner worlds, not as they appear to be to an animal obsessed with survival or to a human being obsessed with words and notions, but as they are apprehended, directly and unconditionally, by the Mind at large–this is an experience of inestimable value to anyone." Allen Ginsberg first gave a public reading of *Howl* (though much of the poem had existed in fragments since the late 1940s), a stunning definition and denunciation of the conformist American machine state.

A state that was celebrated and—in its rigid Catholic 1950's incarnation—undermined by media as diverse as Jerry Lee Lewis and Walt Disney. Disney was a utopian whose mastery of television went a long way toward shaping collective baby boom consciousness. "Uncle Walt's" tales of maverick Americans ranging from The Swamp Fox to Davy Crockett—were in constant battle with tyranny and its fellow traveler, the status quo. In fact, the term "Merry Pranksters" likely came from a Disney movie, *The Liberty Story,* in which Samuel Adams (played by Rusty Lane) says of the Boston Tea Party, "Many of the participants were Harvard students. A college boy is always ready for a prank, and to these 'merry pranksters,' this was the joke of the age."

Kesey's generation was the first touched by the bright grey moving moonlight of television, what historian Daniel Boorstin defined as "a supermarket of surrogate experience," a utopian medium whose elastic realities set—literally—the stage for the dreamscape Kesey would help invent. Television's most important product was the fantasy of fulfillment by consumption. As novelist and critic Marya Mannes wrote, "The constant reminder of what is inaccessible must inevitably produce a subterranean but real discontent…If we are constantly presented with what we are not, or cannot have, the dislocation deepens, contentment vanishes, and frustration reigns. Even for the substantially secure, there is always a better thing, a better way, to buy."

And what better to buy than a dream? As a crown prince of an American lumpen elite—the sons of doctors, lawyers, Indian chiefs and dairy kings—who were provided an unprecedented amount of money, mobility and information—as well as the promise that all their dreams would come true, teenage Ken Kesey lived in a 1950's west coast America in which change was becoming the only constant, Oregonians were "living better through chemistry" (and/or "blinded by science") in a realm where almost no problem could not soon be solved.

"Magic bullets" starred the horizon, "magic bullets" most often imagined as pharmaceutical. Drugs, from antibiotics to Xyclon-B best represented the Cold War generation's hopes and horrors of future technology. It was the dawn of a new age of alchemy whose divine aspirations stretched back millennia—the new age of the elixir vitae dreamed of since the time of the pharaohs. Like the prescient rage Allan Ginsberg had expressed in *Howl*, confluent forces—the power of transcendental drugs fueling the power of a new language, were already combining to produce a many-authored gospel that would redesign the thought worlds of a new generation. Drugs and language born of each other.

Way back in 1935, the year Kesey was born, Aldous Huxley had, in *Brave New World*, forecast his imaginary "Soma" as a sensual social leash that the captives of his consumer super state would gladly embrace in exchange for euphoria. But now a new twist: Banker/magic mushroomologist Gordon Wasson was about to define a real life, real world "Soma" as a psychedelic mushroom able to unleash a wildly expanded mind state, or at least the grand illusion thereof.

CHAPTER THREE: ADAMS AND EVES

"…It was as though the walls of our house dissolved, and my spirit had flown forth, and I was suspended in mid-air viewing landscapes of Mountains, with camel caravans advancing slowly across the slopes, the mountains rising tier above tier to the very heavens…The thought crossed my mind: could the divine mushrooms be the secret that lay behind the ancient Mysteries?"

—R. Gordon Wasson

Psychedelics may be as old as the mind. We remain illiterate of Neanderthal metaphysics, but many if not most "BC and Back" anthropologists find it likely that the earliest hunter-gathers, eating whatever they could lay their hands on, ingested plants with hallucinogenic properties, and acid analogs as a metaphysical "stairway to heaven" date to prehistoric times. Likewise, the tree is the largest living entity to most pre-dynamic people's existence; it also bears sustaining fruit and if it hosts mind-zonking mushrooms, it doesn't take a Yale-educated Bible scholar to understand a logical mythical genesis for the Tree of Life in the Book of Genesis.

Five years before Kesey had hit it big with *Cuckoo's Nest* in 1962, a former Wall Street banker named Gordon Wasson—venerated as the Margaret Meade of Magic Mushrooms—posited the idea that Adam and Eve were ancient Siberians who plucked psychedelic shrooms from birches near the arctic—which became the forbidden Tree of Knowledge that led to Original Sin.[6]

Wasson was no crank. An Honorary research Fellow at the Harvard Botanical Gardens, his vision of a pre-history climaxing in a Soma-inspired Eden is taken soberly. Huston Smith, whose *The World's Religions* remains, after three decades, the standard collegiate text, writes, "In the pantheon

6 Though the godly potential of psychedelics was not born until Wasson's *Life Magazine* article on the religious powers of magic mushrooms, published June 10, 1957, sent Leary to Mexico for transcendental epiphany.

the Aryans brought with them when they swept into Afghanistan and the Indus Valley in the second millennium BC, Soma occupied a unique position. Indra with his thunderbolt was more commanding, and Agni evoked the awe that fire so readily inspired before the invention of matches made it commonplace. But Soma was special…because of what one became: immortal."

In his novel *Brave New World,* Aldous Huxley made Soma a star, a fictional drug which conferred zonked-out social malleability as a useful method of mind control to the helmsmen of his future police state. But Soma existed, in a more interesting form–long lost–30 centuries ago, as a psychotropic plant-god used by poet priests of the original Aryan peoples to endow that race with bliss and immortality, the only record of which comes to us by way of 120 hymns taken from the Rig Veda (1700-1100 BC). This you can learn volumes about from *Soma: Divine Mushroom of Immortality* written by retired banker Wasson who, in his introduction concludes, "In a word, my belief is that Soma is the Divine Mushroom of Immortality, and that in the early days of our culture, before we made use of reading and writing, when the Rig Veda was being composed, the prestige of this miraculous mushroom ran by word of mouth far and wide throughout Eurasia, well beyond the region where it grew and was worshiped."

It is plausible that, across the eons from animal to man, cultural information was installed before birth in the human consciousness. Social evolution suggests leaders, ladies men, bitches and bureaucrats may have been born to the wolf pack. But is it also plausible that it was left to an unknowing Adam to pluck human conscience, free will and Original Sin from the Tree of Life and Knowledge when he ate its trippy fruit?

Consider the serpent's promise from the Old Testament, "Ye shall not surely die. For God doth know that in the day ye eat thereof, then your eyes shall be opened, and ye shall be as gods." Long a symbol of slithering, low-shadowed immortality–Eden's serpent made man die. God placed the Tree of Life in Eden, where its fruit conferred life everlasting. God instructed Adam and Eve that they were welcome to eat from every tree in the Garden, except for the Tree of the Knowledge of Good and Evil. According to Genesis, had Adam and Eve resisted the serpent's temptation to eat from that tree they would have been free to eat from the tree of Life with God's approval and enjoy its benefits.

That fungus or vegetation common to Eurasia which, if ingested, produced profound hallucinations; it might easily have influenced the evolution of religious experience since prehistoric times. In the Spring 1963 issue of *The American Scholar*, not long before much of the young West dropped acid, the poet Mary Ethel Barnard, "looking at the matter, coldly, unintoxicated and unentranced," published an essay, "The God in the Flowerpot," that read in part, "Which was more likely to have happened first, the spontaneously generated idea of an afterlife in which the disembodied soul, liberated from the restrictions of time and space, experiences eternal bliss, or the accidental discovery of hallucinogenic plants that give a sense of euphoria, dislocate the center of the consciousness, and distort time and space, making them balloon outward in great expanded vistas?"

Take this from the Rig Veda: "We have drunk the Soma, we have become immortal, we have arrived at the light, we have found the gods."

These were Gods who later made a splash in the holy waters of medieval religious art. "At the session of the Societe Mycologique de France held on October 6, 1910," according to Wasson, "there was presented to the attendance a photograph of a Romanesque fresco from a disaffected (sic?) chapel that had belonged to the Abbaye de Plaincourault in the center of France…The fresco, crude and faded, is of the familiar temptation scene in the Garden of Eden. The gentleman who presented the fresco to the Societe Mycologique made the sensational statement that, instead of the customary Tree (of Life) the artist had given us the fly-garic." The fly-garic is a fabled Mushroom of Immortality. "A serpent, entwined around a gigantic fly-agaric, was engaged in a colloquy with Eve."

A photo of the fresco reveals at the center a mushroom as big as a small palm tree between a faded Adam and a naked, yellow-haired Eve. Four more large mushrooms arch away from the stem of the central fungus. The serpent is shown entwined around it, a greenish orb hanging from its mouth. Wasson recalled, "From 1955 on I was in intermittent correspondence with Aldous Huxley, and often when he visited New York he would come down to Wall Street and have lunch with me… One day he and I were discussing hallucinogens, and I remember tossing out the fanciful suggestion that Soma might prove to be the fly-agaric, and describing to him the red and yellow phases of this remarkable mushroom, and its role in Siberia, with which I think he was already acquainted. I knew nothing about Soma at the time, and to aspire to the Soma secret was to be reaching for the moon."

Wasson claimed that Adam and Eve had eaten not a forbidden fruit, but a sacred fungus (a speculation portrayed in frescoes of the middle ages, or so he writes, telling us that the artist never had "an inkling" of the fruit's real identity when he "saw a serpent offering a mushroom to Eve in the fresco of Plaincourault"). He concluded, "Ponce de Leon early in the 16th Century was still seeking in Florida the pool of living water that he might have discovered in the Siberian taiga, the pool where Gilgamesh finally found his Herb of Immortality thousands of years earlier, only to lose it again to the Serpent who was more subtle than any beast in the field, the very same Serpent who engaged Eve in pleasant conversation, whose habitation is in the roots of the towering Siberian birch."

There are theories common as crabgrass that civilization occurred only when hunter-gatherer man ate himself out of psychedelics, that until the dawn of recorded history man had existed in shaman-led tribes who tripped the light fantastic across veldt and steppe as part of pre-agricultural "goddess cultures" who worshipped female deities and who might never have sobered up to invent beer, bread, alphabets, the printing press and the atom bomb had they—our great-grand parents to the X power—not run out of hallucinogenic plants.

We can also read psychedelics were the lynchpins of western religious philosophy, that Moses received the Ten Commandments while high on a psychedelic plant and, more famously or infamously, that Christ the Son of God may have been a self-consuming psychedelic cannibal. Today you can't swing a cat at a comparative religions coffee klatch without hitting an acidhead Jesus freak. Thanks largely to John Allegro, whose 1970 book *The Mushroom and the Cross* suggested Christ's invitation at the Last Supper to eat and drink of His flesh and Blood was inspired by a main dish of not bread but magic mushrooms.

Fast-forward about two thousand years. To a time in which psychedelics were perhaps even more appropriate as a main dish. For, shortly after Watson and Crick discovered the double-helix, a stunning triumph for secular science, metaphysics found their last best refuge.

Minus the deepest depths of outer space the only realm left completely unexplained and inexplicable to science was, if not the soul, at least the self. Awareness became the last frontier of the almost totally unknown and the new stomping grounds for endless possibility.

For who knew who or what resided out of sight, out of mind? Intellectuals as various as William Butler Yeats and Aleister Crowley had, during the first half of the 20th century, popularized a theosophical belief in a pagan spirit world dating to pre-Christian mystery cults and before. The McCluhan media made the 1960s the new age of the ether, in which new ghosts, fairies and goblins were, ethereally, possible. A dreamer's, liar's and ad man's paradise brought to you not by Osiris or Odom but Chevy Trucks or 20th Century Fox. Add peyote—and even Carlos Castaneda got a pass.

Chapter Four: BMOC

"One's parents remembered the sloughing common order, War & Depression—but Superkids knew only the emotional surge of the great payoff, when nothing was common any longer—The Life! A glorious place, a glorious age, I tell you! A very Neon Renaissance—And the myths that actually touched you at the time—not Hercules, Orpheus, Ulysses, and Aeneas—but Superman, Captain Marvel, Batman, The Human Torch, The Sub-Mariner, Captain America, Plastic Man, The Flash—but of course!"

—Tom Wolfe

Us versus them. Our array vs. their array. Eisenhower America faced a monolithic Soviet Union, an Orwellian second world techno-state where, to paraphrase the writer PJ O'Rourke, everything not compulsory was prohibited, and where the end of the world was being assembled nuclear warhead by nuclear warhead.

Flip open the 1956 University of Oregon yearbook to gaze upon—rank and file—the class photographs, the black and white pictures of gray to grayer nineteen year-old old maids. Young women who with pale faces and crimped hair already look like elderly spinsters. Another reality. Ancient and distant as Oz. Here we find the 21 year-old Ken Kesey; pretzeling an opponent in a wrestling match; beaming confidently beside fellow staff members on the school newspaper.[7]

Flip a few yearbook pages and see Kesey on stage in *Macbeth*. A man-child for all seasons. Kesey: "The guys on the wrestling team used

---

[7] Kesey enjoyed great wrestling success at the University of Oregon, and late in life recalled it fondly: "Wrestling is the sport of reason. Football, boxing they are all trying to decrease the reason and intelligence of the opponent by knocking him out, but the wrestler doesn't try to knock anyone out. He gets them by the arm and sits them back there and says 'Now listen carefully to me or I'm gonna break your shoulder.' And you reason with them. And writing is the same for me. You get them by the brain and you put a Half Nelson on them and you say, 'Listen, I'm going to reason with you, I'm going to tell you something that might be a little hard for you to understand, but it's correct.'"

to say, 'You write? You act? What the hell you doing over there with those people?' Over in the drama or writing department they were always bugging me about associating with a gang of thumpheads." So what were his motives? The best of both worlds, he was the center of attention in either realm. "I studied acting," he later said, "and I was taught to interpret a character by figuring out, from a detailed examination of his behavior, exactly what he wanted. The theory there is that everything a man does springs from his motivations. In writing, I find myself reversing the process. I know, to *start* with, what a character wants; he exists for me as a kind of abstract creature who wants a specific thing. So, by figuring how he *gets* what he wants, I learn about the sort of man he is."

What Kesey wanted was to be unlimited. By anything. Fair and curly hair no longer than Caesar's, bumper-jawed Kesey appears smiling from dusty pages, grinning at the system, as no freak, no hippie, no prophet— but like everyone else, only a "young adult," an American in training, under the watchful eye of the Mt. Rushmore-like coterie of college administrators, authority figures from a different world, a few of whom would, a couple of decades later, be congealed as coffin-skinned, ash-haired "Dean Wormer" in the movie *Animal House*...

Wrestling at the University of Oregon had been a club sport since 1913, but the university program went intercollegiate the year Kesey had arrived on campus. He had earned a football scholarship. "At U of O I got some other thoughts. At 177 pounds I was too small to play guard, too slow to play backfield, and too stubborn to admit it. After my first season on the bench, coach Bill Hammer, one of Len Casanova's assistants, took me aside and let me know he was starting a wrestling team, and he needed a 177 pounder and I needed another sport—not to mention a chance to end my football career in honor." (Kesey is typically remembered as "big," but the 177 pound figure, little more than the average weight of the average adult American male, speaks to an ability to play larger than life).

Later, he won the Pac Ten championship in two separate years, and received the Fred Lowe Scholarship as the Northwest's most outstanding collegiate wrestler after posting a 11-1-1 record, seventh all-time best. Boyd Harris, who was Kesey's freshman roommate, recalled, "I turned him on to Lord Buckley and jazz; he turned me on to IT-290, peyote and marijuana." Kesey also later served as best man at Boyd's wedding.

"When Ken came to the rehearsal his brother Chuck drove him in a white Cadillac convertible. Kesey arrived wearing a cowboy hat and standing up on the front seat."

1953. Rosa Parks was about to ride an earlier bus. Alfred Kinsey published *Sexual Behavior in the Human Female* and was labeled "a menace to society" by the *Chicago Tribune*, and Hank Williams Sr. died of a drug and alcohol overdose at age 29. Closer to home, Lawrence Ferlinghetti opened City Lights bookstore in San Francisco, Marlon Brando starred in *The Wild One* (Mildred: "What are you rebelling against, Johnny?"; Johnny: "Wha'da'ya got?"), and the author Kesey would come to admire as the most significant writer since Shakespeare, William Burroughs, published his first novel, *Junkie,* under the pseudonym William Lee.

Otherwise, it was pretty much an "I like Ike" Republican America. A young five-o'clock-shadowed Richard Nixon perspiring in the White House, the first year of the Corvette, John F. Kennedy marrying Jackie, a man's world. An unholy triumph of incorporated authority, first by war, then by money. Instant gratification, planned obsolescence, and hidden persuaders under every other rock. Wonder Bread and Miracle Whip, a proto-utopia affirming the failed future that was fascism. As literary critic and author of *Understanding the Beats*, Edward Halsey Foster wrote, "men were supposed to be logical, efficient, and coolheaded, organizing their lives according to their employers' needs."

Though Kesey had yet to describe elliptic roped arcs from the rafters and through the shadows while disguised as Spiderman at the university's basketball gym, he was already headed in a different direction. He talked to Boyd Harris about starting something he called the Free Generation. Kesey didn't smoke or do drugs and told Boyd, "I think they're lying to us about marijuana, if I ever get a chance, I'm going to do it."

Boyd remembers Kesey as "honest to a fault."

One night they talked about the strongest point on a tennis racquet—Was it the yoke? Was it the strings?—for hours. "This was a man you could have a discussion with." Another Kesey occupation: Dong-Dong—"Which is where you would get together with a group of people and take a deep breath and let it out slowly, take another deep breath and let it out slowly, take another breath and make a sound, any sound you wanted to make. I've seen him do that with a few people and I've seen him do it with thousands."

Kesey greeted his muse from a "writing chair" in their room. Boyd would return from class, say he had to write a paper on this or that, and Kesey would sit perched in the chair for a minute , a pencil in his mouth, before he'd start scrawling, tossing papers off his desk, with Boyd picking them up and starting to type. Kesey wasn't tidy. Their room was a mess. "His father used to say after Ken sat down to eat, 'it looked like a coyote had been there.'" So one time, to make a point, Boyd collected all the discarded papers he could find, filled the room about knee high with refuse and waited for Kesey to come back.

"He just waded through the junk and sat down at his writing chair and didn't say a word. But he kept a diary—which when he wasn't around I read—and he was pissed."

For Kesey, epiphanies could come fast and from anywhere. One day he came back from health class and told Boyd, "You know what I learned today? 98% of men masturbate."

Boyd replied, "Well?"

Kesey said, "I don't."

Kesey pledged Beta Theta Pi fraternity and spent his time "playing college wonder-boy."

He and younger brother Joe-Chuck invented a water balloon sling-shot fashioned from surgical tubing tied to a leather pouch and mounted the slingshot on the back of a pickup truck. The future author drove around campus, firing away, launching balloons three stories up to the roof of Carson Hall where girls were sunbathing naked. The bloom went off the rose, however, when they launched a water balloon through a closed window in a society house and a girl was cut in the back by flying glass. Ken dispatched a fraternity brother over to apologize and, happy ending, "The guy ended up marrying the girl."

Down the dormitory hall lived a boy named Conrad, whom Kesey and Harris figured for a communist, but who, more importantly, ate fire. This sparked Kesey to create an "entertainment agency" aimed at the Elks and Kiwanis. "It was a great act. Ken would do adult humor with Dink, his dummy, and I'd play the conga drums while the communist ate fire."

Hypnotism remained the closer.

Kesey would tell the audience, "I have Boyd under a post-hypnotic state. I will say a word and he will become hypnotized." Then Kesey would have someone take a cigarette and grind its hot tip in Boyd's palm. Finally, Kesey would blindfold Boyd, lead him from the room and tell the crowd, "Hide anything you want and Boyd'll find it.'

Boyd remembers, "And I would. I won't tell you how we did it, but it was a great trick."

What price stardom? Could, would or should the love that dare not speak its name thwart or propel or otherwise resolve the ambitions of an incubating leading man whose passion for writing was an acquired taste and who wanted to hit center stage in Hollywood? The summer following their freshman year Kesey took off for Los Angeles and Boyd went down to visit him shortly thereafter. Kesey was hanging around the set of what would be Cecile B. DeMille's last film, the remake of his 1923 epic *The Ten Commandments*. He'd rented an apartment and told Boyd he planned to make good use of it—by installing a girl.

Boyd said, "How are we going to do that?"'

Kesey said, "Easy, we'll just drive down to Pershing Square and find a guy who sells girls and buy one."

They drove downtown to find a pimp. Boyd was trying to cut a deal when up drives a guy in a red Thunderbird convertible. The driver said, 'Ken. Ken. Ken. Come here.' Boyd watched as Kesey strolled over and began talking to the guy, then watched as Kesey came strolling back, to reveal, 'This guy Fred's on *Ten Commandments*. He wants to put me in the movies, so I'm going with him.'

Boyd advised against it, but Kesey said he was going anyway and hopped in the T-bird. There was nothing for Boyd to do but follow the Thunderbird's lights up to a large apartment perched in the Hollywood Hills.

After he'd ushered the two college boys inside, Fred said,"Let me show you pictures of a young man who's done some modeling. I'm trying to get him into the picture." Ken and Boyd looked at the photos. Fred took out more pictures and delivered the punchline, "This is me in Paris. This is my girlfriend in Paris. This is my boyfriend in Paris."

Ken looked at Boyd. Then the guy asked, "Are you two lovers?"

Boyd said, 'No, we're not.'

Which elicited an invitation from Fred to Ken, "Come with me. I want to show you something."

Boyd watched as Kesey was squired off to Fred's bedroom. Figuring it was all over but the shouting, Boyd snatched a fifth of whisky and a carton of cigarettes and took off down the stairs. A moment later Boyd saw Kesey running as if from the devil himself. "Boyd, come here!" Fred shouted from the top of the stairs, "Come here!"

"Don't do it," Kesey implored, "don't do it.'

Kesey and Boyd got back in the car and took off. Harris opened the whisky, handed it to his roommate. It was down the hatch, glug, glug, glug, then Kesey looked at Harris and posed the question: "Have you ever been kissed by a man?" Before Harris could answer, Kesey told Boyd they were going back to Fred's.

Boyd said, "No, I stole his cigarettes," but Kesey had made up his mind, it was back to Fred's, and when they got there Kesey wasted no time addressing the issue.

"Look," he said to fey Fred, "have you ever thought about seeing a psychiatrist about this problem?"

Indeed. "Yeah, I did that, and now I'm sleeping with him."

Then Fred began regaling the two about all the actors in Hollywood who were "queer." And somewhere down the light-in-the-loafers-list Boyd saw a white ceramic motorcycle on Floyd's coffee table and asked, "Where'd you get that?"

Fred replied, "Marlon Brando." Boyd had had enough. "Don't tell me anything more, I don't want to know."

Boyd and Ken's Los Angeles summer was not yet over. They drove to Tijuana to the bullfights and Kesey discovered a shop selling "mimeographed porn" and in need of new authors. "If you wrote a really good one you could get $25." The two conjured "this terrible nasty sleazy thing that ends in orgasmic death." When they returned to the shop, their future publisher read about "orgasmic death," and was not impressed. He offered them only five dollars.

Kesey refused to take the money, and while crossing the border, smuggling two parrots and a bag of cross tops, "Kesey was tossing pages out the window all the way."

Later, Kesey wrote Harris: "I have a fortune-making plan and let's face it, without a plan we are nothing. In fact, we are worse than nothing. Because we once had a plan and let it mildew in the closet beside the discarded jock straps. It's time. I had to spend two months selling and it cramped my mind until it almost smothered. I am not capable of working for a living and actually living at the same time. And I think you are some of the same. It gave us plot and venture. If we lose, we have lost little... So cast off, wash your mouth out, rip the laundry tags from your clothing and come spend a weekend on the Isle of Man's freedom, Keez."

Ultimately, the two were left to more common pursuits, and Kesey's history as a failed teetotaler is somewhat confusing. Though Boyd Harris reports rug-hugging apres-vodka and pop "rootdrivers," according to "Kesey scholar" Bennett Huffman, "He drank on his wedding night when he was a sophomore in college and then he hadn't had a drink (until) he moved to California (as a graduate student)." However, Kesey personally recalled a more intimate early relationship with alcohol, thanks to his first contact with Indians. "I was a junior at the U of O, majoring in radio and television. Our midterm assignment in screenwriting was to write an outline for a documentary about some town we considered particularly unique. Due Monday. I skipped my Friday classes and headed for Pendleton, driving my Nash Ambassador with seats that folded down to a lumpy bed. I wore a black beret and carried a big wine bota so people would know I was there as an artist, not a tourist."

"He was a one man entertainment center," Portland lawyer Brian Booth recalls, "I was going through rush at the Beta House. Kesey had a ventriloquist dummy, he was doing card tricks and magic."

A third generation Oregon Historical society board member—his grandfather wrote several books on John McLaughlin—who became interim director after a career in the sportswear industry, John Herman was one of Kesey's "younger brothers" at the Beta Theta Pi fraternity house. A rangily attractive man who dresses casually and impeccably, Herman was born in Portland, went to high school at Lincoln, went on to University of Oregon and was a Beta pledge in fall of 1956, "We went to a freshman introductory event that was just incredible—I was at the Beta house and had been introduced to Ken Kesey, who had written this whole show—for the entire University which was held at Mac Court. It was mind-boggling, an extravaganza, a huge celebration of the University.

"He was amazingly fit—he would just jump down and do pushups and stuff—we would play football out in front of the frat house and he was rugged and tough, he wouldn't be the first guy you'd try to knock down, because you'd be the one laying on the ground—he had a compelling aura about him very different from everyone else, this leadership quality, but in an offbeat James Jones kind of way, sort of cultish, there was always something I thought I was missing, something he had going on, but I didn't know what it was. Though he was very approachable. He didn't live at the house, at that point he lived at home (but) he was always there, but he wasn't a proponent of any life style that was unusual.

"It was all about sorority girls and going down to the river to drink beer, it was a wonderful time, after Korea, before Vietnam, very upbeat, the fraternity and sorority part very strong, it was the Len Casanova period in football—we went to the Rose Bowl and lost. It was very much a party atmosphere. Though there was a tremendous political awareness, nothing like a few years later focused against the war, because there was no war to be against. But students were very interested in local politics.

"He hypnotized other brothers in the houses, but I never took great credence in it. He would come and sit down in the living room and the brothers waited to hear what he had to say. He played mental gymnastics, not espousing philosophy, toying with people, making people defend their positions.

"It was no big deal that he was married," Herman says, nor that Kesey wasn't a big partier. "He didn't drink around the house—we had a party room in the basement, but…I never thought of him as a drinker at all, that was never visual around the fraternity house…

"We had a dance in the fall that was called the Bacchus Blast, wore togas, as in *Animal House* we had a toga party and it was an absolute blast. The house had many more of me than it had of Ken Kesey, I was a Portland guy from the West Hills who majored in business…there were terms we were on social pro(bation), but not every term."

Kesey later recalled, "I had this record of Ferlinghetti, Rexroth and Ginsberg reading beat poetry. We used to play it out of our loudspeaker system over at the Beta house. Lots of people were into it…I can remember driving down to North Beach with my folks and seeing Bob Kaufman out there in the street. I didn't know he was Bob Kaufman[8] at the time. He had little pieces of Band-Aids taped all over his face, about two inches wide, and little smaller ones like two inches long—and all of them made into crosses. He came up to the cars, and he was babbling poetry into these cars. He came up to the car I was riding in, and my

---

8 Bob Kaufman, a legendary jazz and beat poet of Creole and Jewish ancestry, is often credited with having coined the term "beat"—a shortened form of *beatific*.

folks, and started jabbering this stuff into the car. I knew that this was exceptional use of the human voice and the human mind."

Kesey's junior year at the U of O his instructor in a screenplay writing class informed Kesey, "You need to learn something about story. I'm transferring you to J. B. Hall's fiction class."

Kesey, already a Ray Bradbury fan, loved fiction. Especially if the word "science" was tacked in front of it. Hall had Kesey read Hemingway's "A Soldier's Home" and then explain to the class what the story was about. Kesey's response, "Well, all I can see is it's about this guy Krebs sitting in his mother's kitchen eating breakfast. She's hollering to him about getting out of the house and getting a job and developing some interests now that the war is over but all he wants to do is go watch his sister play baseball someplace—"

"No!" Professor Hall said. "Here's what it's about—here!"

As Kesey later recalled, Hall "strode over in his white shoes and stabbed a paragraph in the middle of my textbook. 'Right after his mother has served him his bacon and eggs and is telling him how she carried him next to her heart…what does Krebs do? What does he look at? Read it again—aloud.'

"The paragraph was only one line long. 'Krebs looked at the bacon fat hardening on his plate.'"

"'That's what the story is about! That one line is the key. That line sounds the note for the rest of the story. The whole composition would be in disharmony without that key to tune it. See?'"

"Damned if it didn't. That key unlocked for me the great resounding hall of real literature, and eventually got me in the door."

CHAPTER FIVE: THE GOOD BOOK

"Me, a stoodunt, gets asked by my buddy, a sighcologiz, dos I wanna go over to the local VA nuthouse, sign up for a government experiment, take some of these new mind-altering chemicals.

"Does I get paid?" I wanna know.

Twenty bucks a session, he says.

All right, I say. Long as it's for the U. S. A.

...and me, a jock, never even been drunk but that one night in my frat house before my wedding and even then not too drunk—going to the nut house to take dope under of course official auspices...

"See anything yet?" asks the doctor.

" Nope,' I tell him, visions swirling indescribable between us."

—Ken Kesey

When wily BMOC *beau ideal* alpha-dog farm boy Ken Kesey got word he'd won a fellowship to the Wallace Stegner writing program at Stanford University he'd been delighted, honored, felt lucky, but not intimidated. Yet Kesey, who once said there was more to be found in an average "Batman" comic than an issue of *Time*, entered a world where he might otherwise not have expected to succeed. An elbows-on-the-table dinner eater who resembled an HO-gauge football fullback more than any looming literary light, he found himself among the writing wing of America's best and brightest: skinny, unconfidently dressed young men (and one woman, Joanna Ostrow, "protected by her elegant Afghan"), whose futures remained hidden in manuscripts as yet unread or unwritten. In his class was Robert Stone—who would soon enter the literary pantheon by way of such darkly realistic novels as *Hall of Mirrors*, *Dog Soldiers* and *A Flag for Sunrise*, that would come to redefine contemporary Noir fiction. More significantly, Kesey's class also included Larry McMurtry, a creative and prolific literary force who'd go on to chronicle the West in a library's worth of wonderful novels including *The Last Picture Show*, *Lonesome Dove*—and more recently, the screenplay for the film *Brokeback Mountain*.

In the anthology *"The Company They Kept: Writers and Unforgettable Friendships"* in his reminiscence about his first encounter with Kesey, McMurtry recalled a half dozen fellow future great novelists: "Like stoats in a henhouse, we were poised to rend and tear," but Kesey "made it plain that he meant to be stud-duck." Kesey, "a figure so Paul Bunyanesque that I would not have been surprised to see Babe the Blue Ox plod in behind him…plopped himself down at the right hand of Mr. Cowley (instructor Malcolm Cowley) and got set to read what turned out to be the first chapters of *One Flew Over the Cuckoo's Nest*. This was stud-duckery indeed."

"Ken cleared his throat, we bristled, and then relaxed and decided to be bemused, rather than annoyed. Why? Because Ken Kesey was a very winning man, and he won us…Ken's determination to be the center of attention: he wanted it so badly; so we let him get away with it, and, with one tragic exception, he kept getting away with it for the next forty-one years, until the day came when he couldn't…when it stopped."

In short, Kesey went from good old boy jock hayseed to fifth dimensional Svengali among a class of literary nerds who became the new giants of American letters; Stanford graduate students soon to be writers for the new age. For starters, an inversion of the underground. Though the keel of the new counterculture was soon weighted with leaden leftist dogma, the existing counterculture, born of the beats, was anything but. Nowadays, Jack Kerouac would be considered politically just to the left of Rush Limbaugh, and at Stanford Kesey, as Kerouac's heir to the throne, was just to the right enough to at first dismiss Robert Stone as a communist.

Though there were exceptions, including an oddly prescient song released by a new and generally apolitical folk group critically acclaimed by only Bob Dylan and millions of college kids, the fresh faced, prototypically preppie Kingston Trio, whose early hit "Coplas" gave America a hint, "Tell your parents not to muddy the water around us, [or] they will have to drink it soon." Paranoia had yet to strike deep but…

Meanwhile in Liverpool, seventeen year-old John Lennon invited another boy, Paul McCartney, to join a band he'd formed called the

"Quarrymen," and in Detroit Ford had recently unveiled plans for the Nucleon, a car which had a nuclear reactor instead of a V-8 and got 5,000 miles to a tank of uranium.

The buttoned-down sky was the limit: Aero was combined with space to create a new word, aerospace; an F-104 Starfighter flew at 1,404.19 mph hour, breaking the world's air speed record; America launched its first satellite, and back on earth, Pope Pius XII declared Saint Clare the Patron Saint of Television. *On the Road*—written in 1951 but published finally the year before in 1957 was flying out bookstore doors and twenty-three year-old Ken Kesey had settled into a Woodrow Wilson Writing Fellowship at Stanford. His first impulse was to write about, if not what he learned, at least what he could discover. On tap, the storied locals. Two years later, by the time Kesey had abandoned *Zoo,* his novel about San Francisco goys gone wild, he'd catalyzed his imagination on US Government inspected LSD.

Your tax dollars at work. Thanks to the provident gods of government lunacy, acid had already enjoyed a colored past. Discovered accidently by Swiss chemist Albert Hofmann just before World War II (Hofmann took the first "hit" and was awarded a very trippy bicycle ride home, where he found himself not entirely appalled at the notion that he was losing his mind), LSD made its way across the Atlantic as a "mind control" drug. Acid's capabilities were soon road tested. Creatively. Take MKULTRA's Operation Midnight Climax, in which CIA agents had San Francisco prostitutes lure unsuspecting men to an apartment where they were given drinks dosed with LSD and then encouraged to attempt sex—as their performances being recorded by a camera operated through a one-way mirror.

The "redemptive" side of LSD was likewise pioneered by the government. Psychedelia may owe its life to CIA super-spook Al Hubbard, "the Johnny Appleseed of Acid," who, while Tim Leary was still parsing Ovid for Undergraduates, was tripping out of his crew-cut mind, and becoming presciently paranoid that his beloved elixir would fall into the hands of bohemian rabble. Director of the Stanford Research Institute Willis Harmon said "arch-arch conservative" Al Hubbard was convinced "if he could give the psychedelic experience to the major executives of the Fortune 500 companies, he could change the whole of society."

Similarly, from the other side of the spectrum, Aldous Huxley had changed his cosmic consciousness tune as well. Beguiled by the ancients' serenades of Soma, Huxley's new Soma, as it was articulated in *Brave New World*, was the key pharmaceutical ingredient in what he felt was soon to be a future utopian anti-paradise that he foresaw as inevitable. From birth—controlled by eugenics—we'd be sculpted, initially by "infant conditioning" then by drugs like scopolamine. Our fates would be controlled from the time we were toddlers, our psyche's numbed by Soma. But by the time Kesey found his own psychedelic muse at Stanford, Aldous had abandoned Soma for the harder stuff, Acid's slightly dumber brother mescaline. Which, unlike the dreaded Soma, Huxley regarded as a true metaphysical savior.

Seismic. Balzac, Voltaire, Kant, Goethe, Yeats, Nietzsche, Aleister Crowley, William Burroughs, Allan Ginsberg and Philip K. Dick were all propelled and/or derailed by various drugs. Coleridge credited opium as his muse (though the Adam of psychedelic writers, Lewis Carroll, was known to be as sober as a storm grate). But acid was different.

As in meta-philosophy so in life, acid would deliver what was later termed "divine schizophrenia" for the coming Aquarian age.

Perhaps only intuitively, Kesey worshipped at the altar of myth. Not the myth particularly of Homer, but the living myth born of his childhood comic books and television. "Everywhere in Kesey," controversial literary critic Leslie Fiedler wrote much later, "the influence of comics and, especially, comic books is clearly perceptible, in the mythology as well as in the style...the images and archetypal stories which underlie his fables are...the adventures of Captain Marvel and Captain Marvel, Jr., those new style supermen who, sometimes just after World War II, took over the fantasy of the young...One might, indeed, imagine Kesey ending up as a comic book writer, but...he has preferred to live his comic strip rather than to write or even draw it."

The director of the Stanford writing program, Wallace Stegner was, however, not a fan of the comic book sensibility. Tall, handsome and dapper in an erring-to-the-side-of-flannel Pacific coast way, Stegner was, like Kesey, very much a man of his time and place, a charismatic novelist whose flagship work, *Big Rock Candy Mountain*, was already a staple of college curricula alongside *Moby Dick* and *The Grapes of Wrath*. Like Kesey, Stegner loved the land, and took the West for the last best place.

In any other era the two might have taken to each other like wise father and errant son. But not at the beginning of this one.

For everything was about to change. Thanks to the good offices of the nearby Menlo Park Veterans Hospital, where the medical powers that be were employing the lesser academic locals to audition a new elixir miraculous. "I had a neighbor," Kesey recalled, "a psychologist booked to do the experiments (one) Tuesday, he chickened out." So for twenty dollars a session, Ken Kesey was presented with a kaleidoscopic array of mind-blowing drugs. For six months.

Kesey waxed philosophical. "The government said we've discovered this nice room, we need somebody to go in and look it over...Eight o'clock every Tuesday morning I showed up...ready to roll. The doctor deposited me in a little room on his ward, dealt me a couple of pills or a shot or a little glass of bitter juice." Then the doctor locked the door, but popped back every forty minutes to see if Kesey was "still alive." He took some tests, asked some questions, left leaving Kesey to "study the inside of my forehead, or look out the little window in the door. It was six inches wide and eight inches high, and it had heavy chicken wire inside the glass."

Sub nirvana but the road to nirvana still, and, thanks to Federal Government LSD, the best Kesey ever had. "They gave me mine—paid me and quite a few other rats both white and black...to test it for them, *started it* so to speak, then, when they caught a glimpse of what was coming down in that little room full of guinea pigs, they snatched the guinea pigs out, slammed the door, locked it, barred it, dug a ditch around it, set two guards in front of it, and gave the helpless guinea pigs a good talking to and warned them—on threat of worse than death—to *never* go in that door again."

Shortly thereafter, Kesey was hired at Menlo Park Hospital to work the graveyard shift, midnight to dawn, as a nurse's aide. Better to kill two birds with one stone, he brought pad and pencil to the chore. As luck would have it, he was put on the same ward as the doctor, Leo E. Hollister (later author of *Chemical Psychosis: LSD and Related Drugs*) who had given him the original hallucinogens. Dr. Hollister was no longer doing the experiments, having, according to Kesey, realized the dangers to "the government" if the experiments were to continue..

But Dr. Hollister, who liked the young lab rat/writer, still had the acid. One night Kesey, who had keys to Hollister's offices, came in and "went into his room, into his desk, and took out a lot of stuff. That was the source of our—all of our drugs—for a long time...there was this stuff all labeled. I already knew a bunch of it. I could see he wasn't using it."

Kesey had found gnosis in a pill. "Not just shock, not just invention," he claimed, "but something that arrives on your familiar wavelength and overloads all your little skinny lines of reason and forces admissions of vistas beyond all those horizons you were certain were absolutely permanent." And no time to look a gift horse in the mouth. He began writing *Cuckoo's Nest* "immediately." As he'd recall forty years after the fact: "You get your visions through whatever gate you're granted."[9]

Kesey had begun the book from a conventional point of view. His own. "I tried working on the novel...from the PV of an aide, me, and realizing how much the narrative sounded like other promising young writers' narratives."

To escape that dismal, rational fate, he took a quantum leap. Or gulp. "Peyote," he wrote in 1973, "I used to claim, inspired my Chief narrator, because it was after choking down eight of the little cactus plants that I wrote the first three pages. These pages remained almost completely unchanged through numerous rewrites the book went through, and from this first spring I drew all the passion and perception the narrator spoke with during the ten months writing that followed. That narrator happened to be an Indian, despite my never having known an Indian before. I attributed this (sic) to the well known association between peyote and certain tribes of the southwest."

Working graveyard, tending the inmates, Kesey "saw it all...I saw the looks on these people's faces...and realized that Freud was full of shit. Something really dug deep in these people's minds, and it wasn't the way they were treated when they were toilet trained; it wasn't the way they were rejected when they were thirteen. It was something to do with the American Dream. How the American Dream gave us our daily energy, and yet the dream was perverted."

An awesome blind vision would soon be his.

---

9 Transcendental lunacy provoked comic turns. Blasted out of his tracks on a "double-ought capsule of pure mescaline" as an orderly, Kesey recalled arguing "so fervently with the big knotty pine door across the office from me that I actually chalked a broad yellow line across the floor between us and told the door, 'You stay on your side, you goggle-eyed son of a bitch, and I'll stay on mine.'"

Chapter Six: Unholy Grail

"It's all God's flesh. LSD is always a sacrament, whether you are a silly thirteen year old girl popping a sugar cube on your boyfriend's motorcycle…or even a psychiatrist giving LSD to an unsuspecting patient to do a scientific study."

—Timothy Leary

Establishing a lair in Palo Alto's bohemian Perry Lane neighborhood, the man soon to be known as "The Chief" quickly also set himself up as leader of a pack even easier to impress than his preppie University of Oregon undergraduate Beta House brothers—America's future literary lions. But the action was elsewhere. "When I was doing those experiments at the Vets hospital, they gave us an enormous array of drugs, and they gave us an enormous array of tests. They tested our motor skills, our memories, our ability to create, to imagine." Of his first acid trips, Kesey wrote, "I grabbed that handle. Legally, too, I might add. Almost patriotically, in fact"…and in an interview several years later, he recalled, "I felt like I was doing as American a thing as Neil Armstrong when he volunteered to go to the moon. There was a new place to be explored and we were astronauts. That exploration of new territory is a very American thing. Say you're doing cocaine, that is not exploration of new territory, that's just titillation."

The magic garden of psychedelics, ancient, holistic, government-sponsored and otherwise, supercharged his vision there at the Vets hospital—he sketched the loonies in the loony bin. Not long before he died, Ken Kesey wrote regarding *Cuckoo* in utero, "Those faces were still there, still painfully naked. To ward them off my case I very prudently took to carrying around a little notebook, to scribble notes…I also scribbled faces. No, that's not correct. As I prowl through this stack of sketches I can see that these faces bored their way behind my forehead and scribbled themselves. I just held the pen and waited for the magic to happen."

* * *

It was at Stanford that Kesey first dabbled in the rewriting of the social contract and the shedding of common social mores.

McMurtry said of Kesey at Stanford: "Ken already had a court; and he kept a court. Courtiers might leave, be chased off, die; but there would be replacements. The Merry Pranksters, once they evolved, functioned as a floating court…To enjoy the strength of Ken's friendship it was necessary to separate him, for a time, from the court, because if the court was sitting, he would play to it."

As a social elixir, LSD made the Martini look like malted milk. "The first drug trips were, for most of us, shell-shattering ordeals that left us blinking knee-deep in the crumbling crusts of our pie-in-the-sky personalities. Suddenly people were stripped before one another, and behold: we were beautiful. Naked and helpless and sensitive as a snake after skinning, but far more human than that shining knightmare that stood creaking in previous parade rest. We were alive and life was us." [10]

Strange brew: Ken Kesey offered his guests to his Perry Lane digs green Kool-Aid percolating coldly in a punchbowl, steaming clouds of dry ice. It looked like "the sort of punch Satan would serve," recalled Malcolm Cowley, former radical Marxist, pal to Hemingway and Fitzgerald, editor to William Faulkner and Jack Kerouac and the man who was about to make Ken Kesey famous, but who declined his student's offer, opting instead for a glass of Kesey's grandmother's bootleg whisky.

Cowley had also been close friend to Ernest Hemingway, and the Hemingway connection was a good one. For, aspiring master fabulist and action figure Ken Kesey was a child of "Papa" Hemingway. Like the author of *our father who art in nada, nada be thy name,* former teenage magician Kesey had dreams of a future as a post-Christ if not post-Christian metaphysician. For young Kesey's enlightenment, Cowley

---

10 Lit up by government acid, the natives were getting restless. "It had been happening down on Homer Lane and Perry Lane in Palo Alto," Laird Grant, the Grateful Dead's first roadie, recalled, "Sometimes there would be parties in all three places…Tripping openly at parties was still six months to a year away. Then it was really secretive. People were feeling, 'Should we let other people know about this?' Then the thing was, 'Yeah. Everybody should do it.' Which again changed everybody's life into a whole different, larger, stranger circle."

quoted Hemingway's metaphysical dreams, as they appeared in *Green Hills of Africa* in which Hemingway's surrogate, Philip Percival, explained to an Austrian companion "fourth dimensional prose."

It was *"the kind of writing that can be done. How far prose can be carried if anyone is serious and has luck. There is a fourth and fifth dimension that can be gotten…It is much more difficult than poetry. It is a prose that has never been written. But it can be written, without tricks and without cheating. With nothing that will go bad afterwards."*

Later, in *Kesey's Garage Sale*, Kesey voiced his own ideas about Ernest Hemingway's transcendental quest, thoughts kindled by a look in the mirror. "Sometimes it's hard to tell if Hemingway was writing the Judy Garland story or if Janis Joplin was writing the Ernest Hemingway story; they're all such tragically similar tales of what happens to people who stare a trace too long into the Spotlight. There are some hints, though, to help the necro-romantic sort the real corpse from the pile of yellow husks: don't be misled by the bodies of bullfighters or the riddled remains of soldiers: look instead for live trout on the bottom vibrating against the clean current, or an old board going sharp into focus through a pair of binoculars; in those delicate transitions where nothing actually moves you may find something of the slow and gentle old giant. Even in his last book, which is, apparently, heavily put down, you'll find the gleaming deposits of these intensely true perceptions. Even when you watch his media-maddened ego begin to lead him astray you still feel you can trust your head to go along with him; he never crossed anybody except himself."

Perhaps alchemy eluded Hemingway, but not Kesey. "There's something about seeing reality with a new light shining on it that goes right from your eyes to your fingertips," he concluded late in his life, "I would not have been able to write as well without LSD. I'll take acid every time, it's a shortcut to enlightenment given to us at the end of the century for those of us who wanted to go on to better realities and understand it with respect: the door's been opened, and this is the key that opened it."

That was Kesey's draft of *One Flew Over the Cuckoo's Nest*, which, in addition to LSD, had been informed by the mystics. "We," Kesey later reflected ("we" meaning he), "had read a certain amount of Oriental literature. And we had read Hesse, and we had a spiritual underpinning of knowing the Bible and knowing the Bhagavad Gita, knowing the Judeo traditions. And that gives you stars to sail by. And without those stars, just thrown into chaos, a lot of people are lost."

As a boy mesmerized by magic and success, Kesey was never shy about thinking too big. Or acting the part. Wallace Stegner, director of the Stanford graduate writing program, pioneer of modern environmentalism, (and writer of such light verse as:

> *There once was a blonde from Nahant,*
> *Whose panties were silken and scant*
> *Her boy was diminutive*
> *And slip his infinitive*
> *You finish this damn thing, I can't)*

novelist of the West and prickly battler of his own demons—his alleged creative treatment of previously published materials got him charged with plagiarism—didn't cotton to Kesey, tagging Ken "a person of more force than mind. I think Kesey is crazy as a coot, and dangerous, and rather special in his charismatic qualities, and with what was once a fairly big raw talent."

Stanford writing instructor Dick Scowcroft allowed, "Neither Wally nor I thought he had particularly important talent. Wally said to me once he (Kesey) was sort of a fairly talented illiterate."

Then Kesey coughed up *Cuckoo's Nest* and it no longer mattered what Stegner thought. For Kesey's part, he was charitable after the fact: "He was better than a teacher. He was like Vince Lombardi, and we were the Green Bay Packers of fiction writing," he told author John Daniel, and spoke warmly of the Stanford faculty, referring to Scowcroft as "so sweet and gentle that he complemented Malcolm Cowley, who was a gruff man." And of Stegner, that the two were on "different sides of the fence. As I took LSD, and he drank Jack Daniels, we drew the line between us right there."

Malcolm Cowley wrote of his student Kesey: "He hasn't ever learned how to spell, and didn't even begin reading for pleasure until he was an upper classman…He went to school on a football scholarship… Last year Kesey nearly made the Olympic wrestling team—he has a 19 inch neck…He's married, has 1½ children, works in a state loony bin in this vicinity…(his) manuscript might just turn out to be something that would HAVE to be published."[11]

Cowley had already read Kesey's first attempt to climb the mountain, his novel *Zoo*, for which Kesey had received a Saxton Fellowship but for which Kesey could not find a publisher. Cowley knew why. "The book was full of powerful scenes, but became sentimental and lost its story line. In this second book the story line is never lost." That was *Cuckoo.* "His first drafts must have been written at top speed; they were full of typing errors, as if words had come piling out of a Greyhound bus too fast to have their clothes brushed." Yet Cowley was tremendously enthusiastic. "He didn't have the fatal notion of some beat writers, that the first hasty account of a vision was a sacred text not to be tampered with. He revised, he made deletions and additions; he was working with the readers in mind."

Cowley was particularly admiring of *Cuckoo's* deaf, except not, and dumb, except not, schizophrenic Indian narrator. "Kesey had his own crazy visions—induced by eating peyote…and those could be attributed to Chief Broom (sic)."

When Cowley submitted the manuscript of *Cuckoo's Nest* for publication, he received much interest from younger editors, less from older ones. "I've been an exception among the gaffers."

Describing Kesey as "an Oregon roughneck," Cowley went on to say, "He's tough, sentimental, and inventive-experimental in matters of conduct. He'll probably end by corrupting the whole Stanford group of writers, among whom he's leader. I'm sure, though, he'll be heard from and write many books."

In *Cuckoo's Nest*, Kesey auditioned messianic themes that would guide his life.

---

11 Later Cowley added, "The faults of this novel…are obvious…Sometimes the narrator, Chief Bromden, talks out of character, when the author wants to preach. The end of the story is false when Bromden kills the wreck of McMurphy and then escapes. If we are to believe that Bromden is really sane enough now to live outside the asylum, he shouldn't commit a murder. Some of Bromden's delusions are overdone: gratuitous dirt and horror. The manuscript could be improved by cutting, but it has enormous vitality…"

CHAPTER SEVEN: BIG MOTHER AND THE WHORES

"A man like McMurphy secretly admires an opponent like Big Nurse, and he will use anybody in his struggle to overpower her. That he betrays himself in the process as a male chauvinist pig hardly matters, to cult followers of either sex. Men see Big Nurse as a combination of Wicked Stepmother, Bitch Goddess, and Grendel's Dam. McMurphy prefers goodtime girls who do not mind helping boys like Billy Bibbit achieve manhood. Nurse Ratched is woman as castrator, and McMurphy flinches automatically in her presence. Female cult followers also identify with McMurphy, and they see Nurse Ratched as a traitor to her sex, the mother who stands in your way, the boyfriend's mother who thinks you're not good enough for her son, the bitchy boss who makes it through the door and then slams it in your face."

—Thomas Reed Whissen

"They're out there.

Black boys in white suits up before me to commit sex acts in the hall and get it mopped up before I can catch them." The opening lines told you that you were in the hands of a mad man and/or a master. Not since Jack Kerouac's *On the Road* would a book have such a catalytic effect. Post modern mythology: McMurphy aka martyred blue-collar Christ versus loony bin boss Big Nurse—groundbreaking hater of freedom, lust and nonconformity—aka the System.

Malcolm Cowley, in retrospect, came to this conclusion: "Artists who succeed are strong characters, which is something different from saying they are saints. Some of them—most of them?—do scandalous and even scoundrelly things."

An author might, for example, steal from life to make art.

While her provenance has been debated—University of Oregon Dean of Women Golda Wickham has long been thought to have provided Kesey at least part of his Nurse Ratched prototype. And, years after *Cuckoo's Nest* made him less a writer than a brand, Kesey, visiting an aquarium in Newport, Oregon, was startled to find himself standing in front of Big Nurse. Not the Big Nurse who sprang from his levitating imagination, but the actual Big Nurse whom he knew, and had re-invented, from the veterans hospital near Stanford.

Try this on for size: *"Her face is smooth, calculated, precision made, like an expensive baby doll, skin like flesh-colored enamel, blend of white and cream and baby-blue eyes, small nose, pink little nostrils—everything working together except the color on her lips and fingernails, and the size of her bosom. A mistake was made somehow in manufacturing, putting those big womanly breasts on what would of otherwise been a perfect work, and you can see how bitter she is about it."*

A big, bad news Barbie? George Orwell, we hardly knew ye. But what did we need 1984 for, if we had 1962? *Those breasts.* Big picture misogyny. The good old boy "combine" in the iron hand of The Matriarchy. Big Brother suckled by Big Mother.

Big Nurse stood tall among the archetypes of the era: the last hurrah of the pre-feminist bad girls, bitches, bimbos, broads, cock-teases, sluts, battleaxes and chicks who were "frigid." Big Nurse, whose skin was as fair, perfect and perhaps even as hard as fine china and for whom soul and lust were buried behind a generous bosom, was an affront to every man's freedom, representing every rule that ever needed to be broken. Yet Nurse Ratched was an odd villain in an era when women were lucky to have the power of butlers and, to strike a best-selling bell, Big Nurse could only represent mother, wife or school marm. The Big Nurse archetype fast became part of American popular culture, inspiring the 1963 Broadway production of *Cuckoo's Nest,* which ran for 82 nights, starring Kirk Douglas as McMurphy.

Kesey was impressed to see how the loons had flown from the nest of his imagination to the reality of the stage. "The actors…capture that nuthouse feeling so completely…that I found myself wondering where some of them had been sprung from. Just, for small example, their movement: inmates have a way of walking that is both piticully (sic) random and terribly purposeful, and peculiar to no other place I know of save the mental ward…Watch Ruckly when he shuffles onto stage; he's been shuffling that same way in those same slippers for centuries…Kirk Douglas was so good it was like I had written it for him."

Kesey had been in the audience opening night—he and Douglas

retired to Schrafft's to await initial newspapers reviews, which were not excellent. Writing in the *New York Times*, Howard Taubman concluded, "How can a thread of compassion stand out in a crazy-quilt of wisecracks, cavortings, violence and histrionic villainy?"

In a letter written in response to a negative review of *Cuckoo,* Kesey began by saying, "The answering of one's critics has always struck me as doing about as much good as fighting crabgrass with manure," and dismissed "people who saw the play as being about a mental ward (as) the sort that would fault *Moby Dick* for being an 'exaggerated' story about a boat."

"The notion that this setting is only a fictional and fantastic one does an injustice to thousands of patients in hundreds of wards almost identical to that ward on the stage…While *Cuckoo's Nest* is…about more than a mental hospital, it is also an attack on tyranny of the sort that is perhaps more predominant in mental hospitals than any place else in our land. It is by no accident that the acute ward was picked for the setting; after working for close to a year as an aide in two hospitals in California, I could imagine no better backdrop for my parable. I only needed to describe what I had seen and heard, what I felt after endless swing shift hours talking with the broken and defeated men of our society, and what I concluded to be the stress that broke them.

"McMurphy is, of course, fictional—a dream, a wild hope fabricated out of need in defeat—but the men he comes to save, and the menace he battles, these are real, live human being (sic). While this world may be fantastic, it is not mere fantasy. Neither is it an exaggeration; when I hear of someone accusing the book, or the play, of 'exaggerating the bad' I think of my last days at the hospital: the first draft of the book almost finished, I had handed in my letter of resignation (a day before, incidently [sic], I received a letter from the superior nurse advising me I was being discharged for 'a lack of interest in the hospital…') and I had only one bit of research left. I had to try shock treatment to get some idea why the patients thought it so bad. And I did. And I found out. And to those who think it is fictionally exaggerated, I only say try it first and see. Because it can never be as bad in fiction as it is in real life."

Kesey later claimed that it was after opening night, driving back across the country, when he learned that John Kennedy had been shot— it was the news of this tragedy that led him to conceive the idea for the cross country road trip to the 1964 New York World's Fair that would eventually metamorphose into the voyage chronicled by Tom Wolfe in *The Electric Kool-Aid Acid Test.*

By the time *Cuckoo's Nest* had established Randle P. McMurphy as, absent Christ, the fictional lone hero template that Kesey would use to establish himself—marginally de-rednecked and the nudie playing cards swapped for an America flag shirt—the lone hero ground had been well ploughed. *Have Gun Will Travel's* Paladin, *Gun Smoke's* Matt Dillon, Davy Crockett, the Swamp Fox, the Lone Ranger, Cheyenne Bodey, The Rifleman, Zorro, Peter Gunn, Mister Lucky, *Rawhide's* Rowdy Yeats ("We don't try to understand 'em, we just rope and tie and brand 'em"), Lassie; the roster was encyclopedic. By 1964 TV had produced enough lone heroes to fill Yankee Stadium. Monkey see, monkey do: lone hero (he who is ready, willing and eager to take the law into his own hands) had trumped President as America's top job. Too, there was a lot of snickering going on behind authority's back.

As novelist (*Rally Round the Flag, Boys,* etc.) and creator of the hit sit-com *The Many Loves of Doby Gillis,* Max Shulman remarked, the average 1950s TV show was about "the whole family getting together to screw gruff old dad." Fathers and leaders were fools. Even the Nazis couldn't shoot straight. Watch the first five minutes of any episode of *Hogan's Heroes* to catch the comic fascist dunderheadedness of Colonel Klink and Sergeant Schultz, the pater-familias of a bumpkin Stalag that could have arisen only on a Hollywood back lot (According to *Mad Magazine:* "If you thought World War II was funny, you'll love *Hogan's Heroes*").

To the extent great novels usually evolve from a trinity defined by character, place and action, *Cuckoo's Nest* was—its inverted locale and red hot lone anti-hero notwithstanding—about the latter, less about describing the symptoms than initiating the cure. By the time Randle McMurphy had worked his martyred magic in Big Nurse's loony bin, Holden Caulfield had spent at least ten years reminding adolescents that the sane were crazy and the crazy were sane. Before and after *Catcher in the Rye*, which was published in 1951, *The Day of the Locust* and *On the Road* had celebrated magnificent empty energy and the terminal restlessness of a motor-headed, empty-hearted Vacuityville that was all about getting drunk on the lost dream of the West and going nowhere fast.

Cuckoo wasn't so much a portrait as, like Christ's ministry, a call to action.

As novelist Gurney Norman claimed "when Chief Broom throws the control panel through the insane asylum window…that was the first shot of the revolution." Add that to reality as a conspiracy, psychedelics as reality, institutionalized insanity, wow. The time was right. Something exciting was in the air.

"We need that Vaseline," they (the "black boys") tell the Big Nurse, "for the thermometer." She looks from one to the other. "I'm sure you do," and hands them a jar that holds at least a gallon, "but mind you boys don't group up in there?" Then I see two, maybe three of them in there, in that shower room with the Admission, running that thermometer around in the grease till it's coated the size of your finger, crooning, 'Tha's right, mothah, tha's right" and then shut the door and turn up all the showers up to where you can't hear anything but the vicious kiss of water on the green tile."

Vaseline in renegade mental institutions is rarely good news for anybody, and this madhouse of horrors was no different. It's been said that *Cuckoo's Nest* owed much of its success to the drive provided by "the great binaries of sane and insane, male and female, free and captive," but Ken Kesey's advice in the 1990s to his students at the University of Oregon was to first find a locale: "What place? The road to Canterbury is long ago loaded, the Mississippi choked with rafts and runaway slaves. Hunting whales on the high seas is out of vogue and Lost Horizons on Tibetan mountain tops out of focus. Let's find a place where people haven't been. Let's go down a hole! Good, at least we know where we're going. Whew! Now all we have to do is find out why these people are going down in this hole, and what happens to them on the way, and what it means to everybody, and we got us a novel.

"On second thought let's not step on that 'what it means to everybody' step: that plank had always been a little squeaky."

As for character, aside from Henry James, men who write novels in this country are usually asked only that their hero play hooky from civilization, kill or mock the boys and fuck or mock the girls and, dead or alive, ride or be carted into the sunset.

"McMurphy comes perilously close to being the clown who will do anything for a laugh and who enjoys defiance for its own sake," Thomas Reed Whissen observed, "a guy who makes a profession out of being a nonconformist and who, ironically enough, inspires others to conform to his nonconformist image. Thus, McMurphy becomes the ideal cult hero, the loner whom vast numbers imitate."

As essayist Bruce Carnes wrote in 1972, "Kesey seems to envision a post-cataclysmic utopia of some kind. He hints in *Cuckoo's Nest,* for instance, that the collapse of civilization will be followed by the establishment of a new kingdom founded by the new Christ... McMurphy.

"McMurphy has assumed the other men's burdens. He discovers, perhaps, that he loves these fellow victims. He is no longer entirely his own man, but a representative of a value system. He is the standard-bearer of humanity against the System. He is Christ, or, perhaps more accurately, Pound's Goodly Fere—not only a cowboy Christ but a Teutonic one as well."

McMurphy's Christ trip has been well documented (*"Cuckoo's Nest* deserves to be recognized as the preeminent literary paradigm of redemption secularly conceived."—George N. Boyd, Assistant Professor of Religion Trinity University), but once more for the record, here are the high points: After provoking Nurse Ratched (who has been elsewhere—on another level, assigned the oceanic identity of *Moby Dick's* Ahab), *"You are strapped to a table, shaped, ironically, like a cross, with a crown of electric sparks in place of thorns."*

And:

They put the graphite salve on his temples. "What is it?" he says.

"Conductant," the technician says.

"Anointest my head with conductant. Do I get a crown of thorns?"

By inspiring Broom to give up his deaf and dumb guise, McMurphy, messiah-like, makes the deaf hear and the dumb speak. However, the unholy jig is up the next morning when Jesus McMurphy and his disciples, all fast asleep, are discovered, and Billy, Judas-like, breaks down and betrays McMurphy, before, Judas-like, slitting his own throat.

After which, Nurse Ratched confronts McMurphy. *"I hope you're finally satisfied. Playing with human lives—gambling with human lives—as if you thought yourself to be a God!"*

Then there was the shocking matter of McMurphy's end. Compare Bromden's description: *"He let himself cry out...when he finally doesn't care anymore about anything but himself and his dying"* with Mark 15:37—*"with a loud cry, Jesus breathed his last"* and Matthew 27:50—*"And when Jesus had cried out again in a loud voice, he gave up his spirit."* Who knew?

On a more terrestrial plane, *One Flew Over the Cuckoo's Nest*, as *On the Road* had before it, certainly filled that bill—and its hallmark quote by Kerouac's protagonist, Sal Paradise, might easily have been uttered by Randle P. McMurphy instead: *"The only people for me are the mad ones, the ones who are mad to live, mad to talk, mad to be saved, desirous of everything at the same time, the ones who never yawn or say a commonplace thing, but burn, burn, burn like fabulous yellow candles exploding like spiders across the stars in the sky."*

If Hemingway's vision had been enriched by booze to reveal the virile loners among the impotent lost, if Kerouac's vision had been accelerated by speed to reveal the seekers in search of the sought, it was left to Kesey to eat his government acid and, courtesy this miracle sacrament, speak with the voice of the schizophrenic Indian Bromden to best reveal, *"a cartoon world, where the figures are flat and outlined in black, jerking through some kind of goofy story that might be real funny if it weren't for the cartoon figures being real guys."*

* * *

Listen: *"There was me, that is Alex, and my three droogs, Pete, Georgie and Dim, being dim, and we sat in the Korova Milkbar trying to make up our rassoodocks what to do with the evening. The Korova Milkbar sold milkplus, milk plus vellocet or synthmesc or dremscron, which is what we were drinking. This would sharpen you up and make you ready for a bit of the old ultraviolence."*

That's fifteen year-old Alex, hero of Anthony Burgess' *A Clockwork Orange*, talking. Published a year after *One Flew Over the Cuckoo's Nest*, it worked psychedelia from the other side of the street—installing psychedelics in the novel itself—in the form of "synthmesc"—though definitely not a peace-love version.

Burgess wrote not in the schizophrenic vernacular of the Chief, but in "Nadsat," his self-invented Russian-spiced street language of 2017 London. The plots of *A Clockwork Orange* and *Cuckoo* reach a similar conclusion: the unruly protagonist anti-hero menace to society is institutionalized and "castrated" of his menacing powers by the state. Whereas, in Kesey's novel the method used was lobotomy; Burgess employed behavior modification courtesy of electric shock. Burgess worked the Christ imagery from the opposite side of the Via Dolorosa.

As critics have noted before, Alex does not imagine himself as Christ but as one of the Crucifiers, indulging in a reverie in which he partakes in "the nailing in" of the savior.

Concurrently, stories of the insane, about the insane or by the insane were standing tall on the page. In 1961, Joseph Heller had published *Catch-22*, whose flying hellhole that was the B-24 bomber dodging German flak and cannon-nosed Messerschmitts, was, for me, a more dynamic realization of the insane asylum and illustrative of a larger, far, far scarier truth:

"There was only one catch and that was Catch-22, which specified that a concern for one's safety in the face of dangers that were real and immediate was the process of a rational mind. Orr was crazy and could be grounded. All he had to do was ask; and as soon as he did, he would no longer be crazy and would have to fly more missions. Orr would be crazy to fly more missions and sane if he didn't, but if he was sane he had to fly them. If he flew them he was crazy and didn't have to; but if he didn't want to he was sane and had to. Yossarian was moved very deeply by the absolute simplicity of this clause of Catch-22 and let out a respectful whistle.

"That's some catch, that Catch-22," he [Yossarian] observed.

"It's the best there is," Doc Daneeka agreed.

A new day was dawning. As Kesey would later write, "Suddenly there was a bunch of us high and we realized we had a chance to see the real books, the Karmic books. They weren't in the Principal's office or down at the City Hall. These were the books that showed just where you stood in eternity."

There were also other vital if more secular tomes. Kesey read *On the Road* three times. "When I first read Kerouac, I headed off and *did* it. Then I saw there was a lot of good writing too, a body of work, all of it literature in which there was a hand moving across the page that went off in my head. Ginsberg, Burroughs, Bob Dylan were all doing the same thing, but Kerouac was the only one who was able to do it in extended fiction. His gift to me as a writer was how to just keep going on, and piling stuff up and not rewriting until you came up with a rhythm that blocked the mind; and that forces you to make connections with your mind that Kerouac was making with his mind. You can't deny his rhythm, and then pretty soon you find yourself thinking from this thing over to this thing, and you wonder how you got through that, and you know how you got through that—through unimaginable wildernesses of synapses. Kerouac would lead you through those things. That's what I learned from him"

Cuckoo's Nest anticipated the Nixon/Manson/Woodstock future: the devil's dance of freedom and paranoia. This novel was, literary merits aside, a prescient and loudmouthed canary in the cultural coalmine. In an end-of-the-Eisenhower-era America, the natives were getting restless. Something was going on, but who knew what it was? *Cuckoo's Nest* was novel-as-conspiracy theory and perfect for its time, the rebel with a cause—to fight the system, which was society as mental institution.[12]

---

12 Years later, when reviewing the film version of *Cuckoo* in *The New Yorker*, Pauline Kael wrote, "the novel preceded the university turmoil, Vietnam, drugs, the counterculture. Yet it contained the prophetic essence of that whole period of revolutionary politics going psychedelic. Much of what it said has entered the consciousness of many—possibly most—Americans."

PART TWO:
THE SHEEP

Kesey turns the camera on the press as a young, bemused Bill Murray
(left, with mike) looks on, June 5th, 1976

Chapter Eight: Holy Land

"American history is totally involved in the attempt to escape European brainlock. Here in the Northwest we are the last chance for that escape."

—Ken Kesey

The Word made flesh. In the manger, the mother of all pregnancies climaxed by the Virgin Birth. Divine, supernatural conception. The Christ child, the new Adam, born 1,955 years ago half a world away to absolve Original Sin, my six-year old wrongs had been swept away by a pill not unlike the mycins that stopped the crazy pain and tiny continents of red on my pillow from my ruptured eardrums. But this pill—"God's body," placed from above on my tongue by the Priest—was round and flat as a silver dollar, light as a cloud, a miracle cure. Dr. Jesus was a superhero, Savior and Avenger, though His message of compassion was lost on me in the near decade since my first communion, swept away by secular signs and wonders.

For now, eight years later, Jackie and JFK were busy building the castle in the air that was Camelot and heaven was here on pioneer earth. Good fortune such as America had never imagined before. We teenybopper future acid eaters never had it so good.

The Portland Golf Club. A New Jerusalem. A look at the supersonic tail-finned behemoths in the parking lot and you knew that, thank God, the worst that could happen, had: lunacy hijacked by technology, cartoon science fiction fantasy mugged by scientific fact, for what was the insane ground-glued fighter plane 1962 Cadillac, with its rocket horsepower and flat suns of gleaming chrome, but the car-kook equal of the Salk Vaccine? Soon, those two ton fuckers could actually fly and…

This was not Ken Kesey's Oregon. A purebred suburban urchin, all I knew about nature was that wood came from a furniture store and tuna from a can. The world's youngest good old boy—my family had only been living out here for six years, but that was an eternity in this nouveau-riche wonderland, I was sure of only one thing: I was lucky, lucky, lucky. The clubfoot, the pinhead innocents elected to impossible conditions, I'd been spared all that. And Kesey's hairy-armed, bull-goose loony cosmos was light years from mine. Yeah, we kids had porno playing cards—who didn't?—but no "hollering" out here in lotusland, unless it was for a waiter (at a white-clothed table, my spidery mitts strangling a steak sandwich drooling blood, I was not presented a bill—only asked to scrawl on a slip of paper, as easy as the number itself, my dad's dining code, 1-2-3).

My father grew up determined to be a golf pro but became, instead, an eye surgeon to make ends meet. So Utopia at the clubhouse for me and mine—the white kid progeny of local doctors, lawyers and Indian chiefs who had been segregated by unbelievable opportunity to live set apart and above, and here in the dining room through the glass brightly—a gently rolling green sea of the fairways and the tan concave islands of the sand traps. And, outside, the moms—American geishas sentenced to a life of mink kimonos, no work and vodka gimlets—a little gassed after drinking lunch, would approach the tee-off on the tenth hole as if walking on the deck of a ship.

Like legions of young churched Americans, I awaited the Savior, who might arrive any day to transport me to heaven or the heaven junior that was the new New Jerusalem, where He'd bivouac the pure souls (we who'd suffered for our sins) for a millennia or two in earthly paradise before zapping us—bodies and all—to Kingdom Come. Christ would descend from the sky or even reveal Himself as one among us, alive with love and solution. It could be anybody.

Yet, already I had questions.

During Mass I'd stare into my Missal at Christ on the Cross, head tipped heavenward in blue-eyed Aryan agony, surfer body flagged with blood, arms extended in that awful T, hair still Clairol-clean under the crown of thorns, and wonder: If Christ had to suffer and die for our sins then the passion play had to be as scripted as *South Pacific* and therefore wasn't traitor Judas just another actor reciting his necessary lines? And though a communion wafer had absolved me of Original Sin, recently

I had escaped the Church. In my imagination anti-evil nuns, their pale lipstickless heads regally encased in starched cloth helmets white as new snow, drove around in drab cars as gray as brains. Trying to track me down.

But they'd never find me. For a new godless day had dawned. Hot light cut from the clouds, putting long suns on the chrome of those tail-finned 300 horsepower ground-bound fighter jets in the parking lot.

The year before, however, three hundred miles away in Idaho, Ernest Hemingway picked up the shotgun (Kesey: "He tricked us into following his mode, then he conked out and shot himself"), and Herman Kahn, America's master planner of nuclear apocalypse—author of *Thinking the Unthinkable,* was dropping LSD at the Veteran's Administration Hospital in Los Angeles. Closer to home, Oregon's new Favorite Son, Ken Kesey, had just had his novel, *One Flew Over the Cuckoo's Nest* lionized in *Time:* "Kesey, 26…has used his empathy…to tilt the reader's comfortable assumptions about the nice normalities, has made his book a roar of protest against middlebrow society's Rules and the invisible Rulers who enforce them."

An orderly era. The organization man in the gray flannel suit lost in the lonely crowd. About the only ones giving corporate Amerika the finger were Maynard G. Krebs and Nikita Kruschev. Rebellion was confined largely to "live fast, die young and leave a good looking corpse," here at a time when Vanguard rockets at Cape Canaveral were blowing up on their launch pads like fire crackers at a Fourth of July picnic, and JFK was touting camouflaged "Green Berets" who'd soon attempt to out-guerilla the guerillas in a "hot spot" called Vietnam.

And then too, there were the drugs. Forget antibiotics and the Salk vaccine, the new wonder drugs were the massmarket anti-psychotics, mother's little helpers, the suave zombifiers like Valium and Percodan. The American dream was about to be replaced by the American dream state and here at the Golf Club under the sun burning a hole in a white sky Kesey's future audience (not so much for the books but the Message), teenybopper soon-to-be members of the Love Generation watched as, on his way to meet fate, my eleven year-old brother stepped from the pool. Light starry water spackles on his sunburned back, he strode toward the diving board. His pre-teen Randle McMurphy-style plan: to boing high in the hot sky off that board, and then descend, his nose speeding an atom's length from the end of that board and splash into the chlorinated water untouched.

Manifest destiny. Designer homes, long, low streamlined wood forts. In Raleigh Hills, love was money. It was as if our Depression-bred fathers had lived like desperate broke bank robbers in a destitute America with no robbable banks, then came FDR and WWII, and suddenly rich easy-to-rob banks were everywhere, and our fathers spent every hour from dawn to dark knocking them off.

There was a threat, of course, that any day we'd wake to a nightmare: any dawn the horizon could bloom thermonuclear flowers with the angels' chorus, the supersonic, superheated hallelujah wind blowing away buildings, houses, trees, cars tumbling like dice, and me stripped to the soul, incinerated, flying skyward.

But, meanwhile: green trees, silver skies, gold Cadillacs, Jaguars, T-birds and Estate Wagons. Raleigh Hills was the color of money, though outside of Monopoly we barely knew what money was—our days were spent at the Golf Club swimming pool, a teeming pond of six to sixteen year old pollywog baby boomers where the world was yours as easy as 1-2-3. Two summers before my newly literate brother "signed" for everybody at the snack bar. My dad, who could click a golf ball off a tee and leave that Titleist 250 yards away and still in the sky (a real feat back in the day when woods were still wood)—got the bill for a 7-Eleven worth of hotdogs, milkshakes, Milk Duds and Jujubes.

Not that he couldn't afford it. The poor son of a handsome Christian fundamentalist saw-sharpener in a sawmill—as a school boy he would walk home in the afternoon to find his own father in the attic of their clapboard home screaming to the underside of the shingled heavens for Christ's return[13]—my dad was founder of Argon Laser, an ophthalmologist who operated on only the worst eyes, and a sort of medical Robin Hood whose very well paid specialty was working the insurance companies so that his patients paid as little as medically possible, which, sadly, was still a lot.

We'd moved from Portland, part of White Flight from the cities to the suburbs. A literate world. The first day of third grade at my new rich kid's school, my pretty, gray haired teacher asked: How do you spell your last name? I had no idea. The T in Christensen stood up like a leafless

---

13 I came from a religious family—on my cousin Jerry's side were Christian anarchists who, at the turn of the century formed a commune and determined to provoke the return of Christ by building a circle of outhouses and having commune elders poop in unison. When they did and Christ did not descend to the center of the outhouse circle, they tried to burn down Tacoma.

banyan in a low swamp of consonants and vowels. Humiliated, I was driven to *Mad*. And when the Catholic Jesus ran beatific face first into Alfred E. Neuman in the lawless galaxy between my nine year-old ears, Christ didn't have a chance. For how could, "upon this rock I build my church" compete with "Rome wasn't built in a day, it just looks that way."

By age ten my classmates recalled miniature adults. Staring out from the pages of my fifth grade Raleigh Hills Grade School year book are boys dressed as I am now—button-down shirts, khaki slacks, tasseled loafers, refugees from a preppie/folk Chad Mitchell Trio concert, already in the uniforms they would enjoy, except for that parenthetical decade devoted to madras cloth, tie dye and bellbottoms, their entire lives.

When my mother got breast cancer her priest told my father that unless he accepted the Catholic Jesus she would go to hell. Now, motherless (surely she floated in clouds light years above me but, by heaven's magic, could see me to my pores), it occurred to me that one day in the not so far off future I'd need a job. So why not The Job? As Christ come back. For however rudely I jettisoned myself from the Church, the smart money said: Maybe it was the singer, not the song. Still, I knew enough about religion that to collect my mail at Mr. Messiah, I'd have to do two superhuman things.

a) Miraculously acquire an indelible understanding of the future. The problem? Every morning the future erupted in front of me like a wild fungus, completely out of my control, in the hands largely of strange adolescents who I called friends. I understood the future the way a snowflake understands its blizzard, and

b) Harder still: Renounce sin.

So, realistically, becoming a mindblowingly awesome writer seemed the next best thing. There had been a story about Ken Kesey in the newspaper that made him sound like the All American Rose Bowl quarterback of thinking. Who knew what this bird watching book *Cuckoo's Nest* was all about but I was no dumb kid and recognized—monkey see, monkey do—the template of the Main Chance the second I saw it. To write a great novel, all you had to do was create a book length universe and say you understood everything. I had a big mouth and a thesaurus, I could do that. A man-child, of course, had to know his limits. *War & Peace, Remembrance of Things Past* and this new *One Day in the Life of Ivan*

Denisovich Al Solzhenitsyn guy? Too much information. Best to just go for the belly laughs.

Inspired by my literary heroes Sergeant Rock and the Combat Happy Joes of Easy Company, plus Superman's nemesis Mr. Mxlzyplk from the fifth dimension, I figured I'd just plagiarize my daydreams and nightmares, string together 10,000 sentences as good as "Don't smoke in bed, the ashes that fall could be you," and become a fourteen year-old best selling beat surfer novelist. I began writing stories about what I knew best: Outer space. Stories laced with "servo-mechanisms"—whatever they were. When a spaceman hit a story-killing cul-de-sac, he'd make deft use of a "servo-mechanism."

My World War II flight surgeon dad said the last great war novel was *All Quiet on the Western Front* because it evoked the hell and shame of war, that Ernest Hemingway sold bravery like a bar of soap, was essentially in the Ernest Hemingway business not the novel writing business, and wasn't fit to polish the chrome on Erich Maria Remarque's Maserati and that—go ask Papa—the future of literature resided not in high Art but celebrity. Fine by me. My interest in Hemingway had more to do with his great divorcing than his great writing—he traded up wives like nobody's business and as someone who already showed great promise as a person-very-difficult-to-live-with, I was taking notes.

Too, I knew my stories, to make me famous, had to be the same but different from all the top science fiction stories before them so, for example, Ray Bradbury's *The Four Horsemen of the Apocalypse of Mars* or whatever he called it (for an obsessive kid I had, oddly, no attention span), well, Maxwell Perkins and the guys could try this on for size: a team of spacemen is marooned on a far flung ice-ball of a planet and, you guessed it, *The Cannibals of Uranus*. Otherwise, all you had to do was call the sun *sol* and fire into space words like "bulkhead," "apogee" and, for the graduate student crowd, "dilatory."

My grandmother said science fiction was in my shirt-tail genes, that my campus queen mother would have married Frank Herbert, the author of *Dune,* had her priest not forbidden the union because Frank had been married and divorced—and I'd be three years older and somebody else. Awesome. But to write a normal earthbound blockbuster, you had to make things up that sounded true, right?

A disease-like word one of my teachers called "verisimilitude." I could make 2+2=5, easy. I'd never caught a foot long trout that didn't measure fifteen inches (An attempted fly fisherboy, I prayed the scurrying wild waters of the Deschutes would yield not only a monster trout but, better, the Unknown Fish), but exaggeration was a trillion times easier than all the macho "verisimilitude" I'd need to out-Norman Mailer Norman Mailer. For the sad fact was, as a liar I was all hat and no cattle. I couldn't even lie about my age to buy cigarettes. Also: How could I become a novelist—able to selflessly envision a whole wide world when all I really cared about was me?

We were blessed. No personal computers, HIV, the end of history and epidemic heroin use among the *Tiger Beat* demographic.

A glorious era. We'd conquered nature. Logging companies were scalping the forests, the big fish corporations were sweeping the Pacific and Columbia rivers of anything with gills. The only "nature" I knew about was the skinny squiggling swamp that was Fanno creek, whose clear but fetid waters were crazy with zooming bullheads and wriggling stuff from 1,000,000,000 BC. Fanno Creek zigged-zagged languidly through the Portland Golf Club's eighteen hole course that was trim and controlled as a tea garden.

On glaring summer days I'd lurk down there with my would-be girlfriend Patty, within its maple-canopied dim and sudden cool, as dark and dank as a dirty cathedral, a feral oasis alive with sex and frogs. There was little wildlife left in Raleigh Hills beyond garter snakes, robins and worms (similarly, the Golf Club had been kept free of Negroes, Japanese, Chinese, Mexicans, even Jews). Moms in Capri pants smoked Tareytons while serving Tuna Surprise, and made jokes punch-lined, "slam bam thank you ma'am, slam bam, thank you ma'am, slam bam, sorry Sam."

After my mother died, my father retained ties with the Catholic Church through his pal Father G. who manifested serious sinkings in my dad's Old Crow supply fifth-by-fifth while the two sat in the dark gold-hued den and negotiated Jesuit-inspired real-estate-deals. So Jesus showered us with heavenly largesse at Christmas time, delegating the chore to Santa who delegated it to my atheist doctor dad who delegated it in turn to the helpful clerks at the new Fred Meyers Super Shopping Center, a citadel of commerce nearly as big as the Vatican.

Two years before, the future had erupted on a cow pasture behind

Raleigh Hills grade school. Huge. A Kitty Hawk of kibble culture, selling anything that could go in one end and come out the other—walls of Budweiser, enough toilet paper to swab an army, *go-carts*—where at age twelve I realized that life was nothing but a long moment with death at the end of it. Sitting there on my racing bike, I plucked a pack of Camel Straights from my shirt pocket. Coffin nails of the Gods, miracle carcinogens charcoaling my lungs, turning my rich boy contralto to manly gravel.

Truly, heaven was on its way. My father dearly loved his motherless children and Christmases were avalanches of footballs, basketballs, baseballs, Etch-a-Sketches, Slinkies, a Supersonic Racer & Smash Up Kit, a Hasbro Pneumatic GI Joe Vampire (sucks Kool Aid blood), electric trains—including a flatbed fitted with a mobile ICBM missile launcher—a chocolate Junior Dynamite Blaster, Whammo Frisbee Flying Saucers everywhere, replica burp guns real enough to rob Fort Knox. Awesome stuff, though by New Years my brother, sister and I had everything broken down to the balls.

The Holocaust may have killed God (who could believe a rational, loving deity would have allowed the murder of six million innocents?) but the Church was doing fine. The nuns who had led my Catholic education gave written proof of and instruction to eternal life. KEY OF HEAVEN was the title of one prominent manual nearly as small and dense as a gem, choices from the contents pages printed on paper that seemed thin and delicate enough to be dissolved by the tongue. *O Salutaris Hostia, Tantum ergo, A Short Table of Sins Have you: Done or commanded some servile work not of necessity? Procured, desired, or hastened the death of anyone? Talked, gazed or laughed in church?*

But, even given all that, did God have the gravitas to rule the universe? 50-50. In school we learned that before the Big Bang in a time before time, when not even nothing existed, everything that across a billion light years we held warm and dear, namely our 100 billion starred galaxy and another 100 billion galaxies like it—had exploded from a "point" as massless as thought.

Times they were a changin'. Science and all its impossible truths were the new almighty and the future was the Jesus of 1963, a savior to make things better forever. TV was the future's church, Saturday morning cartoons the new catechism and Prime Time the New Testament with

Bewitched, I Dream of Genie, The Twilight Zone and *The Flying Nun* waiting in the wings. It was all there in black and white. Miraculous. The Sermon on the Motorola: endless stuff to stare at and then want to buy. Those of us born at this time were cult-bait by the time we were out of diapers, deluged with horizontal information burying the vertical past. Our history was a history of now—liberating to kids, palimpsests waiting for the latest impression, trapped in a pinstriped Amerika where about the only thing overtly wild and creative were—absent Philip Johnson and Jackson Pollock—tailfins and mushroom clouds.

We had all the modern conveniences. Including a rat-like neighborhood child molester named Stu who lived in a colonial house beneath tall firs down the street from the perv's garden of earthly predatory delights that was the Raleigh Hills Grade school, and who entertained boys with pop and beer and *Playboy* magazines—whose larger than life foldouts stood naked, stone still on the page and regal as Statues of Liberty, to be ogled in Stu's bedroom to make sure you weren't queer.

A high school freshman, I was trying to get addicted to cigarettes so I'd have something to do with my hands. Not big on authority, I didn't even like the law of gravity. Rebelling against my father was like rebelling against the Wild Bunch, but I gave it a shot. His mantra was "rules are for toddlers and cops" and he told me I was very bright but, alas, part of a locust-like generation that had spawned countless very bright boys. Future geniuses were doomed to be common as cockroaches. The job of my generation would, however, not require genius: it would be, locust-like, to consume.

Cut to the chase: as a lamb, I was already ready for the slaughter. Not because I ever really had any illusions about the illusionists. But because I realized that if fucking up was the new varsity sport, I could be a first string quarterback. Already a hardcore veteran of fantasyland—Catholic Catechism class had taught me everything I needed to know about miracles and rebellion—I was tailor-made for acid.

By the summer of 1962 LSD was trickling into the public mind as a mysterious, miracle elixir that might "expand the consciousness." My dad guessed that LSD would simply evoke the dream state and, more seriously, provoke schizophrenia in those prone to early onset. *So you two jokers don't ever take any.* No problem. Of the new, bold *Mad*-bred breed, my brother and I had our own dream state. Scrooge McDuck and Jay Gatsby, eat your hearts out. School was over, the sun was burning that hole in the white Oregon sky, while sleek Lolitas in swimsuits tight as painted skin sunbathed around the pool on grass glowing with a green light.

Meanwhile, my athlete/showman/guitar-player younger brother Scott (at eleven, already a master of fuzztone and wah-wah pedal) was about to launch himself from the tip of the diving board toward the sky and an uncertain future based on his own fearless sub-adolescent reality, and I was too distracted to stop him, too busy wondering—what better way to celebrate summer than by figuring out how to dissolve the cohesion between protons, electrons and neutrons so that the universe would by, say, July 4, collapse into super-heated plasma? Or, absent that, and employing a car battery and a "uranium" sample from my Dr. Doom Rock Collector Kit, build a hydrogen bomb in my dad's garage?

Rubber-bodied Scott boinged from the diving board, soared upward, flipped over in white air and then, arms and legs kicking and punching the sky as if engaged in expert upside-down kung fu fighting, plunged waterward, his nose whizzing by the hard tip of the diving board. The idea: to get his speeding nose closer and closer to the tip of that diving board. Every day so far this summer. Inches had become millimeters until today, when Scott's descending nose finally entered the realm of the negative numbers.

—and suddenly there was Scott's eleven year-old nose hurtling past the end of the diving board by about minus 20 millimeters—*kersplat.* Blood on the water. A red-tentacled nebula. Next, blood scrawling the mirrory wet concrete on the side of the pool. Blood on a towel as red as the rising sun on a Japanese flag. Talk about show business. It was the best thing that ever happened to him—destined not to become a kamikaze capitalist but now at least nose kamikaze, the sleek teenybopper sunbathers in their paint-thin swimsuits staring, Scott grinning, immortal behind a blood mustache and goatee—nothing a Camel Straight couldn't cure—waving to the tanned and sunburned mini-masses, instantly a summer star.

CHAPTER NINE: NOTION

"When I first was getting to know him, he was working on Sometimes a Great Notion. The book opens with a scene in which a group of people are standing on a riverbank, and on the other side of the river, dangling from a long pole that's suspended somehow out over the water, is a severed human arm. And it's hanging out there, and all these people are standing on the other side of the river looking at it and hollering to the people in the house across the river and so forth. And I read the first 50 pages of the manuscript and it never explained whose hand, whose arm it was. It never comes up. So when I took the manuscript back to Ken, I said, 'Well, this is wonderful writing, but I don't understand whose arm that is. How did it come to be there? Whose is it?" 'I don't know,' he said, 'That's what I'm writing this book for, to find out whose arm it is.'"

—Ed McClanahan

It is perhaps symbolic—or fitting—that the classic comic tour de lunacy, *Animal House*, which was filmed largely around Kesey's old Beta Theta Pi fraternity house at the University of Oregon, was set in 1962—the same year *Cuckoo's Nest* was published, and the same year that future Oregon Governor Tom McCall produced a film documentary, *Pollution in Paradise*, that revealed an Oregon being destroyed by industrial waste, a film that initiated the national environmental protection movement. It was a year later that the Kingsmen recorded the new national anthem, "Louie, Louie," for $36 in the basement of a Portland restaurant.[14] In the years that followed, *Cuckoo's Nest* went on to sell 7 million copies in 66 editions and has never gone out of print, a perennial bestseller long after its message of liberation and misogyny and enlightened schizophrenia helped open the Pandora's Box that was the

---

14 This siren song was soon subject to an FBI probe to determine if the lyrics were obscene (Their conclusion after 32 months of digging: We don't know).

1960s. And Kesey's next novel, *Sometimes a Great Notion*, made Oregon, or at least the idea of an Oregon, the protagonist; a wild dark-souled wilderness alive with spirits and horrors.

Having seen Ken Kesey's writing from the inside when I was at the University of Oregon in my mid-twenties, I was knocked out. Up to that point I had assumed that novelists wrote of their fantasies the way the rest of us might write of our memories. One version—certainly perhaps sharpened and revised—but one version only. Jake Barnes had lost his balls in *The Sun Also Rises*. There wasn't another *Sun Also Rises* where he'd lost his leg or his mind. But the "true lies" that I believed was the fabric of great fiction were multi-dimensioned in Kesey's hands.

On display at the U of O were portions of the draft for *Sometimes a Great Notion* in which Kesey had written a long scene from three different perspectives. It was intimidating, like reading three different, excellent alibis for the same crime. Was that fair? Didn't the novelist owe his readers the *facts*?

Downsizing from LSD to methamphetamines, in 1963 he quit his courtiers for a cloister, a cabin on the Oregon coast, laboring thirty-hour days, high on speed. In his notes for the book, Kesey wrote, "We start with this boy, 21-24, returning after learning enough to lose God. God is no more for him. He would like there to be God, heaven, hell. Goblins, ghosts…"

Beginning more exactly with the image of gyppo logger Hank "Never Give an Inch" Stamper's severed arm giving the world the finger from the porch of a house that looked like "a wood skull," *Notion* was a horror-show that got me lost in a jerky murk of jumps in time and perspective. A bible-sized tale of Oregon loggers who were, not incidentally, champions of union-busting.[15] Surprising fodder for the leftist multitudes. In *Wallace Stegner and the American West,* Philip Fradkin observed: "What Kesey and others discovered at the time was a temporary condition that gave them the illusion of increased perception, an illusion that did not necessarily make rational sense on paper. His sudden and only success in writing, Kesey said, came from being 'dimensional.' That meant, in his words, 'I saw everything that you see from this position, if you're also able to see it from over there, you've got two views of it.' Of course, this was gibberish to (Wallace) Stegner."

---

15 Kesey: "I want to find out which side of me really is: the woodsy logger side, complete with homespun homilies and cracker-barrel corniness—a valid side of me that I like—or its opposite. The Stamper brothers in the novel are each one of the ways I am."

For Kesey, however, the road was clear. *"Sometimes I get a great notion to jump into the river and drown."*

"The River...water flowing to the sea."

You can read these words in the Kesey archives at the handsome, ivy-hided University of Oregon, where, in a cool and super-quiet chapel-sized room, his voluminous manuscripts and notes are stored as if part of a paper mausoleum. From boxes unfurl the taped-together pages of *Sometimes a Great Notion*, pages wrinkled, stained, dented and lined with Kesey's tight and insistent scrawl, other pages tattooed with fifty-year old hunt and peck typescript. A ghost "o" followed by a cattle brand "t." Whether scribbled as notes or pecked as text, the defiant, worried message remains the same.

"The job of the writer," Kesey once said, "is to kiss no ass, no matter how big and holy and white and tempting and powerful."

So, on to Act Two. *Sometimes a Great Notion* was a veritable paean to not kissing ass. If monumentalizing the pharmaceutically empowered "battle axe" Big Nurse as a symbol of a rising proto-fascist national "matriarchy" on the eve of modern feminism was a hat trick, transforming a dysfunctional family of union-buster loggers into transcendent symbols of American individuality was an even bigger coup.

Especially given that it was such an unhappy book, driven by images of drowning, death and suicide—which came to haunt Kesey, who having returned to Oregon from Stanford, and before moving to the coast, began *Notion* in the lakefront home of a family friend who had recently committed suicide. Although he finished *Notion* in a cabin above the ocean in Southern Oregon, the change of scenery did not seem to improve his mood, as his notes in the U of O archives suggest.

"The river flows out to the sea.

The sea is surrender. Not the sea itself. No, it is a conqueror; it is the giving into it that is the surrender. It waits. It doesn't wait. It tears at the land, at live(sic) of mankind. It gnaws away our coast lives and smoothes out our mountains.

The sea is always after you. The rains tear building (sic) away."

Kesey pulled out all the stops, starts, and most everything else in between. Almost as though he took everything he'd learned at Stanford and everything anybody else had ever learned in any lit class anywhere else, and given it a run for its literary money. "I was staying up 20 to 30 hours at a run. I'd write a piece, and I could see that 'If I change this back here, it'll change this up there.' I began to use this scissor technique, having things happen to me in the present and having things happen to me in the past and future, and have them all there at the same time. When I finished it, I knew I was finished with that form…There are times when you are able to do stuff that is just right for your years and your experience, and I've always known that was going to be the best I was going to be at writing."

On old pages, written with a blue ball point pen Kesey notes: *"We made it up out of the sea, stormed around the land for a time, now the sea is bent on reclaiming us."*

"To jump into the river is to submit to death, the watery nothingness. To give up, and return to death, to nothingness, to nothing."

"More me, the author, into a different dimension. Godlike, able to float across the land and into the minds."

"Big Brother believes: You fight, you struggle, you don't give up, you don't let down, you don't accept death."

"But me. I go on telling the story of what happened when a pacifist brother returns and what he does, how he changes things. Like Bromden tells the story of McMurphy."

Of Kesey's lesser self: *"His conflict: how to reconcile love with death… During the time there little brother falls in love with the wife…He attracts her and makes her love him because of his helplessness and weakness…Lee witnesses Hank's tenacity through the whole (sic) in the wall. Never give up (underlined in red), he thinks, watching Hank finally screw his mother."*

On another page:
"I have lived too long in a
Vine maple glade
My feet are damp with night;
And a heart so long in the dark will fade
Like a plant grown sunless
In the sheltering shade
Blanching limp and white."
Notion was a tale of the Stamper family, a no-nonsense—except when

they were drunk—clan of alcoholic gyppo loggers on Oregon's suddenly mythic west coast. I was fascinated by the voice of young druggie Leland Stamper: urbane, bright, gassy, knowing, weak—a voice Kesey never repeated but which he acknowledged was his, a side to his personality of which he was not particularly proud. Kesey encourages Leland to spend lots of quality time with his belly button and the reader is treated to, if not trapped by, page after page of very high quality post-teenage angst. Veering beyond a brilliant novelist's gift for ventriloquism, it sounded weirdly like a voice if not *the* voice of the author himself.

Leland's older brother, however, was the "other" Ken Kesey. The roughneck as young Noble Savage in training. Our Hero Who Has Suffered.

"When he lost his two fingers in the donkey drum he wrapped the stubs and didn't mention the accident until Viv asked him why he was wearing his work gloves at the supper table. Dipping his head with embarrassment he said, 'Why, I guess I forgot to take them off at the door…' and drew a glove from a claw so mangled and clotted with blood and cable rust that it took Viv an hysterical half-hour to get the wound clean enough to realize that the whole hand wasn't lost as well as three or four inches of the arm."

What Oregon was this? Not the Oregon that was happening at my house. We had Blue Cross. Gushing blood from a neighborhood altercation, my brother, sister and I knew better to await the clotting process purpling the grout of the Danish tile by the back door than leave red snakes on my mother's white carpets. Ours was no ex-wild-west bumpkin Stamper jungleland (sure, up at my father's ranch we had the *Deliverance* crowd, the meth cookers and the "Tansy boys," snake-chested teen brothers who'd arrive at our front door shirtless, their skin ivory even in the August sun, wondering: "Missuschrishionshion, cun we pull suma yer tansy weed?" But thank God for small favors: give'm both ten bucks and I sure as hell wouldn't have to do it).

Sadly, *Notion* flew in the face of an Oregon carpeted by modern life, if Kesey had a clue, these logger troglodite Stampers would have got with the program at Weyerhauser by about page 250, joined the credit union and drawn the curtain happily buying up RV's, ski boats and color TV sets. Didn't the Stampers ever hang out at Nordstroms?

Instead, the existential carne crudo. Ken Kesey was a goldmine; a generation had found its voice before it even knew it had one. He was, arguably, the first writer to speak both to and for the biggest potential market of readers ever. In publishing, your fuel is only as good as your fire. Publish the new New Testament, and if it doesn't sell it's just wet ex-wood. Even bad bodice rippers can burn up bestseller lists, while brilliant closet classics can be lucky to move 1,500. Kesey worked both sides of the street, using a closet classic prose style (which is to say, fresh if difficult) and at the same time rekindling bodice ripper archetypes and Us Against Them plotting into mouthwatering Triumph-of-the-Individual scenarios perfect for the time.

Writing a novel is like juggling bowling balls and soap bubbles—you've got a variously weighted self-invented cosmos to keep rolling toward meaning. Kesey juggled and rolled like crazy. *Notion* was thick as the scriptures, like an experimental novel written by the government, a maelstrom of rainy time, place and point of view, inviting a compass and a road map and graced with the effete speed raps of Kesey's young suicidal druggie alter ego Leland Stamper, the most thoroughly introspective anti-hero ever, who had little to say but said it well in an effective and, seemingly, un-Kesey like voice. Though schooled on the epics of Hemingway and Steinbeck, to me Kesey's gothic Wakonda was about as out of this world as Tranquility Base…

I didn't get it. A few pages back, I said that, so far as I knew, tuna came from cans and wood from a furniture store. In truth, I was more erudite than that by half: By fourteen, I knew wood came from trees. Like my father's. He owned a screaming shitload of them. My dad also had a hand in the logging business, but nevermind a lot of beery "fuck you you fucking fuck" foosball tavern talk down at watering holes for unemployed choker setters like the "Whistle-Stop Inn"—no logger in Oregon (or Washington where, truth in advertising, our ranch was actually located) "hollered" in the "never-give-an-inch" Ayn Rand-as-told-to-the-Beverly-Hillbillies dialect of the Stampers. There was likewise a pitiful amount of union busting. My Republican father had few rules, but "never cross a picket line" was one. The crewcut, tobacco-spitting scarecrows and palookas with tank trap teeth who drove my father's trucks may have been gyppos—Norwegian wetbacks for all I knew. But it was "live and let live," nobody was calling out John L. Lewis to flip him the bird.. You didn't hang severed human arms with rotting extended middle fingers off your front porch, or somebody from the sheriff's office with Big

Nurse from the State Department of Mental Health would drive up and put you in a concrete bird cage. You didn't go out of your way to piss off (or on) your neighbors either. The woods were full of guns, liquor and lawyers. Get Sven upside-down about a property line and he'd likely get drunk and shoot or sue you. Maybe both.

Our rural ideal: a beautiful farmhouse, bulls named Satan and Sweetheart, and the most expensive barn ever, its huge curved wood roof shaped like an inverted Noah's Ark, and log trucks wheeling down the black slalom twists of Little Kalama Road loaded heavy with monster logs, their brakes crying on every curve. Each load worth maybe $10,000. Yeah, I didn't get it. Screw screwing the union. Couldn't the Stampers see the forest for this kind of jackpot trees?

And what was all this Appalachia-meets-Elsinore-number-one-son-sleeps-with-step-mother-so-number-two-son-sleeps-with-number-one-son's-wife, stuff? *Sometimes a Great Notion's* sweeping, claustrophobic vision of rain, doom, and swimming against the tide was an Oregon from a different 1964. Lots of Oregon is green, muddy, unconquered gloom, but it was as if Kesey had dragged William Faulkner's rural and psychic swamp ethic out of Yoknapatawpha County, and stuck it here, among the rain-drenched firs.

Having begat himself as son of the Master, this was clearly the Big Book, a Great New American Bible. But, adrift page after page in the diesel-fumed fog of adolescent, suicidal introspection here in the post-Paul Bunyan, pre-Betty Friedan feminist West, in bed with this brick, I found myself often bobbing lost in a stormy sea of twenty-something angst, hit with dueling gusts of rumination vs. counter-rumination and cross currents of streams-of-consciousness prose, lost to complexities too evolved, or simply too abstract for me to understand.

Notion, however, did not slay the bestseller list as had *Cuckoo's Nest*. Orville Prescott of the *New York Times* sniffed: "His monstrous book is the most insufferably pretentious and the most totally tiresome novel I have had to read in many years." Literature may have literally burned Kesey out.

His friend Gordon Lish saw a sea change. "Kesey was a writer of impeccable discipline when I first knew him, a true champion, a true winner, a most admirable literary artist whose relations with the page were of the highest order. But I think his heart was taken out of him when the New York establishment did not fall all over themselves on that book. I think Kesey wanted popular success too much. I think a lot of the whole gig that followed—the lunacy, the theater—was largely avoidance behavior."

Yet what Lish and others at that time did not realize was that Kesey was no longer concerned about the typewriter, but a much bigger spotlight. For unlike Ernest Hemingway who brought the writer out of the closet and onto center stage to be a star in the new universe of visual mass media, Kesey—whose gifts were literal but whose passions were theatric—was determined to invent himself not only as a famous writer but a rock star as well.

Chapter Ten: Theater of Sheep

"For Kesey, redemptive self-sacrifice is heroic, through the inspirational power of heroism to elicit imitation...Despite Kesey's diagnosis of sloth or weakness as the root problem, there is the division of the world into good and evil, oppressed and oppressors, and all hope for redemption, and even all human compassion, is directed exclusively toward the oppressed...Far from denying the redemptive effect of self-sacrificing love, Kesey celebrates it as a continuing reality, incarnate wherever a man takes up his own cross."

—George N. Boyd

Indeed, Kesey's gothic horror-haunted Oregon was an Oregon from another planet. Not that magic green golf course land terra firma where a fourteen year-old boy might, sunning by the pool, order with a 1-2-3 scrawl a "lady's filet" seared black but revealed quaking jelly-red rare with the slice of a steak knife. Plus, perhaps a Virgin Bloody Mary to wash away the headache of a hard day's Friday night spent ogling the mini-skirted nymphets at the brand new Fred Meyers Super Shopping Center with my pals Scary and Moon. No, Kesey's Oregon, confined as it was to whacks in a whistle-stop insane asylum, was completely different.

For one thing, there was no insane asylum in the Dalles, Oregon, and yet...

I had read Kesey's first novel after his second. But, no matter; had bestselling martyrdom ever witnessed such a master stroke? Picking up *Cuckoo,* I was impressed. Kesey's heroine Big Nurse was an A+ damsel in distress—a single woman alone in a world she never made, prey to heathens, a busty incorruptible hot chick champion of sanity and civil rights protected only by a few semiliterate toy-like black boys, sleeping pills and syringes who does everything in her power to save the misguided.

Then there was Kesey's Rx for his immortal literary anti-hero: kill him before the curtain call. How to top that? As a grim fairy tale, *Cuckoo's Nest* was a barnburner. For Kesey a lobotomy proved his novel's storybook ending, putting a cap on the 300-plus page career of America's new favorite rebel with a Christ-like cause, described by Raymond Olderman as the "Grail Knight" of 1960s literature.

Not that my own private Oregon didn't have a few culturally indicative twists of its own. Raleigh Hills, incubator for the golf club teenage Jacobin revolution of the rich was a ranch-housed Valhalla whose fat cat isotope progeny were typified in ways by a neighbor boy who made *Time* the hard way. He'd put a bomb in his locker at Beaverton High, set his parents' house on fire then stole their Cadillac so he and his fourteen year-old girlfriend could elope to Canada and start afresh.

If you need a better indication of how *diagonal* Raleigh Hills was, consider teenage Paige Powell, the most attractive, sane and conventional of girls, as dark and pretty as a runway model. The Raleigh Hills Goddess of Normal. When I was little we rode to church together in her dad's pickup, and who'd be a better girlfriend? I auditioned hard, protecting her from "Bob" the concrete gray corduroy-coated curly haired pie-faced retard who marked passage of 10th grade by boarding our school bus mornings with a fruit jar filling higher each day with his seed, and from Scary Larry, whose fieriness was then confined to torching bus riders' paper bag lunches with his cigarette lighter, plus occasional harassment by Dick Tator and the Tator Vine Boys—and Paige liked me a lot. Although about the most popular girl in our high school, she was also the least snobby, and I could talk to her about anything. But the problem was Paige wanted "an earthling" for a boyfriend. Still, I wasn't surprised when I learned, years later, that she had been living with Andy Warhol when he died.

Fortunately, Apocalypse was upon us and I was doomed to be the witness to the End, as scripted by MAD, not the magazine, but the acronym for Mutually Assured Destruction. All it would take would be one Chi-Com nuke to vaporize Bonneville Dam, sending the pent-up headwaters of the Columbia River crashing down the Columbia gorge; another nuke on Salem to separate the state legislature into their component molecular parts; and a 20 megaton high altitude air burst over the Steel Bridge, which would blow Portland down as if the whole city were made of irradiated cards. The blast would be cupped and contained somewhat by the West Hills and I might not fry out here on the seventeenth hole, but soon my hair would be falling out...

A little mind blower a couple of years before when freshman football practice got called off after our penguin-shaped coach stood up on a bench in the locker room and informed us that President Kennedy had just announced we might be going to nuclear war with Russia over whatever the hell was going on in Cuba. My pal fullback Moon bit thoughtfully on his mouthpiece and said, not to worry: a little heat, a little wind, a little radiation, then...Lord of the Flies! Free at last, free at last. With our parents freshly indisposed (dead), we could...

The lunatics were about to storm the asylum.

FUCK COMMUNISM. Didn't that say it all? Resplendent in red, white and blue, the words hung suspended like a crucifix above the bed of my rich pal Steve Lonie (imagine a prep school Tom Sawyer/Brian Jones), who lived in the bitchenest hillside, swimming-pooled mini-mansion in Portland, who could rocket a million miles an hour down the local asphalt ski slope Scholls Ferry Road on something called a skateboard, and who had this awesome poster he'd just scored from this magazine *The Realist* where Lonie said you could also order a bumper sticker that read HONK IF YOU SHOT JFK and which was published by this awesome guy Paul Krassner who was, Lonie explained, like God and *Mad* magazine all rolled into one.

So why wouldn't my dad let me hang one above my bed too? He was the wisest father ever, never said no to anything, couldn't care less if I had Miss April, May, June, July and August hanging up there like Cupid's chorus line, so why no FUCK COMMUNISM poster?

Something was up. Krassner's pal Abbie Hoffman hadn't said, "We will dye the Potomac red, burn the cherry tree, panhandle the embassies," or that "girls will run naked and piss on the Pentagon walls"yet—but something humongous was in the air. You could hear it.

On transistor radios. Everybody must get stoned.

Get hit with rocks. Well, according to Bob. Talk about a song with a message. Too Catholic for words. But, I wasn't having any. For despite his real estate deals with the scheming bourbon glugging Father G., my dad said the Holocaust was proof of no god, for no sane deity would allow such evil and that the Old Testament god was, besides, just a ventriloquists dummy for BC patriarchies and plus, just for the record, no rational Christ would ever want to be worshipped, for the desire to be worshipped was an emotion far lower than envy. But if we had no god, at least we had guns and when the shit came down, when those thermonuclear flowers bloomed above the Portland sky, it would be lock and load. For, we were armed to our—or at least my father's— teeth. He had a .45, a Winchester, plus, for hunting moose, a 300 Savage bolt action 30.30. Walnut stock, blue steel barrel and rocket-nosed gold bullets as big as a finger, was there anything the Savage couldn't send to a better place? In the name of horsepower and muzzle velocity our house was hot-rodded and weaponized. We had few problems we couldn't kill.

To me, my father, far more like 007 than any "bull goose loony," was a hero. The best reckless driver ever. Calm as a corpse behind the wheel of his 1959 Thunderbird, flying down the coast highway at night at 125 miles an hour, me beside him in a blue bucket seat, my younger brother curled up behind, taillights we passed in a flash zapping by like red flak. He was also an athlete. The only time I recall ever seeing him ride a bike was one evening when I was about twelve, when he came home to find me and friends pulling wheelies and cutting cookies on Schwinns on our asphalt lake driveway. He got on a bike, pedaled absently, then, as naturally as if climbing stairs, stepped up off the frame and rode the bike across the pavement standing on its seat. Then he climbed down, handed the bike back, walked into the house to, I guess, have a drink.

My dad, who already hated the Vietnam War, said push would soon come to shove. Ascending from the random to the disorganized, by 1965, dissident culture was finding a center. Soon we'd all be dropping primo IT-290, robbing banks and reading Rimbaud. That could work. My father hated everything about money except making it. His mantra: all you needed was a beautiful car, beautiful house, a great stereo and a hand-built 34 foot sailboat.

My mantra: Eddie Haskell's: 'nothing is a dirty trick if it's funny enough.' My oracle: *Mad* and *Mad's* pale step-son, *The New Yorker*, which arrived in the mailbox in front of our long low ranch style house every week to be frisked for seditious cartoons and the new JD Salinger story that is, 45 years later, still yet to appear.

Mid 1960s teenybopper baby boomer reality was horizontal reality.

Who knew anything of anything before Pearl Harbor or penicillin? History was just a government sedative—an agitprop bedtime story to keep me half-asleep in social studies class. But though at that time it was beyond my ability to understand—sci-fi fan Kesey's *Cuckoo's Nest,* his self-described "simple Christ parable," which said the crazy were sane and the sane were crazy, made 1950s science fiction up close and personal, courtesy paranoia. The techno-horrors of Ray Bradbury were delivered to a backwater insane asylum in the middle of the back woods nowhere, a novelist's stage in which all the women were either institutional lackies, ball-busters or whores.

Smoking Lark Filters with my pals, all dressed in the height of 1965 fashion: baggy faded blue or ice white XXL Penney's Towncraft t-shirts bright as a cotton sun, trashed to perfection baggy Levis and green surfer tennies, Clark Desert Boots or Acme "Roughout" cowboy boots, we'd listen to the Stones singing "Play with Fire" on my father's custom MacKintosh stereo in his dark wood-walled den. The Beatles? "I Wanna Hold Your Hand" and "Love Me Do" mere mop-top pop baubles. Our musical nirvana came courtesy of death-door sallow, swizzle-stick skinny Keith/Mick/Brian/Bill/Charlie and the space guitars of David Crosby and the Byrds—eight miles high before they'd even written the song.

And for literary inspiration: *1984*. Big Brother. Awesome. Thought control and sticking it to all the prol whiners and sob sisters. (plus no more godless consumerism: "Nothing was yours except the few centimeters inside your skull'). Tell me I had no future. I was doing things I didn't need my father or the cops, let alone Jesus, seeing. Praying for a godless void, I figured if my prayers went unanswered I could always join the Dream Police.

CHAPTER ELEVEN: I AM A CAMERA

"There was no question of his limitless energy. But, in the long run, some people thought, the practice of novel writing would prove to be too sedentary an occupation for so quick an athlete—lonely, and incorporating long, silent periods between strokes. Most writers who were not Hemingway spent more time staying awake in quiet rooms than shooting lions in Arusha."

—Robert Stone

Ken Kesey's second novel, the lumbering ode to logging and logorrhea *Sometimes a Great Notion,* has been celebrated as "the Northwest's Moby Dick." "The most complex novel of modern letters," wrote Jeff Forester in the San Francisco Chronicle, "it out-Faulknered Faulkner."

Employing "huge" and "sprawling" for ballast, critic Bruce Barcott declared, "*Sometimes a Great Notion* has Shakespearean themes played out against a raw, burly Oregon backdrop. Still the heavyweight champion of Northwest novels. Huge, bold, sprawling, brilliant. Unrivaled, unchallenged, unsurpassed." When it was named the first of "12 Essential Northwest Books" by Northwest writers, critics and booksellers, Kesey allowed, "*Notion* to my mind, is a great piece of work. People sometimes ask me why I don't write something like that again and I reply that I simply can't. I can't keep all that in my head at once anymore. Why, on *Notion,* I used to work 30 hours at a stretch—you've got to have youth to do that." But Kesey's books stood in the shadow of Kesey himself—and Kesey's acid take on alternate reality, and those left to interpret it. "Like Day-Glo Johnny Appleseeds," Jeff Forester wrote, "Kesey and the Pranksters planted a wonderful psychedelic garden."

By which he meant our drug culture, whose revelatory psychedelic seeds seemed to represent a recipe for revolution. Heeding less a call to Art than to Arms, the Boy Wonder novelist turned "original hippie" turned WASP witch doctor, and with two anthems under his belt by the time he turned thirty, declared that he was "no longer a writer," and, in the name of saving the world, detonated the rocketing arc of his literary career by trading high art for a higher God, LSD. Kesey said, "Before I took drugs, I didn't know why the guys in the psycho ward at the VA hospital were there. I didn't understand them. After I took LSD, suddenly I saw it. I saw it all."

For what are novels but fairy tales? These harrowing unreal times demanded not art, but action, a real hero, A Randle McMurphy or Hank Stamper who was more than a phantom confined to paper.

A great protagonist requires a great plot, and Ken Kesey was, if nothing else, a man able to hitch his wagon to big, broad themes. Kesey was a great fan of Joseph Campbell, who famously penned the line, "follow your bliss." Campbell claimed all the world's stories come down to one story, the "mono-myth," whose plot is this: The hero ventures forth from the world of the common day into a world of supernatural wonder; fabulous forces are there encountered and a decisive victory is won. The hero comes back from his adventure with the power to bestow boons on his fellow man.

Kesey took this idea literarily and literally. In *One Flew Over the Cuckoo's Nest*, Kesey alter-ego McMurphy must test himself, enlighten himself and sacrifice himself, Christ-like, to save his adopted flock. In what for him passed as the real world, Kesey saw himself as a man-made-messiah who must be tested by the refiner's fire of his own crusade. And for a millennial generation suddenly infected with the belief that the world could be entirely new with the next sunrise or tab of Orange Sunshine, Kesey was perfect. What he and the other stars of this latest mono-myth—ie. the Tim Leary, Beatles, Grateful Dead mafia—did was, in essence, reinvent the coming American utopia. The 1960s Cash McCall/ Organization Man/Brand X heaven on earth had been all about power, products and prestige; the new and improved post-*Cuckoo's Nest* heaven on earth would be, on the other hand, all about peace, freedom and love.

Via new-time religion. Asked if not a writer, what path would he have pursued, evangelical Kesey replied, "I would have been a preacher."

His perspective was biblical. He saw *Cuckoo's Nest* and *Sometimes a*

Great Notion as moral parables, born from his initial experiences taking Sandoz LSD-25 as a government lab-rat at Stanford where, seated in that room at the Menlo Park Veteran's hospital, he watched the world dissolve and reassemble itself with Godly vision no born-again preacher could afford to ignore.

Similarly, acid was the perfect disconnect for a generation dying for a psychosis to call its own. Take it from Kesey's pal Tim Leary, who claimed trippers "attain a sort of suprahumanity, as if purged of mortal error." Leary had set out to cultivate "the ancient underground society of alchemists, artists, mystics, alienated visionaries, drop-outs, and the disenchanted young, the sons arising."

Baby Boomers provided him plenty of those. "They all wanted the bread of dreams, the flesh of the Gods. And I was charged with the one ring of power in my pocket. I was feeling that miserable pleasure of the millionaire." Leary had already been working the alternate reality room for years. In 1962 Allen Ginsberg dropped acid supplied by Leary and, determined to share the news, reportedly picked up his phone and dialed for assistance. "Hello operator," he said, "This is God. G-O-D. I want to talk to Kerouac in Long Island."

But did the new culture demand a new Christ? In 1965, 30 years after Leni Reifenstahl had produced *Triumph of the Will*, Norman Mailer wrote of the nation's need for new myths starring a "Hero-creator," a "mass man" whom Mailer glimpsed in John Kennedy and Cassius Clay. This hero, made giant and multi-dimensional by the new media, would by force of personality transform the multitudes. For Mailer, trying on the sacred (if he got lucky) robes of his own new self, Aquarius, was writing in a time that gave birth to the messiah, who with his message of separation and salvation promised the Way.

What a difference a daze makes. The government mind control wonks, to whom Kesey may have—at least indirectly—owed his original Whitman Sampler of LSD, thought acid might prove the Tide or New Blue Cheer of brainwashing. But the Central Intelligence Agency never anticipated that acid might ignite a new age of magical thinking. Talking crows, Madame Blavatsky's, Coleridge's, and Crowley's otherworld had found a new stage.

A stage on which the most famous young novelist of his generation found the novel wanting. And you can't fault Kesey for considering literature's known limitations. What is a novel if not a conceit in which a self-appointed demigod awards him or herself power to see inside the souls of a cast of his or her own creation in order to yank them through a rigged fun house or horror house plot to deliver—what?

A man with the passion for the visceral cursed by a genius for the abstract, an aspiring actor whose McLuhan-like Shakespearean ambitions were to take Globe Theater theatrics to the globe itself, Kesey set about becoming not a crooner but lyricist, whose greatest lines would be written not on paper but film. By the time he began to make the movie of himself in 1964, the literature eclipsing-power of cinema should have been obvious to anyone but the dead or the blind. A bestselling book like *Cuckoo's Nest* might sell 100,000 copies while a movie like David Lean's sweeping, hypnotic and sledge-hammer powerful *Lawrence of Arabia*, on the other hand, could easily reach 20 million.

But it was the pure visceral power of film that was so sexy. Any fool could understand a film. Written language had to be decoded, a novel's lettered visions required the reader to match the imagination of the writer, a book was an alphabet swamp. But an expert movie was as clear as the void—all you had to do was see it, and millions and millions of people were certainly seeing epics of the alter-normal like *The Manchurian Candidate*, a knowing paranoia fest in which Red Chinese plan to install a well-washed American brain as a Chi-Com mole President of the United States, and still more saw the French New Wave low-down masterpiece *Breathless*, shot largely with handheld cameras, which championed a glorious breakdown of social mores by way of the brilliant petty criminal antics of its crook-hero star, Jean-Paul Belmondo, the coolest smoker of non-filtered cigarettes ever.

In some ways Kesey, delighted in the fact that the camera did the writer's laborious grunt work of painting the stage, saw movies as a way to return to the days before movable type; film allowed the story teller to take the stage and have that stage appear anywhere and everywhere, and if a movie could prove the medium for the freak-freely message, so much the better. His movie would be a missive from the shaman to the tribe of the medieval future.

Kesey, of course, did not anticipate what was to come, or that his own antics and not his movie, would be the vital source for his incredible influence.

Huxley, Leary, Kesey. It is important to bear in mind that those psychedelic seers were at the very least almost a decade older than the sheep. Abbie Hoffman, Bob Dylan, Jimi Hendrix, Joan Baez, Frank Zappa, The Beatles, The Jefferson Airplane, Grateful Dead, Country Joe, Crosby, Stills, Nash and Young, the Doors, all had at least five years on the audience they were playing to. Kesey was a grown man about to lead a children's crusade; he and his band of acid-dropping shepherds were old enough to have been baby-sitters for their baby boomer sheep. Giving a new twist to the term *in loco parentis.*

Kesey was married and well beyond draft age when the attractions to hippiedom—free love and no death in Vietnam—inspired teenagers a decade younger to buy the dream. For, while balding Faust of Fun Kesey may have joined forces with the Love Generation, he was not of the Love Generation. Demographically no Flower Child, Kesey was 32 by 1967, The Summer of Love. You could argue that Kesey, Leary, Paul Krassner and even Hunter Thompson—who wrote from a meat ax fantasia where left and right ceased to exist—had Messianic natures less suited to baby boomer psychedelic super-stardom than the borscht belt, propelled as they were less by divine revelation than the old school people-to-people carney joys of being a ham—and that Kesey was first and foremost not about psychedelics but vaudeville era show business.

And his Boswell? Tom Wolfe wasn't even a liberal druggie. Wolfe was about as left wing as the America's Cup. Of his one rather dainty 125 milligram acid trip, he recalled: "It was like tying yourself to the railroad track and seeing how big the train is, which is rather big."

With wry hilarity, Wolfe described a national accident about to happen, a clash of cultures old and new, his star instigator, Kesey, now a 28 year-old literary phenom who, after a cross country bus pilgrimage with a band of presciently stoned disciples culminating with collisions with A-list cultural gurus past and future (a head-on with Jack Kerouac, a psychic fender-bender with Tim Leary) and a wild run from the cops across the border into Mexico. On the lam, Kesey declared, "If society wants me to be an outlaw, then I'll be an outlaw and a damned good one. That's something people need. People at all times need outlaws."

The Kesey who starred in Wolfe's *Acid Test* was textbook larger than life. Wolfe had become by that time the Oracle of Now, his books one-stop shopping for running headlong into the present tense. Wolfe's white suit made him at the same time a brand, as easily identifiable as a Corvette Sting Ray or box of Tide, and also separated him from everything around him, further defining him as an observer. Wolfe had an ironic, delightful, pseudo-enthusiastic way of illuminating, embracing and questioning all at once; he clearly loved the Pranksters while at the same time portraying them as preposterous.

Wolfe's top topic was status. The key to status was class. Kesey was living proof that if you wanted to be king of a social class the easiest way to do it was go out and invent a new one. Kesey'd otherwise have to hire Homer to get a press release like Wolfe's jailhouse portrait: "He is standing up with his arms folded over his chest and his eyes focused in the distance, i.e., the wall. He has thick wrists and big forearms, and the way he has them folded makes them look gigantic. He looks taller than he really is, maybe because of his neck. He has a big neck with a pair of sternocleido-mastoid muscles that rise up out of the prison work shirt like a couple of dock ropes. His jaw and chin are massive. He looks a little like Paul Newman, except that he is more muscular…"

Sternocleido-mastoid muscles like dock ropes? Friedrich Nietzsche and Clark Kent, eat your hearts out. In his book *The Hippies*, Burton H. Wolfe described Kesey differently: "hairy, ape-chested, bulging biceps and triceps, bald on the front part of his elephantine head and fringed with curly red locks tucked to the side and back like a doll's wig."

It was as if two representational artists had painted the same man and one painting was of a hero and the other of a clown. Heroes probably sold more books.

In *The Electric Kool-Aid Acid Test*, Kesey stood on the page bumper-jawed, zonked and shawled in the American flag, a brilliant novelist-cum-high camp hayseed who, at the dawn of middle age, had sold himself as the face of Flower Power new youth. Idolatry was where the action was. It was as if Kesey wanted to write like Faulkner[16] and be worshipped like Hemingway. Then—who said there are no second acts in American lives?—he decided to go beyond Hemingway to promote himself from literary savant to Savior.

Novels were make-believe; LSD was real. Small, cheap, trendy, divine, fun—whether you were a hip capitalist or hippie Christ, acid was

---

16 Kesey: "…yes, if Southern Comfort is over-cloying honeysuckle sweet decadence it is still one of the few hundred proofs that a man can sip and not be burned by; yes, Faulkner is my admitted favorite…"

a perfect product: It made all things possible. Anointed a "legitimate religious leader" by the media, Kesey promised paradise for kids for whom heaven was a faraway place that hosted what, besides clouds and their grandparents?

Yet here was a psychedelic heaven. Right here, right now. A heaven, even better yet, providing an ecstasy God himself wouldn't allow in his: Sin. Instant gratification by way of sex, drugs and rock and roll. And the medium—medicine man messiah Kesey, would be the message.

By the Summer of Love Kesey—already on his way to becoming both a cause and casualty of the 1960s—had gone from writing the Word to spreading it. "I think," Robert Stone later observed, "he believed that he could somehow invent a spiritual technology, somewhere between Silva mind control and the transistor, that would spare all the humiliating labor that went into the creating of art."

Or maybe Kesey just once again took a long hard look at the ghost of his literary father Ernest Hemingway, and figured: what America wants was not a new writer, but a protagonist. A Man Among Men. A charismatic leader—athletic, fearless, solipsistic, no servant to the usual gravities. A new man who represented, as Hemingway had, a new—to use his word—"lifestyle." The manly arts: *Cuckoo's Nest* and *The Sun Also Rises*. Shop and compare. Hemingway and Kesey, between impotence and insanity, what else was there? Well, there was—as Hemingway had so dramatically discovered—a new final destination which was not art as art but art as idolatry. Be the hero. And why not add the adjective "super" to the mix? If Hemingway had invented the artist as a heroic man of action then it would be left to Kesey to take that artist of action into the warp zone, and why should the super hero be made out of paper when it could be made out of flesh? His own.

Kick-ass anti-authoritarians were Kesey's central dramatic vehicle, and what Kesey termed "our need for strong men," had already been successfully road tested. Boxing, shooting, deep sea fishing "Papa" Hemingway had harvested the writer-action figure as America's New Man. Kesey simply replanted a mutant Hemingway archetype— archetypes not content to be confined to "the prison of the page." Compare the imaginary personnel of *The Sun Also Rises* to the real Merry Pranksters. Life imitating art—the Pranksters are Hemingway's "Lost Generation" in a fun house mirror. Men behaving like boys—jobless nomads, pushing 30, on non-stop benders, outlaws to the values of the prevailing culture, outnumbering the women around them, trying to live up to an ideal (Hemingway: "Grace under pressure," Kesey: "Freak freely"), each band on a sojourn to a philosophical Alp: Hemingway, to the Temple of Courageous Nihilism at Pamplona; Kesey, to the Emerald City of Oz that was Tim Leary's wood castle crash pad at Milbrook. True, Hemingway's band were ex-pat boozers, the Pranksters—absent the women—largely post-grad school jocks, and Kesey still had his corn-starched balls, but…

The times indeed were a changing. Listen to the Thelin brothers who in 1966 had founded "The Psychedelic Shop," the template for countless headshops to follow with the headshop holy trinity that was "paraphernalia," burning incense, and a meditation room. The Thelins, among the first "hip capitalists" and first hip capitalists to become sick of hip capitalism, closed the "Psychedelic Shop" less than two years later, not from lack of business but because of too much of it. In light of history, some might have taken that end before the beginning as a sign.

"Oh, we were the All American Dream," Jay Thelin recalled. "Eagle Scouts, worked our way through college, invested our money very profitably, saved, started well on our way to becoming an all American success story. Like our father. All his life he worked hard, and that was about it. That was his life. After my first LSD experience, I knew there was more to it than that."

Then, according to his brother Ron, known as "The Dream Merchant of Haight Street," "Suddenly I saw all the bullshit in the whole educational and social system…The Vietnam war was pressing in on me. I couldn't justify going to school with the war on. The problem with our schools was they were turning out robots to keep the social system going and to keep the war going. The psychedelic movement had pierced through the whole thing. I mean, our hospitals, government, and General Motors, the military were all tied into the same system…So, turning on, tuning in, and dropping out meant to conduct a revolution against the system."

What we children needed was a motley crew of post-adolescent patriots, visionaries, communists, and drug addicts ranging from 60s Godfather Norman Mailer—to a more radical light—itinerant protagonist and torch to the torchbearers—Neal Cassady. But Cassady's emeritus years were upon him. "This was the avatar," Kesey said of the great speedy Beat, "Cassady. One of the great failures of all time. I mean, he failed big. But everyone who touched him was influenced by him."

No, the real change, the real dawn of the new world would begin with "hero-creator" Kesey and his Ivy League monster alter-ego on the East Coast. Nitro was about to meet glycerin. Tim Leary, 3,000 miles away in New York, wearing a toga, and with flowers in his gray hair, was waiting in the wings.

For it would not be long before *Life* Magazine reported "psychedelic corporation presidents, military officers, doctors, teachers." Not long before Leary declared, "The revolution has just begun" and forecast state universities having, within a generation, "department(s) of psychedelic studies."

Don't trust anybody over 30. All those truths were out there on the horizon. According to Dr. Leary: "There will probably be a dean of LSD. When the students come home from their vacation, Mother and Father will not ask 'What book are you reading?' but 'Which molecules are you using to open up which Library of Congress inside your nervous system?' However, the bureaucratic requirements will still be with us: "You will have to pass Marijuana 1A and 1B to qualify for an introduction to LSD 101."

The seduction of the consumer by the consumed. Warning against "militant teenyboppers," Leary would soon go on to stump for "a new Declaration of Independence" and concluded, "Everyone should start their own nation. Write their own declaration of Evolution."

Tune in, turn on, drop out. The slogan occurred to a Tim Leary still dripping wet from the shower during which, under the spray, he had previously tried out mottos similar to "Give me liberty to give me death" and "Lucky Strike means fine tobacco."

Leary had been inspired by Marshall McLuhan who had advised: "You call yourself a philosopher, a reformer. Fine. But your work is advertising. You're promoting a product. The new and improved accelerated brain. You must use the most current tactics for arousing consumer interest. Associate LSD with all the good things the brain can produce—beauty, fun, philosophic wonder, religious revelation, increased intelligence, mystical romance…Word of mouth from satisfied customers will help, but get your rock and roll friends to write jingles about the brain."

McLuhan then broke into a parody of a then-current Pepsi Generation jingle:

"Lysergic acid hits the spot
Forty billion neurons, that's a lot."

Meanwhile, back in the universe, the presumptive center of which, America, had been hijacked by a war-friendly elite: between the gray cloth coat competence of Eisenhower and Gerald Ford, three kings of the imperial presidency ruled. Martyred John Kennedy—author of the Bay of Pigs fiasco and nuclear annihilation a push of a button away during the Cuban Missile Crisis, better at adultery than foreign affairs—Lyndon Johnson, who would commit America's sons to the butcher shop that was Vietnam, and, mad as any hatter Richard Nixon—who would keep them there.

The voices of truth—*Mad* and science fiction—told teenyboppers reality was a joke, that our world could be far better than it was, even far better than it had been sold to us to be. The too cool jazz that was listened to by a few passive cigarette smoking loser loners dressed in a lot of black would soon be traded in for the hot rock hallucinations of god's own multitude of activist tribal longhaired potheads dressed in beads, baubles and fake Indian shit. We'd get better court jesters. Wavy Gravy instead of Spiro Agnew. Plus world peace. All we needed now was someone to light the fuse.

CHAPTER TWELVE: AUTEUR

"The Merry Pranksters never verbalized about the Other World. It was the unspoken thing! the weird shit! the zone! And when they did talk about it, it was with comic book hyperbole. The ideal became a place called Edge City, which was that part of the spectrum of being that lay between the ego, with its layers of conditioning, and the annihilating energy bath of the Void. To live in Edge City meant to live totally in the here and now. 'We got so we could do it and be right there, in the present, for long periods of time,' Kesey told an interviewer... 'It was like being in a boat, at sea, drifting, except that powers are available to you that you couldn't find in the past or the future.'"

—Jay Stevens

Art would no longer be held captured and frozen to the page, canvas and stone, but would reflect reality at its best example. Abstract composition would no longer be left to find expression in dead dry paint, but in the living phantasmagoria of the light shows, where the new Guernica could show itself a trillion liquid patterns on a humble hippie bed sheet instead of just one rigid way in some aristocrat's elitist museum. Life itself would be the new true art, as novelists like Gore Vidal, James Baldwin, Norman Mailer and Truman Capote would abandon fiction in favor of fact.

Yet can great action observed ever equal great action committed? In such incendiary times thespian, beatific Jekyll-and-Hyde Kesey was not above shouting theater in a crowded fire. Demi-god or demagogue, did it really matter? Kesey followed the Nietzschian "child, savage, artist, hero" supercharged by Martin Buber's Dick and Jane anti-existentialism. He was on his way, about to take the most radical if not crazy step in the career of any successful novelist in memory. Though, in retrospect, given that Ken may have been less about art than ambition, perhaps it all made some kind of sense.

For God and the novel were dead, Gore Vidal said so—and even if the novel wasn't it was, worse, still in the hands of adults—and how was Kesey to compete with the grown up likes of Saul Bellow and Norman Mailer on the long literary haul? Besides, there was no way in Helvetica the novel was up to delivering the new Word. Just go ask Marshall Macluhan now that he was ten feet tall. Movies—Kesey's super-sacramental cinemaverite in particular—would be the new literature. Far out.

Though the quickly best-selling *Cuckoo's Nest* had proved a money machine—generating tens of thousands of dollars for Kesey almost immediately, Kesey may have been aware of the novel's potential financial limitations as well. Our country reliably rewards intelligence mated to commitment and gall, but novelist is the rare American profession in which hard-working, brilliantly creative souls with outrageous egos can still end up poor.

Best, as Joseph Campbell said, to follow your bliss. Kesey wanted to direct the movie version of *Cuckoo*, so is it hard to imagine that a young writer who also identified himself as an actor and director might want to cast himself in the movie of his own even more unbelievable life? Film as the son of print, the new art leading to the final reductive art of the self.

So, The Movie. To Kesey, film as a medium for the personal story it might embrace, was the meaning of life. His advice: "Get them into your movie before they get you into theirs," and The Movie was to provide documentary record of Kesey, in Kesey's words, saving the world. A bus of bohemians could save mankind? A tall order. It was as if Albert Einstein had walked up and said 2+2=5—your first thought might be: Albert's nuts, your second thought might be: Albert is Albert, so maybe Albert is right. Especially if Albert has a magic pill that when taken reveals the truth and serzenity of a whole new reality. Or think of it this way: as if Christ could have not only starred in but written the New Testament: the Movie. A step up on the original. Because, for one thing, you'd just have to look at it, not have to actually read it.

Propelled by the post-literate possibilities of a whole new and transcendent art form generated by documentary reality, Kesey planned to surf the American swell generated by the French New Wave (not even the Hollywood dream merchants—the fatcat producers who gave us a whole new world of silver screen fantasies were gullible or pretentious enough to believe this—that was left to a higher realm: college professors and, of course, the French), and his self-deification would be delivered by the video testament of his da-da ministry.

The story? Kesey—the post-literate Christopher Columbus of Cosmic Consciousness—wanted to take The Movie *beyond* story.

But a movie is not a creative singularity. A movie requires not only you, but yours. High Art by committee. Beginning with a Right Hand Man.

That would be Ken Babbs.

A great magician always has an assistant. Of Babbs, Ken Kesey later assessed: "He looked like a gleef, a Midwestern term for somebody who's not quite an oaf but is on his way there." Ken Babbs, who would become Ken Kesey's best friend at Stanford and remain so the rest of his life, went to Miami University, where he played basketball and studied writing under Walter Havighurst (author of over 30 books, including *Pier 17*, nominated for a Pulitzer Prize). He then entered Stanford's writing program in 1958 where he met Ken Kesey at an introductory cocktail party thrown by program director Wallace Stegner.

Then a new war. The first big wave from the sea of change came for Babbs when, after Naval ROTC and a year at Stanford, he was commissioned as a First Lieutenant in the Marine Corps. Trained as a helicopter pilot, he found himself in the Republic of Vietnam, and returned to Stanford unimpressed.

Kesey called Babbs "Beelza-Babbs," a moniker elucidated by Burton Wolfe: "Ken Babbs, the alter-ego, the Beelzebub of the Kesey-McMurphy character, the dark that sits in the dark corners brooding or conjuring ways to zap his enemies." Kesey's Major Domo Ken Babbs was the sidekick's sidekick who stuck by Kesey through thick and thin.

In Babbs, Kesey had a one man infrastructure, a Vietnam vet organizer, drill sergeant of the rolling chaos, allowing the incorporated Lost Boys to freak freely in high if not High style, a fun loving kick-ass St. Paul of a guy capable of executing a greater man's master plan...

I as Art. In Kesey's post-literate world cameras and sound equipment would be everywhere. He, we, you were a movie. Meet acid-think. Fast food insanity. Or divinity. Take your pick. On behalf of the ultimate "intrepid trip." Kesey certainly had the right cast. As Tom Wolfe so astutely observed in *Electric Kool-Aid Acid Test*—Kesey's Pranksters were not just a bunch of language-less dum-dums but articulate if occasionally crazed or even crazy social prototypes, a new breed indeed. But that was scarcely all...

In the name of creating the New Man, the unincorporated day-glo super hero of the future whose literary grandma, so to speak, was, not incidentally, Ayn Rand, and who would live in a psychedelic post Great American Novel realm, here soon would be an Eden with Kesey in Adam's role. He would end up spending well over $100,000—most of the money he made on *Cuckoo*—essentially filming the spontaneous "art" that was no more or less than himself and his apostles. The result was not much as a movie, but definitely a primal precursor to the mass media solipsism now known as "YouTube."

High horsepower magic and metaphysics were in the air and Kesey was a hero for a future that fairly shouted his name. Dream houses, dream cars, wonder drugs, wonder weapons, America could kill or cure anything, so why not, next, a dream religion? Fire God and replace Him with yourself. Holy Prometheus, Batman! Your medium? Go with what you know, but with a transcendental psychedelic twist: as star of the Movie of You, on a voyage of total freedom and metaphysical grabass.

You as God or at least His only begotten son: Swashbuckler. Your head wrapped in the American flag, your golden mane rippling beneath it in the wind as you and your Merry Men career through the heart of the country in a bus that doubled as a four-wheeled drug-drenched 24-7 frat party. The Pranksters may have looked like the Kingston Trio on a psycho hootenanny, run by the head fop from the Pirates of Penzance, but they got the job done.

Besides, it was a lot easier to dress up as a cross between Captain Hook and an Easter Egg than sit behind a typewriter. Especially if you held in your hands, courtesy Sandoz Pharmaceuticals, the keys to the kingdom. LSD was first-rate fairy dust for the man on the make. And an even better one making, in Kesey-speak "boogity, boogity, boogity."

Though Kesey was about to find himself in what is often known colloquially as "deep shit," can we doubt his vision? Imagine if 1964 TV technology had the bells and whistles enjoyed by MTV's "slackers stuck in a house fucking around" *The Real World* series. As a "free form" record of trenchant hipsters on the loose, The Movie—or at least the idea of it—predates the best of hipster reality shows by decades. Imagine if 1964 Wonder Bread American living rooms had been wired into the sight of flag-draped Kesey and his sexy hench-chicks as they hurtled across the country looped out of their minds on some Alice in Wonderland Devil's Drug. It would have blown the 1964 American mind.

Up to forty miles of film. Eventually that's how much the Pranksters shot. The Movie would change everything. Save the aforementioned world. Recoup Kesey's hundred grand. But complications soon arose. Namely because:

a) Just because you are a genius of the very words you are abandoning, doesn't mean you'll be a genius at film—no more than Babe Ruth could have been a great quarterback in the NFL.

b) As Kesey was about to discover: Making a great movie about the wonders of acid while on acid is tough.

The problem: in fucking up, as elsewhere, form follows function. In a parallel universe, the young filmmaker Bruce Brown was making a very similar movie to Kesey's. The "plot" was almost identical: a band of attractive, bright young guys embark on a utopian journey seeking Enlightenment and a perfect world. *Endless Summer: in Search of the Perfect Wave*, was a "free form" documentary about surfers traveling the world in search of precisely that—the perfect wave. Timeless, *ES* still makes millions. The difference? *Endless Summer* was about as spontaneous as *Othello*. Scene after scene is carefully set up à la situation, complication, crisis, resolve by a voice-over narration along the lines of "We hiked to Beach A expecting to find gentle three foot waves, what we found instead were monster nine footers, but Gremmie Hangten decided to paddle out anyway…"

In short, *Endless Summer,* as a "free-form" documentary, presented a carefully crafted *story,* and in 1966—about the time a successfully edited Kesey movie would have hit the box office, *Endless Summer* became the biggest—and first—widely distributed alternative lifestyle documentary. *Endless Summer* sold a new vision, the Edenic life of the surfer, to a nation of wide-eyed kids. But, whereas Bruce Brown sought the perfect wave, Kesey's band sought the perfect high. *Endless Summer* left Kesey in the dust. Trying to make a great movie about being fucked up while you are fucked up means you'll fuck up. But Kesey, who bought the illusion that LSD was the end of illusions, was too fucked up to see that.

And besides, Kesey—still a man if not mad man of letters—had an ace up his sleeve. A co-star of literary provenance had landed in Kesey's lap, a living legend who had lately unhitched his bohemian wagon from the tired horse of the beats. When Neal Cassady took the driver's seat of Kesey's bus *Furthur* (WEIRD LOAD bumper-stickered on the back), he had just spent two years cooling his heels in prison for possession of one joint. Allen Ginsberg concluded, "Neal Cassady drove Jack Kerouac to Mexico in a prophetic automobile…one decade later Cassady drove Ken Kesey's Kosmos-patterned school bus on a Kafka-circus tour over the roads of an awakening nation."

Partly truth and partly fiction, Neal Cassady would prove Kesey's exemplar of the new art form. "I saw that Cassady did everything a novel does, except he did it better because he was living it and not writing about it."

A Noble Savage made Noble muse, Art as the artist. Kesey saw Cassady as "in revolution against the tyranny of inertia" and long after Cassady's death offered something of a eulogy: "There's something about Cassady that keeps this nation moving and meeting itself. He's an avatar of the bohemian yesterday." Kesey saw Cassady's "trip" as "the yoga of a man driven to the cliff edge by the grassfire of an entire nation's burning material madness. Rather than be consumed by this he jumped, choosing to sort things out in the fast-flying but smog-free moments of a life with no retreat."

An avatar described by Jerry Garcia as no less than "a tool of the cosmos." The hero escaped from the page, Cassady was said to have stolen 500 Fords by the time he was 16 and to have possessed such a multi-dimensioned mind that he could carry on two or three conversations at once, also so prescient that he could foretell when someone was about to enter a room, their gender and intent, and to be able, further, to rattle off the correct serial numbers of a dollar bill as quick as you could pull that bill out of your pocket. On the road, it was reported that he could name the make and year and condition of a vehicle about to approach from around yonder bend.

As Kesey would write in *The Day After Superman Died,* "Like all the other candidates for beatitude, (I) had prowled North Beach's famous hangouts—City Lights, The Place, The Coffee Gallery, The Bagel Shop—hoping to catch a glimpse of the motor-mouthed character that

Kerouac had called Dean Moriarty in *On the Road* and that John Clellon Holmes had named Hart Kennedy in *Go,* maybe eavesdrop on one of his high-octane hipalogues, perhaps even get a chance to be a bigeyed passenger on one of his wild rapping runs around the high spots of magic San Francisco. But I had never imagined much more, certainly not the jackpot of association that followed, the trips, the adventures, the near disasters—and, worse, danger, the near successes…(Cassady) was Lenny Bruce, Jonathan Winters, and Lord Buckley altogether just for starters. He couldn't have helped but be a hit. But the nightclub format would have pinched his free-flying mind, and no stage in the world could have really accommodated his art—his hurtling, careening, corner-squealing commentary on the cosmos—except the stage he built about himself the moment he slid all quick and sinewy under the steering wheel of a good car, the boatier, the more American, the better. The glow of the dash was his footlights, the slash of oncoming sealed beams was his spots."

CHAPTER THIRTEEN: BLOWS AGAINST THE EMPIRE

"Kesey was already talking about how writing was an old fashioned and artificial form and pointing out, for all who cared to look...the bus.

"...But in July of 1964 not even the hip world in New York was quite ready for the phenomenon of a bunch of people roaring across the continental USA in a bus covered with swirling Day-Glo mandalas aiming movie cameras and microphones at every freaking thing in this whole freaking country while Neal Cassady wheeled the bus around the high curves like Super Hud and the U.S. nation streamed across the windshield like one of those goddamned Cinemascope landscape cameras that winds up your optic nerves like the rubber band in a toy airplane and let us now be popping more speed and acid and smoking grass as if it were all just coming out of Cosmo the Prankster god's own local-option gumball machine—

Cosmo!

Furthur."

—Tom Wolfe

This was Kesey's plan: Instead of publishing words, publish a way of being in the world. Say you're 28 year-old famous Ken Kesey, riding atop your eight ton gnosis-mobile, your bus—painted all swirly, yellow and wild, WEIRD LOAD emblazoned across the back, zooming east into the heartland: what would be foremost on your mind? An exciting world-changing if not world-saving crusade, natch. Iconography on wheels. Long after the dust had settled, Kesey would conclude that the bus "was a metaphor that's instantly comprehensible. Every kid understands it. It's like John Ford's Stagecoach with John Wayne in the driver's seat, just like Cowboy Neal."

But would Kesey have become much more than a less ethereal, more gregarious Tom Robbins had it not been for Tom Wolfe? Wolfe proved the ultimate space-age town crier, morphing low culture into high art. How? Rarely an actual participant in his own "participatory" journalism he was, rather, a great ghost, hauntingly here, there and everywhere— even inside the minds of his characters, and it seemed as though he barely laid his hands on the levers and buttons of his narrative machine. He just watched, and what he saw was a world made new. A new world blessed with a new nomenclature. For Wolfe had abandoned the "pane-of-glass nonstyle" of traditional journalism, abandoning too the pretense of objectivity, which was swapped out for attitude. Of his own craft, he was later to remark, "I never felt the slightest hesitation about trying any device that might conceivably grab the reader a few seconds longer. I tried to yell right into his ear: stick around."

All the better for Kesey if a best-selling pop journalist popped up out of nowhere to record Kesey recording Kesey. As Kesey's Boswell, Wolfe delivered America a kick-ass psychedelic Socrates who preached that the future of relevance, renown and redemption would lie in hallucination and movies as opposed to reality and books.

Flashback to 1964. Tom Wolfe, about to get rich making Ken Kesey famous, was already rocketing to the literary moon fueled by fiery sub-sentences like *'Ggghhzzzzzzzzhhhhhhggggggzzzzzeeeeong! —gawdam!'* his post-Shakespeare, post Joyce, post word take on NASCAR race car star Junior Johnson's race car getting what I would have called in my more common 15 year-old parlance, first gear scratch.

By this time Kesey had already written the epic for the age. But, acquiring Wolfe as his Boswell was the literary hat trick of the 60s. Wolfe was the author of the new Wild West, a Wild West not about six-shooters, rattlesnakes and Bowie knives but stars, cars, bars and guitars. His adjectives (describing the sounds of cars and guitars) like *ffffrrrrnngngah!* And *hhhfdddddrrrashh,* (excuse misspelling) could have been, in a more traditional and less evolved time, the punch lines in a fart joke, but he made reading as neon vivid as—

—real life? Maybe, maybe not; what Wolfe threw on stage was something more like hyper-hilarious real life, that was just beyond the common grasp, and that was populated with hyper real unreal people like Ken Kesey. Who had attracted Wolfe's attention by way of a cache of letters written by Kesey in the third person from his exile in Mexico, one of which concluded with: *"What was it that had brought a man so high of promise to so low a state in so short a time? Well, the answers can be found in just one short word, my friends, in just one all-well-used syllable: Dope!"*

Reading that letter, Wolfe knew he was on to something. A classic story of rise and fall and rise again maybe, if nothing else, in which Kesey became a protagonist for a future that fairly shouted his name, and led to Tom Wolfe's invention of terminally gregarious Kesey as a sort of literary action figure, the voice of his generation, a dada successor to Papa Hemingway as seen in the fun house mirror. This was well before Kesey found himself trapped in the funhouse itself—and Ken's gift for spectacle was, even without Wolfe's help, attracting a lot of attention.

By the time *The Electric Kool-Aid Test* had hit the bestseller list the dream was already over; Love Generation Babylon, aka the Haight, had devolved to a junkies' paradise. But no matter, Wolfe caught the America-changing ephemera defining the fleeting moment, the dogs in mid-bark as the caravan passed, freeze-frames of the rising micro-mini hem of 1960s culture ironically seeming hyper-accurate in its unreality.

Wolfe was writing the headlines, if not the script, of a bold, vulgar new era born of a more innocent age, a world of West Coast surfers, stoners, and custom car freaks. Wolfe connected with Kesey not long after publication of *Sometimes a Great Notion*. Kesey proved the perfect 60s North Star, telling Wolfe that, he'd "rather be a lightning rod than a seismograph."

So best to go on the road in the highway style of the beats, better to install himself as crown prince of the underground future, and in the uncertain time after Kesey was sort of famous but before Wolfe made him really infamous, Ken kept busy taking his world to another world. "The revolt of the guinea pigs," he called it. Which would be memorialized as the new cinema verite.

Many years later, nearly an old man, Kesey offered perspective and intent. "We're the people who planted the seeds. Whether it's artistically valid or not, we have to cultivate the crop." A crop to be planted and cultivated on fertile ground. Burton Wolfe, author of *The Hippies*, identified Ken Kesey as "hero of all the Horatio Algers on reverse trips, making it big and dropping it all for an eternal binge."

But back to the trip. Pioneer "unsettlers"—as Kesey called his Pranksters, heading not west but east to infect America. In Kesey's written documentary, *The Further Inquiry*, Chloe Scott testifies, "I've been on better Mexican buses. With pigs and chickens and drunk drivers who acted more civilized!

"And the noise. And the overcrowding. And no rest stops except breakdowns. And eating nothing but ratburgers…There was always plenty of money but I think they must have actually liked ratburgers. It fit in with the rest of the motifs and décor of the trip."

A trip that was piloted by the Beat Hudson-driving Zen master and original fugitive from injustice himself. The Enlightened Primitive has its fans from Grendel to Alley Oop, and Kesey's embrace of Neal Cassady was classic literary anti-social climbing—inviting America's hippest mystic rogue to trade Jack Kerouac's Hudson for Kesey's bus,[17] and at the same time allowing Ken to go on the road in high style, installing himself on the literary pantheon as top dog on the bohemian porch. A transition that was sketched by Wolfe when he describes the meeting—at the end of the cross-country bus trip piloted by Cassady, of Kesey and Kerouac in New York.

Wolfe observed: "Gradually the Prankster attitude began to involve the main things religious mystics have always felt, things common to Hindus, Buddhists, Christians, and for that matter Theosophists and even flying–saucer cultists. Namely, the experiencing of an Other World, a higher level of reality. And a feeling of timelessness, the feeling that what we know as time is only the result of a naïve faith in causality."

Wolfe was writing what seemed almost to be the unholy grail of the future, implausible (or impossible) as that might sound, and anointing by virtue of his brilliant recognition, our generation with a wonderful feeling of completely unearned and undeserved power. Canaries about to eat the cats in an America that was about to go out of control.

And in Kesey Wolfe had the penultimate American out-of-controller.

Great Helmsman of that whole new era, his image was about to become as ubiquitous as a blond haired, blue-eyed Aryan Chairman Mao. He would end armies, guilt, heartbreak and clocks. Kill the ego, and maybe even the future and the past. Kesey's mantra: Live in the Now. "Go with the flow," emit "good vibes," and "stay positive." Books were over. Kesey told a reporter, "I am not at work on a third book because writers are trapped by artificial rules. We are trapped in syntax. We are

---

17 "The painted psychedelic bus is an American icon like Thoreau's Walden Pond or the Statue of Liberty. It is a modern Ark of the Covenant, rusting in a cow pasture."—Walt Curtis, writing for the Oregon Cultural Heritage Commission

ruled by an imaginary teacher with a red ball-point pen who will brand us with an A- for the slightest infraction of the rules. Even *Cuckoo* seems like an elaborate commercial."

Was he joking? It was as if OJ Simpson had retired from the NFL at twenty-nine, claiming there was more to life than football.

CHAPTER FOURTEEN:
DAYS OF HEAVEN

"Reading One Flew Over the Cuckoo's Nest gives a man faith that the Combine is still buying madmen's work…

"Along those lines I was down at Kesey's house in La Honda last night, bearing witness to one of the strangest scenes in all Christendom—a wild clanging on tin instruments on a redwood hillside, loons playing flutes in the darkness, mikes and speakers planted all over, mad flashing films on a giant trampoline screen; in all it was pretty depressing—that a man with such a high white sound should be so hung up in this strange campy kind of show biz. He MC'ed the whole bit, testing mikes and tuning flutes here and there as if one slip in any direction might send us all over the cliff in darkness. Like a kid's home circus, a Peter Pan kind of thing, but with sad music somewhere up in the trees above the kiddie carols. I drank twenty beers and left sadly sober, remembering Mailer going off that diving board in Las Vegas and all those guys in the press room laughing at the fat boy with the ping-pong."

—Hunter Thompson

Hunter Thompson, a stern moralist at heart, was not an unalloyed bootlicker when it came to his bohemian brothers in arms. Of Kerouac: "I've read *The Subterraneans:* all of his crap for that matter. The man was an ass, a mystic boob with intellectual myopia. If somebody doesn't kill that fool soon, we're all going to be labeled The Third Sex." As for Kesey, in 1963 he had commented to a friend, "I'm trying Kesey's book (*Cuckoo's Nest* had just been published) it's good, but so what? Books like that are like water when you want whisky. Fuck'em."

Thompson's feelings toward his fellow traveler were reflected ambiguously after Kesey's jail break in a letter Thompson wrote to Tom Wolfe. "I'm uncommonly curious about your book (*The Electric Kool Aid Acid Test*) and I'm not sure why. Kesey doesn't need any gratuitous canonization at this point (is canonization a word?)...our general relationship was always so goddamned drugged that I'm not even sure I know what he's like when he's straight. And I don't know how many people he'd want to bring in. A scene like he had at La Honda would have me on death row in two months."

The beginning (Ken Kesey)-and end (Hunter Thompson) of the age of Aquarius met in a San Francisco radio station and afterward drank beers with sundry Hell's Angels, the portraits of whom Thompson was painting in a book-in-progress about the motorcycle gang, a group terrorizing its way into the heart of hip America.

Evangelist Kesey, who worshipped drugs as a sacrament, and atheist Thompson, who took drugs as a joke, were a natural pair: fair-haired psychedelic Jesus meets the Devil's disciple. Kesey was impressed. In tribute to Ken for the Kesey Memorial issue of "Spit in the Ocean," Thompson later recalled La Honda after Kesey invited the gang to an acid bash. "The hordes snarling down the road and amassing near the big welcome banner the Pranksters had stretched across the gate. At the entrance stood the young innocents eager to extend their tribal hospitality. It was quite a scene. People were bursting into flames everywhere you looked. There were speakers everywhere—all around the trees...And there were about six cop cars parked on the road, lights flashing, cops everywhere...And all the while more Angels were coming down the road and being welcomed with great happiness and friendliness. The simple fact that carnage was averted was impressive, but this was incredible."

Young Mr. and Mrs. Kesey's Fortress of an Incredible Lack of Solitude suggested Doctor Frankenstein's lab for lunacy. The original "test of concept" Acid Tests conducted there were often tightly crafted free-form fiascoes—freely freaking from a carefully constructed launch site, but with no known and/or maybe even knowable end in sight. The object: to blow minds.

Kesey recalled that "the most bizarre one" occurred after he invited avant garde filmmaker Kenneth Anger and a bunch of "San Francisco diabolists" to La Honda on Mother's Day. The Pranksters had all blasted themselves Mars-ward, and were draped in—why not?—robes and, according to Kesey were, "playing dolorous music up to the trees." Anger and Co. were "walked" to a small amphitheater constructed among the redwoods up above Kesey's house. Here sat the "thunder machine."

The original thunder machine had been constructed by "Heron of Alexandria" circa 100 AD as a dramatic means of introducing gods and whatnot to Greek plays and Kesey's version had been conjured in similar vein, but electrified.

The thunder machine had been wired to powerful speakers designed to vent a lot of noise and robed Pranksters, thirty year olds going on eight, "banged and clanged" away to excellent echoey effect. A hundred and fifty or two hundred feet above was a tiny hidden spotlight the Pranksters had rigged in a redwood, which shone down magically to illuminate a gold tree stump. According to Kesey: "You had no sense of there being any light. It just looked like a glowing stump." On the gold stump was a gold ax. After much "banging and clanging," the Pranksters lowered a birdcage from the tall tree above. "In the birdcage was a big hen. We…spun this little pointer on what was called the 'toke board.'"

The object was to spin the pointer and whoever the pointer pointed at was, according to Kesey, "going to take that hen out and chop its head off." The needle spun and pointed at Page Browning, who opened the cage and discovered the hen had laid an egg. On tape Kesey said, "You can hear that Herman's Hermits song, 'Stomp That Egg.' '*Stomp that egg!*' So he got the hen out of there and put its head on the stump and chopped the head off. Page threw the chicken still alive and flapping right into the audience. Feathers and blood and squawking and people jumping and screaming and all those diabolists and Kenneth Anger got up and left. They didn't think it was funny at all…We out-eviled them."

Next, the Dead. On their rock, Kesey built his church. Pranksters had discovered "religion," in the persons of the Grateful Dead. Secular saints born the Warlocks—a young San Francisco ex-jug band which, now electrified, spent most of its time playing covers of blues tunes—better to become the American Rolling Stones.

Jerry Garcia remembered, "We were younger than the Pranksters. We were wilder. We weren't serious college people. We were on the street. It was kind of a more intellectual bent than street kids in the present-day sense. It was street kids in Palo Alto. More bohemian than anything else. We were definitely Dionysian as opposed to Apollonian…When the Pranksters took acid, they fucked with each other really. In a big way. We just got high and went crazy…Our music scared them."

Kesey and Garcia were a quick match, and the Grateful Dead vastly enlarged the impact of Kesey's psychedelic circus. "Garcia was as well read as anybody I'd ever met. He understood Martin Buber's *I and Thou*... Anybody who's been on acid and has felt Garcia reach in there and touch them, all of a sudden they realize, 'He's not only moving my mind. My mind is moving him!'"

That Garcia evoked Buber was especially impressive to Kesey. Years later, he declared, "You can read *I and Thou* for two hours and not get over it for the rest of your life. Buber tells you how you stand, either in a dialogical relationship with the creative force, or in a position of 'havingness' where you are a thing bounded by other things...it is a reality that doesn't have any physical form...This is the power of rebellion— the more the government relies on kids to buy Gap, the more vulnerable they are. At any minute, people can stop buying these things. Another thing we learned from LSD is that there are a lot more realities than one. There are a lot of mansions in my house. Christ and Buddha would have shot a great game of pool."

Kesey recalled a particularly effervescent acid test in which Pranksters descended on Portland "like a really crack terrorist group. We could hit a place, get in there, mess it up, and be gone before people knew what had happened." Particular to the Portland experience was a guy in a business suit who was carrying an umbrella and who paid his one dollar/one tab admission price and began to dance. "Somebody hit him with a spotlight and he said, 'The king walks!' And he began to walk with his umbrella and play with his shadow. 'The king dances!' He'd open the umbrella and say, 'The king casts a long shadow!' The Dead were watching this and playing to every moment so he became the music that people were playing to."

Kesey continued to feel movies were a transcendent medium to the end, almost as much as acid. "Movies changed the way I looked at words on paper," he said years later. "So much of the writer's effort is decorating...to putting that sofa over there so it frames the room." On a more basic level, "I thought you ought to be living your art, rather than stepping back and describing it." But the devil was in the details. Not the least of which was that little fact that Kesey did not synchronize the sound of the footage he shot with the film—and that the tape recorder was run off the bus's generator and sped up and down as the generator—driven by the accelerating and decelerating bus engine—sped up and down. The inability to sync sight to sound, Kesey concluded, "finally just broke our back."

Then, boom, he was rescued by Tom Wolfe, who wasn't so much about straight-ahead reporting, as seeing, and telling stories. He just watched, and what he saw was a world made new.

Wolfe got his idea of the heroic Kesey from television. "The Fugitive" was a hit TV show in 1964, fugitives seemed hot and Wolfe saw an open door. In 1968, shortly after publication of *The Electric Kool-Aid Acid Test*, he told Lawrence Dietz of *New York Magazine:* "I thought, gee, this guy's a worldwide fugitive and doing a pretty good job of it." The significance of acid did not ring a big bell before "coming to the realization that this was in a way a curious, very bizarre, advance guard of this whole push toward self-realization…a curious atmosphere developing in which I think people are, in some weird way, beginning to realize that they really aren't needed in the work force in the old way…Everybody's beginning to try and discover what I call The Real Me. It's sort of saying, 'This job I have, at the telephone or whatever they think they work for, that's not The Real Me. The Real me is not the hubby or the mommy. The Real me can come out in some way.'"

From his perch on the kandy-kolored catbird seat, he referred to the German theologian Joachim Wach, "Following a profound new experience, providing a new illumination of the world, the founder, a highly charismatic person, begins enlisting disciples. The followers become an informally but closely-knit organization, bound together by the new experience, whose nature the founder has revealed and interpreted."

By the time Kesey decided to abandon literature for bigger or at least more ethereal things, Wolfe was already using words in a way that had the power of acid and any Ken Kesey Movie combined. For West Coast surfer/hot car/druggie kids in the mid 1960s, *The Pump House Gang* was our reflection in a fun house mirror. Wolfe had discovered a new realm, wild, indulgent, exciting, preposterous. *Us.* No matter that us was cartoon hilarious (Wolfe revealed to me as a 16 year-old hot rodder, that my insanely over-horse powered dream suicide machines were profoundly lethal jokes. Which was so awesome—I was worried they might be just meaningless trash). Wolfe, as literary auteur, was becoming the new culture king and, in the process—never mind the implosion of The Movie—he was about to award Kesey a throne of his own.

Cut to the chase, it didn't happen. Acid proved a sensation not a revelation—or at least a revelation only to the extent that, after taking it, you realized you could be assaulted by sensations as heavy and sharp as concrete and broken glass—yet no new Hamlets, hydrogen bombs or even good tavern graffiti were inspired by psychedelic drug use, and...Movies don't edit themselves, and consider the psychological sledgehammer effect of all that acid.

In *City of Words* British literary critic Tony Tanner wrote, "Kesey's wild bus ride was headed more for nirvana than Entropyville," intent on "finding everything instantly significant without the interpretive superstructures offered by books or theology," then quoted Kesey's belief that, "We're under cosmic control and have been for a long time... And then you find out...about Cosmo, and you discover he's running the show."

Tanner concluded, "Part of the honesty of Wolfe's book is the way it reflects growing feeling that Kesey became obsessed with control, with playing power games, with organizing other people's trips. Some people later came to regard him as a sort of Elmer Gantry, even as a leader with distinct fascist tendencies...(but) Kesey's desire to grasp the pattern behind all patterns is in fact very American. Cosmo is the 'main party' which the Superhero must try to deal with...Kesey's paranoia when he was on the run in Mexico was clearly on a cosmic scale. Perhaps a superhero is never far from feeling himself a super-victim."

PART THREE:
THE SAVANT

Walt Curtis (foreground) and Paul Krassner in the Kesey barn, on the eve of the Hoo-Haw Arts Festival, June 5-6, 1976

CHAPTER FIFTEEN:
KRASSNER AGONISTES

"You got balls of steel for a Jew; you shoulda been a Nazi."
—American Nazi Party Fuhrer
George Lincoln Rockwell to Paul Krassner

B usted.

The savant, Satan or saint who invented the sixties. Seventy-three years old and forced to assume the position while the long arm of the law frisked his jeans.

With his mop of curly brown hair and still baby face of an ancient teenager, here was the wizard who—back when phat was fat, sic sick, ho's whores and the poo still pigs—created *The Realist,* the most important micro media in modern American history. Here was a founder of the Yippies, the comic 1960s revolutionaries who made Richard Nixon's neo-imperialist Amerika a cosmic laughing stock. A macro-visionary who once adduced, "—so-called flying saucers are actually diaphragms dropped by nuns on their way to heaven," Krassner was a man who had long ago excused himself from the America of money and cars, lacking either a fortune or a driver's license.

He was at Fort Mason in San Francisco performing at a benefit for Jack Kerouac's daughter Jan, who needed a dialysis machine. "A friend drove me to the theater where backstage a guy gave me a baggie—I assumed it was pot."

After the performance his friend lit a joint in his car in the parking lot—rolling it from a cigar box under the dash lights. "I saw a police car way over on the other side of the parking lot, saw it driving around but didn't think about it until I heard the rap, rap, rap on the passenger side window."

"Next thing I knew, I was up against the car getting searched, the cop said, 'You got anything sharp in your pockets?'

'No, just my keys, my pen.'

"But I sensed hostility. The cop said 'Okay, but if I get stuck with anything I'm going to be very mad.'

"So when the cop pulled out the baggie and put it on the hood of the car, we both learned that it was a combination of pot and psilocybin. The cop said, 'So you like mushrooms, huh?' In my little thought balloon there was a translation: 'Aha, so you like *the evolution of consciousness*, too?'"

A Mt. Rushmore figure of lost soul sociology, Paul Krassner is transcendent at tapping the source. Charles Manson, defanged and in jail, confided to Krassner, "Mass killer, it's a job. What can I say?" *The New York Times* defined Krassner as "an expert at ferreting out hypocrisy and absurdism from the solemn crannies of American culture." *People* knighted him "Father of the Underground Press," based on his unusual political reporting. JFK unfaithful to his wife? Richard Nixon a liar? In love-it-or-leave-it America people thought he was crazy. But at a time when baby boomers were just waking up to sex, drugs, rock and roll and the fact that the revolution would not be televised, Krassner already knew where all the bodies were buried.

In 1967, he accompanied Groucho Marx on Groucho's first acid trip, and soon found himself traveling in elevated circles. "Phil Spector accused me of killing Lenny Bruce. I was a guest of John Lennon and Yoko Ono in Syracuse, it was at an art opening and it was also Ringo Starr's birthday. There was a group of us sitting in a circle on the floor of a little ballroom singing "Happy Birthday," then the object of the music turned up a notch from Ringo to God, and everyone started singing 'He's got the Whole World in his Hands' to whoever was next to us. Jerry Rubin was on my right, singing, 'He's got the whole world in his hands' to me, and when it was my turn I sang, 'She's got the whole world in her hands' and Jerry whispers to me, 'That was very courageous,' and I said, 'I was just having fun with God's gender problem.' Then we went to another large room filled with people—and at the end of it Phil Spector sees me and he shouts, 'You killed Lenny Bruce!' and all heads turned to see the killer."

After the much regretted collapse of his first marriage and despite the fact that he hated soap operas, Krassner fell in love with *Secret Storm* ingenue Jada Rowland. What he did next was brilliant, sort of. He invited his new beloved to have their photograph taken together by no less than Richard Avedon, to be included in a book of famous counterculture photos. What could be more romantic? There would be, he informed Jada, only two slight rubs. They would be photographed naked, in the neo-classic style of John Lennon and Yoko Ono's *Two Virgins* and, just one other thing, Krassner would be pictured with, so to speak, his genes at attention.

Something must have been floating around in the ozone, for not long after a similar magic media moment occurred: a BJ on the air as the E=MC squared of over-the-top radio. The year was 1971, the place San Francisco. "I'd been a DJ at an underground radio station (as Rumpleforeskin)," Krassner recalls. "Kesey was one of my guests." But problems. "An exec from New York came out and said, 'You gotta stop talking about the evils of capitalism'—which I hadn't been doing—and 'you can't talk about the news after we do the news'—so instead after the news I'd always play the Who's "Won't Get Fooled Again."

"I got fired and then was invited to KSAN to audition for a show there and while I was auditioning on the air, Gene 'Dr. Hip' drops in to the studio with Margo St. James, the founder of COYOTE (an acronym for Call Off Your Old Tired Ethics)—She was going to be a guest on his show."

So, confluence in the heavens, Margo is inspired to give Paul, during the middle of his on-the-air audition, an on-the-air blowjob. "Nobody listening knew whether the oral sex was real or not. All I said was things like, 'Be careful there's a safety pin holding my zipper up,' and 'Would you like to say something to your feminist friends?' to which she disengaged long enough to clarify, 'I'm doing this of my own volition.' I stuck to the rules, did the station break at the half hour and everything: *This is KSAN, the station that blows your mind.*"

Krassner would have been fired had he been hired in the first place. Sadly, however, he was not only not hired, he was banned from the station.

While Krassner never had the public impact of Bob Dylan or the Beatles–because the former musical prodigy *didn't have a band* and you had to be able to *read* to get his message—he was Subversive Zero, the subversive the subversives got their subversions from. After *Life* Magazine published a flattering profile of Krassner, an FBI agent posing as a college student wrote the editor demanding that "Krassner and his ilk be left in the sewers where they belong. He is a raving, unconfined nut."

With perfect punch line pitch, after Ken Kesey threw a bash for both hippies and Hell's Angels, Krassner wrote: "It was a strange alliance. I mean, day-glo swastikas?" As *The Realist's* editor his style was unique. When the *Los Angeles Times* media critic David Shaw wrote about plagiarism, Krassner reprinted part of the story under Pete Hamill's by-line. A thoughtful voice for world peace, freedom of speech, weird science, equal rights and condom use ("encase your porker before you dork her"), *The Realist* was a Whitman Sampler of modern American imagination, idealism and insanity. If you were a sweeping visionary, successful psychotic, outlaw action hero or lethal loser, Krassner was likely your scribe. He dropped acid with Manson girl Sandra Good, and was both touched and slightly terrified when Sandra took off her clothes and invited him to finish his trip with her in her bathtub.

He is great at finding lost quotes. Walt Disney's confession; "I love Mickey Mouse more than any woman I've ever known;" and this from Walt, after Aldous Huxley purportedly gave him pychedelic mushrooms during the filming of *Alice in Wonderland*. "If people would think more of fairies they would forget about the atom bomb." When Patty Hearst was kidnapped by the lethal, loony SLA, her father set up a free food program in San Francisco for the poor as part of her ransom. Krassner recorded then-Governor Ronald Reagan's Lincolnesque response: "I hope they all get botulism."

A guru to the gurus, Krassner was supported, sometimes literally, by the demi-gods. On one occasion his friend John Lennon paid for *The Realist's* entire printing bill. In cash. Once, Lennon, knowing that Krassner was a confidante of Charlie Manson, requested, "Look, would you kindly inform Manson that it was Paul (McCartney) that wrote 'Helter Skelter,' not me." When Bob Dylan asked for an audience, Krassner, curious, had questions, prompting Dylan to inquire, "This isn't an interview, is it?" Krassner replied, no, to which Dylan responded, "Good, because Bob

Dylan is just a guy waiting for me out in the car."

A man for all seasons, Krassner was given the Feminist Party's "Media Workshop Award," only to suddenly be named Publisher of *Hustler*. "I was in the audience at their Christmas party when Larry Flynt announced he'd heard the call of the Lord. The Lord must've told Larry I needed a job, because suddenly he exclaimed to the crowd that I was his new publisher." Krassner's was the first issue of *Hustler* not to feature a strumpet on the cover. He substituted an Easter bunny nailed to a crucifix instead to promote a story lamenting commercialization of the hallowed holiday.

In 2005, at "Wordstock," the annual Oregon Book Fair, I had introduced Krassner, who was there to, in turn, introduce his former father-in-law and last living lion of American literature, Norman Mailer. Somebody said Krassner and his ex-father-in-law did not get along, and backstage, down the hall, in the rectangular light of an open restroom door, I had heard Paul address Mailer, "hello, Norman" and get a "hello, Paul" in return. Then, like a star, a thought, wish or a dream, Mailer, steel wool hair lit by a distant stage light, hobbled on his crutches out of the black toward me. Krassner walking, haltingly, crippled also, behind. Then, in the dark, I sat with the two beside me. It was like having them inside my mind.

Moments later, I stood at the podium above the blinding suns of stagelights and reminded the packed auditorium that without Paul Krassner we might have all been somebody else, that after there was a Lord Buckley, a Lenny Bruce or a Steve Allen, but before there was Tom Wolfe and Hunter Thompson not to mention Howard Stern, there was Krassner—the most dangerous, subversive or funny man in America, take your pick—a man who, thanks to the hilarious muck he raked in *The Realist,* saved the world from techno-fascism, etc., etc., etc. and how he surfed the swelling tidal wave of 1960s zeitgeist long before Ken Kesey or any of the other big cultural wave riders even learned how to hang ten.

To a great if oddly confused crackle of applause, Krassner limped on stage to speak before introducing Mailer.

Relieved to be out of the limelight, I left the podium to the sound of the crowd clapping, walked around the back of the building, and stood in line to get a glass of wine.

Inside the theater, I heard some kind of ruckus and my beautiful wife was still laughing when I took my seat in the audience. Evidently Krassner, during the course of introducing the author of *The Naked and the Dead*, offended his ex father-in-law by way of a complex wiener anecdote.

Now on stage, leaning forward on crutches, Aquarius said. "Gee, Paul, I didn't know how to start tonight, but maybe you got me going. Now, if I ever made that remark, that the reason Jews get circumcised is to keep them from breaking their babies' noses, all I can say is that I must have been down in the lower depths of a very bed marijuana trip. But I think, even at my worst, I couldn't have said that. Paul is the master of hyperbole. He loves hyperbole, for example (when he wrote) Lyndon Johnson 'attacked' the wound in JFK's head."

Actually, what Paul wrote was that Lyndon Johnson had intercourse with the wound in JFK's throat, but…

"At any rate," Mailer continued, his grey curly head as big as a smoking moon behind the podium, "if I said it, I would forgive myself now for having said it, because circumcision happens to be something every Jewish man thinks about every day of his life. It makes us obsessive for a very simple reason. We don't know if it's an asset or a liability. And I'm not speaking of it lightly. I'm speaking of psychic castration that may make us smarter or it may not."

Psychic castration? Smarter or not? Obsessed? Every day of our life?

As a Norwegian touched by the knife, I doubt I'd thought about circumcision six times in my life. What had I missed?

Paul Krassner says, "When you write about acid, you pretty much just report on the experience, but don't make any great claims for the drug as being a source of great escapist new knowledge or anything. Aside from the world turning into crazy shapes, it was never an escape, acid always made me take things more seriously. It gave me ideas I wouldn't have had otherwise. Some good, some—" he shrugs. "It made me understand the structure of music much better."

I asked, "Why don't people take it like they used to?"

"For one thing, they don't make the pure stuff anymore, and young people like Ecstasy better."

Desert Hot Springs, California. A clean and well-lit oasis. Or, perhaps more accurately, hell with a really nice golf course. A Wild West creosote cowboys-and-Indians-scape under a blue oven sky. Wyatt Earp or Beelzebub could live next door. Krassner smiles. "I've never minded feeling the heat, but I've learned to like air-conditioning. They told us that anybody who has a pulse could get a mortgage in this neighborhood, so we borrowed a pulse and here we are."

A "vegetarian who eats fish," doesn't smoke cigarettes, drink alcohol or take any "legal" drugs, he once described himself as looking like "a friendly gargoyle with battle scars." Though born before World War II and tilted by a limp from a police beating, he still has, if not the baby face, the animation and enthusiasm of the brightest 14-year-old ever.

When CBS newsman Harry Smith interviewed Krassner, Paul told him, "I think of the government as the devil, and the devil never sleeps." Smith concluded, "Krassner and his kind were once viewed as radical, even evil. His message has changed little over the years, yet now it sounds somehow conservative."

Krassner expressed dismay. "I was stunned—*shocked,* I tell you— that this was considered somehow conservative." So he told his former father-in-law about it. "'Well,' Mailer explained, 'you have to realize those media guys think that anybody who's against the government must be a conservative.'"

Tough to keep a bad man down. Thirty years after venerated ABC newsman Harry Reasoner fumed, "Krassner not only attacks Establishment values, he attacks decency in general," Krassner, whose one-man show just happens to be titled Attacking Decency in General, is still at it. Desert Hot Springs has adopted him as their official Prince of Darkness, and today the founder of New Journalism is hard at work again—calling a spade a tri-pronged pitch fork, he is dressed as the devil. He has his red devil suit on with his red sequin horns–a Palm Springs devil to be sure—and, riding shotgun in a Land Rover out here on a hell-hot desert highway, is waving from the window on the passenger's side, offering Satan's encyclicals to a van bumper-stickered with the promises that *Jesus Saves* and *God is Love.* The driver is waving back, a Bible in his hand, at America's original equal opportunity offender, and a flock of what are apparently fundamentalist Christian kids in back, are gaga at the sight of God's number one nemesis who, diabolically, looks in his evil suit of lights like nothing more than a curly haired, somewhat road-worn, Halloween-bound junior high school kid.

Krassner's first act of rebellion?

"I was a violinist, the youngest concert artist in any field to play at Carnegie Hall." He was six. "Not long after that I saw Ingrid Bergman in *Intermezzo*. I became obsessed with learning how to play the title theme and told my violin teacher I wanted to learn how to play it. He refused, saying 'That's not right for you.' Which I took to be a declaration of war on the individual, and so I quit the violin."

"Do you still play music?"

"Ed Sanders gave me an auto-harp. I played that for awhile."

"You gave up a potentially brilliant musical career."

"I had a technique for playing the violin and also a passion for making people laugh." Circa fourth grade, a kid in his class got up in front of the class, unzipped his pants, exposed himself and was dispatched to reform school. The next day Krassner got up in front of his class, unzipped his pants and exposed a drawing of, so to speak, himself. "The school told my parents I needed a psychiatrist, but my folks wouldn't go for it. All I was trying to do was show that the boy's punishment far exceeded his crime."

Krassner had to learn the difference between appearance and comic reality. It did not happen overnight. "As a kid, I liked Jack Benny and Fred Allen on radio, and believed they were really having a feud. One day I saw a photo of them in a newspaper sitting together peacefully and the caption read: 'Photo does not indicate presence of armed guards' and I remember thinking: *Wait a second, that sounds a little suspicious.*

"I'd go with my brother every year to the Labor Day free show at central Park to see Milton Berle. I didn't like him. He was snide with the women. He'd say to one of the singers, 'I loved that song, meet me in my dressing-room after the show.'

"My brother and I had a book, *2,500 Jokes for All Occasions*. I studied the jokes for structure. I was obsessed with humor, it became my religion, I perceived the universe through a prism of absurdity—I didn't choose it, it chose me, because I couldn't help it."

While pretty much a normal baseball-playing kid—he even aspired to be a G-man—Krassner also aspired ultimately to a larger world. Enthralled by *The Catcher in the Rye,* he wrote JD Salinger asking permission to sublet Holden Caulfield as the protagonist for a novel that he—Krassner—planned to write. "Silence was Salinger's Zen reply." Krassner went on to write, direct, and star in his senior high school play, earning the description as a junior Orson Welles from his local newspaper. In 1955, "I was still living with my parents, and *Mad's* publisher, William Gaines, gave me a key to the office in case I ever needed to be alone with a girl." At that time he was working as managing editor for Lyle Stuart's anti-censorship paper *The Independent,* and after Lyle joined *Mad* to become general manager, Paul wrote a few freelance pieces for the magazine.

Name a more subversive child molester than *Mad* magazine. Bug-eyed whacks, libidinous Disney ducks and psycho voluptuaries amok (never will you see more perfectly drawn young female breasts) in stories titled—Prince Violent, Mickey Rodent, Melvin of the Apes, Superduperman, G. I. Shmoe!, Little Orphan Melvin and Flesh Garden (a takeoff on Flash Gordon), Lone Stranger, Frank N. Stein and Morbid Dick. For literate kids in the late 1950s, *Mad* changed the classic three R's equation to reading, writing and ridicule, adding punchlines to the American cultural trifecta: politics, media and products. To a core national demographic of grade school and junior high kids, *Mad,* on a playground grassroots—if not seedling level—said rise up, urchins and teenyboppers, rise up, you have nothing to lose but your chains.

Mad's mantra was voiced by a two-headed hydra that said, "Question Authority" and "the country is a joke," and was as revolutionary and effective as *Das Kapital* with a laugh track. In a desert of conformity and jingoism, *Mad* was an oasis of irony, hilarity and mistrust. *Mad's* lingua franca may have been 75% drum roll and grab-ass, but *Mad* inoculated children against hypocrisy.

And what was hypocritical about America? Everything. Through the ice-eyed *Mad* prism we were less a country than a con. During a blindly self-satisfied, tail-finned era mesmerized by money and jingoism, *Mad* made hay imprinting teeny boppers to the fact that their parent's nation was knee-deep in happy horseshit; politicians were greedy, power-mad clowns; movie stars, coddled hot-heads; products, crap. For these efforts *Mad* was selling over a million copies a month, but Krassner found that he could not do stories with adult themes. He wanted to do a story mocking the weird apparent chastity of bachelor comic book heroes, setting his tale at a party where Kerry Drake, Rex Morgan, Steve Canyon, Mike Hammer, and Clark Kent are looking at porn flicks and leafing through girlie magazines. Bill Gaines told him, no—saying, "What if my mother saw that?"

Krassner replied, "But your mother is not a typical *Mad* reader.'

"No. But," Gaines corrected, "she's a typical mother."

At that point, Gaines told Krassner that *Mad* had just hit a million and a quarter circulation.

"I guess you don't want to change horse in midstream.'

To which Gaines rejoined, "Not when that horse has a rocket up its ass."

So, time to branch out.

The Realist. It was like finding the Rosetta Stone for going in through the out door, a paranoid's paradise. The real world decoded to its horrific, apocalyptic base elements. I was not alone. For a teenage intelligentsia suckled on *Mad* and the big beautiful breast of *Playboy*—where "QUESTION AUTHORITY" was tattooed to the collective baby boomer brain, *The Realist* provided the bully pulpit for baby boomer marching orders.

In many ways *The Realist* was simply *Mad* for adults, satire that named names, in which grownup fact replaced teenage fiction—essentially to the same effect. Krassner: "The first Issue in 1958 included a satirical piece about anti-nuclear testing in the form of a child's primer I borrowed from *Mad*...I had space in Lyle Stuart's office for $10 a month, put a (libel) lawyer on retainer for $15 a month and asked the lawyer if he minded if I didn't show him anything until after it was published."

A magazine called *Progressive World* gave Krassner their mailing list of 3,000, who started *The Realist* with 600 of their subscribers. Tom Wolfe was an early and succinct contributor, reviewing Norman Podhoretz' book *Making It* thusly: "Norman who?"

Circulation grew by word of mouth. Steve Allen was his first subscriber. "Allen gave gift subscriptions to a bunch of people, including Lenny Bruce, who gave gift subs to a bunch of people, and that's how it grew, Malthusian fashion." Circulation hit 1,000, then 3,000, 5,000—snowflake tumbled to snowball, snowball careened to avalanche, and, by 1967, Krassner was selling 100,000 copies a month—putting him in a position to make a political difference, a spider for good in the middle of a very influential and convoluted web. "*The Realist* brought me into the psychedelic circle, the conspiracy circle, the prisoner's rights circle, the show business circle, the political circle, the writer's circle—all only connected by the fact they were subcultures…though subcultures often overlap—if Rudy Giuliani can unite with Pat Robertson, there's hope. Now Rudy can get Pat's mistress an abortion."

Realist conspiracy theorist Mae Brussell claimed, among many other things, that one Reinhardt Gehlen, Hitler's chief intelligence officer against the Soviet Union in War World II, had been flown to the United States in 1945 to form the core of a virulently anti-communist CIA, which Brussell claimed, funneled $200 million into secret Gehlen US Nazi spy network. She quoted CIA head Allen Dulles chortling, "He's on our side and that's all that matters. Besides, one need not ask a Gehlen to one's club."

Then there was Manson. "I interviewed a Malibu Sheriff's deputy who was at the bust at the Spahn Ranch that captured Manson. He told me how his department had been told by memos from above to leave Manson alone before the murders even though he'd violated his parole, was living with all these under-age girls, and had weapons there—the deputies speculated these memos were issued because Manson was a racist and the assumption was he was going to kill Black Panthers."

Realist material erred to the side of "admired" rejects. "People would say, this piece is really good—it got rejected by three magazines—try *The Realist*. Sometimes I'd get something really fresh and, I'd say, 'Try and place this in a commercial magazine, but if that doesn't work bring it back'—*Esquire* bought an article like that—I could pay just a little bit. I didn't have a budget. I couldn't afford one."

Like *Mad*, *The Realist* took no advertising but, unlike *Mad*, money was always a problem. "I was very much of an unrealist. There were two guys who had a system to beat the racetrack so I put money from my savings bonds into it. I began going to the track and noticed, besides the nuns with their trays out for people to contribute, that there was a tip sheet called the *Armstrong Daily* that, in addition to race tips, had a column called "Eleven Lively Arts" by Marvin Kitman"—whom he enlisted to great success.

The Realist published Bruce Jay Friedman, and Kurt Vonnegut sent in snippets of interest—like on divorces, a subject with which he was intimately familiar. Richard Pryor wrote a piece about the disproportionate number of blacks fighting and dying in Vietnam, titled "Uncle Sam Wants You Dead, Nigger."

While publishing *The Realist*, Krassner also wrote perhaps one of the most important largely forgotten contemporary satires—pretending to be sections omitted from *The Death of A President* by William Manchester— ever written: *The Parts Left Out of the Kennedy Book*, whose key passage, the passage that provided the template for gonzo journalism, was:

"American leaders seem to have a schizophrenic approach toward each other. They want to expose their human frailties at the same time that they do not want to remove them from their pedestals. Bobby Kennedy privately abhors Lyndon Johnson, but he publicly calls him "great, and I mean that in every sense of the word." Johnson has referred to Bobby as "that little shit" in private, but continues to laud him in the media.

Gore Vidal has no such restraint. On a television program in London, he explained why Jacqueline Kennedy will never relate to Lyndon Johnson. During that tense flight from Dallas to Washington after the assassination, she inadvertently walked in on him as he was standing over the casket of his predecessor and chuckling. This disclosure was the talk of London, but did not reach these shores.

Of course, President Johnson is often given to inappropriate response—witness the puzzled timing of his smiles when he speaks of grave matters—but we must also assume that Mrs. Kennedy had been traumatized that day and her perception was likely to have been colored by the tragedy. This state of shock must have underlain an incident on Air Force One which this writer conceives to be delirium, but which Mrs. Kennedy insists she actually saw. "I'm telling you this for the historical record," she said, "so that people a hundred years from now will know what I had to go through."

She corroborated Gore Vidal's story, continuing: "That man was crouched over the corpse, no longer chuckling, but breathing hard and moving his body rhythmically. At first I thought he must be performing some mysterious symbolic rite he'd learned from Mexicans or Indians as a boy. And then I realized—there is only one way to say this—he was literally fucking my husband in the throat. In the bullet wound in front of the throat. He reached a climax and dismounted. I froze. The next thing I remember, he was being sworn in as the new President."

For Krassner, it still resonates. "I wrote that 40 years ago, it blew my mind, so I had to share it. The important thing is, I wrote it as a seduction—revealing layer after layer of verisimilitude, like peeling back an onion—so it started out with stuff that was totally true, but outrageous to begin with. Like LBJ saying during the 1960 presidential primary that JFK's father, Joseph Kennedy, had been a Nazi sympathizer while US Ambassador to England during World War II-which was true! That set people up. Then I got into stuff that reporters knew. But not everyone else—the Marilyn Monroe JFK connection. *Photoplay Magazine* had run—after the assassination—a poll about whether Jackie should start dating again. So I had a scene of her reacting to it. 'Should I keep my diaphragm in my night table drawer or in my medicine cabinet?' Let'em vote on that!"

"Throughout the early text I was gradually increasing the reader's faith in my credibility as I led up to the climactic scene of Jackie telling William Manchester that on Air Force One, during the flight from Dallas to the hospital in Bethesda, Maryland, she saw Lyndon Johnson fucking the corpse of her husband, in the throat wound. This was done to change the entry wound from the Grassy Knoll into an exit wound from the Book Depository by enlarging it, in order to fool the Warren Commission."

"People read it and didn't know what to think—'That sounds exactly like Jackie!' Paul had carefully mimicked Manchester's style. "A guy actually used one of those monster old-fashioned computers to compare my style to Manchester's—and it matched perfectly."

There you have it: the birth of gonzo journalism.

Kesey was a reader of *The Realist*. They had it on the bus, *Furthur,* and when the issue with "The Parts Left Out of the Kennedy Book" was published, Neal Cassady was reading it, and he handed it to Kesey and said, "Hey Chief, you better look at this."

CHAPTER SIXTEEN:
UTOPIAN THOUGHT IN THE
WESTERN WORLD

"It's bad on the nerves to see a tough-ass in quicksand, and if you read the Cuckoo book, you'll know what I mean. Here he was last night, the Kooky King of the Woodsy Beatniks, orange jacket and headphones and bossing it all while I kept waiting for him to grin and look sane for a minute but he never did. It reminded me of me in my worst hours, and the only excuse I could make for him is the one I make for myself—why bother to make it right when nobody knows the difference anyway?"

—Hunter Thompson

If the road to hell is paved with good intentions, the Pranksters were about to pave an Interstate. National psychosis. Just what the doctor ordered. From a capitalist consumer point of view, as a technology acid did what technology does best: use itself up. And if the self is only a metaphysical boutique, an extra-dimensional, bio-chemical suite living in the meat that is your brain, a bargain basement priced e-ticket to fantasia was hard to beat. Kesey had no problem adding two and two and as a boy who grew up as a "hard-shell" Baptist and science fiction fan, he was about to became a Merlin in the last age of magic, an age that combined science and religion in a way that fit the rationale of neither but the needs of both.

Central to the La Honda-based acid mayhem were the aforementioned Grateful Dead, who were everything to Ken Kesey: "They weren't just playing what was on the music sheets. They were playing what was in the air. When the Dead are at their best, the vibrations that are stirred up by the audience is the music that they play."

Deadheads, according to Kesey, are—or were, "looking for magic. When you see something like that, there's a crack in your mind and you know it's a trick, but you can't figure it out. That crack lets in all the light. It opens up all the possibilities. When that little split second thing happens, when the Dead are playing and everybody in the audience goes, 'Wow, did you see that?' that's the moment that puts them in touch with the invisible."

But it was more than just the Dead. By the mid sixties popular music was moving beyond entertainment or aphrodisiac to mantra and marching orders. The suave crooners of the 1950s—Perry Como and Andy Williams—clones to country club swells in their tennis shirts and golf sweaters, stood for little more than singing handsomeness. But now?

Kesey and Tim Leary's acid mantra might have been nothing but reedy voices in the wilderness had they not been codified and jingle-ized and supercharged by rhymes riding electric guitars, hymns of that newest and greatest of apparitions: the rock god, whose most effective of engines, the power chord, provided the sonic hurricane on which the power of any ditty—from "Row, Row, Row Your Boat" to "Gimme Shelter" might be amplified enormously, so a drug anthem such as Jefferson Airplane's "White Rabbit," soon to be played constantly on radio and stereos, could zoom from idea to tattooed fact: to marching orders for the adolescent mind.

But, meanwhile, what of the end of Gutenberg? As a McLuhan-esque glamorous How-to Guide to the New Hip, The Movie might have made Kesey a monster of the media. But, eager to escape "the prison of the page" as a pioneer of "empowerment," Kesey led the LSD-fueled charge for Anybody-Can-Do-Anything amateurism liberated from the shackles of expertise and sobriety. However, he became stymied by the fact that his new metaphysical gnosis was founded on the notion that, in the new reality, things like structure and schedules and even work—the very things that are vital to the success of a movie—were obsolete.

Not that he lacked the energy to charge once more into the breach. Kesey was a man both before and ahead of his time, less a prototype hippie Adam than a top down leader, boss, guru, dictator of anarchy who literally knew no bounds, insured his own dreams would be torpedoed by their very magnitude. Listen to him speak about his future and fate in 1965: "First, let me make it understood I am not a writer. I haven't written anything since those last drafts of *Notion* and I don't intend to deal with anything else. I have many reasons for this, the main one being that to continue writing would mean that I couldn't continue my work."

In the new multi-media world in which celebrity-hood was already on the chopping block, cut in bits and pieces by a television-led universe that daily allotted less and less time to more and more people, Kesey likely realized that literature was not about the writing so much as the writer, that the future was a secular deification of fame, and that if he could not earn a place in the Bible at least he could spend a lot of time on TV. In short, Kesey wanted out of the novel-writing business and into the Ken Kesey business.

Would that work? Kesey was more interested in power than art, and when it came to power, a novel was an ethereal fist. Sidestepping Great American Novelist to become the Man of His Time, Kesey sought to free the freest society in history from the tyranny of its own consumer ambitions.

Movements are often born of their opposites. Jack Kerouac's *On the Road* was a motor-headed, two-fisted driving in the fast—or at least half-assed—lane account of beatnik babes and brawling, but in reality, Kerouac was a bisexual momma's boy who did not even have a driver's license. Kesey—who, as Walt Curtis said: "Wanted to go beyond novels to become a white knight and cosmic commentator"—created a persona, as black-and-white-as-a-bulls eye, a self-portrait as father of peace and love.

Yet, if Kesey was all about peace and love, it was meat ax peace and love—and what friends he cultivated when not hanging out with the Pranksters! Kesey's "alter-Pranksters" represented a group from about as deep from the heart of blue—or perhaps more accurately, black and blue—collar America as you could find in 1965; rebels who were all about freedom, patriotism, creativity, power and sticking up for your buddies, iron-hard partiers and masters of in-through-the-out door populism, jock bohemians who combined whips and chains with reefer and speed—dirty, strong men brave and true, a sort of hippie SS who had volunteered to go to Vietnam and win the war, men as American as going to the moon, John Dillinger or kiting checks—and what was more sixties tribal than a motorcycle gang?

The Hell's Angels were a perfect match for Ken Kesey. A+ outlaws, free as free could be. In 1965, freedom meant mobile and what was more *mobile* than a chopper? These swastika-baubled cowboys had traded in horses for the horsepower of the gorgeously resculpted Harley 74, the thoroughbred mechanical stallion of the 20th century. Led by Sonny Barger, a savvy Attila the Hun for the Pepsi Generation who was great at laying down the lawlessness, the Angels, like Kesey, were pack animals, outlaw frat boys with bigger muscles and longer rap sheets, kickass cultists whose members, like the Pranksters, traded their identities for cult monikers like "Magoo" and "Terry the Tramp." Also like Kesey, the Angels were all about family, complete with "Mamas," i.e. slinky girlfriends who in photos draped themselves over the Angels like shawls. (Cool, if you were up for love as a team sport. The brothers shared and shared alike—and harbored no reservations bringing home to mother a delicious little anytime, anywhere gang bang-ette.)

But more important than coalescing the counterculture, Kesey wanted to open the American mind and set it loose, unfettered by the conventional constraints of the nine-to-five. All it would take was a national party in which the punch was spiked with the stuff of dreams.

A party perhaps not possible without the arrival of Augustus "Chemistry is theology" Owsley Stanley III, "The King of LSD," whom Timothy Leary identified as "A. O. S. 3, acid king, LSD millionaire, test-tube Pancho Villa…the best known of a band of starry-eyed crusaders who outwitted the wicked, gun-toting federales and bravely turned on the land of the young and the free to the electronic harmony of the future." Sacrament-maker Owsley, whose LSD became the caviar of enlightened psychosis, saw acid as the Answer: "I thought we might survive and the planet with us if we could manage to get enough people to experience the view which the psychedelic sacraments give…(But so) much for the rhetoric of 'freedom of religion' so oft repeated nowadays. So what if the psychedelic of choice is LSD rather than peyote? Is it OK to eat peyote if you are a Native American indigenee (sic), but not if you are white or black or other Native American? Since when's there any difference? Why should there be any barrier to joining any religious group? There is only one answer; we are not allowed to be different, to think original thoughts, to act as if we are really free. We are not supposed to experience the world in any way differently to the way those in power wish us to."

Jay Stevens, author of the authoritive LSD "biography," *Storming Heaven: LSD and the American Dream*, believes that minus "that cocky little boho" Owsley the Acid Tests would have never been more than a pipe dream—simply because nobody else besides Owsley knew how to run an LSD assembly line. Owsley believed, according to Stevens, "the Divine Force had given mankind LSD to counteract the discovery of nuclear fission." He believed acid was magic. "It took you into a place that was like the descriptions in the books by the Rosicrucians and the Freemasons."

Owsley discovered Kesey's acid scene by way of a pal, "a big black dude," who told him he had to meet Kesey and Kesey's new auxiliary Merry Men, the Hell's Angels. Owlsey was taken a bit aback. "Shit, man," he said, "you've got to be out of your mind. And you, a black guy! Those Angels EAT niggers. What are you doing?"

Owsley's friend replied, "Ah, I don't know. It's pretty interesting; he's been feeding them acid, man."

So off they went. "And, Jesus, boy," Owsley later recalled, " that was sort of like getting strapped onto a rocket sled. The stuff that those guys would do to your head, and the drugs and everything else, was nothing like anything I had experienced before. It was absolutely dramatic. And it WAS true. The Angels turned out to be some of the farthest-out people I ever met in my life. They were just cut free by this thing. It was like a key. Kesey was playing with stuff which I recognized as ancient magical shit. But they didn't know it. They just kind of stumbled on it by playing around."

Owsley told writer David Gans, "Kesey was the kind of guy that reached out, grabbed your knobs, and tweaked them all the way to ten. All of them. And the whole scene was running on ten all the time. It was almost as sudden, and as different, as discovering psychedelics themselves for the first time, at another level."

But discovered they were. "None of these people in Kesey's scene had any roots in the shamanistic rituals at all…The Millbrook guys, Janiger (head of the Albert Hoffmann Foundation)…they were more into that. I…never went to an Indian peyote meeting…and I never went to the curandero in Mexico with the mushrooms. But…all those rituals contained a lot of the elements which the Pranksters discovered, or rediscovered, or invented, or something…I told Kesey, 'Hey, you're messing with ancient stuff. And without any maps! You may need to be careful about this'.…And he kind of laughed at me."

Later Kesey said, "All (acid) does is turn up your volume. It don't change who you are, it just turns up the volume."

Owsley was quoted in *Rolling Stone:* "For most people the proper dose is about 150 to 200 micrograms. When you get to 400, you just totally lose it. I don't care who you are. Kesey liked 400. He *wanted* to lose it." Tom Wolfe reported Kesey ingested as much as 1500 micrograms. To get higher than high, he'd take his mind to karmic Everest. But what may have braked his literary output and ascent was the cumulative sledge hammer effect of 400 to 1500 mg. doses. Owsley concluded, "It was sort of like, if you set fire to a skyrocket it's going to be as brilliant as hell, but it doesn't go very far and it doesn't last very long. (The Prankster scene) attracted so much social pressure on the individuals that, had it not been for Kesey getting busted, and the intense amount of social and police pressure on it, who knows how far or where it would've gone?"

CHAPTER SEVENTEEN:
HOLY MAYHEM, INC.

"The man in the space suit is the prince of disorder. His mood is so infectious even those in the crowd who aren't high are catching it. It's powerful stuff and so unstable it's pulling everyone in its wake like a black hole. It's scary stuff for a control freak like Bill Graham. He's met his match in Kesey, a control freak of cosmic proportions. Neither one of them can let go of their bossdom for one second."
—David Dalton

The best of times, the worst of times. For the Angels, all about freedom and each a law unto himself, descending not from the sky above but from the highway below as initiates to the psychedelic New Jerusalem. Unusual. But for authoritarian anarchist Kesey, choosing the Angels as acid emissaries and/or criminal constabulatory made perfect 1960s sense. All about loyalty, brotherhood, individualism, bravery and bad craziness, acid simply took them to a companion universe home to peace, love, idealism, better bad craziness and, as a footnote: thought. Acid made the Hell's Angels contemplate.

They had arrived lock, stock and thundering Harley choppers at Kesey's La Honda retreat. Party time big time. Angels drunk, Pranksters high. Angels soon both.

Former Prankster Lee Quarnstrom provides an aerial view: "We were, in Kesey's own words, exploring inner space without the slightest damned notion of whether we'd get back to home base without going crazy."

Meanwhile, home base was having its own problems. Charged by the police with "operating a disorderly house," Kesey was bailed out at dawn the next day. According to Quarnstrom, the mother of an eccentric "sub-Prankster" who went by the alias of "the Hermit," who—small world—had served as a nurse at the same hospital where Kesey got the idea for Randle McMurphy, threw a copy of *Cuckoo's Nest* in Kesey's face and screamed: "Go back to your cuckoo pad. You should have stayed in the nest instead of flying over it, you big cuckoo!"

Kesey "deftly snatched the book out of the air," and autographed it for one of his jailers. Later on, a back story was revealed: When police, led by one Willie Wong, raided Kesey's La Honda Valhalla, and Kesey threw a buffo wrestling move on Willie before the cops lassoed a bunch of Pranksters and pot and took the whole shebang to jail, Kesey reportedly told the judge: "What else was I going to do? I was raised during World War II. What would you have done? A big Jap jumped on me. I didn't know what was happening. I tossed him off."

Though Kesey's lawyers worked for free (figuring perhaps,—along with a looming legion of attorneys who would make their living defending dopers—Kesey was a great advertisement), money was becoming a problem. Kesey scored $7,000 for an Italian edition of *Cuckoo* he didn't even know had been published, and suggested to journalist pal Lee Quarnstrom that he, Quarnstrom, could sell articles for a higher return if, so to speak, a dandelion was renamed a rose. "You can write it and put my name on it. Write anything you want. We can probably make more money, if they think I wrote it." Quarnstrom: "I think it was merely a case of Kesey the Writer having decided he wasn't going to write anymore."

Paul Krassner met Kesey for the first time in 1965 at the Vietnam Day teach-in at the Berkeley Campus which, Krassner said, "I was MC-ing. He walked up to continue a conversation which had never begun. 'Faye said that so and so, and that such and such,' like we'd been talking all along.

"Then he got up on stage, played the harmonica, started dissing the marchers, which pissed people off. And I said to Jerry Rubin, one of the organizers, 'If you don't like what he's saying, you shouldn't have asked him to speak—that's what happens with celebrity fucking, you know, maybe we can get Kesey...'

"The next night at a local theater I got up on stage and started mimicking him, playing a harmonica and saying. 'Thou shalt not march' or whatever he said and he jumped up on stage and it was like he was

Flash Gordon. 'I protest!' he began, 'These wars have been going on for 10,000 years.'

There was a storied Argument between Kesey and Allen Ginsberg after a Vietnam Day demonstration in which Kesey, perhaps not to offend the Angels, was dynamically noncommittal. "If WE can't talk about it…how can the diplomats involved talk about it," Ginsberg demanded. "Both sides have to be willing to start mediation soon or it's gonna' be hell."

"It's gonna take more than talk," Kesey insisted, "People have to walk away from the war."

"You mean like you did at the rally?" Ginsberg sneered.

Meet "Big Nig," tall, gangly, affable, the guy who wanted to sponsor the first Acid Test. Kesey and the Dead had decamped at Big Nig's house, Big Nig planted at the door—ready to charge one dollar cover.

Prankster Paul Foster wrapped himself in bandages to become a Grateful Dead mummy (Dead Head Lou Tambakos: "At its peak moments, the Dead's music is violent and out of control. It's ugly music with an edge—really nasty shit."). They started playing and fuses started blowing like lady fingers, Big Nig running in and out of his house replacing them as fast as they could pop…

Good fun according to Jerry Garcia: "The Acid Test was the prototype for our whole basic trip. But nothing has ever come up to the level of the way the Acid Test was. It's just never been equaled…What happened was light shows and rock and roll came out of it (but) something much more incredible than just a rock and roll show with a light show; it was just a million more times incredible. It was incredible because of the formlessness…We'd play stuff and the Pranksters would be doing stuff and there was an incredible cross interference and weirdness."

And there was the New Music. From above or below, The Grateful Dead, Kesey's church choir, sang acid-blasted inverted hymns of deliverance and cohesion. But the Dead were not psychedelic or, even particularly, about peace and love. Their music wasn't half as spacey as David Crosby's, the Beatles or the Electric Prunes. I know of few Dead love songs, fewer Dead political songs—the themes that stagger to mind lean more to the side of drug bust, arrest, and incarceration. However, Garcia and company were, unlike almost any other musical entity, about community. They provided the one force of gravity for the otherwise weightless hippies. Who were willing to pay for their grounding. As a product, the Dead were endlessly recyclable—an "average" Deadhead may have gone, over time, to 300 Dead concerts.

The night he got busted in North Beach, an arrest that would propel him forever if not for better from fair-haired Messiah to martyred culture king, Kesey described himself (in the third person) as already not feeling so hot. "The man has all the usual stigmata of the bohemian in vogue of that period…a bohemian crowding that age when 'it's time the goddamn ninny stopped acting like them snotty Vietniks and dope fiends and acted his age'…He has partially balded and has been sick long enough it is difficult to know if he is 25 or 35. Hair boils wildly from his head in thick kinky blond locks. His neck and torso are thick and muscular though he is not as those built thus usually are. His face is excited but tired, lopsided with the strain faces show after too long forced to smile diplomatically."

Nevertheless, in 1966 "Outlaw" was a great franchise—better than boss, doctor or movie star, especially if, by "Outlaw" you were—in the parlance of the time—a "fugitive from injustice." The quickest way to become an Outlaw is to get thrown in jail. Kesey did it like this: Hippie entrepreneur and future famous publisher Stewart Brand (*The Whole Earth Catalogue*) had come up with a way to take the Acid Tests to a next level—stage a huge "come one, come all" public bacchanal in the Longshoreman's Hall. Of the Trips Festival stage in San Francisco in January, Kesey waxed reasonably: "The general tone of things has moved from self-conscious happenings to a more jubilant occasion where the audience participates because it's more fun to do so than not. Audience dancing is an assumed part of all the shows, and the audience is invited to wear ecstatic dress and to bring their own gadgets (A. C. outlets will be provided.)"

The Grateful Dead and Big Brother and the Holding Company were booked, and the night before blast-off, Kesey, Brand and Kesey's new love, the large and large-eyed young voluptuary Mountain Girl, decided to retire to the roof of the Longshoreman's Hall for a communal smoke. Kesey then got the idea to invite himself onto the roof of the house next door. Pot smoking on the roof of some stranger's home in 1966, even in San Francisco, was risky and, cut to the chase, the cops showed up.

Kesey freaked, and nearly "chokes to death" trying to swallow the weed. Failing to get the pot down the hatch he tried to throw it off the roof, but one of the cops intercepted it. Kesey started throwing blows and the cops began hitting him with their flashlights. Then, according to Grateful Dead manager Rock Scully, "One of the cops pulls out his gun and says: 'Okay, stand clear! I'm going to blow his head off.'

Mountain Girl grabbed the cop, pleading, 'No, no! Don't shoot him! Peace!'

So a night locked up in jail instead. Kesey didn't miss a beat. The next day, out on bail, he showed up at the Longshoremen's Hall wearing a gold lamé space suit.

And who does he run right into but Bill Graham who, clipboard in hand, is guarding the door.[18] According to Scully, Graham "won't let Kesey in. He's not on the list! Where did this deranged control freak come from? He's shrieking orders and throwing people up against the wall. He's hitting people…Kesey is already tightly wired from spending the night in jail." Scully reports Kesey telling Graham, "I'll tear your fucking head off if you put your hand on me again."

Graham replied, "Go ahead. You're still not getting in," which elicited from the astonished Kesey, "It's my show, asshole."

"Says fucking who?"

Bill Graham recalled the fracas differently, that, prior to the show, he was standing in the hall when he saw bikers being let in through the back door by a guy in a space suit. "A full body space suit with a helmet on top…I ran to him and I looked at him and I said, 'Why are you letting these people in? Are they working here?'

"The space helmet turned to me with the visor up. Two eyes looked at me and then he turned back without a word. I said, 'Excuse me, excuse me' and he just kept letting people in. I tried to get the door shut but I couldn't because people just kept pushing through, all strangers coming

---

18 Re: The Trips Festival, Graham had a bone to pick with Kesey from the beginning: "I remember the Merry Pranksters were there and they were pretty spaced out. (But there were)… a lot of very decent people out there. I had not seen the acid thing in full force. That night, I did. It shocked me. They might as well have been offering hand grenades to people. When LSD exploded inside the body, how did they know how much damage the shrapnel could cause? They had ices spiked with acid, available to all, children as well. There were big tubs on the balcony and downstairs for anyone to consume. From the outset, that has always been my one ongoing argument with Ken Kesey. There has to be a warning. If people don't know, how can you assume their body can take what yours can? How can you know that?"

in with no tickets."

"I said, 'WOULD YOU MIND ANSWERING ME? WHAT THE HELL ARE YOU DOING HERE?' Finally I said, 'Are you Ken?' I had seen his picture before. Inside the helmet, it was Kesey's face.

'Do you mind telling me what the hell you think you're doing?'"

Without replying Kesey simply flipped the visor down. "I didn't even have to touch it," Kesey later recalled, "I just nodded and it went plop."

According to Kesey, Graham "wanted every nickel out of all these people coming in that night and there were lots of people who were part of this Acid Test retinue that didn't *need* to pay. They were already part of it. He really took issue with this, saying, 'No, no, everybody pays.' This is where he began to make his real Bill Graham reputation. Which was a cross he had to bear for many years. Until finally he crawled up on it and decided to rule from there."

Bill Graham, however, was looking at the acid tests from the other end of the telescope. As he told Burton Wolfe, "The first full rock dance concerts were held right here, before Kesey or (Chet) Helms came in this place. I mean, you want to talk about Acid tests, Trips Festivals, hippies, it's all a crock of shit…What is Trips Festivals? People dancing and having fun, that's all. These things were never exclusively for people with long hair or beards freaking out on the floor. They were for everybody. A guy with a tuxedo could come in here with a half naked blonde bitch, and they could wiggle their asses all over the floor and do their thing and nobody would give a damn."

By this time, Kesey had a warrant out for his arrest. Forget facing the music, time to blow your life. The Pranksters exited stage south.

After Kesey established a hidden-in-plain sight hide out in Manzanillo, he had Faye and the kids fly down.

Kesey claimed to have done "the most outrageous things" while in Mexico. When broke he and the Pranksters would catch fish in "forbidden waters" and sell pot. Profits would then be reinvested in the purchase of marijuana by the pound, "the purest grass I've ever had." After they'd smoked their fill, the rest was often baked into brownies which Kesey claimed he and his carried "back across the Mexican border."

Time to beat the reaper: "It was a peaceful, relaxing time in Mexico, "but I had to come back and face the man. I let the others drive the bus, and I rented a horse and rode over in a red cape and a big sombrero. The border guards asked me for my visa, and I told them, look, man, what do you mean visa, I don't know anything about visa, I've been fuckin' drunk since I came to Mexico, what do you want from me. And they kind of nosed around me and laughed and waved me on, and I rode over the border in the sunset on my horse and then I put the horse in a taxi and told the guy to drive him back to the owner. I picked up the bus, and we drove on up to Monterey, where we fed the marijuana brownies to a cow."

Before Kesey went to jail he spent time on the farm in Eugene, where, on a horseback ride with his young son Jed, the boy was hit by a train at a railroad crossing: "I thought Jed was zapped out for good. The kid had stopped breathing, his heart had stopped, it seemed like he was gone. And so I knew I had to dig deep into my power and draw on every resource, yelling out: 'Don't let him die, don't let him die.' And he started breathing again. It's like we're all supermen changing into clothes from the phone booth when we're called on to do a superhuman job."

CHAPTER EIGHTEEN:
THE JAIL INTERVIEWS

"Oh trials, trials, Man. They're a horrible experience. Besides, I thought it might not be a bad idea to go to jail anyway. There is a certain value in getting inside a penal institution where you can talk to men and get them altogether and learn things from each other and then teach the cops on the other side. I mean, you say to the cops: look, we're all in this same situation together. We're both confined to this institution, you have to serve time here as well as we do, we're all one, so let's cool it together and see if we can work this thing out to make life easier on everybody. In that way I can turn some cops on, and hopefully the vibration will spread to other institutions."
—Ken Kesey interview with Burton H. Wolfe

Locked up and loaded. Perhaps a little lese majeste was good for the soul. Or so it might seem from reading Kesey's very likeable *Jailhouse Journal,* which reads something like *One Flew Over the Cuckoo's Nest* written from the inside, but with crooks instead of crazies, narrated by an alter-McMurphy, the author himself, not a redneck roustabout this time, but a psychedelic outlaw on a vacation from hero-hood, placed in the work camp shadows away from the burning light of his brand new red hot celebrity and able to do best what it's a shame he didn't do more often: humbly observe the unreality around him.

Never mind the Kesey culture growing like magic mushrooms after a rainstorm in the real world beyond the gates of the California hoosegow where he'd been locked up for essentially a political crime if not simply political theater—pot smoking in public—in *Jailhouse Journal* Kesey combined his electric talents as an artist to create a words and pictures portrait of a 1960s America in psychedelic transition. The fact that Kesey brought the psychedelia with him took little away from the fun of seeing a bunch of America's minor bad boys behind bars getting an acid introduction to the brave new world.

University English professor Bob Williams offers, "I'll tell you a story of Jimmy V., Kesey's fellow inmate when Kesey was in jail. Jimmy was going down the stairs as Kesey was coming up. Kesey held out his finger and said, 'Suck, Jimmy,' and as Jimmy was passing, he sucked on Kesey's finger—his finger was coated with acid—and Jimmy said he really got off."

"There was always grass in jail," Kesey recalled, "and speed. Sure glad I didn't take any speed. Took psilocybin in jail and had a good time. There are dues. Speed is like throwing kerosene on a fire. If you keep taking dope you can't keep getting the same flashes. You've got to lay off and pay a lot more dues before you get that same flash again. The biggest thing I've learned on dope is that there are forces beyond human understanding that are influencing our lives."

In stir, Kesey was able to kick back and put the world in better perspective. Burton Wolfe (whose idea of Kesey and Jerry Garcia was this: "Both are basically scholarly men who have deliberately adopted the loose Negro style of life and slang. Both have taken their minds apart with drugs") visited Kesey in jail, where, over an inmate's lunch of pea soup, cheese, bread, egg salad, tea and stewed prunes, Kesey revealed, "You know, I have a theory about all this. It relates to there being so many Jews at the head of the hippie movement. My theory is that the Jews were responsible for World War II. I mean, look at the German mentality. Here as a people conditioned for centuries to develop their superior race concepts and penchant for war. But there had to be a scapegoat for the Germans to start the holy war they wanted, or else it could not have been started, and the Jews were the perfect fall guys for it. I mean, this was a people destined to be martyred. From their ancient Biblical stories, they prophesied it. They were the chosen people, and they were determined to expunge the sins from mankind. But they became a separate race, living apart from the Christians in their own life style. And this enabled the Germans to sanctify the murder in their systems, because without this scapegoat they probably would not even have been clever enough to do that—there's no people as stupid as the Germans...you can relate this to what's happening to the hippies because of their position in the straight society."

And to listen to the great new American novelist who no longer planned to be one, it sounded as if jail offered almost a welcome return to what amounted to a "normal" life he'd otherwise long since left behind. "Our boss is an old white-haired fart known as Bushie," he wrote. "A retired county-works supervisor come outa retirement to offer his expertise to young hellbents don't know one end of the shovel from t' other. Pretty good at it, too. He showed me how I was supposed to hold a handsaw: 'Hold it like it was a gun butt, keeping that pointing finger pointed straight down the saw like it was a gun barrel. And don't cut on the push, cut on the <u>pull</u>.'

"Jail didn't hurt at all. I liked it. Time doesn't hurt you. We can do time better than the cops. We," he said, referring to the guards and inmates, "were up there in the same situation. Ate the same food…The cops can't do time as well as the cons. The only thing that hurts you is the trial. Bobby Seale will come out of this whole thing clean. He's way ahead of everybody else because he hasn't been frightened by the time he's going to have to do. That's the trip. They get you there and frighten you of the time you are going to have to do. So you freeze up. You begin doing things and saying things for them. It burns you inside in a way—well; you begin to play their script. You're in their movie and in terms of their movie ours is invalid."

When Burton Wolfe asked him why, here in jail, he had abandoned writing, he replied. "There are too many things to be done. Until the final earthquake, the big zap when we're all one again, we've got to play a dual role. But it's coming, things are changing. We've already moved out of the Age of Pisces into the Aquarian Age. The millennium started some months ago."

Kesey further explained to Burt Wolfe his decision to quit writing novels. "Well, like take McMurphy. He was just there, like antimatter. I didn't have to create him; the patients built him for me. But the Indian was different. I don't own the soul of that Indian. He just appeared while I was on peyote, and the first chapter of that book was written by him. So, that makes me wonder am I as talented as I might think or as others think? Or am I an instrument picked to make a statement, and after the statement is made, should I assume I've got the right to make endless statements? Oh, I like to write. I will write a poem for a friend on the occasion of getting married and I will put everything into it. If I were to write longer things now, I wouldn't sign them. I'd just write them and send them in to the publisher and have him put them out there for anybody to read. See, I know now that the Indian in *Cuckoo* was not my Indian. He was brought into being by some higher power to tell America where it's at.

"Of course, I've been chosen to do that, too, and if I ever get the call to write something else, I will. But the call must come first. I will not write just for the money. I don't need money. With my two books I've already earned my stripes. They have enabled me to go around and do other things that will have impact because I'm an important person, while when others do it they have no impact. Until the public knows we can take dope and paint buses and do all these things out front and still carry on business, they will go on arresting hippies and putting them in jail. It's like running from the bogeyman. When you stop running, when you say take me, now you've got me, now what are you going to do with me—then they don't know what to do with you. This is what the hippies have got to learn. They've got to stop running and just give in, let them see how many they can arrest and what they will do about them. They watch me close here to see if I will be a shit disturber, but I play their game rules, I'm quiet. I follow orders, and then I do something like put flowers in a shop, and their minds are blown."

In jail, Kesey waxed philosophical: "Romeo couldn't have made it in a tribal scene. There are people who are inevitably mated, in the stars, and when they get together, they are the lucky ones. Those not mated but married are the unlucky ones. Faye and I are among the lucky ones. She doesn't take dope; she's never used it. But we are mates.

"As for my children, I consider myself a devoted father. I've given my kids acid several times, so now they know what it is, they know where it's at, and they don't even want to take it now…I've put them in with the Pranksters so I know there will always be someone to take care of them no matter how high I am, and I am often high. They think they can keep me from getting high by putting me in this jail. They don't understand that anything that gives you a sudden flash is dope. I'll take a flash wherever I can get it: from acid, pot, people, music, jail, anything."

While still in the work camp, Kesey waxed optimistic, "The movement is growing and will last a long time. One reason is that it's based on a life-pulsating rhythm, an upbeat that is vibrating through the universe turning on people. Iambic is the natural meter in all music and literature. You find it in the temple, the Bible, Shakespeare, all the classic works." Result according to Kesey of a "vital meter" differentiating the greatest generation for its hippie sons and daughters. A "total impact, then decay" trochaic: life-death, life-death, life-death meter had been replaced by a new "regeneratively iambic" death-life, death-life, death-life meter. "These kids have a certain upbeat that makes them unlike anyone before them except Neal Cassady, and they will be that way forever."

Cassady, for his part, was, not long after Kesey's release, to discover times had changed: "We used to be equals. Now it's Kesey's trip. We go to his place. We take his acid. We do what he wants."

Vowing to "rub salt in the wounds of J. Edgar Hoover," Kesey had found it useful to hedge his bets. He advised his national flock to "move beyond acid."

"More and more," William Plummer wrote of Ken Kesey in *The Holy Goof*, "he saw himself as someone like John Kennedy or Jesus, who was charged with a mission to change the world."

CHAPTER NINETEEN:
SEA CHANGE

"What the Kesey thing depended on was who you were when you were there…It was open, a tapestry, a mandala—it was whatever you made it.

When it was moving right, you could dig that there was something that it was getting toward, something like ordered chaos, or some region of chaos…Everybody would be high and flashing and going through insane changes during which everything would be demolished, man, and spilled and broken and affected, and after that, another thing would happen, maybe something out (of) the chaos, then another… Thousands of people, man, all helplessly stoned, all finding themselves in a room of thousands of people, none of whom any of them were afraid of. It was magic, far-out beautiful magic."

—Jerry Garcia

MAKE LOVE NOT WAR; HELL NO, I WON'T GO; IF IT FEELS GOOD DO IT; UP AGAINST THE WALL, MISS AMERICA; SAVE WATER, SHOWER WITH A FRIEND; WAR IS GOOD BUSINESS, INVEST YOUR SON; REALITY IS A CRUTCH; THERE'S HOPE WITH DOPE; WITH BOOZE YOU LOSE; FREE THE INDIANAPOLIS 500 and my Vietnam era favorite CHARLIE DON'T SURF.

Laws would be illegal and money would be free. Such was the sound bite sensibility circa 1966. Ken Kesey was cooling his winged heels in a prison farm. Après the Acid tests, the Chief could not have been more pleased. Asked about the meaning of the Acid tests, he replied. "I got aboard a spaceship one time, and I saw I was to be taken to outer space on a trip by myself, and I would have to spend the rest of my life in what society would consider an insane asylum, and I would be sad and lonely. So I saw I would have to take everybody with me, I would have to turn on the world."

"They'll have to take LSD," Kesey concluded in his interview with Burton Wolfe, "and go through the same mind-blowing experiences we have, that the hippies have, and then they'll either see it or they won't see it. To understand, they will have to turn on. The whole world will have to turn on."

So LSD, how bad could it be? My father said it evoked the dream state and might provoke schizophrenia in kids so inclined. So? I lived the dream state already and felt like a thousand guys all at once anyway. Ken Kesey was not the only one sending new signals. Because there was a new and very popular kid at school: Murph the Surf. The hair-do god, Murph was the New Man, creation of a young Californian, Rick Griffin, a long-haired blond, proto-hippie destined to become the greatest acid artist ever, whose caricature Murph—with his great swoop of yellow hair—graced, in replica, the notebooks of my fellow surfer wanna-be's who'd likewise seen The Movie. Bruce Brown's *Endless Summer: In Search of the Perfect Wave*. (Which, unfortunately, was not to be found on the shores of an Oregon Pacific Ocean where putting a slender white 17 year old finger into the surging hem of tide water at Short Sands Beach was like sticking your finger into liquid frozen concrete).

Murph was not hanging ten anywhere around here, and not that I was ready to throw the devil under the bus, but Hawaii was the place. Dying for redemption, I determined to score some acid, fly to paradise, and in no time I'd be hanging ten on twenty foot milk-warm breakers with cabbages and kings.

If Alice fell to Kesey's New Wonderland from space that year, He, She or It would have plunged toward an American rabbit hole generation-gapped between the old and new, where growing your hair as long as George Washington's or Thomas Jefferson's,[19] was as un-American as homosexuality, and the young American dream was to snap the fascist shackles of the pig establishment—tyrannies which held us down, like income taxes and stop signs. Burn baby burn, all power to the people, the revolution will not be televised—The summer before the Summer of Love, before hip capitalism ate the Revolution and excreted it as bell bottom pants and $30 shag haircuts, before a blown mind became a

---

19 In 10th grade, one of my high school pals, Billy, was literally put in a mental institution for growing his hair to his shoulders (though it takes force from the story to reveal that Billy was, actually, crazy).

corporate commodity, before science knew there were more stars than sand on every beach, when Apple was about to be about the Beatles but not yet about a billionaire, there was 1966. Micro-mini-skirts, white knee high go-go boots, 350,000 American soldiers in Vietnam, LBJ in the driver's seat and Richard Nixon waiting in the wings—clearly, the center could not hold.

* * *

Picture this: Bright stars above a spotless Portland, handsome downtown edifices scrawled and dotted with neon and street lights, where, on any Saturday night, a tall, rich boy built along the lines of a daffodil could zoom downtown in a brakeless Chevy, Ford or space ship with Moon, Scary, Loog, Scherz, Big G Little O, Ronny Joe, Smacko or Jimmy H., score matchboxes of weed that no doubt was at a beatnik squat and gobble owned by a transvestite (married, perhaps, to himself) and, outraged when the "pot" left us calm and sane as prize virgin school marms, go berserk and kick parked cars until sirens started screaming.

O, my brothers and sisters, those were the days. There between world wars was and world wars would be, a new world was waiting. Trapped in a delicate bubble of peace, we'd soon be atomized by plummeting Soviet ICBMs. Next: From irradiated rubble would arise G. U. M. department stores where once had stood Nordstrom's. Display window mannequins draped in Ferragamo and doused in Chanel No. 5 would be replaced by Zil tractors, hobnail boots and fifths of must-buy (It is the law!) potato vodka. From each according to his ability, to each according to his need. Given that mine was daydreaming and a free lunch, Soviet style Communism actually sounded pretty good. Otherwise unshaped by plot and unmotored by motivation I decided my best bet was to rebel.

So how?

Flunk out of high school might be one way. My report cards depressed me. Like an episode of "The Three Stooges" with that numbskull Shemp instead of, nuk-nuk-nuk, the sublime Curley Joe. My problem was, I could learn, but could not be taught. Another problem: Great books were worse than booze. Their dreamscapes became your life. The novels which inhabited my teenage years—*One Flew Over the Cuckoo's Nest, The Story of O, Catcher in the Rye, Catch-22, A Fan's Notes,*

The Collector, Lord of the Flies, The Bell Jar and *A Clockwork Orange*—were, to varying degrees, glorious testaments to insanity or the insane, for the insane or by the insane.

Still, could you eat a book, drink a book; use a book as a blanket if you were cold? Could a book, more specifically, pay a mortgage? My father, who auditioned the latest groundbreaking literature—from *The Collector* to *Catch-22*—as quickly and dismissively as if they were rock concert flyers ("Nobody, including probably Joyce himself, has actually ever read *Finnegan's Wake*"), had news for me: the novel and god were indeed dead, the future of fiction was the soap opera and the future of creative art was architecture and design.

That certainly wasn't the message I was getting from the finest teachers tax money could buy at Beaverton High. Named, I believe, America's 17th best public high school at the time by *Parade*, it was as socially rigid as a jail cell, like a posh state penitentiary run by the post office. If you had money, came from a doctor, lawyer, Indian chief family, were wily, violent, had eyes, nose, mouth and ears arranged on a regular geometric grid and had been around forever, you could find yourself King Shit, and go through cars and girls like candy-wrappers. For us adolescent round pegs facing a lifetime of square holes, there was nothing too good not to trash.

One can wonder the extent to which the failure of the holy trinity God, father, and state led us, the American kids growing up in the 1960s, to abandon traditional social structures, to worship instead at the altar of new gods, and new fathers. As for the state, not so much, for the United States of America wanted its sons in Vietnam.

In a world where God said sex and rock and roll were bad, almost no one I knew was, by age eighteen, involved in a church. And, I was just about the only boy in the neighborhood who got along with his dad. Perhaps because our fathers, who had been raised during the Depression and had been saved by a post World War II cornucopia they could not have imagined before Pearl Harbor, resented the indifference their sons had for all the luxuries they worked so hard to provide.

One may also wonder to what extent the "free at last, free at last" psychedelic satellite had been lifted into orbit by the first-stage rocket of the civil rights movement, to what extent young white kids—rich but essentially powerless—had identified with the spirit of Rosa Parks— never mind that we "suburban urchins" had never seen six blacks in our lives who were not cleaning ladies, on TV, or playing on a football field or basketball court.

It was a new no rules world. Some boys were intimidated by the new women's movement. Not me. For one thing it kicked the shit out of the traditional high school ladykiller—the 'my way or the highway' football playing Strong Silent Type.

Hot, hip, newly gnosticated girls had caught the Alienated Zipperhead flu. A high school hallucination, who two years before was little more than a longhaired UFO, could now score big as a local Kink, Zombie or Rolling Stone. As for drugs, I did not seek nirvana. I sought a way to make a six foot three inch tall 145 pound speechless waif magically transmogrify into a towering fast-talking giant able to zonk mini-skirted girls into seeing that imaginary creature, and say to that creature nothing but yes.

CHAPTER TWENTY:
THE RISE AND FALL AND RISE AGAIN, MAYBE, OF THE HIGH IDEAL

"A new man was born smoking pot while besieging the Pentagon, but there was no myth to describe him. There were no images to describe all the 14 year-old freaks in Kansas, dropping acid, growing their hair long and deserting their homes and their schools...The Marxist acidhead, the psychedelic Bolshevik...Heaven's demon...A street-fighting freak, a dropout, who carries a gun at his hip...A long-haired, bearded, hairy, crazy motherfucker whose life is theater, every moment creating the new society as he destroys the old."

—Jerry Rubin

So how high was high? Acid. There it was. In long-haired San Franciscan hippie prince Eric C's open turned up palm. Just a little pill, baby-pink-pastel, innocent as aspirin. LSD. There to drop, free, at no cost to the consumer. Which would be my pal Moon, about to take over as social chairman at Ken Kesey's former fraternity, the Beta House, inhabited now only occasionally by Kesey's living ghost. Legally blind without the glasses he was usually too vain to wear, Moon squinted at the tiny tab, looked at Eric, resplendent in a baggy t-shirt that appeared woven from a regurgitated rainbow, swashbuckling bell-bottomed top germ of the hippie plague that had spread up here to Kesey's alma mater, at best a petty felon's take on Beaver Cleaver middle America.

So: to drop or not to drop? Acid by weight was now more valuable than gold, Owsley's assembly line having made him the Henry Ford of pharmaceutical psychosis, and Kesey having embarked on a loony-tune, dose-the-cosmos loaves and fishes program to make LSD the new "Breakfast of Champions."

"You want it?" Eric C. asked. Not Moon, but me. Tempting. Given especially that I was, like my Savior, on this world but not of this world, at college but not in college. Turnkey psychosis. A swallow and I'd be oooooooooming the tantric night away with a holographic Suzie Creamcheese, tripping the light fantastic in the Disney Fantasia between my ears.

We knew because Tim Leary just told us so. At the same venue where ten years before Kesey had swung from the rafters as Spiderman, Leary appeared dressed in a toga, flowers in his hair, and, flashing his sunshine smile, he gave us all the news: tune in, turn on, drop out. "Each person will become his own Buddha, his own Einstein, his own Galileo. Instead of relying on canned, static, dead knowledge passed on from other symbol producers, he will be using his span of eighty or so years on this planet to live out every possibility of the human, pre-human, and even subhuman adventure." Plus! "An enormous amount of energy from every fiber of your body is released under LSD—most especially including sexual energy. There is no question that LSD is the most powerful aphrodisiac ever discovered by man."

Already on academic probation, also on social probation (ie. banned from fraternity membership), I was recently informed by my Honors College advisor, the head of the journalism department, that he would not counsel me as a matter of personal principle. For I had no business belonging to honors anything, Vietnam was likely my next institution of higher learning and while that storied jungleland was likely to be little more than Beaverton High School with machine guns, dragon ladies and palm trees, I gazed at the little pill wistfully and deferred to Moon, "Better not gild the lily, it's all yours."

Frat and freak culture about to collide. We were freshmen, but Moon's reputation had preceded him. His specialty: the collapse of western civilization and, re. mayhem, his policy was "think globally, act locally." His fingers, nails bitten uniformly to the quick, hovered over the pink dot on Eric C.'s palm. Moon on acid seemed as natural as Hiroshima under the "Enola Gay." Well groomed—starched Gant button-down shirt, khakis pressed to razor creases and mirror-shined Bass Weejun penny-loafers—Moon looked as all American as high noon, a Mr. Right prototype, America's young fair-haired idea of itself, a spotless endorsement looking for a perfect product.[20]

His motto was, like mine, Eddie's Haskell's: "Nothing is a dirty trick if it's funny enough," and his philosophy: "Nothing's better than doing something really wrong really well." Others may have designed the detonators, but Moon was a top explosion. Forget that his hair was rarely longer than Jimmy Carter's ever got, and that bellbottoms on Moon would've rivaled pink on a Porsche. Moon was a powerful force for chaos, yet as a populist visionary BMOC, rightful heir to Kesey's Beta House throne, he was still getting his sea legs where total social dysfunction was concerned.

For our world was changing in a flash, re-peopled by a new species of bohemians, an Army of Adams and Eves descended from the new Oz of sex, drugs, and unreality that was, until Kesey's abracadabra, San Francisco.

The sexual revolution was upon us. Potential transcendental lasciviousness had taken a quantum leap. Take "Impetuous" and "Cat Woman." Hubba hubba could not begin to describe the tempestuous black hole gravities of their allures: hookah dream Love Children, hallucinatory hot house flowers, the ethereal apples of our four eyes from the new Eden, a kosmic step up on the ladder from the clerk-eyed, bourgeois, capitalist roader Beaverton High Barbie Dolls who, on their way to score a suburban Dr. Rich McDreamy, had availed us (or not) of their favors. Neither Cat Woman (who, like the real comic book Cat Woman, had smoldering, yellowish, evil eyes, possessed in Moon-speak "lush kazooms," and dressed neck-to-ankles in a black spray paint leotard with a micro-mini in the middle) nor Impetuous (who favored diaphanous, beguiling, tent-like Mother Hubbard micro-minis, a lanterned-jawed little cutie all long eyes and pillowy chrome red lips) was from California. Odd, given that each represented a forbidding Alp of take-me-I'm-yours new hippie sexual freedom. Also strange: neither, while shoulder to shoulder, tray to tray, in the dorm lunch line—our identical quaking Jell-O cubes cut from a red, chopped celery sea—went too gaga when greeted with a friendly, "Hi, I'm a Gemini, mind if I rip

---

20 Moon, (aka the WASP and "Wally Cleaver from Hell") would soon set the bar for the co-writers of the movie Animal House, camped in that same Beta House to adapt Moon's End Times gospels ("One crime at a time." "Cotton uber alles." "Fight the Zeitgeist." "I pay, I take," "Forget about your enemies, worry about your friends." "The other shoe will always fall.") in more civilized form for the silver screen.

your dress?"

No, each represented the standoffish one-chick bohemia from little nowhere goat-roper middle Oregon towns, each incubated in rural isolation. The problem: Cat Woman and Impetuous had near identical pizza-skinned but goat-roper tough boyfriends, "Abominable" and "Reboziating," who did not cotton to Moon and me one little bit.

Still, Moon was optimistic. He calculated there had been only "eight" goddesses in all of Beaverton High, a school of 2,400, and one didn't count because she was his sister (what made a goddess a goddess? To review: 1. Perfect angel face; 2. Lush kazooms; 3. Legs that go on forever), and by Moon's count I'd been picked up and spit to the street like ABC gum by three and a half. Humiliating failure not to be sneezed at. "When thrown off the horse, or horses, you have but one choice—spelled: back in the saddle.

"You must once again evoke"—Moon spoke four words so their first letters stood as capitals, "The Call To Eros." Then, the fine print: "You and Catwoman? No fucking way. I heard her tell Abominable that you looked like a too tall, baby-faced, beach-rat Vampire thug who weighed less than a doorstop and, besides, no way'd she'd ever get her ends wet with a dude born between May 22 and June 21. But you and Impetuous? Gangbusters."

Her real name was Annikka Popenloppenos, Joan Smith or something in between, cartoon curvaceous erring to a tad squatty, born of elite Polish potato pullers. A hippie marketing major, she flaunted her deliverables in the cafeteria line—the black V of her "next-to-nothings" ghostly behind the gauzy paisley of her haute "Straight from the Haight" Mother Hubbard micro minis, she spoke in a tongue freighted with, *ashram, backassward, blow, blown mind, bogart, bong, boogity, boogity, boogity, bummer, busted, can you dig it, catch my drift, class struggle, clean up your act, cold turkey, come down, commotion lotion, connection, contact high, cop out, cowabunga, crash, crash pad, Crisco party, crystal, dharma, downer, doob, do my thing, drop out, dude, dude-ette, far out, flashback, flower power, freak-out, funky leather stud, geeze, gig, gimmefive, godhead, goin' to a go-go, go with the flow, group grope, hang up, happy feet, hassle, headshop, heavyosity, hunky, if it feels good do it, joint, karma, kosmic, lid, light show, luv muscle, mainline, mantra, maxed out, mellow out, mindfuck, muff dive, narc, needle freak, negative aura, nirvana, off the wall, off the pigs, out of your gourd, outasight, plastic phantastic, prong, pusher, rap, re-fi, ride the rude rocket, right on, rip off, roach, satori, scarf, score, shine it on, smack, sock it to me, sock it to me, sock it to me, soul brother, space case, spade, speed, stash, stoked, stoned, stone fox, straight, tieoff, toke, tranqs, trippy, tubular, turn off, turn on, uncool, uppers, uptight, vibes, you suck, zap and zat U Santa and zonk*—intimidating when all Moon and I had was *bodacious, starry veks, ribbit, pick two, stupercalifragilisticexpealadocious, fugly, yowser, yowser, yowser* and *eat shit and die.*

Everywhere, signs and wonders: Here in the Oregon fog between 1966 and 1967—all those ivy-hided elm-shaded brick walls that signified the perfect cross of paradise and penitentiary—whirl would soon be king. Toward a new bespoke reality, *Playboy* had named the University of Oregon America's top party school behind Parsons College—less a college than an Arizona barf fest with a campus attached. As social chairman of the Beta House, master of the toga party Moon (Moon in his sheet resembled Caligula on 'ludes and our hallowed halls rang with his "Toe! Ga! Toe! Ga!" long before that glorious refrain was given to the lips of John Belushi) was flying high. Soon, according to his plan, the Beta House would be a wanton wonderland—the devil's heaven: legions of Rose Festival princesses downing Chivas/Mad Dog shooters before, with ruby red lips, inhaling hot popsicle chasers.

Former Beta brother Ken Kesey said, "The purpose of psychedelics is to learn the conditioned responses of people and then prank them. That's the only way to get people to ask questions, and until they ask questions, they are going to remain conditioned robots." But ask yourself: did Moon fit the robot mold? "I have magic powers," he said. Though the Beta House isn't where he said it. Where Moon said he had magic powers was in the back of a Greyhound bus packed with a college football team, the captain of which—whom Moon addressed as "Converse" after the brand of the captain's tennis shoes—had just been invited by Moon to go fuck himself.

Back Story:

Witness the "Sporting Club," created coincident with outdoorsman Moon receiving, through the fillings in his teeth, a "Call to Action" by "The Great Elder" McQueen or McCain. The Sporting Club's object was to "bring normal to its knees" through "rites of passage" and at Christmas break Moon said it was time for a deluxe ski vacation. A complete fucking disaster. Our pal ski patroller and/or ski lodge dish-washer the also fair-haired Steve Lonie—who in high school had presciently assessed, "God's not dead, he's drunk," and whose grandfather had been mayor of Portland and whose parents owned matching baby-blue Cadillacs—had a big comfy ski patrol room at Mt. Hood.

Oregon was in the middle of a state-crystallizing ice storm. Moon had crashed his parents' cars, my hot rod Chevy was a smoking pile of metal ruin, so we took the bus. Not one with a WEIRD LOAD bumper sticker on the back, but a Greyhound packed with a local college football team. It was a dark and stormy night. We got stuck in back, Moon, muttering, "On the road," armed with Jack Daniels and tequila "refreshments." Snow laced from the sky as, across the river and through the woods, on the twisting frozen road out of Portland, Moon, bored, had a glug, glug, glug "chat with Jack," before, as I mentioned, confiding, "I have magic powers. Watch." Then he addressed the burly captain of the football team sitting at the front of the bus. "Hey Converse! What's that shit on your crew-cut, jizz or Butch-wax?"

Say what? We were outnumbered sixty to three by a football team—and Moon's existential assessment, "No Exit!" brought a dour assessment from Lonie, the bravest kid ever: "We're fuuuuuuuuuuuuuuuuuuuuuuuucked." Moon, waving the Jack Daniels like an inverted baseball bat, kept hooting, "point, counterpoint, jock fuckers!" The football guys, at first mystified, got the gist and, pissed, started evaluating us. As in: "You're dead, freaky preppie shitheads!"

Slowly, as the bus slithered up the mountain on and on into the snowy night, the unfair reality of it all sunk in: Lonie and I weren't freaky preppie shitheads. We were simply genial rich suburban urchins trying to put one foot in front of the other in a world we never made. So *why oh why oh why*? We beseeched Moon. "Rites of passage," he replied.

Thinking: In the alternate universe, I could be, should be on a surfboard, skidding down the face of a perfect wave, in the dark I saw the nightmare team get up and, with the bus still plummeting into the icy night, advance towards us. Gentle reader, ask yourself: how had it come to this?

* * *

"If Shakespeare were working now," Ken Kesey informed the world, "He wouldn't be working with a quill pen. He would be working with whatever the cutting edge of theatrical technology would be. And this is where literature is headed."

"When people ask," he said, "what my best work is, it's the bus. I thought you ought to be living your art, rather than stepping back and describing it."

A sentiment that had spread like an aura or a stain. Escaping the prison of the page, living in the Now, for post literary Beta brother Moon, life was not Art but, better yet, Spectacle.

"What?" I barked, ready to cry, "are we gonna do?"

In the back of the bus, right behind me in the dim, a reassuring voice, "How should I know?"

His Jack Daniels extended as if it were a fifth of kryptonite against the legion of superbluto football players lumbering down the aisle of the Greyhound to where we were trapped in the back, I saw the slash of Moon's smile and what-me-worry shoulders shrug, "Firewater, Kemo Sabe?"

Something strange, aside from the teenage Bronco Nagurskis now within spitting distance of my skinny face, was happening to the bus. Like it had exchanged its wheels for ice skates. Steve Lonie, a boy who, like Moon, would fight anything from dogs to gods, slid from his seat and muttered: "Fuck it." I crouched up behind him in the aisle, ducked down and began clawing my way forward, getting whacked and slammed and feeling the bus sway weirdly as more football guys spilled into the aisles pushing against me toward the back. The bus driver and coaches were shouting "Sit down! Sit down!" Chaos within, chaos without, lunging upward, I could see among dark and flailing arms, the football team was fighting with itself. They couldn't tell us from them and were falling over the bus seats, beating the shit out of each other, as the bus bumped, bounced and flew off the road, tipping way over to one side.

So what was to become of us, and who was to blame?

Now, here in the middle of the frigid mountain night, by a literal miracle I'd been borne from the black battling womb of the halfway tipped over Greyhound, punched, but not *well* punched, eerily A-okay, lost in the spill of football players tumbling from the bus door to the black ice-rink that was the road. Out here in the 0 degree Oregon night, another miracle. Under street lamps that painted the landscape in swathes of snow banks on either side of the highway, I could see the ski-workers' lodge, a squared off log cabin type place. Big, basic and above all *there*. So, at least in theory, we could just melt into the night scot, as they say, free. Because I could hear the sound of cop sirens—somebody was going to jail for this mess and...

...unbelievable. Across the street I saw a neon sign that said, among other things, CAFÉ. And under that sign I saw ski-parka-ed Moon, without an apparent care in the world, slipping through the front door. The big twin stars of a police car's headlights swung up beside the listing Greyhound, the cruiser pirouetted to a sliding, skidding stop, its roof light revolving. Red light jumped and sighed across the silver tilted flank of the snow-beached bus. It was going to take God's own tow-truck to get it out of the dirty white ditch.

I saw Steve Lonie beside me. "We gotta beat feet," he said, 'before somebody recognizes us."

"Moon," I said, "went inside the café."

"That's where the cops and everybody else'll be in about two seconds."

A brainteaser. "So what do we do?"

Steve said, "Go get him."

Then we'd be trapped in there too. Even for Moon, this was over the top. Doomed, Steve and I skate-walked across the road and tramped inside the restaurant. In the cold fluorescent light above red formica tables Moon's left eye was going red, white and blue and swelling Chinese. His nose looked redesigned by Picasso and the maroon numeral II was drooling from his nostrils to his mouth. "What happened?" I asked.

"Converse landed a lucky one." *Wunderbar.* As soon as somebody simply saw us, we'd be in the back of a patrol car spelunking through our pockets for dimes to call our dads' lawyers.

"Moon," I said, "they'll know that anybody who isn't them, is us. Look at your face."

"No way," Moon smirked, "I've got magic powers."

No exit. You set the spark that tips over a loaded Greyhound bus, and you'll be eating fish sticks and government mash potatoes for six months, easy. Lonie leaned over the restaurant table, and said, "Moon, be cool or the cops'll be slipping the cuffs on our fragile extensions."

"They're gonna do that anyway. Rise above, my brothers. For those not busy being born are busy dying," A white paper worm was forming in wiggling fingers. "This'll turn your frowns upsidedown."

What was he doing?

Lonie shrugged, "Search me. Rolling a jay?"

* * *

The best of times, the worst of times. But even before the bus trip, mostly the latter.

See the boy: In a jail cell dorm room whose shiny linoleum floor reflected the barely cleaned up site of an explosion of Trix, Wheaties, Captain Crunch and who knew what other kind of breakfast kibble, Fat Shit Larry. Fat Shit's uniform rarely varied: white long sleeved shirt soaked translucent at the armpits, black unironed slacks, black boatlike brogues. A blimp, as tall as I was but twice as wide, his white face blood-rouged at the cheeks, he had hamster eyes, greasy black hair and his lower lip was as red and extruded as a berry. He looked like he was going to start crying any second, and probably—lonely, lost, disliked—he was. A tattletale, Fat Shit was why I was on social probation. He'd ratted me off to our dorm counselor for an exploded beer bottle. A total lie. I'd dropped a brewery worth of bottles down the dorm staircase—it was fun to watch them flutter and zip thirty feet to starry galactic brown explosion—but I didn't drop that one. But now? As soon as I got arrested for this bus fiasco? I had no student deferment and was only boot camp and a 707 away from a ticket to Firebase Sucking Chest Wound.

"Good news!" Moon enthused, rubbing his hands together as if with invisible soap the way he did when he figured he was going to *get* something. "Impetuous just dumped that grease ball Reboziating. So it's your chance to step to the psychedelic love plate."

What planet was he living on?

Soon, he said, I'd be tying tantric sex knots in a cumulus cloud of fine Oaxacan.

"Moon," I said, "how are we gonna get out of here?"

Cops and football players were milling all over the cafe. Moon sat there, face bloody, looking like he'd just gone ten rounds with Godzilla the Wolverine. "Easy," he replied.

And it was. Three days later I was sitting in handsome, Ivy League-ish Mr. Meinke's office, safe and sound. Despite my shit grades I was the only freshman exempted from English Comp and allowed to enroll in Creative Writing. My instructor, Mr. Meinke, who was in some kind of beef by mail with Lawrence Ferlinghetti and who said most men live lives of quiet desperation, suggested I find an "alter ego." Who? Sadly, the happy idea of myself stored safe in my head didn't survive well released to my typewriter. No, that guy did not seem to know the difference between courage and recklessness, confidence and conceit, that guy treated people like chewing gum. My expository vacuum was made emptier given I knew nothing of life not having had one yet and Mr. Meinke said it wasn't enough for me to describe a bad bus accident I'd been in or knocking up my beautiful girlfriend even in fictional terms, unless the wreck or the horrors of teenage fatherhood *meant* something,

"And you just walked out of the restaurant?" he said, gazing at the papers that contained my new story as if those papers were a failed crystal ball.

"Yeah," I nodded. "There was so much confusion, nobody even noticed us." Indeed, in the mountain café, Moon lit his crooked branch-like joint, exhaled a mushroom cloud of smoke, stood and squinted blindly at the chaos of football players all around us, no-necks and mouth-breathers born unknowning from the lightless womb of the halfway tipped over Greyhound bus—and said, "I have magic powers, brothers. Let's be gone." And we were.

Fine, Mr. Meinke said, but the bus crash still had to *mean* something. Otherwise it was just an event—and events, like remarks, weren't literature. Oh.

"I'm hanging on by a thread," I said, "playing without a bench. I'm eighteen. All most guys like Moon and me have going for them is getting their girlfriends pregnant in high school. Moon got that part right, but I'm still waiting for the rabbit to die."

* * *

So to drop or not to drop? And that acid resting still in Eric C.'s open palm? I didn't need acid, I needed paradise. I wanted to be a surfer, not a psychotic.

As for Moon? Eric C. said, "What's up with your face? It's all scabby."

"Rite of passage," Moon replied, staring at the tab of acid.

"Far out," Eric. C. said. "So, what's it going to be, eh?"

Moon shook his head. "I'm not taking it."

Eric. C. asked, "Why?"

A slash of a smile. "Because I'm already there."

CHAPTER TWENTY-ONE:
FANTASY ISLAND

"We're not in Wonderland anymore, Alice."

—Charles Manson

California. Paradise 1967. Nineteen cent tacos. Orange Sunshine for 25 cents a tab. Fast food fantasia.

Butterflies staggered the bottom of the sky, where in an "All You Need is Nirvana" world there was no problem under the sun that could not be cured by love, karma or tetracycline, and the long haired "Lords of Acid," aka "The Brotherhood of Eternal Love" passed out hundreds of dollars every day to hippies, surfers, space-age Gidgets, bikers and homeless wanderers who dreamed the impossible dream in the Jack in the Box parking lot at the ragged hem of the Pacific.

Laguna Beach. A gilded Oz, where even the rich had good taste. A recent arrival among them: A+ List neuronaut Timothy Leary, who claimed LSD—the wildest letters in the alphabet—would allow women to experience hundreds of orgasms, evoke God for all mankind, make that God as real as any Chatty Cathy doll and be—according to bi-sexual Tim—"a specific cure for homosexuality." And that was just for starters.

A new day, a new dawn: The Age of Aquarius. One twelfth of the 25,800 year-long cycle, this was to be an era to supersede the dying Age of Pisces, which had dawned concurrently with the birth of Jesus Christ. Now a new and hyper-miraculous age defined by a 30 degree sign of the zodiac, the Age of Aquarius would be a 2,160 year-long "time of New Beginnings," or mass extinction to the tune of global earthquakes, volcanoes going off like firecrackers and skies streaked with meteor showers. We were about to hit the hell or high water trifecta: Armageddon, the End Times and Judgment Day in which a celestial zoo of "Masters, Avatars, Saints and Angels" would descend from the sky, and…?

…perhaps join with "interdimensional, multidimensional and hyper-dimensional beings" in a new world that would no longer know sickness or injury, in which the multitudes would enjoy a sudden higher consciousness and possess telepathic powers and be able to tell the future.

The Age of Aquarius would be ignited, according to Dr. Tim, by the illuminated, "neopagans, neochristians, agnostics, witches, wizards, pagans, psychics, priests, parapsychologists, mystics, mediums, magicians, astrologers, diviners and occultists." The earth might be united with a Galactic Federation; all good things would be possible and perhaps even guaranteed.

A great time for a messiah to meet his moment. Just a few years before, thirty-nine year-old Harvard lecturer Dr. Leary had been "a middle-aged man involved in the middle-aged process of dying." When on vacation from an America that was becoming "an air-conditioned anthill," lounging by the swimming pool of his rented "villa" in Cuernavaca, Mexico, he found himself, "being swept over the edge of a sensory Niagara into a maelstrom of transcendental visions and hallucinations" toward "the deepest religious experience of my life." Courtesy "sacred mushrooms." Though it was ironic that Leary, after he and his troupe took their first Mexican magic mushroom trip, did not declare he'd found The Sacrament, but rather, "We're all schizophrenics now and we're in our own institution. But for the first time I understand James Joyce."

But it is Leary's recollection of his first acid trip, several years later that is far more revealing. He discovers, "all forms, all structures, all organisms, all events, were illusory, television productions pulsing out from the central eye. Everything that I had ever experienced and read was bubble-dancing before me like a nineteenth century Vaudeville show. My illusions, the comic costumes, the strange-ever-changing stage props of trees and bodies and theater sets. All spinning out from the momentary parts of the central God-eye-heart-penis light."

Clearly, Tim had scored the good stuff. It delivered the illusion that life was an illusion as a sort of revelatory anti-fact. The message: All bets were off. "After several billion years I found myself on my feet moving through a puppet show. Where does Timothy Leary belong in the dance of illusions?" Reminded of his children, Leary walked upstairs, made his way across the second floor landing and opened the door to his daughter's bedroom. Where, rock and roll blasting from her stereo, he found Susan with her hair up in curlers sitting on her bed, a school book on her lap, "frowning in concentration," the "classic" thirteen year old. "It was pure *Saturday Evening Post* cover Americana. The puppet doll teenager glanced up. 'Hi, Dad.' She was biting a pencil and looking at the book. I slumped against the wall, looking with amazement at this marionette stranger, from assembly-line America. She glanced up again, quickly, 'Hi Dad, what would you like for Christmas?' She went on biting the pencil, frowning at the book, waving slightly at the beat of the music. In a minute she looked up again. 'Hi Dad, I love you.'

"A shock of terror convulsed me. This was my daughter and this was the daughter-father game. A shallow, superficial, stereotyped, meaningless exchange of Hi, Dad. Hi, Sue. How are you Dad? How's school? What do you want for Christmas? Have you done your homework? The plastic doll father and the plastic doll daughter both mounted on little wheels, rolling by each other around and around on fixed tracks. A complete vulgarization of the real situation—two incredibly complex, trillion-cell clusters rooted in an eternity of evolution, sharing for a flicker this space-time coordinate. And offered this rare chance to merge souls and bring out the divinity in the other, but desiccated and deadened into the Hi Dad, Hi Susan squeaks.

"I looked at her beseechingly, straining for real contact. I was stunned with guilt."

Notwithstanding the fact that in this dramatic recollection of his first LSD experience Leary makes the acid argument for the uncoupling of reality—which acid reveals as not real at all—with the necessary (according to Tim) uncoupling from the emotional and spiritual "robot" reality of early 1960s middle-class America, the narrative begs big questions. Like what's wrong—in fact what could be righter—than to have your daughter remind you that she loves you and wants to know what you'd like for Christmas? How is that "desiccated" or "deadened" or a "complete vulgarization of the real situation"? Did Leary expect the two to be twined in ecstasy and transported to the sixth dimensional

Oooooooooooooom state to enjoy an eternity of acid super bliss?

Who knows, but this says everything about Leary's acid gospels especially, if oddly, the bit at the end about being "stunned with guilt"—because it's Zen prankster Leary telling the truth by not telling the truth—acknowledging that he was to his daughter a distant (if doubtless genial) authority figure in the standard early sixties mold, but blaming it on zombie Americana that had left him a robot.

But now, thanks to acid…

Leary was in grey flannels and crew cut when, in 1960, he first met Aldous Huxley and Humphrey Osmond, who coined the term "psychedelic" and dismissed Leary as "on the square side." He would soon trade up to LSD-25, which he predicted would become "the spiritual equivalent of the hydrogen bomb," and it was not too long after that Huxley wrote to Peggy Lamson: "If only Tim cd (sic) get to a Summit meeting and give some mushrooms to the two Mr. Ks–the result might be world peace through total lucidity." Big on Big Think, Leary emitted more signals than a Telstar communications satellite, foretelling a United States regulated by acid agencies. There would be acid studies in universities, even acid universities—plus utopia and its fellow traveler, what was later defined as "the deification of psychosis."

"We consider our religion to be highly orthodox," Leary claimed. "LSD is ecumenical. God is not a Christian. He doesn't speak Greek or Latin. When you contact God as we have, you realize that His energy and His blueprint were going on long before man worked out these verbal formulas." What's more: "In our religion the temple is the human body…We expect millions of Americans will be licensed to use these sacraments." (Of the October 1966 performance in *The Reincarnation of Jesus Christ as Timothy Leary*, Abbie Hoffman's wife Anita recalled, "On stage, to my amazement and horror, Tim appeared to be playing the role of Jesus Christ! I thought that was unconscionable [although I'm not a Christian]. What hubris to play the Divine! As I recall, the dramatization ended with Tim on the cross, arms outstretched. Shameless!")

If you were old enough circa 1966, you may recall tune-in-turn-on-drop-out "Acid Thinking" as anti-intellectual, pseudo-mystical, happy horseshit, the idea that the tripper's illusion of power and omnipotence made acid a wonky pharmaceutical Scientology. Yet acid thinking, as a magic mantra for me and mine that "questioned the sanity of facts," was as powerful as Japanese Emperor Worship. Bohemian power brokers imagined acid to be a deified flagship for the drug culture, potential franchise, compared to which, McDonald's and the Catholic Church would look like lemonade stands.

For Leary, a brilliant, well-meaning quack—who might offer you "a packet of aromatic hydrocarbon sticks" for what looked like cigarettes and who proclaimed, "Late terrestrial species architecture, mostly silicon fusion and inorganic slab construction, erected by the musculotoic legions of the late twentieth century industrial feudal dynasty," as his take on Boulder, Colorado—had revealed acid as an *elixir miraculous*. Salvation by psychosis. Take past lives. Regarding his own incarnations, Leary had witnessed, "Moments of propagation—scenes of rough ancestral sexuality in Irish barrooms, in haystacks, in canopied beds, in covered wagons, on beaches, on the moist jungle floor—and moments of crisis in which my forebears escape from fang, from spear, from conspiracy, from tidal wave and avalanche."

Nirvana's last big chance. The Wonder Drug in the age of wonder drugs. In 1961 Wilson Van Dusen wrote in *LSD and the Enlightenment of Zen*, "It has been called satori in Japanese Zen, moksha in Hinduism, religious enlightenment or cosmic consciousness in the West…The drug LSD appears to facilitate the discovery of this apparently ancient and universal experience."

Nevertheless…

"Take it from me—it was no illusion," Tim Lott of the *London Independent* wrote on the occasion of LSD's inventor Swiss pharmacologist Albert Hoffman's death at age 102 in 2008. "It ripped the filter off my perceptions and showed me what I thought of as reality was merely a mental construction, limited by habit and conditioning." He went on to lament a "pop culture (that) reduced these insights into silly Day-glo art and psychedelic music, while frightened authorities outlawed LSD as a threat to established order. Imagine how much we could have learned if mature adults had been free to tap the drug's full potential."

The devil has always depended on the gullibility if not the outright kindness of strangers. It was to be the last great age of gospels, Zen West.

The transformative vision? Like the Nazi space program, as preposterous schemes go, the so to speak "from-on-high," hippie master plan wasn't a bad one. We would see the end of dehumanizing cities and god-fearing godless suburbs, America dissolved into a mostly WASP kibbutz; the family abandoned in favor of the tribe, the nation atomized. Heaven on earth. Or vice versa. Via the new doors of perception hawked with godless religiosity.

For if love was an illusion could not an illusion be love? The quintessential 1960s dewy, pinned-pupil-eyed lysergic love lyrics were penned by Huxley and Leary, not Lennon and McCartney. And these lyrics played perfectly in southern California, when in 1964, Ken Kesey's brother from another planet, Tim Leary, had first found himself parked in low earth orbit above sun-gilded Laguna Beach. Leary holed up in "Dodge City"—known to local unpsychedelic civilians as Laguna Canyon—a one-way-in- one-way-out worldwide headquarters of the "Brotherhood of Eternal Love," where acid god and piety gnosis were already taking a more earthly turn toward money and guns.

Leary was a light who attracted odd moths. The Brotherhood had grown rich making Orange Sunshine—high horsepower LSD. Like most common pharmaceuticals—and unlike less ethereal products like Chevies or condominiums it was almost as cheap as flour to make; free money to those who sold it. A dime to blow your mind was, for most enlightened young consumers, a no-brainer. Especially given that the Brotherhood who hawked it claimed that "Orange Sunshine" had been endorsed by no less than God.

So what exactly was The Brotherhood? Think the eco-spiritual-holistic Wal-Mart of ball-busting psychedelics. A network of over 2,000 young acid dealer/freaks—located mostly in California, Oregon and Hawaii. According to Brotherhood alum Bob Stubby Tierney, "There was nothing in the world that could get you high for twelve hours for just ten cents…We were totally spiritual, religious people. Acid (was) a sacrament to us." Vehemently against the Vietnam War, the Brotherhood existed in its own collective mind "like soldiers"—determined to use Timothy Leary to connect to famous musicians like Crosby, Stills and Nash, the Grateful Dead, Jimi Hendrix, and the Jefferson Airplane. "So we'd have control of the music," Tierney explained. "We really had power." The Brotherhood became kings of discount psychosis, generating $200 million, their bylaws declaring the intent, "to bring the world a greater awareness of God through the teachings of Jesus Christ, Buddha, Ramakrishna, Babaji, Paramahansa Yogananda, Mahatma Gandhi, and all the true prophets and apostles of God, and to spread the love and wisdom of these great teachers to all men," to anoint Leary Pope of an acid religion, and to incorporate an island utopia.

Located 700 miles off the western coast of Mexico, Ile de la Passion was a two-mile wide volcanic atoll that lacked fresh water and whose only natural resource was guano. A table scrap of the French Colonial empire, Ile de la Passion had proved a veritable gold mine of bird shit, but was otherwise uninhabited. A Brotherhood of Eternal Love emissary had been dispatched to France with a $2,000 down payment. Fascist Amerika would soon be an acid theocracy and the Ile de la Passion its psychedelic Vatican.

Here's a good Brotherhood of Eternal Love story: One Laguna Beach night rich, gregarious, Jesus look-a-like surfboard maker John Gale, a small, young man with dark shoulder length hair (whose passion was to give away those aforementioned hundreds of dollars every day at the aforementioned "Jack in the Box" and the Brotherhood's vegetarian soup kitchen, "Love Animals Don't Eat Them," and who was said to have also been distributing up to 100,000 doses of Sunshine a day) sold a bag of dog shit to undercover detectives and then bolted into the bushes with the cops' money. Those cops pulled guns and started shooting—missing Gale but nearly hitting an unrelated group of drug agents conducting a sting operation down the street. The agents freaked and began screaming at the other cops—which drew a crowd of people who started Ooooooooming in celebration of what was later termed "the cop clusterfuck." Then more cops arrived on the scene and started billy-clubbing people.

Gale meanwhile was hiding in the scrub counting his government money.

Elsewhere, an alternate reality. For a nation of teenyboppers weaned on Drs. Seuss and Spock, earth would soon be as it was in heaven. In fact, as mentioned earlier, acid analogs as a metaphysical "stairway to heaven" and as sacraments of the prophets date to pre-history. As "psychedelic sociologist" Terrance McKenna once said, "Shamanism without psychedelics is like wife-beating without alcohol, it just doesn't happen."

By 1967, acid had become the astral communion for a Pepsi Generation on its way to the moon. Subtract the fear of nuclear obliteration and 150 boys dying every week in Vietnam, the hope was each day might be a better day. Doubt it? All you had to do was turn on Top 40 radio and listen to the Zen Commandments delivered by 100 decibel Fender guitar-wielding rock gospels.

Thanks to the good oval office of Richard Nixon, corporate oligarchs threatened to turn the United States into a police state. William L. Shirer, author of *The Rise and Fall of the Third Reich*, had declared of the Nixon administration, "We could become the first country to go fascist through free election." While, in a less ethereal realm, America's foremost war planner and thermonuclear acidhead, 340-pound Humpty Dumpty Herman Kahn, was refining MAD, his ever-popular plan for, if not winnable nuclear war, "Mutually Assured Destruction." For Kahn, who "war-gamed" apocalypse after taking LSD, all was context: "War is a terrible thing. But so is peace. The difference seems to be a quantitative one of degree and standards."

The Revolution had yet to run into herpes, AIDS and Hunter Thompson and—take a toke and think about it: Wouldn't the moon be mellower if Cream ran NASA? Launched by our fathers, we were about to conquer, if not the heavens, heaven's cold cousin outer space.

CHAPTER TWENTY-TWO:
HIGH CRIMES

"Consider the basic metaphor of the 'shepherd' and the 'sheep.' 'The Lord is my shepherd; I shall not want. He maketh me to lie down in green pastures.' Now if the Lord is your shepherd, who the fuck are you?"

—Timothy Leary

Acid. How can we miss it if it won't go away?

Evoking "incense, candles, flowers, bells, beads, yoga, meditation, Sufi dancing, shrines in the home, kinetic multi-channel art, Hesse, Tolkien, Bosch, acid-rock, Hinduism, mantras, mudras, Tantra, psychedelic mating, leaving the city, avoiding plastic, walking barefoot and laughing-eyed, chanting love-seed delight" plus…"the Beatles, Pure Vedanta, divine revelation, gentle, tender irony at the insanities of war and politics, sorrowful lament for the bourgeois loneliness, delicate hymns to the glory of God," Tim Leary suggested that a single pound of LSD was all it would take to "blow New York City's mind."

Leary had got his psychedelic sea-legs, in fact had earned his captain's stripes, operating the International Federation for Internal Freedom (IFIF) in Zihuatanejo a few years before as "an experiment in transpersonative living" which embraced a sort of communal "Tennis anyone?" A good time was apparently had by most all. A Mexican immigration official observed, "Senor Leary must be either crooked or crazy; he could get $1,000 a month for this, and he charges only $200!"

By the "Summer of Love," the Harvard psychology professor once tagged "Theory Leary" was part of a Team Almighty vying with other other-worlders Ken Kesey and Alan Watts for coronation as Acid Christ.

Aldous Huxley, Gordon Wasson and Timothy Leary served as rivals and co-conspirators as they sought to define a near future "Soma" world. But, by 1967, Kesey had elevated himself from America's Favorite (if only latest) Literary Son to psychedelic demi-god. More than anyone else, handsome frat-boy-jock-cum-golden-goy hippie Kesey marketed acid as an Atlas (or at least Charlie Atlas) like elixir of the mind that would make you, once you dropped it, the New Man. Meanwhile, in Laguna Beach the Brotherhood of Love was raking it in. "Orange Sunshine" was selling like indulgences on Judgment Day (A Brotherhood lawyer had successfully filed papers with the California Franchise Tax Board granting the Brotherhood tax exempt status as—and why not?—a church).

Though Leary's apostles had hit bumps. The Ile de la Passion utopia-site envisioned to host his reign as acid pope wasn't bearing up under inspection. For one thing, fresh-waterless, it resisted human habitation. Though envisioned as a fertilizer gold mine in the 1856 Treaty of Guano, the last people to live there were fifteen women and children and a lone male adult lighthouse keeper who, in 1917, had declared himself king and gone on a rape-rampage, only to be killed by one of the few surviving women. The French had even rejected it as a site to conduct hydrogen bomb tests.

Closer to home, acid Appleseed John Gale was reported killed in a car wreck when his Porsche veered off the road—an accident said to have been a bizarre fraud. Many believed Gale had acquired a corpse and that Gale's father had extracted his son's teeth and made it appear, for the purposes of identification, that the teeth belonged to the stiff. Leaving a supposed "undead" Gale free to go about his business, now a truly free spirit shed of, if not his body, at least the cops.

From eight-tracks and transistor radios, The Doors crooned of strange days and weird scenes in the gold mine. The Lizard King reminded Jack-in-the-Box tourists, victims and loadies that while we got the guns and we got the numbers, when the still sea conspires an armor, true sailing is dead.

Hippie heaven on earth. According to the "Post-Competitive, Comparative Game of a Free City," published by Paul Krassner in the 1967 issue of The Realist, that called for creation of Free Cities within all the western world's metropolises:

"Every brother should have what he needs to do his thing…At this point in our revolution it is demanded that the families, communes, black organizations and gangs of every city in America co-ordinate and develop Free Cities where everything…food, printing facilities, transportation, mechanics, money, housing, working space, clothes, machinery, trucks, etc…can be obtained for free."

It began on a high note: "By now we all have guns, know how to use them, know our enemy, and are ready to defend. We know that we ain't gonna take no more shit." These free Cities were to be composed of free Families "(e.g. in San Francisco: Diggers, Black Panthers, Provos, Mission Rebels and various revolutionist gangs and communes)."

The free Cities would each require:

*"high-style, hard-nosed, top-class lawyers…no honky, liberal bleeding heart, guilt-ridden advocates of justice, but first class case winners…turn on the best lawyers who can set up air-tight receivership for free money and property, and beat down the police harassment and brutality of your area.

*"A free hospital…a house converted into bed space and preferably with a garden and used for convalescence and people whose minds have been blown…

*"A free food storage and distribution center…should hit every available source of food–produce markets, farmers markets, meat packing plants, farms, dairies, sheep and cattle ranches, agricultural colleges, and giant institutions (for the uneaten vats of food)–and fill up their trucks with the surplus by begging, borrowing, stealing…This gang should help people pool their welfare food stamps and get their old ladies or a group to open a free restaurant for people on the move and those who live on the streets.

*"Scavenger Corps and Transport Gang responsible for garbage collection…as well as liberating anything they think useful…They are responsible for the truck fleet and especially aware of the economic strain if trucks are miss-used by tripsters.

*"Free City garage and mechanics…to repair and maintain all vehicles used in the various services…The garage should be…free to tripsters who only create work for the earnest mechanics.

*"A free environmental and design gang…gangs of artists from universities…should be turned on and helped in attacking the dank squalor of the slums and most of the free City Family dwellings…paint landscapes on the sides of tenements. . .fiberglass stairwells. . .make crazy

(sic)…Big warehouses can be worked on by environmental artists and turned into giant free dance-fiesta-feast palaces.

*"Free City Housing. . .a strong trio of serious business-oriented cats should develop (our) liberation of space within the cities…one of the main targets for space are the churches who are the holders of most real estate and they should be approached with a no-bullshit hard line.

*"Free City Stores and workshops.Space should be available for chicks to sew dresses, make pants to order…The management should all be life-actors capable of turning bullshitters into mud…no trace of salvation army/st. vinnie de paul charity rot. Everything groovy. Everything with style…must be first class. It's all free because it's yours!"

Utopia, 1960s style. A wilderness was already becoming a zoo. Revolutionary spontaneity replaced by devolutionary ritual. Ken Kesey should have known that, by then, whatever was supposed to have happened, already hadn't, that no amount of primo Oaxacan was going to turn Wally Cleaver into Baba Ram Das or The Flying Nun into Grace Slick and that all we baby boomers had to hope for was big licks and belly laughs.

CHAPTER TWENTY-THREE:
THE ABUSES OF ENCHANTMENT

"The utopian sentiments of these hippies was not to be put down lightly. Hippies have a vision of an ideal community—a psychedelic community to be sure—where everyone is turned on and beautiful and loving and happy and floating free. But it is a vision that, despite the Alice in Wonderland phraseology usually breathlessly employed to describe it, necessarily embodies a radical political philosophy: communal life, drastic restriction of private property, rejection of violence, creativity before consumption, freedom before authority, de-emphasis of government and traditional forms of leadership."

—Warren Hinckle

Literature has the power to anoint and ignite. If the Jazz Age was codified by F. Scott Fitzgerald's *This Side of Paradise*, and the Lost Generation was memorialized by Ernest Hemingway's *The Sun Also Rises*, then it's fair to say that the 1960s were kindled by *One Flew Over the Cuckoo's Nest*—and, further, that the end of the 1960s were announced by Kesey soul brother and antithesis, Hunter Thompson and his opus, *Fear and Loathing in Las Vegas*.

Thompson was the key to the undoing of the Kingdom. His news: the Love Generation was "a generation of swine." By New Year's Day 1967, hours after the sorry conclusion of our (Moon's and my) mountain bus trip, Thompson announced he'd already had enough: "The head generation...a loud, cannibalistic gig where the best are fucked for the worst reasons, and the worst make a pile of money feeding off the best. Promoters, narcs, con men—all selling the new Scene to *Time* and the Elks club...The handlers get rich while the animals all get busted or screwed...ride the big wave: folk-rock, peace symbols, long hair..."

Thompson fumed about a Lenny Bruce hounded to death by cops, about 300,000 people in jail on marijuana charges in a country and a world "controlled by a stupid thug from Texas…A vicious liar with the ugliest family in Christendom," and that California was in the hands of "a governor straight out of a George Grosz painting…Ronnie Reagan, the White Hope of the west." Meanwhile, Owsley Acid was worth its weight in gold and guess who among our University of Oregon heroines threw in with Prankster Zonker and flew a million dollars worth of it to Aspen tucked in her panties?

Cute as a ladybug, Sara H. had no sooner checked her luggage (kilos of pot Zonker bought from a guy named Spidey) on a plane from San Francisco to Aspen when she heard on the radio that—Holy Synchronicity, Batman!—there was about to be a big drug bust in Aspen. So she flew the whole way thinking she was about to be arrested. But what the hell? Go with the flow.

Sara grew up in Eugene, her family owned a timber company, and she had three brothers. Pretty much nothing but normal, until she met Kesey in the fall of 1967. This, after she was walking across the campus at the University of Oregon and Prankster Mike Hagen drove by and said, 'I had a Technicolor dream about you last night, get in the truck.' So she did. They went out to the farm. Kesey had just got back from Mexico and Sara fit right in: "We drew a huge horoscope on the floor of the barn, twelve by twelve feet, cut into 12 pie shapes—one for each sign of the zodiac. Everybody who Ken (Kesey) wanted got to paint something inside their sign."

"The main M.O.," Sara said, "was doing useful work around the farm. Hagen and I weren't too strong in that area." A lot of time was spent simply taking care of the people who just showed up. "Kesey came home with this guy he called the Cloverdale Flash because he picked the guy up hitchhiking at the Cloverdale turnoff. He didn't work out. Faye was a great disciplinarian, she could clear people out in a heartbeat."

Sara H. says, "Then Ken and Mike Hagen decided to drive to San Francisco in the white Cadillac. So we headed down to San Francisco. It was really cold out—the fall of 1967. We went to 710 Ashbury which was where the Dead and everybody and their dog were living at the time. Ramrod's baby son Strider had just come home from the hospital with Strider's mom, Patty Cake. Ramrod worked for the Dead his whole life, until he died—all these boys with the Dead were from Pendleton.

Ramrod was the 'Man.' Head roadie."

Everybody wore fur parkas. Sara decided to stay. Dead keyboard player Pig Pen lived downstairs. Dead manager Rock Scully's office was there, Janis Joplin was in and out, "it was like the Hee Haw gang." Then the Dead and the Airplane bought the Carousel Ballroom which became the Fillmore West and Sara moved from the city out to Mickey Hart's ranch in Novato. "Everybody had horses and guns. Stephen Stills was there—he used to be a jockey and was very short and had a tummy on him, a very small man but in very good shape and he was a major rider of horses. That was one of the reasons he was staying at Mickey's ranch was because of all the horses. David Crosby would come over to see him." The barn was being turned into a recording studio. "It was a musical village, 25 to 50 people. There was a big house, long table, everybody ate together, if you had a bed you were really lucky. Marmaduke and David Nelson were there—starting up New Riders of the Purple Sage."

Then Sara moved to Colorado, to Aspen—where she lived in a mining cabin for about six months with her friend Georgia Baum. Her uncle was L. Frank Baum who wrote *The Wizard of Oz*. "We were the Girls in the Hood." They hit the road in Georgia's bus and came back to Mickey Hart's ranch, zigzagged to New York to stay at the Chelsea Hotel, then back to Aspen, then back to SF then back to Kesey's farm. "Then Kesey comes back from England where they'd been at Apple."

Not a half bad landing zone. "There was the cook house and the gas house—where the nitrous oxide tanks were, the big bedroom, the barn. It was extended family. I grew up in a male dominated family of brothers, and that was the attraction."

* * *

Meanwhile, when Sara got to the Aspen airport she ignored the cops and picked up her luggage anyway. And nothing happened! Nobody busted her.

Cosmic. Home free. "Except for one detail. The pot that could've got me thrown in jail forever was all male plants. Totally worthless. You can only get high off female plants. We'd been burned. Zonker was so pissed he got in a fistfight with Spidey. The pot dealer. But we made a million dollars on the Owsley acid. All of Aspen was high for a month."

CHAPTER TWENTY-FOUR: .000001 AND MUCH, MUCH MORE

"...the other end of the rainbow was Haight-Ashbury. The Capital of Forever, where beautiful people cared for each other, where all would be provided and everyone would do their own things without being hassled."
—Martin A. Lee and Bruce Shlain

The Haight.

Love Burgers were going for 25 cents and soon: the death of money. Here .000001 of a gram of acid could be bought for a dollar, and put your teenaged head in another universe.

Oberved most particularly by two Wolfes, Tom and Burton. Of the two, Burton was in some ways the more interesting. Tom Wolfe—who, with his passionate detachment and droll prose shot through with exclamation points has everything fluffed and folded—but Burton tended to lead with his chin.

Consider this dire warning in *The Hippies*. "It was interesting for me to find Negroes and some of my beatnik friends down on hippies because of their way of living. I talked to some Negro men who turned down the chance to sleep with white hippie girls because they were too dirty. One of the most well-liked beats in North Beach, Shig, a Japanese co-manager of City Lights Books, tried it once and regretted it.

"'I picked up a hippie chick myself just to see what it was all about' he said, 'and I let her stay in my pad for several weeks. Man, I'm telling you, never again...She stayed high on drugs...and kept reading and chanting Hindu mysticism, and she was just way out of this world. But bathe? Man, I'd get into the shower and she'd come into the bathroom and say: 'What are you putting that water on you for? You already bathed your body yesterday. Why do you spend so much time washing your body? You should spend your time washing your soul.'"

Obviously, but…

The reality?

In our more pragmatic 21st Century drug world of date-rape facilitators like Ecstasy, LSD has become the Hula Hoop of elixir vitae, everywhere forty years ago, now—I wonder why—practically unicorn rare. I go see Walt Curtis, poetry editor of Ken Kesey's anthology *Spit in the Ocean*. Walt received his invitation to this position by mail, in 1975. An envelope arrived at his apartment known as "The Lawn" in Portland. Inside the envelope was a triangle of Swiss cheese and a note from Kesey: "All we can really offer is shelter, lunch and infamy. Even so, you are my No. 1 draft choice."

Due to poems like this:

THE LEPER
When the leper comes to our house,
I am frightened and curious, Mother.
He is so unprepossessing!
Can't we catch his condition?

No, daughter. That's an
Old wive's tale.
Now mind your manners. And serve
the soup.

His skin is dark-spotted,
And one finger is rotted off,
dressed in white linen.
When he touches the silver,
won't it be forever contaminated?

Shush up or I'll let him
fondle your breasts,
you racist little bitch!

You were always too snooty
for your own good.
The leper is my lover.

I have grown tired of the other fellows.
I need some different stuff.

To brighten my bedroom culture,
increase the sticky
filthy bacteria count, daughter dear.

When reading his poems aloud, Walt's delivery suffers in translation. Thin, of average height, he is nervous on stage, often reading as if he is seeing his own lines for the first time, swaying from side to side, one hand holding his papers, the other making slow-motion diagonal karate chops through the empty air, in time with his voice. Often, his face will take on a shocked unease, as if horrified where his own poem is taking him. Wincing self-criticism, à la "I can't believe I wrote this shit," is, in mid-poem, not uncommon.

In the first issue of his self-published anthology, *Spit in the Ocean*, Kesey presented his wiry, balding poetry editor Walt Curtis as a one eyed Jack on a playing card with four photos of Curtis smoking a cigarette, and presented Curtis's biography his way:

"Our Syxx-eyed Jacky Butts was brought nekked from the wombe in Olympia,
Washington. He shalle be this minnitte
Found swimming in thee Clackamas River,
Nekked yette.
His slogan: 'It's thee water makes thee wette.'"

He is the Unofficial Poet Laureate of Oregon, a brilliant man whose selfless love of boys is profound enough to make him, if, while certainly not a pedophile, at least a priest. Writing for the Oregon Cultural Heritage Commission, Walt allowed, "I realize it's too soon to evaluate such a great writer and legendary human being. But I'm gonna take a shot at it! The spirit of Kesey is total freedom, and the right...to challenge the cosmos and the forces that be. What do I mean? Well, on Valentine's Day—Oregon's birthday—Marty Christensen, Lorna Viken, and I drove to Pleasant Hill with Ken. We talked wildly in the car about 'Venusians'—folks without auras—Wilhelm Reich, UFOs, orgonic energy, and the burning of the library in Alexandria. Just back from Egypt, Ken was excited about the struggle for the human soul. Because we humans were compassionate, we would win, he emphasized. The hair stood up on the back of my neck. Marty and Lorna and I thought the car might pull off the road of its own volition."

It's summer 2007. A sign says DRINK HERE. Walt lives on the carlot-carpeted, light industrial side of Portland beneath "The Noir," which operates as an alcoholic embassy for "gothic post-punk death rock plus New Wave, Dark Wave, Cold Wave, Bat Cave" on the placid east side of the river. Walt's apartment looks like an explosion in an art gallery. His paintings, largely of people, angels, devils and whatnot having sex, are scattered everywhere among wine bottles and books. In his bedroom, under a cloud of blankets, somebody is sleeping. It's three in the afternoon. Walt keeps whatever is the opposite of bankers hours and, anyway, today he has a guest.

Tom McGovern is a fit, trim, casually well-dressed man about sixty who was born in San Francisco. Now he buys and sells rare books, but back in the day, he sold the dream elixirs that made San Francisco the New Jerusalem. In Walt Curtis's basement apartment below the "Noir Tavern," amid Walt's paintings and books, sitting on a spidery chair, McGovern said, "I had friends who were bohemian—acid freaks part of the Santa Cruz crew, I was hanging around a little place called the 'Café International' out on Ocean Avenue or down in Union Square… guys started crashing at my house who'd been to acid tests and were part of the Santa Cruz scene—Les Dozier and Curt Berry first and through them people who became a big deal in the psychedelic movement, Bob Lindsay, Chocolate George, President of the San Francisco Hell's Angels. He went about six seven, big guy."

I ask, "Was Chocolate George a nice guy?"

"Well, he was a Hell's Angel. He was very polite to me. At least initially. But Hell's Angels turn on you at the snap of a finger. You'll be talking with one, it's fine, then another Hell's Angel walks up and it's two

Angels or three, and all of a sudden you're just a nameless asshole. Your friendship of moments before is forgotten. I was talking to Chocolate George one day on Haight Street—I liked George, we were kind of buddies—I just bumped into him, hadn't seen each other, we're talking, I think he was just sitting on his bike, and then another Angel comes out, and another, and he said: 'You should go now. Otherwise you might get stomped.' I sort of told him off—I said, 'Then I'm just not going to talk to you anymore'—and he was shocked, because, according to Angel etiquette, he was being polite.

"He didn't live much after that, six months or a year, he got killed in sixty-seven or sixty-eight—ran into the back of a semi or something on his bike."

Wiry Walt, wine glass in hand says, "One of the things Tom feels is that little flower child thing they had going in San Francisco was only nice for about a year."

Tom McGovern says, "It was never nice. You have different images of what it was like. Well, it was very gritty, from about the beginning. You know, you take some acid and you have this ecstatic experience but you have to understand that the people you're hanging around with, the general medium, is pretty polluted. We were mostly young criminals and juvenile delinquents. The youth culture was really a big criminal element, we're gonna drink, we're gonna smoke, fuck the cops—you didn't rat people. The culture we started with was a very productive field in which to plant the criminal element—which matured in a pretty big way. Hell's Angels smoked dope, so they were all right. Ex-murderers and other people we hung out with, we didn't know how they were exactly, but that they were other people who took dope and that made them okay. That was your ticket into the counterculture—people you'd smoke a joint with. It's like how the alligator on an Izod sweater makes you part of the same club. Smoking grass, dropping acid, taking amphetamines were sort of medallions to make you part of the same club.

"The first time I dropped acid was when I was seventeen, it would have been 1965. I remember when we got it, we went over to the "Blue Unicorn" a few streets over from Haight, the hippie acid Mecca, and my buddies bought some sugar cubes and we took 'em and had a fantastic trip, it was wonderful—very ecstatic.

"Owsley got into it early—to have acid for the acid tests you had to get it from somebody and, oddly enough, Owsley had it. I knew his buddy Alex—Alex was the big speed dealer. He's as famous, more famous than Owsley probably—at least in the speed culture."

Was there a central lack of idealism early on?

McGovern says, "I think we had a sense we were on a quest, I don't think you'd call it a spiritual quest—because that language didn't exist in American culture at that time—a spiritual quest for some, a quest for early death for others."[21]

I ask McGovern how he met Neal Cassady. "We were living in Santa Cruz and we were down there, probably looking to score some pot and there wasn't any and we went into the 'Catalyst'—this was a big deal, there was a bookstore where at one time you could buy LSD out of the refrigerator, next to the bookstore was the St. George Hotel. At the St. George Hotel was the Catalyst. The Catalyst was a big counterculture place to meet. We wandered in there and I think Cassady was sitting with Danny—one of the Santa Cruz guys. Most of them became junkies later. It was a heavy drug culture and it evolved as heavy drug cultures do.

"I knew the Santa Cruz guys, they'd crash at my house, we got high together, we scored for each other. Danny jumped up and introduced us to Neal Cassady. I was with my buddy Jerry. We had a car. Cassady wanted a ride. So we drove him to San Francisco with us. We stopped mid-way, in Palo Alto I believe, and Cassady jumped out of the car and scored us an ounce of pot. A big bag of it. He knew it was okay because we were fellow criminals. It was good pot, maybe fifteen bucks and we drove on to San Francisco. He was begging to drive the car and I was saying fuck no, because he was crazy—really a very strange guy.

"I didn't make the connection with *On the Road*, he was just some nut we'd met. As time went on people told me he was a big deal, but I never thought of him that way—he already had been driving Kesey's bus. Generally speaking he was horrible, he was high on speed, babbling a million miles an hour about nothing. And I would say that behavior, if you go back and read *On the Road* and read between the lines you will discern that Cassady is a maniac, that he talks for hours about nothing because he's high on speed all the time.

"He wanted to impress people, he wanted to feel important. He wasn't

21 Owsley had just had bypass surgery. McGovern says, "It makes sense Owlsey would have been up for a bypass as the inventor of the all-meat diet."

at the level of Ginsberg or Kerouac, he was Ginsberg's love interest and Kerouac was astonished by his immorality and maniac behavior—"

The 20th century version of the Noble Savage?

"That's what they projected him as. I liked him when he was straight. He'd show up and he could be extremely charismatic. To be a con man you have to be. He'd smile and, 'Hey, great to see you! It's a real pleasure! I've heard so much about you.' He could come on like that, and just beam. But you got the impression he was never really being straight with you. It was, like, weird being around him. He used to come to score speed. I always had speed, I always had a lot of drugs. For a little while, we had suitcases full of pharmaceutical stuff from a guy down at Moss Beach—kind of a mob place. There were wise guys in Moss Beach.

"I would sell him what I had, later maybe some crystal meth. And he brought the Pranksters, and he brought Allen Ginsberg to the house and Jerry Garcia and Kesey came to the house once—but Kesey came up to the floor we were on, looked around and disappeared into the night. Too hot. He might have been a fugitive. People were getting arrested for marijuana in those days. The sentence in California was six months to five years."

"How did you get out of this?" I ask.

"Everybody died. I lived in the Fillmore. It was a good spot for Cassady to come by. Most of the time I lived in the Fillmore. I lived within a few blocks of him, but I never went to his house, because I wasn't welcome there. Because of my relationship with Cassady. I was considered a bad guy."

"You were corrupting the devil?"

"That was it," McGovern says. "Somehow people could put that on me, that I was a speed dealer. Neal went out and he came back high." McGovern was only 17 or 18 at this time. "People were dying all the time. Next to where I lived was the Kirkland Hotel, also known as the Greta Garbo Home for Women. Wayward girls. Boys too. There's a song about it, maybe you've heard it:

My name is Jack
and I live in back
of the Greta Garbo Hotel

"A horrible speed house. A drug hotel, full of methamphetamine and crime (Now it's Japan Town, in the Western Addition, all destroyed by redevelopment). Haight-Ashbury was devastated, by late 1968 everything was boarded up—the political structure of San Francisco did not want this counterculture in Haight, to them it was an alien presence. They never offered police protection, the Hell's Angels ran rampant, people using more and more and heavier drugs…It got hard to make money since the economy of Haight-Ashbury was based largely on selling marijuana—the pyramid could only build so far before it collapses— when there aren't any groundfloor customers anymore the business has to implode. By '68 or '69 it got pretty crappy in San Francisco, I was a long-hair. It got so long-hairs couldn't walk on the street anymore, we were targets for robbery and police. I moved to Marin in '69. I lived in Sausalito for a few years, then moved farther out.

"I never got high on speed a single time after Cassady died. We weren't particularly close, but I saw him just a few days before he died. He came to my house, he actually went to visit my downstairs neighbor who had some liquid dexedrine. It wasn't very good, but he supplied it to Cassady in aluminum foil, not very hygienic, Neal is sucking it up, licking it off his fingers…He's there with a couple girls from Oakland. Pillhead girls from Oakland, they looked like girls I'd go out with, long dark hair and depressed and big purses. Neal came in and it was, 'Oh Tom! Little Tom!' Shook my hand very friendly, he bought some speed from my buddy and I asked him how things were going and he said, 'Better than ever, better than ever!' Things are great, blah, blah, blah' and he went out the door and a few days later word came back that he was dead. He was on his way to Mexico so I imagined he jumped in his car and drove to Mexico and it was within a week we heard. My buddy knew a crazy guy in Sacramento, as queer as a three dollar bill. Apparently this guy supplied him with some dexedrine of crappy quality which theoretically he made, supplied it to my buddy who supplied to Cassady, and that was his exit speed trip.

"The coroner's report said he had cirrhosis of the liver, I remember that last time he came back from Mexico with a woman named JB, and he came back to San Francisco and I was walking down the street and a white van rolls up and there's this mad man wildly gesticulating, honking his horn at me and he needed a place to stay and I had a little extra room. He and JB stayed there about a week—quietly. I wasn't particularly well at the time, I had had trouble with my liver. When I told Cassady about it, I remember him looking at me very strangely, as if frightened, or disturbed. Shortly after, he was dead."

The Holy Goof, eaten alive by amphetamines, was buried. But a new day was dawning. God or the Anti-Christ had changed zip codes. Not long after LSDeity Leary had fled the east coast to become Jesus II or governor of California—whichever came first. In the interim, Dr. Leary parked himself at the Brotherhood's ranch in Idyllwild in the mountains above Palm Springs.

Each morning the Brothers—who had also bought a ranch in Oregon and land in Hawaii—rose at dawn and, before embarking on their day's labor (mending fences for their until recently wild horses or dealing millions of dollars-worth of LSD) they would spend an hour in religious meditation scored by rock music or recorded Buddhist chants. Leary began work on a screenplay which would map the creation of an acid-blessed utopian state.

CHAPTER TWENTY-FIVE: MANCHILD IN THE PROMISED LAND

"School sucks. The white honkie structure that has been handed down to us on a plastic platter is meaningless to us! We don't want it! Fuck God in the ass! Fuck your woman until she can't stand up. Fuck everybody you can get your hands on. Our program of rock and roll, dope and fucking in the streets is a program of total freedom for everyone...We breathe revolution. We are the LSD-driven total maniacs of the universe."

—White Panther Manifesto

Paradise, 1967. Hawaii.

The future was already out there someplace. The Bee-Gees had released their first album, Ken Kesey had, on the advice of his lawyers, long since declared, "I think it's time we graduated out of acid. LSD has reached the state where Babbit begins to take it. It used to be Hell's Angels and bohemians, but now the son of the hardware store owner in Des Moines is taking it."

But here, unknowing, the surf rolled in, white tumbling line after white tumbling line, each spilling off a fresh steep peaked wave, a speeding water roof of an ocean house, crashing toward sand as white as salt. Waves as symmetrical as an A-frame, water as clear as dirty air and as warm as mother's milk, rushing in snow white hems before chalk and lobster-skinned tourists and tan bikini-ed college chicks on the beach. The shepherds may have been ready, on the advice of their lawyers, to dismiss acid as water under the bridge, but the psychedelic tsunami had yet to hit the the nation of sheep.

An eight-year-old boy slithered aboard the big "learner" board, and pushing the flat fiberglass log by its skeg, I eased him into the crashing shore break. The big board shot up, the kid clutching its rails. Stupid barge. How to get the boy up on it? Six months before, I could barely spell surfboard, let alone ride one, and having me teach this child to surf made as much sense as having Ptolemy teach him about the universe. But the Vietnam War had created a teenage surf instructor labor shortage. So there I was.

The boy paddled, I pushed. The wave splashed over my head, and the kid was off, and up. I saw the boy's head bob above the speedy foaming wave.

Time to make something of myself. How? Easy. I'd put use back in uselessness. If I could not become a man of action, I could at least become flotsam of action. Time to settle for the more down to earth: utopia, and here in the sandy emerald sky-ed ($1.98 yellow-lensed John Lennon granny-glasses tincturing God's earth a weird sickly green) ground zero of the future of whack I saw absolutely nothing—in all dismal aspects of the word—wrong with walking a la Johnny Potseed down Waikiki Beach with a grocery bag of zip-locked lids, hawking pot to anybody who maybe wasn't a sunbathing cop. What Richter scale of idiocy could measure that? If any bikini-ed airline stewardess had declined my pitch: "Twelve bucks for an oh zee of fine Oaxacan" and called hotel security, I'd've been sharing shower soap with Oahu's Most Unwanted for six months.

Time had come today. Take this from the *Berkeley Barb*: "In unity we shall shower the country with waves of ecstasy of purification. Fear will be washed away; ignorance will be exposed to sunlight; profits and empire will lie drying on deserted beaches; violence will be submerged and transmuted in rhythm and dancing."

Two years later, writing in *The Great Speckled Bird,* Tim Coffin got down to particulars: "Dope not drugs—alcohol is a drug, pot is DOPE; nicotine is a DRUG, acid is DOPE; DRUGS turn you off, dull your senses, give you the strength to face another day in Death America, DOPE turns you on, heightens your sensory awareness...gives you vision and clarity, necessary to create Life from Death...the difference between Stupor and Ecstasy is the difference between Jack Daniels and Orange Sunshine, between the Pentagon and Woodstock...we all have to make our choices."

I'd certainly made mine. Hair brushing my shoulders, my pupils erring to the size of atoms or bowling balls, I could see the obvious: Serpent Amerika was shedding its skin. With the Lizard King in the Oval Office and Wavy Gravy's finger on the nuclear trigger, power would soon be transferred from the executive office, Supreme Court and Congress into the hands of the nation's 10,000,000 most capable nineteen-year-olds. Free at last, free at last, the revolution would save me from the unspeakable tyranny that otherwise awaited me: a job.

For Ken Kesey culture had brought radical change. Suddenly, guys had the right to wear their hair as long as the Founding Fathers' and you could buy any drug you wanted on every other palm-shaded street corner to take you from drooling lassitude to speeding hysteria and back again, cheap. By this time LSD was old news, a Johnny-come-lately to manhandled mania, and who needed all the psychedelic sales jive? Besides, acid scared me. Time to get real, to start thinking about the future. I'd graduate college and get, say, a job as Executive Vice President in Charge of Thinking at the Testor's airplane glue factory. Because, face facts, were there two sexier words in the English language than toxic inhalant? A fifteen-cent tube of that shit and you were as high as, reasonably speaking, anybody really ought to get.

Love might steer the stars but I didn't need Eden between my ears when I had an ungodded heaven before my eyes. Not the Eden imagined (and perhaps, I prayed, enjoyed) by my mother in heaven—but the Eden of my father's South Pacific. Hippie Heaven on earth. Home to royalty. During whose reign, Waikiki was once site of surfing parties held outside the King's beach house, where the "merry…intelligent, warm-hearted, musical and athletic" Kalakaua had held court. In those days Waikiki was a rolling ocean of flowers planted by the Hawaiian Royal family. Now it was a more populist Eden, an angular hodgepodge of tourist hotels and hippie crashpads, a confused, ungodded honky tonk Garden-full whose Adams, Eves, Cains and Abels were mostly drugged-out hippies, angry, hulking dark-hearted Samoans and—just after the bloody Tet Offensive—terrified GI's on R & R from Vietnam, but an Eden still, where the Beatles, fresh off their Kesey-inspired Magical Mystery tour, were the Walrus and here in Waikiki my job was to grow my hair as long as Ray Davies on the cover of *Kinks Kontroversy*, and sell grass that probably was.

The morning surf was so crowded with boards that you could practically walk across the waves. The good news though, was that society was falling apart. Revolution was in the wind. Far off, on another radio, I could hear the Stones song "Street Fighting Man"—that was that year tattooed to the air.

Student riots: up at the university. Nights before, I'd dodged a club-waving conga line of Hawaiian Metro Police as they turned a mob of SDS'ers into hippie goulash. Fortunately, I'd smoked enough Moroccan dog biscuit to realize that love was just "evol" spelled backwards, and the world could all blow away for all I cared. Except for the beer and birth control factories, and McDonalds, so I could still eat. But flower power, that liar Carlos Castaneda, beads and having to eat sprouts? I didn't like being a hippie much even when I was one. All I cared about was surf.

I had left my board leaning against the hau tree under which he-man novelist—*The Call of the Wild, White Fang*—Jack London had sat sixty years before, in the summer of 1907, watching the members of the Waikiki Swim Club surf.

"Where but the moment before," London had written, "was only the wide desolation and invincible roar, is now a man, erect, full-statured… not buried and crushed by these monsters, but standing above them all, calm and superb, poised on the giddy summit, his feet buried in the churning foam, the salt smoke rising to his knees…he is flying through the air…a brown Mercury. His heels are winged, and in them is the swiftness of the sea…"

Had St. Christopher actually been an eighteen-foot-tall, toga-wearing dog-headed cannibal who'd carried the "enormously heavy" Christ child across a river and saved Him from drowning—the facts didn't bother me. It was the rumors. That the Vatican was about to strip St. Christopher of his powers to protect "vagabonds" because St. Christopher had been canonized "too late" or some god awful thing, which would mean the St. Christopher medal I wore around my neck, a medal I had "inherited" from my mother would no longer protect me from the police, VD, myself or the water.

Miraculously unarrested, I walked two blocks down Kalakaua Boulevard, stepped out onto the beach at Queens, flopped my nine-four Hobie in the water and scrubbed on wax. Status here was a great board, and, though mine was soon to be obsolete as a crew cut, I had one. Bought spotless, a dingless Hobie from a kingly local Moke, Earl, perfect as a wish and scored for $40 which, if I had it today, might be worth Kelly Slater's mortgage payment.

Brown wire-thin arms thrashing through quaking glass-clear sea, I could see the cluster of palms below Diamond Head that marked the site of the Outrigger Canoe Club. Where I paddled out to the lineup to bob among an edgy school of haole freaks, moke locals and GIs. I heard the sound of a breaking wave—a throaty hiss, the roar of a far away crowd. A dark blue line of water was rising, slashed with ice-white feathering foam, rolling toward us.

My board rose, lifting me up to the big blue sky. I dug my arms deep in the water, my long lozenge-like Hobie shot forward. This was a big wave. I jumped to my feet, swung around, the too-long nose of the Hobie whipped east toward Diamond Head, the board dropped arcing across the face of the wave, and unreal: It was cresting right above me.

Warm foam and water plopped and poured and jetted all over my face, shoulders and back. I looked into the face of the wave, it was a wall. Green Coke-bottle translucent. I was in the tube.

This had never happened to me. It felt as great as a girl.

I paddled back into the lineup. Wow. The waves. Not the usual rippy little curls, but a big set. Two guys started to paddle and, as the breaker rose up behind them, both stood and took the drop. One guy's board hurled stabbing into the other and they went flying, kersplat.

The wave roared over them, its crest a deep, long snowy peak of tumbling, racing foam. I paddled, rising up and, as I stood, I shot too high and was suddenly falling as fast as if I'd jumped off a building. I tried to crank the Hobie's long nose around, but...

WHAM! I hit the water, was dragged under it, tumbling end-over-end. My knee hit coral. A problem out here. Big waves in shallow water. The coral could cut you to sushi.

I paddled back out. The waves were almost overhead. Another loomed. I dug my arms into the water, looked over. Foam was skidding down the sky-blue face of the breaker. Next, I was way high up on the lip of the wave and my board was flying straight down to the water. The surfboard knifed beneath the face of the wave. Zillions of pearl-like bubbles poured over its nose in silver flames. I tumbled to razored depths.

Paradise found. I'd been inspired by the phenomena of *Endless Summer,* the hugely successful surfing safari documentary which, like the Ken Kesey ministry, suggested a fabulous career in simply existing. If Kesey and *Endless Summer* were the future, I could just be Mark Christensen for a living: me and mine would embark on a video surf Chautauqua for the next 40 years, the play would truly be the thing, morality boiled down to fighting weight—most sins obsolete, the Ten Commandments slimmed down to "don't lie, murder or steal" and, anyway, I had learned my lesson. T-shirts, boxer shorts, board shorts, that's all you needed.

The illusion of power and riches beat the reality of power and riches. Real power and riches were work. Keeping track of mansions, yachts, thoroughbred horses and trophy wives a pain—Ferraris and private jets just more stuff to break. As for fame, say, as a rock god? Traveling around all the time being worshipped by yo-yos, having to trash hotel rooms and get cooties from groupies? Forget it, better to be America's Guest. *Su casa es mi casa.* Light the herb, kick back on your couch, leaf through the latest issue of the *Paul is Dead Gazette...*

...I slogged from the water, hoisting the treacherous log that was my Hobie surfboard under my arm, my knees and forearms flecked with stoplight-bright, red tailed cuts that looked like bloody sperm cells. Coral cuts everywhere, but did this beat the running of the bulls at Pamplona or a lobotomy or what? As a writer, might I not represent the Every Freak, provide the madman-on-the-street perspective?

Anything to escape the country club, Cadillac conformist machine. Aside from the moon, the country was going in the wrong direction. Oh, there were some good things: no-fault divorce, convenience caesarians, token blacks. But, mostly I was about to fall into an America made out of bosses and rules.

My mind as open as the void, I'd flown to Hawaii with a trio of "virgin nymphomaniacs," The Blondes. Charlie's Angels from the Dog Star Sirius. The best bad news any boy every had. Shapely, mouthy, vivid as neon danger signs. I'd inherited two thirds of the Blondes from high school, a good hearted yellow-haired pair whose questionable answers to the plush boredom of Raleigh Hills were alcohol, big mouths and crashed cars. The third Blonde, statuesque and glowing, had descended from the mothership of the Hanford Nuclear Reservation in Washington State.

The plus side of the Blondes: the constant companionship of gorgeous girls. Quality of care common to rich invalids and prize poodles. The minus side: nothing but trouble. I got a North Star to my future when we arrived at Waikiki Beach. We left our hotel room and had just hit the sidewalk when sailors in white sailor suits and wearing round white sailor hats started whistling and doing the "haaaaaaay baaaabeeeee!" stuff and a Blonde shouted back, "Who shit and put a Dixie Cup on it?"

The sailors ran across the street. We dashed back in the hotel, into an elevator and back into our room. Cool. No autopsy, no foul. Except next the Blondes were out on the lanai shouting fuck yous to the white hats four stories below, and minutes later there was pounding so loud furious wild horses could have been stampeding towards our front door.

My idea: surf the Revolution and, as their own personal pilot fish, I enjoyed among the Blondes the status of a god or a dog, deemed variously too transcendent or stupid to be be engaged in the shopping, laundry, cooking aspect of life. Yet I was expected, like a god or dog, to provide protection for them; while I may have appeared as fatless as a frog, my anorexic Quasimodo bonafides were otherwise spotless.

We rented a studio apartment below the university above the mirrory waters of the Alawai Canal. All of us in one room, and though I slept with the blonde who wore negligees as thin as a dream, it was water, water everywhere, but Jesus…"If. You. Ever. Squirt. Baby. Batter. On. Me. I. Will. Kill. You!" The sexual revolution from the other side of the mirror. I'd wake to find Blondes flouncing around in their next-to nothings and hear hard candy takes on sexology: "Mark, do you know if every time we screwed we dropped an M&M in a mayonnaise jar, that jar would fill up in no time, but when the jar was full, if we took an M&M out every time we screwed it would take the rest of our lives for the jar to be empty?"

The good news? These willowy, buxomy fair-haired young vixens of the west loved anything not "shitty or boring"—and would have gladly enjoyed gymnastic sex with any really great looking surfer dude who passed them on a sidewalk, so long as they didn't have to touch him. Marketing majors like Impetuous (or was it Catwoman?), they lived to flaunt their deliverables through The Schooner, a big Waikiki bar, a sweat factory packed shoulder-to-shoulder with drunk longhaired surf freaks, GI's and sumo-sized Hawaiians. Bosch's portrait of a rainbow coalition slave galley or human Noah's Ark. Here, as elsewhere, nothing was a dirty trick if it was funny enough. I'd pop from the men's room to see the Blondes standing in spiderweb bikinis before a platoon of burr-head Marines/GI's/sailors, hooting "Mark! These fucking jarheads were oogling our hot bodies—sic'em!"

In our apartment arid desert of water, water everywhere I was so spaced I could not even talk, flat on my back on the couch, with the Blondes' three angelic faces, plus the face of just exactly the kind of big, horndog guy I was supposed to protect them against, looming above me, as big as four planets.

"What's wrong with him?" the guy asked. "Is he sick?"

"No," one of the Blondes replied, "I think he just has a blown mind."

Though Tim Leary had big news for me and mine (from High Priest): "Listen! Wake up! You are God! You have the divine plan engraved in cellular script within you. Listen! Take this sacrament! You'll see! You'll get the revelations! It will change your life! You'll be reborn!"

I wasn't sure I wanted LSD to make me God. This shit was surely more than a magic communion wafer. My step-mother had sent me a newspaper headline that read NINE DROP ACID, GO BLIND STARING AT SUN. Scary and, anyway, even given the price of admission—death— heaven was too pie in the sky.

But tonight I'd smoked something completely weird. Discombobulation a go go. I could understand language, but could not speak, everybody looked like their own reflection in a fun house mirror.

A man-child must know his limits. A buddy of mine had given me a joint of something that turned the world to Oz. Above me where I lay on the couch, one of the Blondes began to cry, and tears trickled down her perfect cheeks, each as big as a fish bowl.

CHAPTER TWENTY-SIX:
HEAVEN ON EARTH

"...the summer of love...thousands of surfers engaged in activities that seemed to explicitly ignore the maxim, "Kill the head, the body dies"...those stolid, volan-glassed tail blockers wallowing in the tar pits, their gazes fixed on the Owsley-fueled meteor rocketing towards them.

"The days of T-bands, competition stripes, and signature models were done. No more opaque panel-jobs. No more cut-lap obsessions. Time had come today. Break out the squeegee and catch the joy of a full-length acid-bath resin-flow color job. Delve into the realm of the first airbrush fades. Fry on the faux-marble, and trip on the Dashiki cloth inlays. These weren't props for Fresno car clubbers. These were mixed-media vessels driven by W.A.V.E. S.E.T. fins, their psychedelic opacity capable of harboring a traveling pound of pungent Moroccan kif from the hungry eye of the X-ray at JFK International. Those suckers TURNED."

—Scott Hulet

Hit by the lucky bus, thanks to my new best friend Frank, who had given me the twelve-word Rosetta Stone to the language of love. Otherwise this could have never happened. Fired as lap dog/bodyguard by the Blondes, bummer, but now—tall and tan and young and lovely the Girl from Ypsalanti had big beautiful eyes, the flat symmetrical face of a $1,000 cat, a body to stop a clock and sitting on the sand with fellow longhaired yo-yo surf freaks and aquatic Adonises, down the curve of Waikiki beach a familiar irresistible sashay, bikinied Cindy getting bigger and bigger and bigger and then, like getting hit by miraculous love lightning, there she was practically her-nose-to-my-nose with a smile as wide as the horizon, some charming girlish small talk from stop light red lips and a bizarre command, "Let's go out."

Which left the yo-yo Adonises and surf freaks—watching Cindy's perfect Valentine butt sashay away with the swing of a metronome made flesh—speechless.

With reason. For at no other time in history would such a celestial dream being have taken me for more than a non-boring sustenance node, but during acid think, Katie bar the door. Pharmaceutical discombobulents plus the collapse of reason could equal the Artist Welded to His Godded Vision who was also as malleable as ABC gum. But when I went to pick her up at her apartment, an impediment: her boyfriend. Not some rockjawed stud mirror of celestial Cindy but a chubby little lisping elf. Who, seeing me, threw a *who-the-fuck-is-this, you traitor-bitch?* shit fit so explosive that Cindy yanked me into her bathroom, and slammed the door. Which he started with bite-sized fists to pound on. Then kick.

"Question," I said, "Why are we in here?"

"He has a black belt." Cindy was no intellectual skyscraper, but funny. Leaning close, her voice a whisper of carnal promise, she breathed, "You're screwed."

Think about it: Was Ken Kesey the Promised Land's promised new man, the messiah to lead us out of the Wilderness? Or wasn't this the Promised Land, and hadn't I been led out the Wilderness already?

So, anyway, here I was: In hippie heaven, led from the robotic techno Amerikan Wilderness to a tropic sub-Shangri-La where we longhaired surfer lunatics truly ran the asylum, a utopia for boys and girls who barely needed opposable thumbs to survive in bong-centric high style.

That very morning, in a dream state stoned and staring through rose tinted granny glasses at the sun, an angry red ball through the lenses, I had the new New Testament on my fatless, tan- as- a- football stomach.

The Electric Kool Aid Acid Test. Though you might argue that who needed acid-blasted Merry Pranksters for models when you had the much hipper Hawaiian mysticism to fall back on, (what could LSD do compared to the ancient Kahunas—each high priest's high priest—each able to "pray a man to death"?) the fact was Tom Wolfe's revelatory tale was about far more than Ken Kesey and his bad magic ministry. While I admired that they went to jail a lot for crimes unrelated to the Ten Commandments, there was something corny farm boy and too-insistent about the Pranksters, men acting like funky children—and as a self celebrator of the bumpkin ideal guiding-light, Kesey seemed a day-glo good old frat boy who—like most revolutionary frat boys from Adolf Hitler on down—was in the revolution for the driver's seat.

No. Wolfe's message to me and mine transcended Kesey. Wolfe's real message was about us, and it was the most vital message of all: YOU EXIST.

At least for the moment. What's-his-face, Cindy's lisping little Black Belt Elf, continued to pound her bathroom door. And shout. "Come out and faith the music you thtupid thun of a bitch, I'll kick your ath!"

Bad news. But, signs and wonders: for looking behind me—perhaps there was a backdoor to celestial Cindy's bathroom, new gnosis, her vanity was an altar to booze. A glass forest of well-sampled fifths: wine, scotch, bourbon, something pink either rose' or perfume.

So, time to think. Should I stay or should I go? I chugged BV Cab Sav '62 thoughtfully. A brain teaser. Though already half-wasted, I was able to address the issue to myself in simple terms. Put in language dogs and kitty cats could understand: I was a good bully. If we could get out of here we could go back to my shoebox apartment and Be as One. But if the elf knew karate?

"So what," Cindy asked, a slinky bare arm on mine, clearly far less frightened than excited. Sex or violence, what did she care…"are you going to do?"

What I did best. A) Get drunk or drunker, B) Absent that, absolutely nothing.

Indeed, *Acid Test* was nothing less than the Word to legions of recently ex-teenyboppers who, to the moment of the book's publication had been, like me, useless naïfs impotently in tune to the gospels of the consumer apocalypse, doomed to end up either corporate tax attorneys or the kind of alienated artistic type who spends his or her time scratching 666 on shopping mall walls. Then, out of nowhere, Wolfe had given us, through the power of his sacred pen, the greatest gift of all: Identity.

Mine was: Lucky Boy. At each brink of nirvana the rocking boat of love gave Cindy, how else to say it, an "anti-gasm." She'd scramble, hand over sputtering mouth to the john where—wild the wine a girl could hold— erupted a purple Niagara into my toilet bowl. Then she'd brush her teeth until her mouth was foaming like a rabid dog and: reprise. My ability to avoid reality had paid off in the biggest way. All I had to do was drink myself fearless in her bathroom—which took, I dunno, maybe two hours—open her bathroom door and—nothing. The Black Belt elf was gone. He'd stopped kicking her door probably ninety minutes before, but to be on the safe side I'd waited him out and now, wow, we were back at my apartment and though our love had revealed itself as a passionate puke fest, drunk Cindy, who by this time was calling me Tom, said I was the sexiest guy she'd ever met.

And from identity would soon come power. Before *Acid Test,* I figured I'd end up in Portland, twenty stories above the Willamette River, an anonymous executive nobody, gazing out at lucky gulls tipping this way and that, flying free high in the Oregon sky, while I sat for forty years imprisoned in a corporate corner office with a Gucci Horsebit silk-tie noose around my neck, all my time and money spent in or on fancy restaurants, a Mercedes, mansions, alimony and...

But now, the Good News: I was saved, absolved of my Original Sin of Ruling class Nobodyness. For Tom Wolfe had discovered that, from the cocoon of suburbia now flew hot-rodded, hallucination-headed surfer butterflies beating freak wings high in the sky: New Boys vital and ridiculous about to conquer the world.

* * *

There It was. The Answer. The tiniest surfboard ever. A screaming toilet seat cutting a breaker to confetti. Testors airplane glue was copasetic (I kept my glue sock under my pillow), but waves even better. No rules. Gnarly peace and love. Nothing to get tackled, punched, conquered, humiliated, damaged or killed by (Except myself—I'd already nearly drowned at Sunset Beach, after trying to ride a water mountain). Out there, beyond the swells that were lifting me up, up, up then setting me down, out there beyond the subtle curve of the horizon across the Pacific Ocean a quarter of the way around the globe: the U of O. Here, a swell rose behind the surfer. His arms stabbed into the water. Two strokes, three. He hopped up, then did everything but sign his name on the wave. Exhausted and trudging up the beach toward my apartment, I felt a warm trickle down my shin. A snake of neon red blood from a coral cut slithered from my knee. Under my arm my beautiful Hobie felt as heavy and cumbersome as a world.

The little sawed off board.

That was It. I had seen the light, and it was very, very bright.

The sound of one hand clapping, and soon I could be getting a standing O. New gnosis. Rock god reknown as the Orville and Wilbur Wright of toilet seat-sized surfboards. The Main Chance. And yet and yet—all I'd been hearing lately was Kesey, Kesey, Kesey, Kesey. This from my new roommate, surfboard-shaper pot smoker Terry, who could actually *make* the gnarly little slivers but who, antithetical to fiberglass nirvana, hated the "system." His take: Reality—with all its tricks, obligations and dire conditions—was for capital pig millionaires, cyborgs and losers, and for Terry his new guru was--better than a Beatle, Kink or Door—not a peace/love flower power Kesey but a WASP golem Kesey who took zero shit from planet earth. Terry said Keze said that microdot shit was the pablum of toddlers and cops. But an oz. of Orange Sunshine down the hatch and, boom, kosmic Krakatoa. Yet, somehow re: blowing my mind versus not blowing my life I remained on the fence. Tiny-board giant or dream state basket case? Sunshine Super Freak or revolutionary surf savant? Talk about a brain teaser. Sure, acid wouldn't zap me into Jesus or even Rick Griffin. Those daze were over, bro. Still, a blown mind could be hard to beat. For somehow, despite all my efforts, however altered, I'd so far always retained a thread, albeit microscopic, of common horror and comprehension, and was still a virgin to the psychic equivalent of having a hand grenade go off between my ears. In 1968 the very definition of lame.

Nevertheless, you still could make the case that in shortboards, not Orange Sunshine, lay the future. This I got from Terry's best friend, our next door neighbor Bill Cook who also took me to hippie boot camp. A crew-cut former Marine minus his surfboards, he had maybe ten possessions, including his bicycle and toothbrush. Like a refugee from 4,000 BC hunter-gatherer barter culture, he lived off the land, picked mangoes and papayas off trees, we'd go to "Love's Bakery" and get day old loaves of bread for ten cents. He was married to the most beautiful woman ever, Marie, whose suit of lights was a string bikini made out of barely that, and who had cotton candy cumulus clouds of platinum hair, big batting eyes, a red mouth half of the perfect kiss, and was heartbreakingly nice. For Bill the object of life was to surf. He rode waves that rose up like watery Everests, and he had no use for drugs or money.

Hawaiian sun cutting bright lines through the open door into my cracker-box Waikiki apartment, the perfume of solvents in the air, white fiberglass dust all over the linoleum floor, a beheaded white shark of a sawed-off surfboard—

seeming to float suspended in the air before me, my bare sun-teak feet up on the plastic couch, the floppy V of the recently re-read paperback *Cuckoo's Nest* open on my swimsuited lap. "A roar of protest against middlebrow society's Rules and the invisible Rulers who enforce them," according to *Time*. "A glittering parable of good and evil," said *The New York Times*.

That much I got off the back jacket.

My new "big gun" surfer roommate Terry who, eight years older than me, resembled a muscle-bound young Woody Allen and whose occasionally combed explosion of reddish yellow hair suggested a head on fire, and who might flash any new cute girl he met a rectangular smile with the news, "I'm sexist, racist and rotten," was among a new legion of Kesey freaks in a world for whom soft core hobbits and Hesse had nothing on redneck nirvana or common cause with bull goose looneys who never gave an inch. Terry was at war with the inanimate world. A chair would, for some reason suddenly piss him off and he'd tear it apart. He considered Ken Kesey a sort of kick-ass Jesus, a Jesus whose Angels had names like Magoo and Terry the Tramp, a Jesus you could (if, say, Ken teleported Himself to the cinderblock and linoleum pleasuredome that was our apartment) "grok" with, a Jesus who said fuck, a Jesus who...

...Actually I could see Big Nurse's logic: Personally, a lobotomy might be just the ticket.

My new mantra: Lethal inhalants, use, not abuse. The Blondes were gone. Celestial Cindy gone. I'd found my new god, here in my new apartment house to revolutionize surfing. I needed a little platform, not a barge. And thanks to Terry's amputations, I was about to get one.

It sat before me, a sharkie little slab of styrofoam glistening with a still wet coat of fiberglass, perched between kitchen chairs in our cinder-block living room. Which now resembled, surfboardwise, Dr. Frankenstein's OR. Resin-splashed newspapers all over the floor, a fine snow of fiberglass dust covered our vinyl couch, and—between the kitchen chairs—an ever shrinking monster. A surfboard whose nose was a fresh white scar of exposed fiberglass.

Terry was a sometimes math teacher and, at twenty-seven, a surf and girl fanatic who'd wake before dawn and paddle out to greet the horizon on his "gun," a spear-like surfboard, and go tsunami hunting. Because his surfing prowess was limited to a straight line shot-from-a-water-cannon descent down the face of a monster breaker toward rocket speed nirvana or oblivion, he sought the biggest waves. A good morning was any morning he didn't drown.

Terry, like our next door neighbor Bill Cook, was a disciple of belly-boarder George Greenough, a surf cult guru who held that surfboards were, according to Terry, at least too long by a third. If you'd told this to most any great surfer of the day—as Terry informed Phil Edwards—that boards under seven feet long would soon rule, that great surfer would say, as Edwards—paddling beside Terry on a board as long as a coffin—said: *You're nuts.*

The product of Terry's insanity lay on the floor of our living room. Like most ambitious surgeons, he lived to cut. His board began life as a nearly ten-foot, dish-nosed behemoth "Wardy." But Terry had been whack, whack, whacking away. To perform his surgeries he used a hack saw, a two x four wrapped with #80 grit sandpaper, and many syrupy cans of resin.

My job, as Terry's Igor, was to "test" the shrinking Wardy. If I could ride it, anybody could. Usually, I'd get out of bed at dawn, brush my teeth, then go out to our lanai to select from my quiver of one: That pretty and unwieldy Hobie.

This morning, however, I picked up the chopped off Wardy, eased outside and down stairs. Country Joe and the Fish wafted across a potholed Paokalani street already warm from the sun.

"Oh, it's one, two, three, what are we fighting for?
Don't ask me, I don't give a damn.
Next stop is Vietnam."

We lived in a neighborhood known as the Jungle, a petting zoo of surfers behind the big tourist hotels and, hey—Who was that down the street by the Catholic Church, looking as if he had just grown up out of the sidewalk?

"And it's five, six, seven, open up the Pearly Gates…
Ain't know time to wonder why,
Whoopee, we're all gonna die!"

It was my surfer junkie pal Glen. Not too stoked this morning, it didn't look like. Glen was huddled up in a corner on the concrete. I asked, "What's happening?" and he told me he'd dropped a drug called STP, that helicopter blades were spinning above his head, and if he looked up they would shear his face off.

Trippy. I left Glen to his devils and walked down to the beach toward two familiar mokes. Samoans. Brothers. Not tall, but big. Brown and slope shouldered. Generous, friendly, violent young men. Happy to knock an inconvenient GI/freak/chalk-skinned tourist off his board, pick up that board and deliver, whack! whack! whack! nine from the sky. The brothers represented a subculture I was more at home with than the love generation: thugs. Good friends to have, considering that the biggest thing on me was my mouth. I was six three, but weighed only 150 pounds. Carrying a TV set.

One brother asked: "What da fok you do to yah board?"

The other said. "Bra, you amputate you board. Dumb guy, what went wrong?"

Absolutely nothing, and when it rains it pours, I had discovered beyond home-hacked midget surfboards a second set of keys to the kingdom: Frank Merlino. The best new best friend ever. God's own hippie. The New Man child: Psychedelic America's Favorite Son. Though we had grown up 1,200 miles apart, we were from the same tribe. We talked the same (a nasal drawl) and thought the same ('Fuck, dude, I dunno.'). Tall and slender, Frank could practically be me looking at myself in a mirror, people mistook us for brothers and as a lab rat for the evolutionary-revolutionary concept that was the Freak Freely Generation, Frank was a great guy and had it all. Freedom, drugs, money, and girls, girls, girls. He claimed to have fucked fifty women. How many had I fucked? Nine or ten I said, lying by seven or eight (humbled, I was tempted to make a truthful argument for quality over quantity, revealing, for example, that though my numerical experience was dwarfed pitifully by his I had, for example, already almost started a family).

He was sixteen, a skilled surfer from LA who had a deft, lazy style, and who for some reason no longer had to go to high school. He had eyes as big as those in a Keane painting, and looked like a rock star. We looked out for each other. Separately we were just two tall skinny kids, but together—Frank had a temper, had arms from surfing and wasn't afraid to shake it up.

Frank's nice, angry architect Dad designed all the Baskin Robbins franchises and carried a gun. Frank's girlfriend, Darlene, had been a Mouseketeer and was on The Dean Martin Summer Show, his older barroom bouncer brother Danny's blonde 37-23-35 wife Dee Dee Lynn was the most pneumatic Playboy bunny ever, inspiring "Little Annie Fanny." Frank's big mesmerizing eyes spoke the language of love: *Your thoughts matter.* He listened to these girls and, for that celestial favor, they became his. It quickly occurred to me that movie-star-handsome Frank could be an amoral hippie chick goldmine and, bonus, I soon discovered that he came equipped with superhero friends. As for the bad news…

* * *

Hitting the guy was no problem, I was hitting him plenty, nine from the sky, but the problem was it was like hitting a fire hydrant, my knuckles could have been hitting iron and meanwhile the beefy little stump was nailing me in the side of the head, over and over and over, each blow an explosion and, thank God, I was about to be saved by the power of mindblowing drugs.

I'd just returned to Honolulu from Oregon, where on the night before Christmas I'd gone to see three pals who for some reason I'd agreed to pick up by the railroad tracks in Beaverton. My headlights were illuminating: speed had clearly hit Raleigh Hills like a hurricane, ripped my pals crazy svelte, the three glowing in my headlights like 111. Somehow that number seemed to represent a message, and, anyway, while I was home running around with my pals Moon and Big G Little O, I got in a beef with some stump outside a bowling alley. I was used to this equation: What I hit hits the ground.

But not this time. I cracked this guy on the side of his head and I doubt he even blinked. Instead, he started using me for a scarecrow punching bag and I probably would've been dead right there had the bowling alley managers not come running out threatening to call the cops. The upshot. The grinning stump wanted me to meet him two days later in front of—of all places—the Beaverton movie theater to finish things up right there on the sidewalk.

So dead in two days.

Sunny Big G Little O drove me to the theater so that, instead of having to pay attention to stop lights and speed limits, I could sit in the passenger seat of his spotless mirror-blue 1965 Pontiac Lemans convertible and concentrate on how many teeth I was about to lose and how whatever was left of my nose would soon be flush with my face and, then, a miracle. At the Theater, no Stumpy. Just two of his friends I recognized from the bowling alley disaster. They had fantastic news. Stumpy had fried his brain on paint thinner and was, presto, a vegetable in a mental institution. Unbelievable. Boy, did the Catholic Jesus ever love me to engineer a *deus ex machina* like that!

Otherwise, life hadn't been going so hot. I'd failed German and Latin and couldn't get past "donde esta bano?" in Spanish but, worse, I had become the first white kid ever to fail the spoken English language test at the University of Hawaii. Still, I was nineteen, and, what with my action-packed family, Moon, the Blondes and Celestial Cindy, etc. under my belt, best-selling novels should've been flowing Stephen Crane-like, from my fingertips. I was a good typist. All I should need otherwise was an agent with cracked shoes and a beaver hat and…

Tall and tan and young and loony, having boiled English down to the existential yes and no-ness polarities of "fuck you" and "farout" under the transcendent umbrella of "gimme that," my schedule was like this : 8 am to noon, surf, 12:00 to 12:05, remember I was in college, 12:05 to 6:00PM with a pencil practice the drum solo to "Innagoddadavida," 6:00PM to 6:20PM, walk four blocks to the International Market Place and eat teriyaki Spam-on-a-stick while telling sun-fried tourist girls my entire life story. 6:20pm to 8am: fire up, dream the Impossible Dream, and then hit the coma zone. Repeat.

Copacetic. But with Frank along for the ride, life in paradise got a lot more interesting. Like a sixteen year old Robin Hood Frank came equipped with merry men, not only his big tough big brother Danny but burr-headed astronaut-like Jim Coverdale, the toughest guy in the world who, when he wasn't punching somebody's lights out (sometimes, bored, he'd let a guy thump on him for awhile before tearing the poor schmoe a new one) aspired to become, like me, a famous writer and, anyway, Frank soon had girls coming in and out of my apartment as if it were a sex Seven-Eleven. Sort of stressful, actually. On the mainland doctors were prescribing sedatives and stimulants at the rate of 150 million a year and here in the Jungle, Frank, to slow down, favored reds. Seconal. And to speed up, whites. Amphetamines. Good to know. But I worried something must be wrong with me, because reds just made me feel stupid, and whites, worse, just more like myself.

Meanwhile, over in Southeast Asia, things weren't going so hot. George Will and other conservative baby boomers have since dismissed the 1960s war protest as a hissy fit thrown by privileged longhairs too chicken to die for nothing in Vietnam. After all, American wars are essentially good wars fought—if occasionally by the wrong means—for the right reasons. Though from where I sat on the sand, it looked as if, somewhere over the curve of the Pacific horizon, the wheels were falling off. For on March 15, 1968—Lieutenant William Calley, a clueless newbie to mass murder, really fucked it up: finessed the gang rape and killing of at least 347 unarmed Vietnamese civilians, old men, women, children and babies within ear and camera shot of the press.

At the International Marketplace, Frank and Terry and I fell in with a couple of GIs in Honolulu on R&R who, with their shaved heads and Ozzie Nelson Sears Roebuck civvies, stood out like Ken Dolls in Eden. Their tales were not those of Sergeant Rock and the Combat Happy Joes of Easy

Company; the stories they told were of being scared to death all the time fighting for corrupt people who hated their guts.

Disturbing, given that my draft board was after me. And next, more signs and wonders. This could not be happening. Frank had dropped acid for the first time. We found ourselves in a house in the hills above Waikiki, Keane paintings everywhere—all those waifs with black pupils the size of bowling balls—it was like being in the Louvre of kitsch. Keane paintings were what the popular art was all about in 1968 and these were not fakes. What was up? Frank was about to lose his mind.

But not just yet, not in this house that was, acid magically, an art gallery of waifs with famous bowling ball eyes. Lady's man Frank had somehow fished from the hippie chick cosmos the daughter, younger sister or wife of the top pop artist of the psychedelic moment: Mr. Keane, and the insane fact of that, the unbelievable serendipity, made me suspect that acid had the power to hijack reality. Though it also occurred to me that losing your mind by taking a pill had a potential down side. Local mokes had, Hawaiian style, really taken to it. A big rumor flying around the Jungle was that one young Hawaiian couple had, in fact, taken so much acid during the woman's pregnancy that her baby was born with a finger growing from its forehead.

Out there on the sawed off Wardy, I screamed at a burrheaded GI on a rental board for dropping in on me and then got screamed at by a burly local for dropping in on him.

Then reality by Moke. For I'd done the dropping in on the freshly chopped down Wardy and, my, it was slick. Cut down three inches a day for over a week, it remained stable, as maneuverable as a tongue—I couldn't make it nose dive to save my life.

The brothers paddled over.

"You lookin' gooooood," one brother said.

"Lemme try that," another one said.

I shrugged, slipped off the Wardy. He climbed aboard. A big swell came rising and rolling in. He whipped the Wardy around, paddled, took off. As he slid down the crest, he hopped up, the board's wake splashing a roostertail above the wave…

…I knew I had it made about a week later when one of the brothers paddled beside me one early morning out at Queens and, as a nice big fat feathery curl came slouching shoreward beside us, invited me to help him rob a jewelry store. He'd even provide me a gun. "Will it be loaded?" I asked.

"Yeah, brah," he nodded, "jus in case sumthing go wrong."

"This is completely and totally lame. She knows shit I never taught her!" Frank, long dark hair falling like wings on either side of his tan handsome face, eyes hidden by the black lenses of his aviator glasses, was sky high on the top floor of a Honolulu parking garage where he had been reading between the lines of a love letter from his movie starlet girlfriend and getting a bad secret message. Since his first acid trip, things hadn't been going so hot.

We'd been at the Ala Moana Shopping and Shoplifting Center and now we were spiraling down from the roof of the parking garage, Frank at the wheel of the tin can Morris Minor mini-stationwagon we'd bought for $80, tires screaming, parked cars flying by and Frank, dressed in a baggy snow-bright T-shirt and baggy long surfer jams, shouting about how he could tell by the words in Darlene's letter that, back in Los Angeles, she was "screwing another guy."

Frank's evidence—aside from the confession written in invisible ink: he'd flown back to LA for the weekend and to repeat, as he was repeating now, "She did stuff I never taught her!"

Since his acid trip, he'd gone, and abruptly, from sleepy, casual, drawling confidence, to wild-eyed paranoia. Though weirdly—aside from the business about Darlene—he was more paranoid on my behalf than his. People, he confided, were plotting against me, not him.

To regain his sanity, Frank was eating reds—seconal—like these downers were M&Ms. And wouldn't it be easier, he wondered, if he cut out the bureaucracy of his stomach and simply shot the seconal straight into his veins instead?

Lightbulb: Frank's whole sense and pride of who he was was tied to his ability to fuck any attractive girl he met and not get fucked over in return. Oddly, it didn't strike me as a terribly selfish emotion, but could one tab of acid invert your whole world? The end was near. I went with Frank and Terry and a couple other guys to a party above the beach down by the Outrigger Canoe Club. Frank's burly brother Danny and Jim Coverdale had flown, broke, back to the mainland but I was late for the revolution: It skipped my mind that without the two of them as bookends, I had lost my free pass to a loud mouth.

At the party was a very pretty bronze-haired girl who'd just been crowned Miss Young Hawaii and who was extremely impressed how good I was at agreeing—after I nodded through her entire tale of woe—what jerks her parents were. Somebody had the stereo on a continuous "Innagoddadavida" loop, thumping drums and guitars and zombie vocals and awesome drum solo drowning most everything out but the look of love, like or lust in her 3-D eyes and I didn't hear the voices until somebody called the cops.

I went outside. It was night and at first all I could see was, under a street light, mokes pushing somebody—

—Frank. I said something like, "Wuzzup, dickheads?" and a moke grabbed me by the hair, threw me over the front of a car and and began smashing my head on the hood, a skull drum solo and I had just enough time to think: *I'm dead* before the guy went flying off me.

Frank had nailed him. Hit him on the side of the head so hard he was lost to the night and that's when the blue lights came flashing out of nowhere and bronze haired Miss Young Hawaii beckoned like a desperate angel: "Come on! Let's get out of here."

We ran, me thinking: what about Frank? The next morning we were still in bed in my apartment when Terry popped in, pissed. Frank had been thrown in jail last night, and why the hell hadn't I gone downtown to bail him out?

Terry shaped the smallest board ever. It had the heft of a Communion wafer and was like trying to surf on a pumpkin seed. I carried it more than I rode it. It afforded me a May Fly celebrity there on the beach, for in weeks short boards were everywhere, common as sand.

CHAPTER TWENTY-SEVEN: BURBANK BABYLON

"The cybernetic age entails a change in our frame of reference, man. The traditional spatio-temporal concepts are inadequate...The digital computer is easing us into the electronic/automotive age just as the steam age pivoted us into the industrial revolution. In those days it was gin. It flowed like water. Kids were suckled on it, societies campaigned against it. Now it's acid. LSD is for us what gin was for the Victorians. It lubricates our acceptance of the new age."

—Pete the Coyote, a Hell's Angel

Time to get real. Tim Leary's important advice: "When you turn on, remember, you are not a naughty boy getting high for kicks."

No, far from it. I was a boy trying to figure out how to get high for good. But there was more. "You are a spiritual voyager furthering the most ancient, noble quest of man." Tim, you know me so well. "You leave LBJ and Bob Hope; you join Lao-tse, Christ, Blake. Never underestimate the sacred meaning of the turn-on."

"To turn on, you need a sacrament. A sacrament is a visible external thing which turns the keys to the inner doors. Today the sacrament is LSD. New sacraments are coming along."

And then? "Quit school. Quit your job. Don't vote. Avoid all politics."

And then and then and then and then? "You must start your own religion. You are God—but only you can discover and nurture your divinity. No one can start your religion for you. Write down and define your:

Goals
Roles
Rituals

Rules
Vocabulary
Values
Space-time locales
Mythic context."

How in paisely hell had he read my mind? I read on. "You will find it absolutely necessary to leave the city. Urban living is spiritually suicidal. The cities of America are about to crumble as did Rome and Babylon... Grass will grow in Times Square in ten years. The great soil-murdering lethal skyscrapers will come down. Did you know they were stage sets? Didn't you know they had to come down? The transition will come either violently (by war) or gently, aesthetically, through a psychedelic drop-out process...Go to the land. Go to the sea...Turn on, tune in, drop out. Then you are free to walk out of the studio—a god in the Garden of Eden."

Which is more or less where I was, wasn't I? Barbecuing my throat, reading Leary's just published hymnal. *Had I not,* Tim wanted to know, *questions?* Sure I did. Like was LSD the fuse but not the blast? Was acid the answer or just a metaphysical ponzi-scheme that promised to deliver the undeliverable, a grim fairytale at a time when ozone-weight writers were dining in high style off the unlettered enthusiasm of young readers for whom literature was otherwise just the crap they had to read in high school? Except now with Carlos Castaneda in a crow suit, cawing, "Nevermore, gringo."

Eight miles high and falling fast. Trading up paradise for Gomorrah. Still tens of thousands of feet over the Pacific, five hours out of Honolulu the jet liner was sinking toward the amoebic sprawl of Los Angeles. As the Lizard King said not long after drinking his Orange County model girlfriend's blood, "The West is the best." California culture ruled the world, hammocked between the Beach Boys and psychedelia, Oswald and Owsley, the Kennedy assassination and acid when America really was California dreaming, beginning in glory and drowning in drugs, Californians living the Life when there really was one.

Bye-bye, Honolulu. Hello, Hollywood. Just before Manson, just after Sirhan Sirhan. I'd been in a Waikiki apartment with a really cute girl I'd known forever sitting on my lap in a bikini made of red string who suddenly announced she really liked me, when suddenly on TV, even more shocking news. Bobby Kennedy shot at the Ambassador Hotel.

Now the real new America. Kid culture. Surreality sculpted in steel. Kandy-kolored '32 Fords with motors as big as chrome doghouses. A '57 gasser Chevy standing cartoon-high above skinny spoked front wheels that looked custom-made for a midget's covered wagon. Surfer dudes with the baked teenage faces and flags of long yellow hair picking at French fries while leaning against slammed mirror black-nosed and decked '40 Fords and monster-motored bucket-Ts, painted as many colors as an oil slick. Toluca Lake, California. The heart of the height of hot rod culture.

Most of my nights of summer 1968 were spent sitting in the front seat of Frank Merlino's '57 panel wagon, his 283 V-8's incompetent mufflers burbling, jetting hot smog through their rustled baffles, the motor idling at Bob's Big Boy Drive-in Toluca Lake, Jim Morrison preaching to us over the radio:

"When I was back there in seminary school,
there was a person there
who put forth the proposition
that you can petition the lord with prayer,
petition the lord with prayer
You CAN NOT petition the Lord with prayer!"

while sixteen year-old Frank smoked a joint as if it were a Marlboro, and flirted with the teeny-bopper carhops.

Los Angeles seemed made for a West Coast generation that, in writer Charlie Haas's words, grew up under an incredible lack of oppression: the Promised Land. Extraterrestrial. The Pearly Gates writ in hookah smoke. At 19, I had died and gone to the next heaven, resurrected surf flotsam, New Jerusalem by way of yesterday's paradise. Getting off a plane from Hawaii, I saw LA for the first in the form of two new white Lincoln Continentals waiting for me, and my new girlfriend, Suzie, who had a dandelion poof of platinum pale hair, red bee-stung lips, and who called her mom Jeanie.

The two Lincolns were suave white barges of unreality, blatant reminders that LA was a blatant world. There was something going on, but I didn't know what it was, that made Jeanie instead of Mom not ridiculous. As Jeanie passed the smoking wand of a Kent filter to her daughter, I realized, poof for poof, bee sting for bee sting, Jeanie was pretty much Suzie, just more etched. Same hip-hugger bell bottoms, pot-smoker languid mannerisms and far-out mind. My emotional vocabulary did not include middle-aged teeny-bopper, but, hey, why not?

From the back seat of the Lincoln, I could see we were driving up a local Mt. Olympus. Hard blue sky above, a chrome bright sliver of Pacific Ocean through the smog below. Jeanie pulled into the Appian Way that was driveway to the most impressive home I'd ever seen. The Parthenon in Pacific Palisades for a Greek construction god. Doric columns as wide as tree trunks beside a massive front door. Inside, miles of marble floors.

I was introduced to Suzie's father. I cut, for Dad, quite a figure. Two plus yards of human coat-hanger wire, hair brushing my shoulders, wearing pretty much my entire wardrobe: a blue rag of a T-shirt and Levis stitched from laundry lint. Simion the Stylite with a worse haircut. From the look of horror that congealed around his wrinkled eyes as he shook my hand, for the first time since I got off the plane I saw something Norman Rockwell normal: A terrified father who loved his daughter and who looked under this meet-the-zombie circumstance, a million years old.

I was handed a goblet—Sprite, not hemlock. Suzie said she wanted to go see the mom of a friend. We drove to a ranch house of aircraft-carrier majesty. Suzie knocked on the front door. When nobody answered, she let us in. In the foyer was a life size oil painting of Bob Hope. But nobody else was home. Where were we? Phyllis Diller's.

I had left paradise for LA, bored. Water as clear as the air and as warm as blood, salt white sand, pretty girls who—gone native—would do *anything* (what happens under a palm tree in the middle of the night in Kapiolani Park stays under a palm tree in Kapiolani Park) even excellent fast-food violence thanks to a volatile mix of pissed off Hawaiians, druggie longhairs and GIs on desperate leave from Vietnam wasn't enough.

I wanted to trade paradise for the center of the new universe. Bobby Kennedy had just been murdered here, and Charlie, Tex Watson, Linda Kasabian and Squeaky Fromme had picked the City of Angels to stage the shock concert of the century. This was where it was coming down.

In short order, I got what I'd paid for.

I had flown from Waikiki with Frank. I got to meet Danny's Playmate wife Dee-Dee. Danny and I returned to the apartment where he had more or less abandoned her months before, and found Dee-Dee downstairs by the washers and dryers in cutoffs with beer can rollers in her yellow hair, no longer a sacred foldout, just another busty Yankee Farm girl with an armload of dirty shirts and sheets.

Big, muscle-bound, ox-like Danny said, "Dee Dee, say hi to Mark." She looked at me, all eyes and mouth, said, "Hi, Mark." Then Danny said, "Say bye, Mark, and she said, "Bye, Mark" and that was it. I couldn't figure why Danny would leave the nation's number one sex goddess, until I realized, *because he was bored.*

Danny, burly, post-adolescent sage, knew the secret of living here in heaven: *Never settle for the best.* What a life. Frank's other brother Bobby owned fourteen pairs of sunglasses with identical wire frames each with a different shaded lens, and was the promotion genius behind the hit song "MacArthur Park," which, along with the California National Anthem, "Good Vibrations," and "Riders on the Storm," wafted through the air everywhere that summer.

Stars, cars, bars and electric guitars here in the Hereafter. Plus enough drugs to OD Bedlam. Move over, Rover, and let Jimi take over. Hendrix had ripped the Organization Man a new one and the bikinied, body-painted, delicious nymph Goldie Hawn was available everywhere, on TV and in your dreams, hand-in-hand with the mini-skirted ghost of the near future: Sharon Tate. Ditzy land of undying fame. Angelic, beautiful street freaks. Manson family values.

Castles in the air, tacked to the sky, and plenty of fairy sawdust off the three ring circus floor. Auden's Great Wrong Place. A bitchen Old Testament city of the future. Fires, earthquakes, floods, all the rabbinical trimmings. Sam Goldwyn, David O. Selznick and Phil Spector wouldn't have it any other way. Acid noir, the gilded tie-dyed yo-yo farm, a petting zoo of too-rich, too-famous and too stupid to be.

Puffing on zonk tubes—empty toilet paper rolls that had crackly, fire-tipped joints stuck in the ends—barely obeying even the law of gravity, drinking wine to the tune of "Alice's Restaurant," Frank and I would drive down Sunset Boulevard—no longer Raymond Chandler's property but Frank Zappa's. We'd hang out at the glitz Gomorrah that was "Pandora's

Box," rapt to the howitzer concussive guitars and machine gun drums of Canned Heat, then go to a Warner Brothers Records warehouse to throw around record albums from man-high stacks as if they were frisbees.

Maybe, I should've paid more attention to the lyrics, Bob Dylan had already faded into his own parade wandering ancient empty streets too dead to dream, and, fuuuuuck. Frank was a great friend. As I may have mentioned: when he became a paranoid schizophrenic he thought people were out to get *me,* not him, but then he started shooting Seconal and we spent hours at night sitting in his hotrod Chevy surf wagon listening to Jim Morrison croon, "The End," watching his girlfriend's house for other guys to show up. They never did, but Frank took one of his father's guns and blew his brains out anyway.

Apocalypse then. Frank is buried at Forest Lawn. Pallbearers Danny and I, crying and joking, nearly dropped the front of the coffin. No longer immortal, all I knew was: try to keep funerals a spectator sport, for the secret to life is that it ends.

Part Four:
Sheep, The Sequel

William Burroughs (left) and Marty Christensen outside the Kesey Barn,
June 5th, 1976

Chapter Twenty-eight: Working on My Fantasy

"The escalation of the war so completely dovetails with the introduction of psychedelics that it becomes analytically impossible to separate them. Larger and larger amounts of people were having the experience of a different reality, of a different sense of human possibilities. Whether in a political or metaphysical sense. LSD was loaded with a sense of opposition, risk, departure from ordinariness—it was really 'Break on Through to the other Side,' and for many it took a political form."

—Todd Gitlin

Meanwhile, back at the ranch. Jeannie Whitman, whose family gave their name to Whitman College in Washington State, and who had grown up as a Pendleton, Oregon blueblood—which in Pendleton meant no linoleum floors in the living room—was living 300 miles south on Kesey's 80 acres. She got there by way of the Grateful Dead's No. 1 roadie: "I met Ramrod (Larry Shirtliff) when I was 14. He just got out of reform school (MacClaren)—out of Hermiston. He was the local bad boy, and a year ahead of me in high school. He got a call from Johnny Hagen—and somehow went down and met Kesey. Ramrod ended up in Mexico with Kesey—in Manzanillo he and Kesey got busted. Ramrod ended up doing some time. Kesey had a joint on him or something. Kesey ran away—Ramrod took the blame and went to jail—he was only about 19.

"The first time I met Kesey," she says, "was when they were first back from Mexico in 1966 or 7. Ramrod picked me up in Eugene, we went to Boyd Harris's house in Portland. They had a tank of nitrous there. Chuck was there, Boyd (Harris), Kesey and Mike and Johnny Hagen. I hadn't smoked dope, taken acid or much of anything—Pendleton is a beer-drinking town.

"Anyway, I got on the tank of gas with Kesey and like—flash—he looked up at me and said, 'Gas Girl!' And that name stuck forever. But that was the first time I'd met him and I'd not read his books. He was just some asshole as far as I knew—a guy with a huge ego and it was like: Who is he playing, God? Everybody is kow-towing. We butted heads from the beginning—I could never get over my feeling of: Who died and appointed you God? We came to love each other but I could never get over the ego."

Nevertheless, the two formed a bond. "I was on the farm when Kesey was in jail and I was there after he served his time. It was very rough. Kesey and Faye were living in the little pump house (no longer there). All the rest of the crazies were scattered around trying to make nests for themselves. The Space Heater house is what Ramrod and I fixed up for ourselves. It was just a little room with carpeting on the wall.

"There were 15 to 20 people living there, Hagen was there, he had his mail truck parked outside. I was into cooking, so they liked me. I had dough, I liked to cook and I cleaned up after myself, so it was heaven. I remember staying at Chuck and Sue's, who became like my aunt and uncle, that first Christmas. Everybody would come over to watch *Star Trek*—there was like nothing at the farm, there was running water, that's all. The bathtub was a cheese vat that came from the creamery, something they used to make cottage cheese. We were sitting around, they would pass a joint, I'd take a puff, peer pressure. There's a knock on the door. It's the state police, and I hear a voice: 'Is Jeannie Whitman here?'

'Well, your mother wants you to come home.'

"I wasn't even eighteen."

Those were the days. "The Summer of Sergeant Pepper, the Summer of Love," she says, "suddenly people on the road, all these loser people, suddenly it's all free and all I have to do is show up and they'll give me the dope and a place to sleep. At first Ken and Faye tried to be open—but soon we'd be serving dinner to 30 or 40 people. Sometimes 50. Chuck and Sue had cows and would have cows butchered and they had a freezer full of frozen meat and Ken liked my cooking because I could make a roast go a long way with gravy or whatever. He did not like brown rice and vegetables."

There were, here on the farm, some entertaining mouths to feed, however. Jeannie said, "I was in awe of Paul Krassner, he was so smart, funny and twisted. I had the complete opposite feeling as I had with Kesey. I fell in love with him immediately." She loved Allen Ginsberg too. "We had Owsley, Blue Tabs, White Lightning, Mysine."

"I was around when Fred (Kesey's father) was still alive. He instilled competition in those two boys. He liked to see them compete against each other. Survival of the fittest."

Sara H., who was also living on the Farm at that time, recalled: "I got angry about a couple of things—when you get people high you are karmicly responsible in the big picture…my point where I got pissed off was that you don't have the right to play God and you can't go around arbitrarily drugging people up because you're responsible for their consciousness. The drugs become more powerful than the consciousness. Ken could go back to the farm and there was no place to go for those other people in San Francisco—Georgia and I could go back to the mountains. But the people who got stuck in the city with no way to get away, some of those people never fuckin' came back.

"Owsley was around making the best acid on the planet…Oh my god, I hated him. I'll tell you a great Owsley story. Owsley had this house it was up in the hills and he had a pet owl. I don't know how I got up there, God only knows, but there were alchemical symbols above the fireplace and stuff and I got stuck up there—by having to go some place and pick something up and blah, blah, blah and so I'm in the bathroom and Owsley had this little owl—it was Owsley's pet and Owlsey's owl came in the bathroom with me and I'm like oh my God I'm stuck up here and Owlsey's in the house and he was nasty and—he wasn't nasty, he was just Owsley and I wouldn't trust him any farther than I could throw him, I'll put it like that. He was everywhere. And his acid. It was everywhere and the purity level was really high. This was my experience, Owsley had this girlfriend Melissa who was the sweetest person on the planet and, you know, I had three really good acid trips up in the mountains in Colorado. I also got dosed on stage in San Francisco. I was freaked out. I remember being on stage with the Airplane and the Moody Blues in LA and we were throwing acid out to the audience. But I wasn't very good around a lot of people, not a happy camper, I had a very bad trip and I didn't know where to go. Veronica, Pigpen's girlfriend comforted me, and then I said, 'Patty Cake, I have to go home,' I wanted to go back to the ranch. So Johnny Hagen, Mike Hagen's brother, drove us back to Novato—Johnny was a road guy from Pendleton and he drove like a bat out of hell and he scared the shit out of me and I was like glued to the door going God, get me home and Patty Cake was going shhhhhhh because if you exasperated Johnny Hagen he would drive faster. I love Johnny Hagen but that's just who he was, one of the guys, so I got home and then, ohhhhhhhhhhhh I went back to Colorado with Georgia and Laval, who was a big black drug dealer who dosed a bunch of people up at the farm with STP and we were just walking around for four days and, oh God, Kesey was so pissed and Laval he was just nasty. Bad, bad, bad news. STP is like acid except without the fun. Like a bad dream not a good dream, three days of being high, it wore you out, there was no light at the end of the tunnel."

"This was '69," Sara said, "And Frankie was there and we just walked around going what the hell? It was terrible, terrible, terrible and then Georgia and I went back to Colorado and Laval came there and he dosed me, and I was like working as this little cocktail waitress in Aspen and we were just like *girls*. I had more fun being around the Dead but not being on acid."

Psychedelic England, 1969. Ken Kesey had his wife, kids and Cadillac all there. The two Bobbies, Miller and Sky, "brothers by different mothers," met Kesey at Apple. Arthur Miller's son Bobby was 21, a production assistant who'd just completed "winter exteriors" on *Midnight Cowboy*. Filmmaker Bobby Sky was, according to Bobby Miller "fearless, he could get anybody on the phone, talk anybody into anything." Sky had set off to set up an office next to Ridley Scott's in London, where Miller met Kesey. Who was working for—or at least getting paid by—the Beatles. The next year Miller was bouncing around the country, going to LA a lot with Sky to chase film projects, then found himself invited to fly up to Kesey's farm. Where he was met at the Eugene Airport by Pranksters in the bus and "that was the beginning of the gypsies stealing us from what we thought was regular life."

Which for Bobby Miller was growing up with Marilyn Monroe as his stepmother and having a father whose plays, "Death of a Salesman," "The Crucible" and "A View from the Bridge" had become North Stars of American theater, constellated on high school curricula before they'd concluded their stellar runs on Broadway. These were plays that had defined the American 1950s, just as Kesey *Cuckoo's Nest* had precipitated the 60s.

Bobby moved from the east coast to Oregon in 1970 with his first wife after they'd lost a baby. Not a good time, but Bobby had talked to Kesey, who said, "Why don't you just come out here and hang for awhile?" So Miller and his wife drove out and stayed in the Space Heater house where Sky and "Tangerine" were living. Miller and his wife stayed there for five or six months, then bought a house in Eugene. They had another child, and Miller did a lot of work outdoors. "I got the tractor running, got the haying going, it was a good summer for me."

Viking published both Arthur Miller and Kesey, and Bobby sent Ken Kesey's *Garage Sale* manuscript to an editor there, including Kesey's big and self-lacerating screenplay, "Over the Border"—the "story of the 60s" that told the story of Ken's run from the law in 1965. "Viking looked at *Garage Sale,* and it was like 'What the hell do we do with this?' I thought "Over the Border" was really good, though you'd have to cut 25-30%. Kesey may have asked me, 'Do you think your father might want to write an introduction?"

Bobby's father had previously come to Oregon with his third wife, Magnum photographer Inge Morath. Now, a second trip. After a trek through the stone-walled Columbia Gorge, the trees of Sisters, the sands of Tillamook, post-McCarthy Broadway realpolitik met freak freely theater over "a great dinner" at Kesey's where "everybody was on their best behavior," and a torch of sorts was passed from Miller, the Conscience of the 1950s, to the Kesey Consciousness of the 60s.

Today Bobby Miller, tall and thin and in jeans and a long-sleeved western shirt more cowboy than hippie, lives in Laguna Beach with his wife Jeanie in a sprawling house perched on the side of steep hills that open toward the ocean. "My father," he says, "didn't get the sixties at all."

Jeanie Miller, sitting in the kitchen, says, "When he was asked to write about the revolution of the 60s, he said there was no revolution."

"I think it hurt him in some ways," Bobby says, "he was very political, an activist and thought he'd lost touch with that audience. To my father the 'revolution' was just a lot of goofing around, abdicating responsibility…responsibility was what he thought was most required. For my father, writing and work were the same, and work was life. If you couldn't work you might as well be dead. By seven o'clock in the morning he'd be up and showered, go down and have his eggs or cereal and by 8:45 he'd be in his studio and wouldn't come down at least until noon and if he was on to something, you wouldn't see him until much later. Five, six, seven days a week. Sometimes I'd go up there and he'd be reading or listening to music, but he'd be in that seat every morning. If he wanted to do something else he'd do it, but if he was on to something you couldn't get him out of there if there was an earthquake."

I asked, "Did you feel the force of his celebrity?"

"Being married to Marilyn, how could you not?"

"Was his celebrity good or bad?"

Bobby said, "A lot of good and not so good. A lot of the not so good was his limitations as a dad."

"Like?"

"That he could keep his own hours bothered me. If you can do as you please, why don't you spend more time with us?"

I asked Bobby if he knew why Kesey had given up on writing novels. Bobby leaned forward in his chair. Through the window, I could see a hawk tip across blue sky. "Kesey felt that writing no longer spoke to the audience he wanted to reach. He'd be writing for the old folks and they already had enough writers. Wallace Stegner writes for them, Norman Mailer writes for them. He was trying to speak to his followers, and writing wasn't going to do it."

So, by the time Bobby and the other young movie people arrived at the farm…All the king's horses and all the king's men couldn't put the Movie together…"This suited Ken's fantasies," Bobby said. "Great, we now had sound equipment, and people who knew how to use it. As opposed to the Pranksters who had squandered this opportunity—and part of the fantasy was to go through the Prankster footage and see if we could make something out of it—it was a convergence of symbiotic interests, needs and talent, for Ken to start fantasizing."

It didn't happen. "If somebody started a narrative outline, created a dramatic through-line, they could have used voice-over narration, even animation, but it was too much work, nobody had the patience for it—that's really what it came down to. If somebody had said, 'Here's the script, here's where we'll start, we'll wander through here, flashback there—but the Movie was all the past, we were in what we were doing now—writing our own kind of stories. We all treasured it, thought there was something great there—but we wanted to do today what we wanted to do today. It would have been a huge effort, taken a lot of money, a lot of time and anything that took much longer than it took to smoke a joint didn't seem to happen. Who wanted to sit in a little room with a bunch of editing equipment when you could be on a bunch of inner tubes floating down the river?"

I asked Bobby again whether he and Kesey ever discussed his writing, or lack thereof. Bobby replied, "Kesey said, 'The time I spend writing is no fun for me, it takes me away from the things I'd rather be doing, it's a waste of my time. When I get this down you'll see what I mean.' He thought he was going to take his act out on the road, do a road show, like Buffalo Bill. I said, 'If that's what gets you off the way that writing and drugs used to, that's what you should do.'"

Jeannie said, "He said when you're writing you're never in the present. 'I just want to be in the present.'"

Kesey had the history of hippie-dom in his genes—if acid could not take us to heaven why not return to till earth? The farm, the rural Holy Land. We would have to come down out of the clouds. Acid was being evicted by the rural ideal. Dirt was where the action was. Kesey's heaven was now a heaven on earth which, if me and mine went along for the descending ride, would likely leave me on my dad's farm knee-deep in my Edenic pig sty feeding ancient celery and tomatoes to my enlightened holistic pigs.

Before decamping for Woodstock, about 60 hippies living on Kesey's farmland left a memento—a lit candle next to a dry pile of hay. Ken later recalled that a firestorm was not something he wanted to bring down upon his wife and kids; so he tacked a sign at the foot of his driveway that simply read "NO."

After he got out of jail in 1969, commune pioneer Kesey got out of the commune business, evicting everyone from his farm. "I don't want to knock communes or anything. They're just not for me. I just don't think much serious thinking gets done when there are a lot of people around. When you live in a commune you can't have your friends over because they're already there."

"Rednecks" had burned a cross in his lawn and shot up one of the out-buildings. In February 1970, and while still on probation, Kesey reflected, "The revolution, I think, is America trying to break away from those forces—getting too much, trying to stash more than one person's share, trying to rule things, trying to keep stashes safe from all those guys who don't have quite enough."

"It's a simple thing that doesn't have anything to do with hippies or squares," Kesey continued, "Take the school nurse. She comes out here and tells us Jed isn't doing too well in school because she thinks he might have worms, because there was someone out here she knew who had them last year. We took him to the doctor, he didn't have worms, but we went ahead and got him some stuff for his cold. It was nervous (sic) for her to come out here. And I was trying my best to be nice to her because I realized that she had me. If there was any competition going on she was gooder (sic) than me that day because I was just laying around. She was out there doing her business trying to make kids healthy. If there is a revolution going on, that day she was a whole lot more revolutionary than I was."

On a soiree south, Kesey continued to confront the powers that be. Though those powers were a-changing. Try this on for size: "The quest for the Apocalyptic Fusion will find optimal conditions only in a Classless Society, the absence of classes being the sine qua non for the existence of a Unitary Society in which the Unitary Sexual Image can be achieved," a brave new world in which hubba-hubba could not begin to describe the liberated white woman's attraction to Panther-style black men. The sex Rx? "What wets the Ultrafeminine's juice is that she is allured and tortured by the secret, intuitive knowledge that he, her psychic bridegroom, can blaze through the wall of her ice, plumb her psychic depths, test the oil of her soul, melt the iceberg of her brain, touch her inner sanctum, detonate the bomb of her orgasm, and bring her sweet release." This from Black Panther Minister of Defense Eldridge Cleaver's bestseller, *Soul on Ice*.

Outlaw literary lion meet outlaw literary lionnette. Petite Jean Genet, homosexual outlaw son of a whore who had been saved from a life of prison and chance restroom encounters by art, fairly shouted the love that dared not speak its name. So for the author of *The Thief's*

Journal, perhaps the Black Panthers represented a gay erotic ideal. In a 1960s America where prejudice was considered often more logical than outrageous, the Black Panthers often had the instincts less of civil rights heroes than savvy criminal businessmen who leveraged their portfolios to retail politics when the market demanded it. Ask Stokely, Huey and H. Rap—revolution moved fast off the shelf.

Of the Panthers, Ken Kesey told his pal Ed McClanahan, "It's a cop trip, and it's a big mistake. They shouldn't be trying to out-asshole the assholes, they should try to be the good guys." So time for an object lesson. A great thing about Kesey, was his Joker's ability to expose petty and important boob authority and pretense and then fuck with it. In Tom Wolfe's book *Radical Chic,* Wolfe reveals the elite pretensions of the New York literati as they served canapés to the Panthers. Kesey upped Wolfe's ante—screw observation, he got involved.

First, a suit of lights. On his way to meet the Black Panthers, Kesey was dressed for excess in Ed's favorite shirt. "But this is not a commonplace shirt," Ed wrote, "this is my Frisco Fag-store Bebop Buccaneer Blouse, my Polk Street Sike-O-Deelic Swashbuckler. The silky, silvery one with the shiny blue paisley and the mother-of-pearl buttons big as quahogs and the huge, billowy sleeves and the tight three-button cuffs and the cantilever collar and the gullet to sternum décolletage, my Saturday-night-at-the-Fillmore shirt."

But that was not all. Keze—north and south dressed to the nines, tens or elevens in, as Ed described, "his neon red and white striped hip-hugger bells and his bugeye blue reflector shades and his American flag front tooth and his new twelve-tone hand-painted day-glo sneakers."

Kesey was off to mediate a meeting of the tribes—America's suppressed black masses as represented by the revolutionary Black Panthers, and Western Intellectual Thought as represented by Jean Genet, whom history, or at least the internet, shows had, the night before partied a little too hardy and ended up dancing in front of the Panthers in a negligee.

Kesey walked to the meeting of the minds soiree—a room full of drab professors and Panthers dressed in no-nonsense anti-bourgeois combat chic—even Genet was afforded a Black Panther black leather jacket, though he was so small he had to be specially fitted to a boy's size twelve—and Kesey was as vivid as the sun. Announced as the "famous

Ken Keee-Zee" he quickly ingratiated himself to the crowd by observing, "Fame is a wart."

Radical times. "If it takes a bloodbath to silence the demonstrators, let's get it over with," Ronald Reagan said April 7, 1970, "No more appeasement." Ed McClanahan, noted that "It is a judgment of history and the considered opinion of the Black Panther Party that this country ought to take a good blood bath every so often, whether it needs it or not," and quotes Black Panther David Hilliard—with a bemused Kesey looking on—telling the professors, "You have to pick up guns and you have to move against the criminals, against the disturbers of the peace, against the lawbreakers! And that! Is your *judges,* your pol-lice *officers,* and your other *symbols* of the *state!*"

Aghast, a professor shouted, "Wait a moment!" and it was at that moment that neon Kesey stepped forward to continue his parable about "the spades" on his brother Chuck's basketball team. "Now my brother has a creamery up here in Springfield, and there's a basketball team, and the team is made up of my friends and my brother and people I know well, and…"

His call to race war bizarrely one-upped by this huge day-glo honkie hallucination, Hilliard, shouted, "Order! Order!" but Kesey continued, "So these two spades from up there, these two Negroes up there that I knew well, they were…"

"Get out of here!" Hilliard shrieked, "We didn't come here to talk crazy, we came here to talk about…"

"I think," Kesey concluded, "they were looking for a bunch of zombies. And some of us just don't qualify."

A more innocent time in which the gods and goddesses were seen through the mist on the barnyard Olympus. Michael Goodwin wrote of Faye Kesey in Rolling Stone: "Her image is water gushing forth from the earth, its steady flow filling up the deep places blocking its progress." Today, not even Angelina Jolie or Laura Bush gets that kind of press. And her hubby? "His voice is soft and gentle, but it grows out of an inner strength—invisible in times of peace, but always ready for use as a source of power. Kesey's image, like Faye's, is water flowing on and on. Water doesn't shrink from any dangerous spot or from any plunge, and nothing can make it lose its essential nature."

So what of the Movie? "What comes to mind," Kesey reported,

"is when Hagen was working on the bus a long time ago, doing a lot of speed, doing a lot of grass, doing a lot of thinking and rushing around, trying to turn something out of all these hundreds of hours and millions of feet of jiggly bus footage. He used to take a break by curling up on the floor in a corner with his eyes squeezed shut, obviously too wired to sleep. When anybody asked what he was doing, without opening an eye: 'I'm working on my fantasy.'

"And just a few months ago," Kesey continued, "a decade and a half after Hagen used to lie down and curl up, I found myself at the Koasthaus (the Kesey family vacation home), working on the film, the same film, the most famous film yet never completed. 15 years in the process, the great bus movie. *Further.* I had been at the coast for days working on it, hours and hours on end, looking at 15 year-old images of myself and my friends' selves, and trying to make the 16 mag tape match up with the 16 mm film on the editing machine, stuff shot and recorded 15 years ago, high, at a time at a time when we didn't know what edge numbers were, or synch marks, or the difference between speeds on the camera and speeds on a tape recorder…Moving back and forward, the images rushing in fast forward, then stopping, slowing, then rushing backward and fast backwards, the sound rattling and trickling and jibbering trying to find the lips. After hours and days I gave up and went in and lay down on the pool table, with my mind spinning, head on a pillow, in the old Hagen position, working on my fantasy."

CHAPTER TWENTY-NINE:
THE REVOLUTION HAS HAPPENED

"Kirk," Kesey wrote Kirk Douglas, "what's happening with Cuckoo's Nest? The reason I ask is because I was regailed (sic) by the rumor that you were bowing out and letting your kid star in it."

—Ken Kesey in letter to Kirk Douglas

One Flew Over the Cuckoo's Nest first left the page by way of Dale Wasserman's play, on which Kesey collaborated: "I was supposed to have deep intellectual discussions with Kesey," Wasserman recalled, "But we never got around to it. We talked about lumberjacking or about jails we had in common."

Kesey was wowed by Wasserman's production: "Beautiful. Outasight. I'm amazed. It takes over where I left off," just a little less wowed by the Broadway production. Though, given that Kirk Douglas, who starred in the play, expressed his enthusiasms in red, white and blue. "Good or bad, all aspects of this one are American. I'm getting sick and tired of everything that comes over from Europe being hailed as great. It's giving me a complex."

The prospects for a movie version of *Cuckoo* seemed to Kesey excellent. Douglas had called *Cuckoo* "the most strenuous role I've tackled—it requires a different set of muscles from the screen," and Kesey, eager to prime the movie pump, had encouraged Douglas to drive up to San Francisco to see what he called an "amazing" new stage production of *Cuckoo's Nest:* "They've not only gone back to the book, making a lot of changes in the Wasserman script, but they've gone beyond the book, bringing a lot of the colored aide talk up to date, making Billy Bibbit a hippie." After which Kesey concluded, "I'm fat and fine and the morning glories are in bloom before me. I been writing pretty steady and sticking to my vow not to ever show the stuff to anyone. It feels nice to whiz around inside of fiction again without my miserable name anchoring me with the importance.

"My oldest boy and I drove forty miles the other night. Couldn't find the correct place in the dark, back and forth and up and down the road until the car cut out suddenly and we coasted into this drive, slept on the ground, got up at dawn and waded into the river and caught thirty trout by noon."

Still, Kirk Douglas had his own fish to fry. Threads of *Cuckoo's Nest* rights were tied up in litigation with playwright Dale Wasserman, and earlier he had written Kesey: "I have had to go through two crappy arbitration procedures which took a couple of years. The second one ended only a few months ago. I want to make a movie out of your book—a good movie. Tried to do it as a play and I gave it a lot of time and effort. I know the mistakes I made doing it as a play, but the biggest was in timing. We were too far ahead. I think the timing is right now and I'm ready to go."

Or not. In a letter dated September 25, 1970, Douglas's producer, Mark Rubin, wrote Douglas, acknowledging Douglas's "okay" to "unload *Cuckoo's Nest*, or at least explore these avenues. Don't you think you might be throwing up your hands in a moment of uncertainty? Someone is going to make either one of the worst or one of the best films out of this first-rate material" as a "metaphoric microcosm of what goes on in the real world."

Two months later Douglas, who visited Kesey in Springfield, (and was impressed to be reminded that both had been "undefeated wresters in college") had decided to stick with the project. He'd received another letter from one of his producers, Norman Kurland who had met with Kesey and screenwriter and novelist William Peter Blatty, author of *The Exorcist*, and had been impressed with Kesey. "What must be done, he feels, is to involve the audience in the experience to a much greater extent than they have ever been involved before. His ideas...include shutting the back doors of the theatre with a loud sound and turning off the exit signs when the audience sits down, puffing actual foggy gas into the room at the time the fog actually begins to permeate the Chief's mind, and having the lights come on for several minutes while the voice of the big nurse tells the audience to sit quietly while the film is being spliced together."

Kesey told Kurland, "from his experience in an asylum, the most terrifying sight are the attendants going through the wards with Vaseline-dripping rectal thermometers, trying to 'spear' geriatric patients."

"Personally" Kurland found no "visualization that would be more empathic to the audience that would make them squirm with the remembered discomfort of rectal thermometers, and that would drive home the helplessness of the inmates.

"…Ken thought of telling the entire story from (the Chief's) viewpoint, even going so far as to use him as the camera," Kurland wrote Douglas. "What Ken is looking for is a barrage of sense-messages that will build the world of horror in the minds of the audience."

Kesey bemoaned the fact that once you are granted the skill, you simply poop out your novels the way Walter Keane pooped out his paintings. That nothing new had been written for 100s of years because of "the trap of syntax." Though he had recently been involved, at least peripherally, in script talks for "The Lenny Bruce Story" and had developed a skepticism for "Hollywood talk versus Hollywood action," a movie of his most popular novel represented a more attractive option than trying to write another one. "The thing about writing is that writers never seem to get any better than their first book. This bothers me. This bothers me a lot. You look back and their last work is no better than their first. I feel an obligation to improve, and I worry that I won't.

"I talked with Norman Mailer about it, I talked with Arthur Miller, and they agreed, they worry about it too. I've got a lot of writing to do. I wrote about fear in *Cuckoo's Nest,* and despair in *'Notion.'*

"The jail novel is about anger. There are two more I want to write. One about vanity and then one about attachment. But I wonder to myself is *Cuckoo's Nest* the best I'll ever be?"[22]

Meanwhile…"I'm not through with my work on acid, and nobody I know is either."

---

22   Kesey may have been by now more comfortable with the paragraph than the page, but he could still toss off great lines like confetti. Of a favorite Nevada bar: "Something of the rusted mining machinery lying baffled in the desert sun, of the wind rattling the bored sage and the sky so blue it might have been mined from the very mountain it covers like an armor plate, some secret alloy dust of Nevada's bleak motive that is tracked into the big drafty clutter of the saloon and sifted into the very beer."

The year was 1971, and by Kesey's lights, it was all over but the doubting. "The revolution has happened. Now we are all hanging out waiting for its maturity." Youth, he claimed had discovered God and formed an ethic, "available to anyone." So that "you can walk into a room and put pressure on its occupants without uttering a word."

Cosmic. "If you're not connected to the yearly protein resurrection, the calves being born, the plants pushing up after their long winter, you have a hard time having any real hope for anything. I watched my cows staring at a newborn calf, and I felt I knew what it meant to them.

"I saw it in their eyes, that it was proof of renewal, that it was going to get sunny again. I'll stay on this piece of land as long as I can, when I work out there I know the land is what it's all based on."

But these were perilous if not apocalyptic times. "I was down at Stanford for a reading, and I was sitting around talking with a bunch of guys about the way things are going, the food supply, population explosion, pollution and so on.

"Now these are the guys who can save us, the cream of the crop, smarter than I ever dreamed of being. One of them is one of these big, tall, gangly guys, you know, with his glasses taped together in the middle. He's kind of hanging there in the door listening to us.

"I knew he had a bombshell. I could see he was just waiting for his chance. So I looked over and he says, 'You know, in 20 years 91% of Africa and 84% of India will be dead. It's simple arithmetic. There's no way around it.'

"Nobody said anything, just sat there. I said, 'Wait a second, don't you guys realize the future is open, that we can do anything we want if we just put our minds to it.' They all just shook their heads. All that incredible education is teaching them there is no way out."

In 1970 Paul Krassner got a call from Stewart Brand saying he planned to publish *The Last Supplement to the Whole Earth Catalogue,* which Kesey had promised to edit if Brand could enlist Krassner as co-editor. "I moved to San Francisco in February 1971," Paul Krassner later recalled, "Stewart picked me up at the airport, and we drove directly to Palo Alto where Kesey was staying. Working with Kesey would serve as my decompression chamber from New York. I had been living in a loft where, when it was 15 degrees outside, it was 15 degrees inside. I learned to type while wearing gloves. I also learned how to trip on acid during rush hour in the subway—marveling at the moving footprints of everyone who had ever stepped onto a train in that station—but I had forgotten how to breathe. I read that breathing the air in New York was the involuntary equivalent of smoking two packs of cigarettes a day, and I walked around the city constricting my lungs as if I were right behind a farting bus."

Before he flew out from New York to SF, Krassner received a note from a reader with a card enclosed from a doctor exclaiming the virtues of a most remarkable muscle, the anal sphincter. Krassner put the card in his pocket, and, after Brand picked him up at the airport, the two drove to where Kesey was staying in Palo Alto. Kesey was sitting out in the back yard in front of an electric typewriter which was powered by an extension cord plugged into an extension cord plugged into the outside wall of the house. His parrot was squawking up in a nearby tree and a typewriter key had just stuck so that at the moment Brand's car approached the front of the house, Kesey had written "Kkkkkkkkkkkkkkkkkkrassner is coming," and when Krassner approached Kesey looked up and said, "Hey Krassner, I was just sitting here thinking about the anal sphincter," and Paul, astounded, reached into his pocket, took out that card with the doctor's little treatise about the anal sphincter. Handed it to Kesey, and said, "My Card."

It was a magic moment. Krassner recalls, "My religion has been a mixture of humor and coincidence—It was at that moment the line between coincidence and mysticism began to blur..."

CHAPTER THIRTY:
THE DREAM MUSEUM

"This book and the mindset it speaks for posit a destiny of utter truthfulness, by letting it all hang out by means of drugs, prayer, or whatever, the flood of impulses merge into a morally undifferientiated receptivity to life, tropism pure. As though evil were merely a fear of what we have within. And so it is that Manson becomes an ambiguous villain, for he went the whole way, and if repression is the only enemy then Charley was incarnate liberation. And not merely because he killed or psyched out his little witch band to kill, but because the dead were people he did not know and had nothing against personally..."
—from Arthur Miller's introduction to *Ken Kesey's Garage Sale*

Poor Mexico, as the old saw went: so close to the United States, so far from God. Fall 1969. Exciting times here in Mexico City, where the Revolution had one year before arrived with a bang. The mock democracy that was Mexico was Nixon's Amerika times ten. Better repressed, better censored, better cheated of basic rights, Mexican students were far better able to deliver upon themselves the kind of apocalypse upon themselves that the would-be martyrs of the SDS back home could only have dreamt about.

By way of the Tlatelolco Massacre October 2, 1968 when up to 5,000 Mexican troops and riot police supported by 200 tanks surrounded approximately 10,000 student protesters gathered in the Plaza de las Tres Culturas and opened fire, killing as many as three hundred. I met a girl who claimed to have been trapped in the bell tower at the University of Mexico and had her ears clanged deaf when revolutionary students rang the huge bells—bells as big as cars—over and over and over for twelve hours straight, and here on the home front a year later my roommate Sally E. said that at the ranch house or whatever it was, with my handsome pal

Jeff tied up outside, "When they asked: do you sleep with your boyfriend, I knew it was all over."

Dopeland. The seven Mexican "freaks" who raped Sally in Acapulco were rich, like the rich Mexicans at the University of the Americas, Mexican hippie mutants known as "Spirals," (named for the school notebooks they all carried as part of their disguise) who weren't students but sexual predators who cruised the little campus looking for American girls too dumb to know any better.

No problem. The student body was a freak-freely hallucination to populate a library of Robert Stone novels. Lost souls by the 707 load, seriously altered Vietnam vets, teenage LA rubes, beautiful girls, plus the kind of rich young expatriates who'd spend afternoons plotting fantasy pot deals while emptying clips from semi-automatic weapons into the jungle backyards of their rented haciendas.

Colorful people. I can remember on one of those afternoons sitting upstairs with the fair-haired young heir to a Hawaiian sugar fortune, watching as he fired a .45 out his upstairs bedroom window, and chortled between blams about how the year before he had, drunk, hit a Mexican with his car and how that Mexican had, "popped off my front fender like a chip shot."

Home from Hawaii and Los Angeles after Frank Merlino's funeral, I had spent my summer mostly cooling my boot-heels at the Portland Community College parking lot, drinking $1.99 Spinada wine in my brother's pink four-door Mid-Day Rambler, a bumper sticker that read WHO CARES ABOUT APATHY? on the back—Moby Grape's "8:05" lilting asthmatically from Scott's eight-track. We were surviving the Revolution pretty well. My well-groomed honor-student, junkie pal Big G Little O was in the National Guard and spent the riots down at Portland State during the Days of Rage in the dark of a canvas-covered Army truck sitting behind a fifty caliber machine gun. So it was great things didn't really get out of hand.

Then, for me, it was off to Mexico City, an ancient city that smelled like a bus garage and sported gorgeous new skyscrapers, rectilinear slabs stabbing the exhaust-blue sky—a new Mexico City rising out of its own old adobe and ashes.

At first I lived on the tree-shaded Paseo de la Reforma near Chapultepec Park in an elegant plaster-walled rooming house where you could, like a teenage Graham Greene, while away afternoons drinking gin and tonics at the stately Hotel Geneva down the street, or eat pot brownies so potent that you were left clinging to your bed for hours as if on a life raft in tossed and crashing seas, and where my boardinghouse mates included the tall, wire-thin stepson of Jesse "Big Daddy" Unruh, Speaker of the California State Assembly who was dating Racquel Welch and about to run against Ronald Reagan for Governor.

Big Daddy's stepson's girlfriend was Miss Mexico City and, recently, to settle a strange grudge, he bought a small cannon, filled it with explosives and pebbles and nails, and blew a hole through the front windows of the Philippine Embassy. Anyway, he introduced me to Miss Mexico City and said they were engaged to be married. I replied I was amazed. She didn't look like a beauty queen, but more like a busty brown little cow, so how could she be Miss Mexico City? Easy, he said. Because her father owned a ranch the size of Rhode Island.

Then I moved into a little chalk-colored hacienda in a six-chicken village above the University of the Americas which, in turn, inhabited a former resort above Mexico City. I lived with my friend Jeff, who I knew from Hawaii, and his wonderful, tough Texan ex-topless dancer girlfriend Sally, whom he'd met on campus where, pretty much, the ex-pat hippie freaks unrestrained by American law or order, had taken the Revolution to the ungravitated max.

For example, one of the student body officers was a charming, ice-eyed towering rangey felon in bell bottoms, who, recently shot silly in a dope deal gone way haywire, cutting his losses, decided to run for office as "the ripped rep." When I wrote in the University newspaper that, as a succinct surrogate for a campaign speech, he should stand before the assembled student body, tie off and shoot up, he was not mad, but glad, so impressed he stood on the plaza in front the university's front doors, pulled up his shirt and gave me a guided tour of his entry and exit wounds. What had happened? He'd gone to score a Winnebago-load of fine Oaxacan from "badass beaners," and a good thing he brought not only money but a nine millimeter, because, next things went from green brick retail to the OK Corral, and he ended up nearly bleeding to death in the jungle. He suggested I become his new campaign manager so we could, together, "run the fucking school like a fucking peace and love banana republic."

But that didn't happen. Because Sally E. got raped. After finals she and Jeff went to Acapulco and were hitching in front of Sanborne's Pharmacy when they were picked up by a rich Mexican kid in a Volkswagen. Next they were stopped by other rich Mexican freaks who claimed to be cops. Seven in all, who took Sally and Jeff to a ranch where Sally was enjoyed by one and all. She went limp during the assaults and afterwards when the Mexicans took them down to the beach and said they were going to be shot, Sally said, according to Jeff, "Fuck you. You're not going to shoot us; you're going to take us back to our hotel." And they did.

When Jeff and Sally got back to school, Vietnam vet students and armed undergraduate drug dealers determined to return to the Mexicans' ranch and kill as many as luck and ammo would allow. The idea was that about twenty of us gringo vigilantes would, armed by the "ripped rep," descend on the Spirals' ranch house with a gun in every hand, and blow the rapists away. The President of the University held a meeting at our chalk-colored hacienda to plea against that plan. He told us *Time* Magazine was on to the story and that the Mexican government would bring the rapists to trial if Sally and Jeff agreed to co-operate.

* * *

But it didn't turn out like that and here, back in the United States, months later, seeking divine perspective, I took two purple tabs just to be on the unsafe side, got in a car when the world began to float apart, and went for a drive. Behind the wheel, time, unclutched by the present, let me recall catastrophes past and future and, too, thanks to that crap acid I:

a) realized that writing a novel, even one based on exploits of enormous criminal ineptitude, can leave you trapped inside yourself, confined by the walls of your own narrow imagination, but

b) I had the germs of future job skills. One more super big pot deal and…Becoming an expert at listening to a John Mayall eight-track, I saw myself under the street lights as one of the new seers—rock critic, interpreting the gospels of the new shaman, Dylan, Hendrix, The Seeds, The Weeds, ? and the Mysterians, the same way T.S. Eliot might disembowel *The Iliad;* as a rock critic, I'd be like kids who play doctor to the same effect and satisfaction.

And shifting up and down the 4-speed H-pattern, I re-discovered the promised old warhorses:

Your thoughts matter
Your dreams will come true
It's not your fault

as the interior of my car warped into terra incognita, made a dream car instead of a junker, powerful instead of gutless, a joy to drive instead of a rolling time bomb until, light bulb, and I realized all of a sudden that I wasn't driving my Chevy shit-mobile but my friend Lance's gorgeous yellow 300 horsepower 1967 SS Camaro.

Days or weeks later peaking, dying or both, sky high on acid supercharged with strychnine, with Pete Townshend towering right above me in red kaleidoscopic light, close as my own image in a mirror, his blood, sweat or tears raining from the stage at this Denver roller rink packed with a hell worth of stoner longhairs, packed so tight that I could barely move and all I could see behind me was what looked like Country Joe and the Fish times 4,000 staring up at The Who on stage, who'd been playing nonstop for maybe three days straight, an endless loop of "See Me, Feel Me, Touch Me, Heal Me," scarecrow Townshend's endless arm a wind-milling propeller crashing across the strings of an electric guitar as loud as a moon-bound Saturn C rocket...

And, here later at the University of Denver, a brick and ivy-hided Ivy League manqué made psychedelic romper room, deciding enough was enough and too much was plenty, I found shelter from the storm in the curvaceous person of Molly P. Molly P. was something. Expertly faded designer jeans, delicate black alligator fetus Gucci slippers, Easter bunny soft cashmere sweaters and the dot of a diamond at the bottom of each ear, a beguiling owl-like face, big Betty Boop eyes, cute beakish nose, lush wide only vaguely predatory lips and hair so platinum she could sell it.

Molly P. had a radical, revolutionary idea: It was time to grow up, before I ended up dead or worse. Because, back from Mexico, I'd thrown in with bigger, better dope and gun people, and things were going bigger and better haywire. She had seen my future and it wasn't psychedelic. Forget marinating squares of LSD-soaked newsprint in order to supercharge the high. Her dad was the industrialist Mister Mega and, talk about late for the evolution, her news: blotter acid was yesterday's papers, not the secret to life.

Which was?

Don't touch principle.

Wait, didn't she know that Abbie Hoffman had just changed his name to FUCK and was about to levitate the Pentagon and that the plastic fantastic ray gun my pals had liberated from the fence who had liberated them either from the Green Berets or F.A.O Schwartz would jump start the revolution? Didn't she realize that the gold standard of revolutionary commitment was represented by having in your hot little hand a hot burp gun (or not. For this was no normal stolen burp gun, but a *stolen* stolen burp gun. For Big G Little O had ripped it off from a fence and it came without clips. So we couldn't blow away anything to make sure that— even though it looked exactly like something my dad would leave under the Xmas tree—it was real. Bummer).

That's what I loved about rich girls, they were so naive. Shortly, after a chaste if relatively complicated first kiss, she predicted my future: I'd go to work for her father and we'd live happily ever after on six figures a year for the rest of what sounded like our very unnatural lives—me cooped up in an executive suite and having to drive around in some barge Mercedes pig-mobile.

Not long after, slumped as loose as blankets on either side of the shapeless brown couch in our shapeless brown living room, "Roxanne" hissing from a kilo-financed stereo system that cost as much as a new car, one of my entrepreneurial, pony-tailed roommates reached across the time-space continuum to pass me a joint. Not just any joint but a different kind of joint…

"What is it?" I asked.

"Some new shit. Called Angel Dust. It'll take you to a brand new place."

Awesome. Because I really needed, drugwise, some fresh perspective in order to keep up with the ever-changing cosmos. For dig it: soon colleges, buildings and roads would all be obsolete and, following a confluence of the corporate and the divine—my longings and aspirations practically buyable in a blister pack, depending on which way the wind blew—I'd start a chain of Garden of Edens, move to LA and open a Day of the Locust-land. Or, parsing stars and Martians try my hand at social climbing. Though occasionally I was besieged by doubt. Perhaps I was setting my sights too high. Better to have ended up Oooooooming-out on a cool Marxist, Leninist, Krassnerist, Keseyist commune? At worst I'd've been force-fed Herman Hesse by cute hippie chicks who in exchange for tofu or trust funds, would do pretty much anything, all around psychedelicized, amoral, delicious girls to burn, who needed to know that I was an artist with soul who had no idea the difference between reckless and brave, and who took direction through the cosmic voices broadcast via the fillings in my teeth.

I held the joint in long, thin fingers. Angel Dust. Cool name, but what was it? Only one way to find out. So to puff or not to puff? That was the question.

* * *

The belly of the Rocky Mountain Revolutionary beast. Afternoons, me and my posse—landlubber pirates Big G Little O, Doug, Dougie, and Charlie W. might descend on the local Safeway grocery to liberate chicken, beer and rice from its capitalist-roader shelves, and on the way out, the front of our zipped-up down ski parkas pregnant with raw fryers, Budweiser and jambalaya mix, pass shaggie-haired pouter for the proletariat Jane Fonda picketing in the parking lot against—what? Nixon? Agnew? Something. But who really cared?

Because it was time to get stupid. Fun (with only one little glitch, forgetting to get drunk, I'd taken bad acid that took me *to* instead of *from* reality—acid that suddenly made me see I'd taken terrible advantage of my parents, friends and girlfriends, and managed to acquire, in the process, the 20th century job skills of a 50,000 BC French Neanderthal cave painter) and a year or two later I would complain bitterly to my creative writing teacher, the novelist Seymour Epstein—author of *The Dream Museum,* which included me as an inspirationally dislikable longhaired phantasm ("Sorry, Mark, but that's how literature works")—that our shared vision of my generation (Seymour was a casually regal man old enough to be my dad) as callow, shallow and selfish was being hijacked by New York publishing barons so that acid-blasted hippies could be better sold to themselves by writers like Ken Kesey's Stanford classmate Gurney Norman, whose new bestselling novel *Divine Right's*

Trip was an idyllic marshmallowy ode about acidhead David Ray and his talking VW bus—while here I was back on planet Earth as a real freak, learning a real freak's real life's lessons, like when, recently at the Denver police station I was asked: Did I know that, in prison, the term "boyfriend" took on a whole new meaning?

Spring, 1970. More men on the moon and me trying to get my pot Mafia pal Charlie's Irish setter unconfiscated, an affable, admiring Clark Kent of a detective checking my arms for tracks ("you got arteries like garden hoses") dying to know what came down when Mr. Vest pulled the gun, and did I think the Denver PD could be fooled by all that shit hidden in the bottom of a trunk flown from Panama or Columbia or outer space?

The Denver cop, probably at worst a bargain basement imitation of the father figure I no doubt desperately needed, said he knew all about me. He knew that me and mine were flying all kinds of "crazy shit" all over, he knew because he had two of my best friends cooling their heels in the county lockup. He also knew that, should he get a warrant, the Denver PD would find a Christmas morning's worth of Class C felony presents in our current crash pad, so maybe he and I ought to start talking, because he really knew a lot—even, for instance, that my girlfriend had just dumped me.

So how cool was that?

In his office, pictures on his desk of a very attractive, plaid, smiling mom-son-and-sis cop family, the square-faced detective, not a bad person, said, "Your phone's been tapped. So what kind of crazy shit are you going to say to let me let you go out my door? Otherwise, how'd you like to think about five to fifteen? "

Fortunately, what the cop didn't know and what convinced me that he was seriously behind on his indictment-making intel was that I'd been awarded, bolt from the blue (actually bolt from the DU Student Union, where, I guess, I had been admired from several tables afar), a new girlfriend, a pneumatic, divorced at twenty-one, flower child whose father was boss of all the sewers in Massachusetts. She came equipped with an ex-husband and, like Molly P., an Italian sports car, but a model so exclusive that I'd never even heard of it. Besides, he didn't know I enjoyed an expanding social circle, young blue bloods here in a shimmering oasis of irresponsibility. My new stoner pal, compact goateed Worley, back from 'Nam, could eat glass. To get girls. Still in his fatigues, he'd drink his beer and eat the stein. But somehow, stoned here at the cop shop and just wanting to get my buddy's Irish setter out on bail, little did I know the bloom was about to be going off the sex and drugs and rock and roll revolutionary rose.

* * *

For millennially speaking, it was getting to be a shit-or-get-off-the pot end-of-the-old-beginning-of-the-new world. Tim Leary—convicted of various drug charges—had broken out of jail. Abetted by members of the violent revolutionary Weather Underground, the former Harvard professor, a little older if not a little wiser, took time to reflect and wax philosophical: "To shoot a genocidal robot policeman in defense of life is a sacred act. World War III is now being waged by short-haired robots whose deliberate aim is to destroy the complex web of free wild life by the imposition of mechanical order...blow the mechanical mind with holy acid...dose them...dose them...stay high and wage revolutionary war."

To which Ken Kesey replied, "Don't misunderstand me, Doctor; I wish in no way to cool your fervor. We all know what is at stake. Unless the material virus that has been burrowing for decades into the spirit of the country is somehow branded and checked, unless our I/It lustings are outgrown and our rapings of the earth and each other is stopped, in short unless we become gentle and enlightened people we all know ourselves capable of becoming, we shall surely lose not only our life and land but, like Esau, our birthright. And worst of all, the birthrights of our children.

"In this battle, Timothy, we need every mind and every soul, but oh my doctor, we don't need one more nut with a gun...What we need, doctor, is inspiration, enlightenment, creation, not more headlines."

Leary denounced the letter as a fraud, "We don't believe Ken Kesey wrote it. We think the FBI and the Federal Bureau of Narcotics ripped off his energy...hard work, suffering and atonement, that's what it said, right? A revolution's going on. Our guru is Huey P. Newton, go down and tell him about suffering and atonement. Far out! Sounds like the old white racist ethic to me."

The fact that he had not met Newton did not slow Leary down. "Read the writings of Huey P. Newton or look into his eyes when you see him. He's a complete turned-on holy man, a golden black Aquarius tuned into the central energy. It was always an acid dream of ours to find turned-on blacks who could leap over the whole middle-class integration trip and define a new culture. That's what the Panthers are."

As for guns as a means to remove those in power. "It's inevitable. Their system is based on guns. The Weathermen and I have rapped through this on acid and agree totally. Arms (are) one of their weapons...Anyone who's been through the LSD experience with us is an acid revolutionary now. Dynamite is just white light, the external manifestations of the inner white light of the Buddha."

Shortly thereafter, Leary went for the belly laughs, telling interviewers on WMCA radio in New York: "My advice to the Weathermen...was that they should not continue bombing ROTCs, that they should escalate the violence, they should start hijacking planes, they should kidnap prominent sports figures and television and Hollywood people in order to free Bobby Seale and in order to free John Sinclair." A little far out, and the soul of Soul Reality Black Panther Eldridge Cleaver was worried. In response he wrote: "To all those of you who look to Dr. Leary for inspiration, or even leadership, we want to say that your god is dead because his mind has been blown by acid. If you think that by tuning in, turning on and dropping out, you're improving the situation...it's very clear that you are doing nothing except destroying your own brains and strengthening the hands of the enemy."

We were about to enjoy violent revolution. The LSD-inspired Weather Underground would provide a fresh, fatal wind, a toxic breeze to waft through our Shopping Mall Amerika—and maybe blow it right down. High fashion loony Bernadette Dohrn was about to become the People's Republic of Amerika's Paula Revere.[23] Bitchen. The world—the Amerikan part of it, anyway, was staring at the prospect of national fratricide.

Accelerated by the combustibles of desperation and TV attention, LSD-

---

23 One Weather Woman even managed to become more Catholic than the pope of radical feminism Robin Morgan. Revolutionary one-upmanship reached a storied alp when Morgan, while breast feeding her infant son, was confronted by a Weatherman in the offices of Rat Magazine and—after evidently being reminding that all white babies—having been tainted with the "original sin" of "skin privilege" were "pigs"—was told by the Weather woman, ergo: "You have no right to have that pig male baby." When Morgan, astonished, replied, "What should I do?" the Weather woman instructed, "Put it in the garbage."

fueled revolutionary soundbite rhetoric reached warp speed, supersonic edicts, from "anti-monogamy" revolutionary women: "Revolutionaries who fight together fuck together" to the earnest hilarity of a *serious ode* ala *Mad* Magazine to Korean Dictator Kim Il Sung sung to the tune of Maria from Westside Story:

I've just met a Marxist/Leninist named Kim Il Sung
And suddenly his line
Seems so correct and fine
To me
Kim Il Sung
Say it soft and there's rice fields flowing
Say it loud and there's a people's war growing
Kim Il Sung
I'll never stop saying Kim Il Sung

"As for this 'don't trust anyone over 30, shit, observed James Kunen, "I agree in principle, but I think they ought to drop the zero."

* * *

Here on the revolutionary home-front: Dust. I held the joint in slender fingers, stared at the tiny red sun that was its burning tip and decided, no, whatever Angel Dust was, I didn't need any of it. For my plate was full. For example, I was helping, in a grammatical way, to foment Revolution. In a DU student union parking lot that had more Porsches than Volkswagens, the local poor were served by young Black Panthers there to solicit money. I liked the Black Panthers, at least the rookies my age whom, to help ice their revolutionary savoir-faire, I reminded there was a T in "breakfast fund." "It's actually spelled B-R-E-A-K-F-A-S-T, not B-R-E-A-K-F-A-S-S." The young Panthers—more mocha than black, smart guys dressed in the height of revolutionary fashion in leather jackets so glossy you could see your face on a sleeve, who seemed to know more about *Mad* than Marx—got a kick out of that.

Good times. My friend, the suave, impeccably dressed (no hippie shit, but starched khakis, pin-striped long-sleeved shirts starched flat as paper), rodent-like Strauss the Mouse had a party where he tried to get

Teddy Kennedy on the phone, generally no problem given that Strauss's parents evidently owned May Company. But when Ted didn't pick up, everybody went out, led by me, and kicked the shit out of their BMWs, Mercedes and Porsches.

Then there was twenty-year old Dean L.'s first acid trip. Dean was sort of a cowboy, by way of Chicago. With a shiny surf of slicked back black hair, he resembled a beakier-nosed James Dean. Dean thought of himself as a redneck. He hated hippies and dope, even though all his friends were longhaired drug dealers. Dean's dad Fat Sam owned a bra factory in St. Louis and Dean had been hired by Charles Kettering, Junior—whose father or grandfather had founded General Motors—to take care of their horses.

The summer before in Hawaii, Dean had written his girlfriend Laurie, a whale rider at Sea World, that to be honest, he planned to screw as many other girls as possible and he hoped she could handle it, to which Laurie wrote back: no worries, she was already screwing the guy who trained the porpoises and Dean, heart-struck, climbed Diamond Head with the idea of jumping off but, instead, returned to Denver where he lived in the tack shack next to Henry Fonda's house in Cherry Creek.

We'd gone to a big demonstration at DU, thousands of protesters, Army helicopters whizzing above us like monster dragonflies, troops with bayonets thrust forward at stern diagonals everywhere—me in a T-shirt spray-painted FTA, which I wanted to stand for FUCK THE ARMY but which everybody mistook for FUTURE TEACHERS OF AMERICA instead, where we swilled acid-spiked wine, and suddenly redneck Dean was a hippie—gone from God, guts, guns and glory to flowerpower in a flash, back there in the tack room talking peace and love in horse with Henry Fonda's palominos...

The stuff was truly transformative. Though much if not most of the acid the "suburbanurchins" got was rotgut chemistry in a tab, cooked up likely by some freak teen Lavoisier whose previous chemistry experiment was pouring Ovaltine into a glass of milk. We were not warned about but, in fact, promised our acid would come laced with strychnine—better to give the weak LSD we were getting a stronger kick.

I learned my lesson after dropping two tabs at once to make sure I got the job done. I went home where my friend John Case came into my room and bounced a ball that took on the properties of flubber; though "learning my lesson" took unique resolution. By "learning my lesson" I didn't reject acid. No, I dropped lots more but took the precaution when the world began to flex itself concave, convex, or inverted, to also get really, really drunk.

* * *

Alas, Promethean utopian Acid Think was getting down to seeds and stems. American kids had been brought up in a real world in which if you did this, this, this and this, you could expect to get that, that, that and that—yet the problem with Acid Think was that you couldn't spend dreams, you couldn't hallucinate your rent check, a mirage a day did not keep the ennui away, and some avatars of psychedelia found themselves hitching their starry wagon to a more earthly paradise: sex. After his attempt to have 1969 declared "Clitoris Appreciation Year" hit the skids (figuring out who was to do the declaring proved to be the rub), the Sexual Freedom League's Fuck (born Jefferson) Poland, sent a press release to the *Berkeley Barb* declaring, "A new sex/pot church will attempt to bridge the gap between suburban swingers and hippie heads. This Psychedelic Venus Church, chartered Nov. 24 by the Shiva Fellowship, worships Aphrodite as our symbol of hedonic pleasure, in her psychedelic aspect symbolizing direct spiritual revelation. We see her presiding over nude orgies of fucking and sucking and cannabis: truly Venereal religion."

The Psychedelic Venus Church aspired to eclipse the Catholic Church by 2000. It didn't. Yet by then, stoner college girls, subtracting meta from the physical, opting for body over mindlessness, were finding heavens on earth, assembling extensive erotic biographies, ignited by new Holy Grails not written by Ken Kesey or Tim Leary but Free Love feminists like the anonymously libertine "J" whose blockbuster best seller *The Sensuous Woman: The First HOW-TO Book for the Female who Yearns to be ALL Woman* had unlocked the primordial floodgates. Freak freely was being seduced by touchie-feely and for hippie chicks now less inclined to feed their heads than to give it, *The Sensuous Woman* was paint by numbers Eros unlimited. "Proper love today is uninhibited and harmonious love carried out with consummate skill and grace. Does that mean I'm going to tell you to do some pretty wild things? Uhmmmhmmmm. I'm going to tell you exactly how to do the wild, delicious things"[24]

The acid revolution was being commoditized into Encounter Groups and Nude Sensitivity Training in what author Jane Howard termed the Bod Biz ("In the hagiography of the Bod Biz there were many saints... Each had an evangelic clientele, convinced that its idol was possessed of some mystic entrée to true and total awareness.") and what was this? Check out *The Harrad Experiment,* a bestselling hippie bellwether of a novel that championed Love Generation promiscuity as if practiced by the post office. On a utopian college campus where students represented "a new sexually oriented aristocracy. . .free of sexual inhibitions, repressions and hate," romped the Harrad College campus plugging into each other with naked abandon, *The Harrad Experiment* defined monogamy as a barbaric shackle to a new generation "who can and must relate to their sexual drives and needs for one another into a unified whole so that the act of sex is a perfectly wonderful consummation of a much larger ecstasy and pride and joy and respect for the amazing fact that each of us, man and woman, are human beings."

If girls were learning how to get fucked, boys were learning how to get fucked-up. Growing up, I had seen so many of my friends become junkies, heroin and speed turning them into blobs and coat hangers. My visionary alternative to the status quo: severe oxygen deprivation. Self-suffocation could be the bathtub gin of the revolution, the people's champagne. Totally non-addictive, yet so prudently economical. A puff of Acapulco Brass or fine Oaxacan, breathe into a lunch-bag until you were totally oxygen-starved, and there you had it, a whole night on the town just floating around your apartment more or less dead for three or four hours. Nirvana.

Though I'd gone to movies that lasted longer than some of my girlfriends, I was doing very well otherwise, living with the flower of the flowerpower generation: big-time pot dealers. One had made a $13,000 softball—$20, $50 and $100 bills rolled up in taped-together plastic garbage-bag skin—which we'd bat around our little weedy back yard. When we weren't doing flowerpower business. Elite pot dealer freaks would leap from my $89 '62 Chevy station-wagon like clowns from a

---

24 A quadrant from the road map: "When a man enters a woman, she's not supposed to lie there like a rag doll, she's supposed to meet and become enmeshed in his thrusts, entice his penis to throb and hunger for the depths of her and make him feel that the center of the universe is her pulsating and maddening vagina. That takes muscle."

clown car, run into Stapleton International Airport, wave $20 ounces of fine Oaxacan in front of servicemen, grab their money, and run out before there was time to realize what a mind-blowingly stupid thing that was to do.

My roommate Charlie was point man. He had pale straight hair whacked to a bob, wore bib overalls and looked like the kid on the Dutch Boy paint cans. Kind and smart, he loved dealing. Even when greasy pot wholesaler Mr. Vest pulled a gun and robbed Charlie of $1,000.

Plus, I was a very smart boy, a doctor's son, and as far as the Clark Kent Denver Detective went, I knew and he knew he was the middle class tail and I the upper class dog. No way he could keep me in his office or county for five to fifteen.

When I said "I'm going home" he didn't make a move to stop me.

Things were looking up. Sort of. My pal Big G Little O had come up with a plasticky thing which looked like Darth Vader's Saturday Night special and/or something made by Mattel that shot bb's that I used to find under my Christmas tree. I'd enlisted "Conan" as our enforcer and top sales thug. A Vietnam vet in jungle fatigues and combat boots, he had red frizzy hair to his shoulders and a waterfall moustache. He spent his time reading "Conan the Barbarian" novels, hence the moniker. Big and muscle-bound, but peaceful. He assured me that if anybody ever pulled a gun like Mr. Vest he—Conan—would, like Conan the Barbarian, "revert to type."

But those revolutionaries. "They weren't cool," Conan reported, a mushroom cloud of dope smoke ascending in front of his hairy face.

"Why not?" I asked.

"They weren't like leftist freaks, man. More like right-wing freaks. Hippie Kluxers."

"How do you know?" I asked, confused.

"The crucifix with a swastika in the middle of it on their living room wall was a clue."

"So what if they shoot up Mass at a black church or—Or what?"

Conan shook his electric red frizz. "No man, they just want to replace Richard Nixon with a freak Grand Dragon. Big dif. I mean, if you think about it. But shit."

"What if they attack the White House? Why didn't you 'revert to type'?"

"There were too many of them. Besides, this is really good dope."

Chapter Thirty-One:
California Girls

"Every woman has built into her cells and tissues the longing for a hero, sage-mythic male, to open up and share her own divinity. But casual sex encounters do not satisfy this deep longing. Any charismatic person who is conscious of his own mythic potency awakens this basic hunger in women and pays reverence to it at the level that is harmonious and appropriate at the time."

—Timothy Leary

Who'd done this? The Girl of My Dreams in a sad weird bow to modesty or, even weirder, the Random Ooooomster in a sad, sick act of—what could you call it—chivalry? When I got home from a trip I discovered that photos of my father and mother were turned down face first on the night table next to my bed.

* * *

What do women want? Beautiful young Cannery Row Californian feminist Ms. America said that since Adam screwed Eve men had called all the fucking shots, but now, guess what?

It may be sexist, racist and rotten to say it, but maybe LSD and all its mind-bloviating brothers and sisters didn't improve white girls' take on reality. In a brave new world where the rule was there were no rules, by 1970, fantasy had shot beyond custom toward law.

Before herpes gave cold sores a bad name and when AIDS was just a headache for lover-boy frogs and monkeys, when any girl over eighteen still a virgin was not virtuous but ill, and when too much was rarely enough, as a Cain or Abel in the freak freely Garden of Eden (if not a sage-mythic male aware of my own mythic potency), a boy with friends to burn, I was not a good influence on those around me.

A pal for whom one Coors tall boy was satori, and for whom acid came from chemistry class now, following my example, fell down the rabbit hole so often he'd meet himself walking the other way down the street.

Nevertheless, as a pure proto-type of upper middle class Flotsam Chic, (I had a spoken vocabulary to shame a Gray Parrot, and one heartstopper swooned, "The sexiest thing about you is that you're fairly stupid") I had a lot going for me. I was an expert at being manipulated and had, too, an appealing, squeaky-clean take on sex—like, think what you could do with soap—and the New Feminism didn't bother me a bit: so what if I got stuck staring at a plastic chandelier during Ride'em Cowgirl? And so what if what was good for the gander was now going to be even better for the goose?

What had the demi-gods wrought? Prior to my last year or so at college sex was at best or worst a sort of leapfrogging serial monogamy—and Free Love could have been, so far as I knew, just another capitalist gag to sell cigarettes and shaving lotion.

So, say you were between the Summer of Love and *Deep Throat* and Deep Throat in low earth orbit above Hawaii, Portland, San Francisco, LA, Mexico and Denver, beginning to wonder what was to become of yourself, and who was to blame? Yet hopeful because your stories about beginning to wonder what was to become of yourself and who was to blame were getting published and, say, also, you'd met the Girl of Your Dreams, who mirrored the armless Venus, had a smile to light a city, wore tomboy jeans, was wholesome as Holy Water and as loyal as Lassie. What happens if you get very, very, very, lucky, lucky, lucky: a first place 34-22-34 trophy to take home to Mother, proof her stepson hadn't flushed his life down the toilet.

But a trophy with a soul can be complex. An artist who knew 10,000 blues, Ms. America, one stop shopping for love at first sight, was competitive. Risk or Russian roulette, she hated to lose. She was also very generous—if somebody needed $50 somebody got $50—and to the point (melting against my arm after a night out: "Sorry, but I'm too fuck to drunk"), she had friends from toddlerhood and fidelity was an eleventh commandment.

Help others before yourself, save the world, Burger King no, heaven on earth yes. The hippie ideal. Aside from a Bible-thick stack of traffic tickets, no sin. No envy, no gimme, gimme, gimme, no malice. Angel-faced, she could turn more heads in jeans, a SMASH THE STATE t-shirt and tennis shoes than a stack of *Cosmo* cover girls. At the Playboy mansion (long story) two playboys, one sober, confided Ms. America was more beautiful than all the Playmates put together. She read novels, not just wrote them, and told me I took her "out of this world"—her feelings, at critical moments, seemed to go beyond love to epilepsy. A seeker, she had texts written in a Swahili-style language called Cyrillic and, aside from serving drinks at the "Lettuce Inn" Vegetarian Booze Boutique, she worked either selling ads for the *Paul is Dead Gazette* or tutoring language theory. Something bookish.

Too, Ms. America begged questions. Like: was she proof of an ungodded cosmos? No just God would award me like this. We'd go to concerts and be swept backstage (a special shout-out to Joe Walsh). Night after night the essential frictions rendered my humble populator an elbowed bloody war zone, forcing me to confide to my physician father, "I think she broke it." His Rx: "Lay off."

Heart and soul as rectilinear as a crucifix, Stone Tablet values—right was right, wrong was wrong and never the twain shall meet—shy except when she wasn't, our courtship took, by freak freely standards, forever… three weeks. Then I was hers. Ms. America was mine. That was it. She said God meant us to be. Thank God for God. I was "the one and only," no other Romeos, Casanovas or Supermen, only friends, brothers and dads and sons. If she saw a handsome guy her take was Catholic, as in: "There goes Joe Mona Lisa, wonder who does his hair?" (Not that she lacked a knack for bohemia. Big G Little O reported she'd had a heroin dealer boyfriend. Shocked, all I could think to ask was: what'd he look like? Big G Little O: "You, but as a vampire").

As exquisite as she was, to me the sexiest thing about Ms. America was that she was as normal as a new moon. And if I was not the man-child of her dreams I was the next best thing: a cool gizmo with fun parts for her to play with. Though she erred to the unkinky side and our sex was nothing if not Norman Rockwell wholesome, little après-the-Revolution you couldn't put on a Hallmark Greeting Card.

But she was challenging. Beds had to be made, dishes washed, rugs vacuumed, bills paid. She could be like being in the Army. Also, she spoke in shorthand: "He says to meet them there before the rush or it'll be too late." He? Them? There? Rush? Too late? For what? Likewise, thinking, possibly, made her sick. She'd given up acid because she didn't want a mind by Picasso, but got migraines from all her books and then, catastrophe, there was a run-in with a girl and an incident involving a nightclub parking lot, a car, a bartender and a lot of lying.

* * *

In the hills above our neighborhood, a huge squat wood and concrete UFO, "Foxy O'Squack's," landed over night. Best go check it out. Outside, through the cracked windshield of my 1967 Mustang convertible with the top slashed so a triangle of dirty black cloth hung above the transmission console, we saw sun-shiny new BMWs, Porsches and Mercedes. In a single flash, the sudden news: Hippie days were over. The parking area was a luxury car lot. Inside, the New Church of the Polyester Anti-Christ, a hallucination to make Tim Leary puke. Everything big, shiny and all these guys with big frizzy hair and gold chains, like white Mister T's in neo-Edwardian suits and platform Oxfords. Beer pimped in neon scrawls all over the walls, syrupy effluvia called "soft rock" leaking from hidden speakers. One look at this plastic piss-hole and I knew I was dead.

Because, according to Ms. America, she could make a "fortune" here cocktailing. Foxy's manager described the red-walled Foxy's as a "gold mine," more specifically a "meat market" and he wasn't talking about their gummy filets. Gone the acid queens in their caftans, flowers and lace, now replaced by high-heeled Harvey Wallbanger sippers in outer spacey spandexy, faux call girl platinum. The staff wore blouse-like shirts with little hearts all over, the bartenders tri-corner hats. Love Pirates here at Captain Hook's corporate cat house. Selling twenty-something capitalist piglets in bellbottomed pinstripes McSex, a place to get your ends wet and put the tab on your Visa card (Unlike the wino/biker/street freak bar where I was, for two dollars an hour, pulling beer for pinball wizards with tattoos and integrity—real hookers and pimps).

Inside the menu, news from a Foxy O'Squack cartoon mascot, a pink potato-like creature who spoke in cartoon balloon, *"Yo, bro! Cecil the*

Trouser Snake here. See the bombshell sittin' down the bar? Like to jump those little bones? Well, order her a Foxy O'Squack 151 rum jalapeño depth charge and the next thing you know, she'll be panting in the dark, shaking hands with the one-eyed dude." But, instead of let's-beat-feet-out-of-here feminist umbrage, when I showed Cecil's entreaty to Ms. America, all she said was, "Sounds like something you'd write."

The fix was in. For, according to my beautiful beloved, we needed money. That we barely had enough for food, rent and five hours a night six days a week spent in clubs and bars, and, besides, she was tired of being poor. She filled out an application and what did I think? That we'd crossed our Rubicon, bye-bye peace and love, this corporate plastic shit-hole was an emissary from tomorrow, the tackiest thing God would ever make, the 1970s, and I vowed on the spot that if she took a job cocktailing at Foxy O'Squack's I'd never darken its door (the second biggest mistake I ever made), but, hey, as long as she didn't make her money staring at the ceiling, she could be my guest.

* * *

Indeed. We still lived in an if-you-do-this-this-and-this-you-get-that-that-and-that world, and among many young liberated women, the search for the Holy Acid Grail was now for the Magic Penis, an inner glass slipper for the 1970s Cinderella, perhaps a red plastic projectile resembling less Johnny Wadd's awesome implement than a pulsating 1:200 scale model of the Starship Enterprise. But that's getting ahead of the story.

I wasn't getting invited over for chalk talks at Anais Nin's, but I had been to the city and seen the elephant. Just before I met Ms. America a friend had invited me to a Michigan ski resort where, no sooner had I sat down in the lodge, he told me I was to be "guest boyfriend" of a prim Junior League style college girl whose fiancé was at that moment gathering his ski equipment on the other side of the room, leaving for a Las Vegas "vacation" on the week before they were to get married, and tonight I'd be sharing her bed, because this was her last chance to have fun. So I, Boy Toy. Given the mail-order rude rocket aspect, what, I asked, were her expectations? Easy: that I be cute, clean and, after six days, gone.

Free love. Back at DU, within a half hour of meeting a girl whose brother was the drummer in the band that recorded "Bird, Bird, Bird, the Bird is the Word," we were on a half- hour honeymoon. Next I ran into a very attractive school marmish Little House on the Prairie style girl at the DU cafeteria, all calico, cashmere and curls, who I'd nearly run into on a ski slope in Vail and who, between selecting her sun-lamped Mystery Meat and sun-lamped apple pie, invited me to spent the weekend. No Carol Doda wanna-be staggering around in dagger heels and a leather bustier, she looked as x-rated as Wonder bread. Still, at night Venus and Aphrodite were benched in favor of Marilyn Chambers and Rube Goldberg, the carnal evoking the carnivorous, expert enthusiasms to make Linda Lovelace blush. Disconcerting. Lovemaking seemed to me, I dunno, *personal,* inviting accelerating affection and hope, but…

Truth be told, I was free-loved out. For one thing free love wasn't nearly as lascivious or salacious as I had imagined. The Little House on the Prairie insatiable school marm notwithstanding, not a lot of strip teases to crotchless panties and nipple rings. In fact, it often seemed less about lust than loneliness; for many girls, getting screwed seemed just the price of getting held. And, weirdly, though all I asked of a one night stand was that she be brainy, beautiful, honest and funny I nevertheless, despite my attractive hygienic Play-Doh qualities, experienced what seemed like light-year long Saharas of girllessness. Still, I managed to catch nonvenereal urethritis three times in a year and my urologist said next time antibiotics probably wouldn't work and he'd have to stick some kind of pipe cleaner up there to ream me out. That or filet me open like a just caught trout.

Meanwhile, Ms. America, for whom romantic love was the meaning of life, gave and expected to get loyalty. By luck of the draw, I was attacked by an internationally renowned violent person and before my knees even hit the ground she jumped on the guy's back, went triple OJ and you never heard *no mas! no mas!* faster in your life.

But she was fickle. *I love you, I love you not.* I'd go from god to devil in a blink.. Today Jesus in the manger, tomorrow Rosemary's Baby. Plus: she was fiery (from day one a voice in my head said: *never cross her*) and though her goals were heartbreakingly simple: "I just want someone to love me," and though I'd conjured as many words for yes as the Eskimos have for snow, somehow we could agree on anything and argue about everything

("You're crazy. It was six, Mark, not a half dozen!").

We'd make love to stop fighting and lie still on our backs afterwards, as if the bed were a coffin, our eyes leaking, desperately unable to figure out why we couldn't get along. Quizzed, I did not receive, as a swordsman, a standing O. Why go to bed with all those girls? What had I been trying to prove? I heard words like "sad," "foolish," "lonely," "dehumanizing," though I'd like to think others like "revolting" and "predatory" escaped the mix. She considered loveless sex a tacky Disneyland for which, thank God, no one had given her a ticket.

If you'd been some yo-yo trafficking in drugs and walking kilos of suitcased pot between cordons of cops at airports, breaking bread with fences whose apartments were pawn shops, blasted out of your tracks on whatever you could swallow, snort or smoke, suffering perennial mind freeze from bad hookah pipes, a super-smart, beautiful young woman whose most attractive aspect was traditional middle-class Judeo-Christian morality natural as her heartbeat was bound to be irresistible. Nevertheless. Sensitive as a moth's wing, moral as the Stone Tablets, more about soap than perfume (possibly unleashed from bodily functions—I don't think I ever saw her go to the john), honest (at tax time I watched her track herself down to the last nickel), Ms. America was also rash.

I've driven dragsters so fast they're stopped by parachute and ridden with blind drunks like Moon who play bumper cars with bridge abutments, but behind the wheel at night, she made the world a video game, everything in front of us, wham! Nothing but slashing lights and fiery blobs; too fast was rarely fast enough. There were no brakes in a Ms. America car, only gas pedals. A delicate hand atop the steering wheel, she'd fly into curves while diving into her handbag to look for directions. Maybe she had eyes in her knuckles, but I was impressed—Mario Andretti and Jeff Gordon may shoot through S-turns at 90 mph, but not while rummaging through their purse. A rough-draft Danica Patrick before Danica Patrick—but sadly, you can't make an omelet without breaking eggs and, once she crashed.

While her $400 British Racing Green Varoom-mobile was getting fixed she said wanted to hitchhike downtown to buy a Japanese lacquered box. Hitchhike? Color me apeshit. I was terrified. What could she be thinking? She'd end up Poopsie sushi. But I wasn't the boss of her, so next a lacquered box. Fuuuuuuuuck. Then days later she confessed maybe just maybe she'd been too chicken to stick her thumb out and had taken a bus—though, even if she had hitchhiked maybe she'd say she hadn't. *Why?* So I wouldn't worry. *Why II?* Because it wasn't that she *had* hitch hiked but that she *could* hitch hike. And I couldn't stop her. Oh. So either she was hitchhiking and *wasn't* telling me, or wasn't hitchhiking and *was* telling me, I had no idea.

She was less about truth than truths, used words like magic wands and cattle prods, and was a Houdini of pretzel logic. We knew a dog, a dog that was sort of a friend of ours, who had a continence problem. My take: A dog is a closed loop system, less water in, less pee out. Ms. America was aghast: pee was a constant, the only way my plan would work would be to deprive the dog of water entirely, which would be inhumane—to which all our hookah-smoking caterpillar pals agreed, suggesting her best future might not be saving the world but serving as legal counsel to brashly incompetent Mafia hit men.

There were other issues. She lived in a civilized world. If it had atoms, I'd eat it. To me, a grocery store was meat, booze, bread and vegetables—soup was soup—all the same swill from the capitalist roader pork/cow/carp consortium—what difference did a *brand* make and why eat halibut when pork sausage was ten times cheaper? "ARE YOU JOKING?" Well...

...While okay when getting what I wanted (an advantage of growing up spoiled rotten), when I didn't I wasn't. I resented the fact she liked me more than my writing. True, I wasn't typing a cure for cancer or world hunger, but still. I'd flown to Utah and been bumped to an empty first class section whose flight attendant enjoyed dramatic allures suggesting a movie star playing a flight attendant in a first class blockbuster. She'd read a story I'd written about an ancient giant lake in Idaho that had "exploded" and sent a small nation-worth of rocks and water blasting west to form the Columbia Gorge.

I was *that* Mark Christensen? Soon seated at my shoulder, she realized for me that I'd written a Dante/Rimbaud/Henry Miller-level allegory for Father Earth making apocalyptic love to Mother Nature—making me, thus, a Word God, and though she was married she'd fly back with me so we two could Be As One. Though I left her unadulterated (husbands have guns), I had to unclaw her hand from my forearm when Ms. America met me at the airport and the point was: that's how Ms. America should be reacting to my writing.

But it wasn't. *You don't write about the real relevant world.* Possibly not, but considering I was working for a paper where it was understood that all prisoners were political prisoners and North Vietnam represented a pinnacle of Jeffersonian Democracy, reality and relevant were relative terms.

Ms. America claimed that if I got a grip I could be almost as good a writer as Carlos Castaneda or the Divine Right's trip-talking VW bus guy and, how could anybody not know how to Osterize?

So? I wasn't domestic. I couldn't spell Osterizer, let alone operate one.

Imagine Jim Morrison's younger, dumber, less drunk brother—skinnier, taller, tone deaf, broke. Probably my problem was not too much acid but too little Ritalin. Saturdays I could be found staring at (minus my tooth brush, beater Mustang, Lucacci cowboy boots, worn Sperry Topsiders, Rossignol racing skis and my Keith Richards-joins-the-vice-squad leather waist jacket) all I owned spinning in the local laundromat drier: boxers, t-shirts, alligator golf shirts for weddings and funerals and navy issue bellbottom dungarees. It was so incredible to just sit there and watch your whole universe spin forever in front of your face, and by the way, Ms. America, Carlo Castaneda is a fucking liar and Volkswagen buses don't talk. I grew up around coyotes, have taken every dream pill God, Sandoz or the Brotherhood of Eternal Love have ever made, and, guess what else, coyotes don't talk, lizards, crows and kitty cats don't talk either and…

…After euphoriants, a tiff at a beach. She ran to the water, leapt expertly from rock to rock, surf crashing after her, sea water exploding white against the night sky—just another knockout immortal 21 year-old. Screams to "get back to the beach or you'll drown" provoked a middle finger. I wasn't coordinated, smashed, brave or murderous enough for rescue.

So a few cracks in the love basilica.

Change was gonna come. In honking counterpoint to her general ladylikeness, she'd blow her nose like a one hippie chick elephant's graveyard, allergic suddenly, she said, to all her dusty books—which for sneeze reasons and otherwise, seemed to have begun to annoy her—and, anyway, for Ms. America, the present often shaped the past. When I was "bad" she'd do things like threaten to join the Peace Corps and one day when I was extra bad she claimed she'd signed up and would be off to darkest Abanisabjubistan tomorrow morning. But tomorrow morning, after a night of my genuflections, it was like nothing had happened, which it evidently hadn't, she was back before noon at the Lettuce Inn Vegetarian Booze Boutique serving Saturday brunch Bloodies to her beatnik college professors.

There were, on reflection, other clues to the looming perfect storm. She loved utopian promises hitched to farfetched plans—like that some day we'd buy a house. She also liked experts—i.e. generally anybody whose opinion you had to pay for. I had a minor legal problem—made major by my lawyer. "He couldn't have been wrong." "Why not?" "Because you paid him all that money." She also took shortcuts to certainty: "It makes sense, so it must be true." So how stupid could I be? While she didn't drink a lot, it only took a little. Though her watchwords included "Wodka makes me Womit," put a martini in front of her and watch inhibitions evaporate drop by drop. So, re. Foxy O'Squack's, Ms. America on a nightshift at a firewater factory was nuts.

One evening we'd visited friends. We arrived early; they were in bed, their bedspread covered with skin magazines open to naked nymphs in every stage of spread-eagled undress.

It seems the guy, just years out of high school, had a problem getting his rocket ready for launch minus a super charge from the 12th grade staple of his sex life: stroke books. Never mind his embarrassed girlfriend was a yellow haired Grade A sprite—a local teenage Cheryl Ladd—to humble any balloon-boobed *Swank* magazine pinup. A point, emboldened by bud and Bud, I made—rhapsodizing that if he couldn't rise to the occasion, I sure could. Which, helpfully, the Sprite amended with a doe-eyed "feel free."

Big mistake. As big as my entire cosmos. Ms. America was on fire with horror and disgust. "Betrayed," humiliated and furious, she stayed furious dawn to dark—*what creep cad swine would say he wanted to screw another girl right in front of me?* The Sprite, formerly Ms. America's worshipping apostle, was excommunicated. (What had I said? Given that it exploded my life, it was arguably my most effective piece of authorship, but I recall none of the text).

Ms. America said all her hopes and dreams had been pinned on me.

Deep at night her soft shoulders quaked, and one morning after she got up I found her pillow and sheets damp, and realized her eyes had wet our bed. I felt like I couldn't breathe, and anyway…

Soon one o'clock, two o'clock, three o'clock in the morning—she kept working later and later and later at Foxy's, where she'd been anointed a "Wench," Foxy O'Squack for waitress, coming home in her Wench miniskirt and hearted blouse and soon smelling like Burt Reynolds' cat, and I guess if I was smart and wanted free rent for the rest of my life, I'd've gone up to Foxy's at the end of her shift with a tire iron, but I couldn't see the ugly forest for the beautiful tree and soon there was the ghost of another presence.

With a freaky twist. For there was no misty eyed staring out to Ernest Hemingway's "middle-distance" where might float her new Mister Right. No. It was almost as if I'd been replaced by a new toy, as if this wasn't about the moon in June, but ready, aim, fire. I faced simmering rage dawn to dusk, but in bed in the wee hours after her longer and longer late night O'Squack shift I felt a temperature of another sort; it was, in oven-speak, as if she'd been pre-heated; she no sooner touched the sheets than it was five, four, three, two, one blastoff, then…*encore*—until one night she came home crying and out spilled what should have been obvious for weeks (lost on previous late nights to the blue smoke and mirrors of: "I'm up there working my butt off serving vodka zombies to sweaty-palmed plastic punk stockbrokers drowning in Jade East." [Though what I smelled was more like Old Spice]. "Accusing me of that is crazy, insulting and soooooooo hypocritical, it's you who wants sex with other people, not me!"). Presumably she'd been either parsing Cyrillic over a glass of Cold Duck or, I dunno, maybe yo-yoing away the afterhours in the back of a Love Pirate's Dodge Econoline honeymoon suite. Anyway, with that, whatever it was, she was gone.

I'd made my own bed, and she didn't have to sleep in it, but I was blown away. I barely knew what planet I was on. It was like getting a dear John letter from the Virgin Mary and when we were reunited in her new apartment a month later I found a whole new world. Bye-bye jeans and t-shirts. Hello a stunning and stunningly brief snow-white knit dress that made her the sexiest girl ever. It was summer and what legs. Perfect skin as poreless as maple syrup, no more tennis shoes but patent leather blue high heels, she'd gone from Becky Sawyer Hippie Chick to Ultra Vamp.

Her new bedroom recalled Hef's ashram. Gone were the collegiate baubles like the smiling pictures of her with her fresh-faced stoner girlfriends and the old stuffed blob that I think used to be her teddy bear, now replaced by diaphanous Indian blankets, scented sheets, candles, which sent slithering light and slinking shadows up the walls at every corner of her bed, on one wall an erotic cloth print that appeared to depict an ancient Buddhist ode to eight-armed cosmic 69. A shrine to tantric orgasmia. What—had she ditched the Love Pirate for the Dalai Lama?

Then the particulars. Everything in a rush. Shock and time have lost the verbatim, but the gist was that when I said I hadn't called because I knew she hated my guts she looked at me like I was crazy and said, no, wow, she'd really, really missed me, but that so much had changed. Indeed. Like the universe according to the Big Bang theory—nothing relevant before was relevant after.

The good news: indeed Foxy O'Squack's and the Love Pirate were history—how could she have ever even walked into this plastic place? The bad news: on to bigger and better things. I was right, she was wrong. She'd found religion. Mine. All the things she'd said about being disgusted about me screwing the other girls being sad, indulgent, creepy, etc., etc. etc., had been completely backwards. Before, other guys were abstract and invisible, they didn't even exist. But now, wow. Before we met, she thought sex was all about love and commitment but, thank God, thanks to me, she'd wised up. The reason we fought all the time was because she didn't really love me, she just loved having sex with me, we were just about lust and obsession, which was no reason for narrow-hearted monogamy but now, free at last, free at last, released from guilt, fear, hypocrisy, possessiveness and jealousy, we would be in love, our lives all about happiness, openness and bliss, because she'd no longer be weirded-out by the tyranny of we-own-eachother-exclusivity which had, among other terrible things, convinced her there was a floozy under every rock plotting to get her hands on me.

It would be pretty to think so, but *what?*

Several of her most attractive girlfriends—who she'd once been jealous of—would, given, half a chance, rip my id a new one. Including the uber-Viking vixen Supreme Poopsie X, the ice blue eyes of whom Ms. America, pre-free love, would have scratched to their sockets.

Supreme Poopsie X? The tall curvaceous flaxen-haired humorless pea-brained Nordic Mantis who hated my guts and who—

—had all but stalked me. That was another problem she said: I lived in a dream world. Supreme Poopsie X was just playing hard to get and had practically Vowed to the Multitudes that I'd be her next man-child *hors d' oeuvre,* she'd gobble me up and spit my bones on Ms. America's doorstep- but now it would be A-okay if we Became as One because… because…because Annie Alpha said so.

Fuuuuuuuck. Annie. The New Guru. I shoulda known.

* * *

Follow your bliss. From empty promise LSD heaven back to feather-bedded earth. Psychedelic delirium junked for an even more absurd between-the-sheets reality. Fuck who you want, where you want, when you want, as much as you want. Forget acid: The sisters were doing it for themselves. Empowerment through ecstasy a go go. But in fucking up, like architecture, form follows function. Best to design into your fuck up floor plan a big back door, plus an anti-gong for unringing the bell. I'd been fucking up since second grade, while, sadly for my brash beloved, she came from a rational, loving middle of the middle class family big on logic, and had only been fucking up for a few years at the most.

We were in San Francisco, the Promised Land, where the Haight had gone to hell and heaven had returned to earth. Think about it, Ms. America said. We knew we wanted to "be together" the minute we met, but due to fear, repression and hypocrisy she waited three weeks to sleep with me, weeks we'd never get back, so why hadn't we just gone to bed "instantly," wasn't that how I felt?

Yeah, about twenty times a day. "I see those 'instantly' girls on street corners, in cars, department stores, 7-Elevens, on front stoops, their lush spread wings man oh man oh man just waiting to happen."

Lush lips became a red line. "Are you patronizing me?" As one who rarely knew how he felt before he heard himself say it, I "instantly" wished to unsay that, but, wait, miscalculation, all was well, for that just proved her point, why not, if you saw the right person, do it "instantly"? Leaving me to wonder: in cobra vs. mongoose, who hypnotizes whom?

Loss of religion isn't loss of religious need. Ms. America: *Mark, you know all about the how of sex but not the why.* So what's the why? To escape the patriarchal prison of monogamy and make soul-to-soul connections. To the several parted question: "Are? You? Out? Of? Your? Fucking? Mind?" she sighed, "It's spiritual." As in the Virgin Mary finds her inner horn dog? Hello the emotional bends. This was a girl recently reluctant to introduce me to her parents because that implied these-are-lips-that-might-have-been-kissed.

But now? One boy, one girl—evidently that ship had sailed. What did Kesey say? Get them in your movie before they get you in theirs. Well, guess what? This was somebody else's movie. Or a dream or a joke. Because the human psyche is not made to operate on a moral swivel, able to do a 180 overnight. But, whoever Ms. America had been, she was not that now. Thanks to new gnosis. Delivered by a new guru. More free love sales jive, but now from on high. As in Annie says women did not need the "addiction" or "projection" of romantic love. Annie says sex for sex's sake can be really sexy. Not about guilt or god, just sex. Annie says not wanting to sleep with other guys was sick. Annie says, Annie says. As if Ms. America were Annie's ventriloquist dummie, I was soon drowning in a fishy touchie feely/feel good/ Bermuda Triangle of psycho babble in which, like Oakland, there was no there there, free of the sanity of facts, all about "unlimiting yourself," "internal eternal awakening," "auras," "upliftment," "destiny points," "the understanding of the lack of understanding," (a Ms. America favorite) and, by the by, "What is your next level of greatness?" And, now she was free to make, if not mad passionate love, at least mad passionate <u>like</u> with anyone she pleased.

Pussy-power metaphysics. Ms. America had made a glamorous new friend at Foxy O'Squacks, the "Wench-in-Chief"—her manager, basically, who'd channeled erotic human potential acid think into a *your place, my place, or right here?* New Testament. A free love bromide goddess, honey-voiced, honey-haired Annie lived by slogans like "be your fantasy" and "explore the possibilities." I'd been sold crazy bars of soap and in theory, didn't mind the Everybody Gets to Screw Everybody Theory, so long as the right Hegel, Kierkegaard or Kant was flying the Everybody Gets to Screw Everybody plane, but guru Annie Alpha suggested a cross between a St. Paul of the New High Church of Fucking Strangers and a lobotomized mini-skirted Margaret Sanger.

Yet for fiery seeker Ms. America, AA was just what the doctor ordered: a boss. I think that Ms. America, like a lot of militant 1960s free spirits, secretly missed hierarchy and gospel, wanted to once again tell or be told, to control or be controlled. Sadly, I'd starve as a doormat and if you want me to control you, best be a lawnmower or a dog. Ms. America believed that Annie Alpha, unlike me, had a "vision," held, in fact, close to her impudent young breasts the capital S capital T Simple Truth: Sex need not be about love or commitment, just passion and fun. A friend to those who had no friends, kind to everything from paramecia up, imagine a pro bono version of the $1,000 an hour Beverly Hills call girl with a heart of gold, Annie, as with a lot of basic bosses—like mammies and drill sergeants—put an implacable *don't-argue-I-have-the-answers* face to the world.

So, a showdown. Though I'd yet to be published in *Rolling Stone* or *Playboy,* I'd already received enthusiastic rejection letters from two top literary agents (their twin upshot: try to get published in *Rolling Stone* or *Playboy*). Had Annie Alpha ever darkened the door of a community college? And, if you think it was no contest, you're right. I never had a chance.

Gone her chaste "Mary Poppins" white cotton nightgown, replaced—if replaced is the word—by a micro-mini negligee slightly less transparent than Mississippi River water. Ms. America and I were about to conjoin, Annie Alpha "sensual fantasy" style.

A whole new world.

For a culture going from communes to cults, from John, Paul, George, Jimi and Bob to Werner, Bagwan and Reverend Moon, on its way from saving the world to selling it, all about certitude, bliss and permission, pre-EST-Eve-of-the-new-New-Age Annie Alpha was drop-dead perfect. Owning the implacable élan of someone secretly famous, she'd spread to conquer in *Cherry,* a garden hose squirting her ground zero, worried the photos weren't "sexy enough," and held that when it came to cute guys, three was not always a crowd. She told Ms. America it was time to "shake the money tree" and opened her eyes to a love in which love wasn't necessary, just like, gnosis as simple as a railroad spike, the fast track to Pleasure-ville.

I'd already been introduced to the Annie experience. Like most centers of the universe, Annie Alpha was divinely incurious. You were Q, she was A. Aside from standard boilerplate (like: "Don't you have a home?") on the occasion she asked me anything, her bottomless almond eyes went away as soon as the question mark flew out of her perfect mouth. The smiling, big-eyed look of rigid, radiant Barbie doll self-satisfaction never had it so good and I knew that, while barely old enough to vote, I was a dinosaur.

A breath before our lips met, a trill. Ms. America reached across her bed and picked up her phone. "Annie!" A smile to light a city. "Nothing much. Yeah, he's here. Really? Wow, see you in five."

"So we're not gonna?"

"Later, we need to be over at her house right now. She's dying to see you."

I bet. It was as if we had been granted an audience with the Pope.

No longer a church goer, removed from her middle of the middle class parents, Ms. America found in Annie an ideal guiding light. Big Nurse as New Age Penthouse Pet. For Annie insisted the rules were that there were no rules, except, of course, hers. In my memory Annie greeted us at her platinum front door in a diaphanous toga hemmed at her crotch. But that can't be true. Her apartment was decorated in, her words, "casual elegance," walls clean bare-breast cream, vulva-pink pillows all around, no books, a home that was a slap in the face to my cozy Appalachia West—I lived in a matchstick cracker-box built to burn down with extra-terrestrial porch monkeys whose idea of a quiet night at home was a gangbang in the basement.

Immediately, as was Annie's wont, we went shopping. In Annie's company you enjoyed the liberating freedom of choicelessness. Your day could have been mounted on railroad tracks; you simply went where Annie wanted to go. Left on our own, Ms. America and I would mull forever the choice of a restaurant. The Future Poop Steak House or Eat or Die? Eat or Die or the Future Poop Steak House? Quality of the food, service, décor, distance to and from, autopsied fore to aft. But with Annie you just went, she made decisions instantly.

Boutique after hip café after hipper boutique, Annie's formerly drug-sotted, food stamp-fed neighborhood had become a trendy utopia. Talk about a song of seduction—it had taken Annie no time to get Ms. America between the psychic sheets. By putting Ms. America in her debt.

Literally. For Annie possessed the new yuppie magic wand, a "Gold card." That afternoon when Ms. America made a purchase—gum, a magazine, a dress, each required an approving nod from Annie, then, "I'll put it on my American Express. You can pay me back later." And it wouldn't take Dear Abby to see who wore the pants in our new ad hoc nuclear family. I went from man-of-the-house to stepchild in the bat of an all knowing almond eye.

At a "restaurante" that looked like the inside of a wedding cake, we got something that called itself coffee but was more like a scalding hot little milkshake. Mesmerizing gorgeous Annie held forth. Better to be talking in tongues at some Arkansas Reverend Feelgood's Baptist circus tent church, my hand in a bag charming rattlesnakes, than listening to: there was no sin, only "bad life decisions," and right and wrong, good and bad were all relative. Gospel, though, for the now thought-free love of my life, suddenly a true believer, redeemed from her orgies of introspection by feel-good New Age Answers simple as a swastika.

Not that my humble opinion was appreciated, and on the drive back to her apartment Ms. America's prognosis: I'd argue every side of every issue, but Annie just *knew*. I was lost, Annie was found. Annie serene, I chaos, Annie positive, I negative, Annie had no ego (!), I was all ego, Annie was spiritual, I godless, Annie yes, I no (!?), I funny, Annie serious (a breeze, given she had no sense of humor) I was about questions, Annie about answers and how dare I portray her as a sweet, whack power freak estrogen head whose brains were south of her belly button? I could make all the funny ha-ha mocking jokes I wanted but Annie was "together" in a way I'd never be. I'd grown up in a country club cocoon and knew "ab, so, lute, ly nothing" about real life. Annie had grown wise facing "life's challenges," a childhood of dysfunction—even now half her family wouldn't talk to her—and had realized stuff like: what were books compared to "intimate experience"? That it was less important to think than to feel.

So what did I feel? That Annie was an anti-intellectual train wreck waiting to happen (and believe me, it did) and free love would be, pardon the pun, a fucking nightmare. Ms. America said you don't need God's IQ to see the obvious.

Indeed. Ruler of reality Annie, granter of Big Permission, had a wizard's grip on the new buy low sell high post-sixties, post peace and love undress for success courtisanship—boy toys would soon be traded for sugar daddies and, anyway, hippie Ms. America was poor; yuppie Alpha Annie was not.

Annie Alpha's boyfriends, and there were many, were not no-necks and mouth breathers but, worse, handsome squared-away Ken dolls from the new normal—a he-harem well groomed in the new bouffant Donnie Osmond meets Black Sabbath, hip capitalist style, sturdy Jacuzzi-ites, like Annie—yuppies not hippies, twenty-something Joe Namaths, Ted Bundys and Geraldo Riveras. Civil, civilized suitors, young brokers and managers, elite worker bees with sexy stuff like barbers and health insurance, the male mani-pedi folk who populated the fashion spreads in GQ. The new All American lady killers: known in some unenlightened circles as "heterosexual faggots."

I know, I know, but there you have it: Babes in boy land. There was only one Annie Alpha. Do the math. The best that could happen would be that Ms. America would somehow escape the worst things that had ever happened to her: me and Annie Alpha, find her Dr. Rich McDreamy, the prince she so richly deserved and…

…imagine a five star cathouse where the kitties are free, Ms. America said free love would allow her to escape her "fear set," and spread, so to speak, her wings, and wouldn't it be neat for us to live together, "no strings—so if I saw a guy that I liked at school or you saw a girl you liked you or I could just bring him or her home to bed?"

I suggested she could find 10,000 guys happy to get her ends wet, there were probably dead gay quadriplegics up to the task. But who could live like that—a lot of people from my proctologist on down considered me a sociopath, but I couldn't—how to maintain a relationship when you had a turnstile at your bedroom door?

Once again: I did not understand. Maybe because I was "from Oregon." But Annie's girlfriends and spiritually evolved boyfriends certainly understood. As a boy "from Oregon," I'd thought that for most young women bimbohood was a predicament, not an ambition, but this was not sleazy slutty ungodded fishnet stocking, pushup bra Spanish fly-ed promiscuity, but wholesome, clean-cut, California Girl Scout, right off the Wheaties box *spiritual* promiscuity…

Everything that was up was down, plus now minus, white black. Even with every cop a criminal and all the sinners saints, no strychninegoosed acid could deliver this trip. The death of a thousand cuts. Ms. America said she still despised "your little slut" and, while "slut" now seemed relative, revenge takes many forms. All I knew was that whoever she'd been with the night before wasn't me and whoever she'd be with after tomorrow night wouldn't be me either. Back at her apartment, I looked at her bookshelf. Bye-bye James Joyce, Tolkien, Sylvia Plath and William Faulkner. Hello Hesse, Krishnamurti—*Freedom from the Known, Thought is Your Enemy, At the Feet of the Master* leaning against an orphaned copy of *The Heart is a Lonely Hunter*—

That night, however, she held onto me like a shipwreck victim to a life preserver, eclipsing passion to a connection like I'd never felt, our souls One, a sleepless dreamworld ride to Heaven's Gate—or maybe it was just half the sad super nova that can occur when you both know all your hopes for each other have exploded. But the next morning, in shops and bars with that smile to light a city, she admitted I was indeed 99% totally sweet, only 1% moody, arrogant, selfish, insulting, criminally reckless, lazy, remote, thoughtless, snobbish, controlling, patronizing, scary, and about as lovable as borax, and not one argument all day long. A record. Then, that evening when I said this had to be love, and *thank God this idiocy is about to blow over,* another fall down an elevator shaft, for when I said what do you want to do tomorrow night, she replied, "Be with somebody."

You mean there'd be another guy sleeping in her bed?

Of course.

Like a slow motion shotgun blast, the impact of this madness finally hit home: the priceless at the unpayable price.

No longer part of a joke or a dream, I could've been Ptolemy arguing with Columbus. I could possess her totally because I could no longer possess her at all. She was all mine because she could be others' as well. Or something like that—but we'd "lose everything" if I didn't change. We'd live on earth as in heaven, I as a One for All and All for One bonus baby in the he-harem.

I asked, "Do you love him?"

"Who?"

"The guy you're going to fuck tomorrow night."

A look cousin to horror shadowed her angel face. "No way."

So who was he?

"Just a guy. Nice." Slight shoulders shrugged. "Fun. It's nothing. Why do you seem so threatened?"

Be still, my beating heart. For that crazy Q there was no rational A. Here was a girl for whom, until very recently, lights out, under the covers, missionary position had been one step below starring in a stag movie. No longer. And that night between gymnastic nirvanas I got, chapter and verse, the low-down on the new one night stand love-minus-love gospels. Musical chairs sex as sacrament, Holy Grail of a new morality.

There was no turning back, it was her way or the highway, and I'd be either on the free love bus or off it. If I moved in with her and she didn't come home at night, so what? And the same for me, because hadn't I said sex was the most beautiful thing ever? Had I changed my mind? I didn't think sex was dirty, did I? Something to be ashamed of? Free Love was salvation. If we followed the Path we'd be "a hundred times stronger." We'd do it "together." "Not *together* together, but together, if you know what I mean."

Are you serious?

Delicate hands flew to a delicate face. "Ohmagod! I'm turning red! No! I'm joking—joking, joking, joking. You should've seen your face! But, still, what if?"

What if what?

Oh, and one more thing. I needed to learn to meditate. On what? "Mind change."

Ten Thousand Light Years from Home, miles from my front porch, I had no idea if this was the truth, a hoax or, somehow, both and, forget acid, had I heard of the new "love drug" MDA?—which makes you "melt no matter who you're with."

I said this is crazy, you could get cooties from a choir boy—that if she got colonized by the varsity squad she'd be napalming everything from her navel to her knees, that MDA was great if you want to screw on elephant tranquilizer—and when I said: what next? I sit on our living room couch, *Time is on My Side,* on the stereo, cheering from the cheap seats while she wrecked her diet blowing her lunch time study date?— she freaked.

"How can you say something that? Go home and screw your little slut."

That aspect was not going so hot. The "little slut," whose lovers, including me, numbered two, was on her way to a nervous breakdown—driven half crazy with guilt by her "betrayal" of Ms. America—she considered Ms. America a hero who broke her beautiful back at the Lettuce Inn Vegetarian Booze Boutique so their bad-ass butch bitch beatnik boss could sit on her bad-ass ass, and stood up for all the other's waitresses' rights, including the Sprite's. Her hips developing a *Dancing With the Stars* mind of their own, the Sprite had concluded that, conjoined, we were literally fucking Ms. America over, and denounced herself as a crash-pad if not home wrecker, as if she were a hookah-smoking Jezebel from the Freak Freely Hansel and Gretel-scape who'd betrayed the Pepsi Generation's Cinderella Madonna.

A Catholic, the Sprite believed the best thing about sex was that it was sin. We were watched and damned. As if Jesus and Ms. America were looking down on us from above, horrified and heartbroken. "We betrayed her," the Sprite said and were on the highway to hell.

After that it had just got wilder. Weeks before the mere term BJ had elicited a terrified torrent of tears, now—to settle a family feud, re: "freedom," the Sprite, her hair the color of fresh cut wheat, and conducting some sort of Freudian jihad with her family, had demanded that I have sex in her parents' bed and then more sex on their living room floor in front of her for some reason hated virgin younger sister.

But that was then, this was now. "Don't you understand?" Angel-faced Ms. America said, rotating her wine glass by its stem. "It doesn't matter what other guys I go to bed with. Other guys are just—"

Dick appliances? Like fun Osterizers, except with bodies attached?

What part of complete incomprehension didn't I understand? I could twist anything upside down. Why'd I suddenly gone from happy, idealistic, confident and funny to mocking, sullen, cynical, it was just sex, and why oh why by the bye was I so insecure?

I dunno. Maybe cuz three thousand years of Judeo-Christian morality were gone in a flash, a girl weeks ago as pure as the Madonna who I imagined I'd one day marry, booking random guys into her bed the way she'd make a restaurant reservation and, wait a sec, hadn't she just said what she just said?

That I should be the only one? Mark: Shop and compare.

What made me think that among the world's billion guys, I was the best? What E equals MC squared of the essential frictions did I have? Having to love a guy to sleep with a guy was crazy; you didn't have to be in love to make love. Free love, or at least free like, the freedom to "connect" with whoever was the most essential freedom of all. Monogamy made people property—and doesn't he look graceful?

Say what, what and *what?*

She'd taken me to "Meet n' Fuck," a former freak freely sweat lodge turned fern-jungled singles bar that once served roadkill and sprouts but now something called keesh, and Ms. America was gazing, as if absent-mindedly hypnotized, at a longhaired cowboy at the bar: bellbottomed paisley-shirted ectoplasm with cubist-cut, pubic hair sideburns.

She said that before, she'd considered me "the only one," that before she knew me she barely knew what sex was, but now, once her motor got started…

Had I been the hippie John Wayne she was looking for—the Man with the Answers not the boy with the questions—I' d've said, "I'm your prince and this shit has got to stop." But I wasn't and it didn't. The fact that she was "still angry" notwithstanding, "Because you were gone, and weren't using it" was not my idea of an explanation for why, while I was out of town, she'd brought some hole-in-a-doughnut Oooooooooomster over to my house to share my room for two or three nights.

Why oh why oh why hadn't I been nicer to her? Attempting perspective, I said that I'd tried to have more than one girlfriend, once I had two and a half and, maybe because I wasn't Mormon or Mick Jagger, it was like sticking my finger in a moral light socket—I felt like shit—and when I said we had an incredible night last night, why not call up tonight's funky leather stud and tell him to go fuck himself, she said while she loved lobster and caviar sometimes a hot dog could really hit the spot, and why was I so possessive? "You used to be so sure of yourself."

So what if sex was just an indoor thrill ride, nothing but X-rated social discourse? (Later: "ARE YOU JOKING? ARE YOU OUT OF YOUR MIND? I can't believe you believed all that stuff. What kind of trailer trash do you think I am? You're so gullible. I knew the conniving Little Slut wanted to A your B the minute she laid eyes on you. But you never even had a clue. And just for the record, Supreme Poopsie X would never give you a second glance." "But what about the Love Pirate and the Random Oooooooomster and...?).

When times change fast someone can become someone else. The girl of my dreams took my hand in hers the way a 19th century British missionary might have taken the hand of a pagan Zulu. "You're the only one who could ever take me out of this world; you taught me everything I know." A pause. Her eyes had ticked elsewhere to the cowboy at the bar. "Boy. What arms," she sighed while I sat, hopes ghosts, mind blown, as silent as a scar.

CHAPTER THIRTY-TWO:
SCEPTER OF DEMOCRACY

House organs proliferate espousing fervent aims and enlisting energetic members to voice rabid cause, whereas the BITR Reality furthers no special interest, but like a bleary-eyed buzzard, soars on outspread wings above tiny-seeming stiff-necked do-gooders, eager-footed scurrying money makers and earnest-voiced humble guru-becomers to spot a bloated carrion (victim of fossil fuel blight) about to burst, releasing stench, maggots, sickness and death across a befouled-enough land.

Fold wings! Plummet! Talons strike! Buzzard's beak pierces! Gagging air rushes! The balloon is pierced (did it do any good?). The bubble burst (did anyone notice?). The boil pricked (yes dear, someone up there cares...down here, too).

The buzzard grins, a Madison Avenue seventy-dollar smile that could sell coldcross buns at Newberry's. He's a satisfied bird. Croaks happily and pushes sluggishly into the air, lilting wings raise him to high feathered (sic) where he perches on the edge and disgorges daily tidbits to gaping-mouthed buzzardlets. Even corruption gets recycled.

—Ken Kesey's *Bend in the River* "Official Policy"

I f the sexual revolution was moving in one way, all power to the people was moving—Ken Kesey's hand groping at the tiller—in another. Toward truly revolutionary change in the political process. Arguably Ken's biggest and best—if not also most strangely overlooked—idea ever: a way, post whack acid dreams, to save Amerika if not from the Combine, at least from itself. What Kesey's brilliant plan called for was a complete overhaul of constitutional democracy.

Out here in the middle of the west Oregon nowhere, under skyscraping fir trees, a wood nymph's paradise if there ever was one, big, tall, healthy Lloyd Marbet, who might best be described as what mountain men might look like if they were college professors or, absent that, simply a man possessed of the down-home bookish élan of a senior logger promoted to the timekeeper's shack, told Walt Curtis and me,

"Oregon had been the second state to enact Initiative Process."

All about transparency, Kesey's "Bend in the River" advised banning of nuclear power plants. Issues would be televised, then a ballot provided in the daily newspapers and people would vote.

Sun cutting into the woods. The Clackamas River sighing and hissing out there through the trees somewhere. Under a cathedral canopy of Oregon firs grown to the sky, branches furred with bright green moss, squats Marbet's homestead. Lloyd's rural digs reflect less a conventional home than a tiny "town" of connected clapboard structures, recalling a grounded wood International Space Station, or if the Swiss Family Robinson only had propane tanks and solar panels.

Lloyd has been living here since 1977, about three years after the conclusion of Ken Kesey's attempt at the radical reinvention of the American political process, an event in which Lloyd came from out of nowhere to run a four minute mile on the road not taken. Through the nascent medium of Kesey's "Bend in the River," Marbet attempted to stop further construction of nuclear power plants if not in the United States, at least here in the progressive state of mind otherwise known as Oregon.

Now, thirty-plus years later, he can look back with satisfaction. Thirty miles away the Trojan Nuclear Reactor is an atomic ghost town, shut down for years. Despite numerous attempts by local power utilities, no other reactors have been constructed, partly because of Marbet's often largely single-handed efforts. Tacked up out front, one of Marbet's better known aphorisms: "If our youth are tried for their conscience, when will our leaders be tried for their lies?"

Marbet could have sprung whole as a figment of Kesey's imagination, an eco-intellectual who lives in a world where coyotes run in packs and spidery vines crawl over maples and a forest floor woven with nettles…a tree fort with a "huge" picture window stands just above head high, its old maybe eight by ten-foot floor triangulated between the thick trunks of three firs that have grown side by side by side, while grapes glisten like green chandeliers from their vines.

Marbet's benefactor, a Texas libertarian, told him that he was free to stay on the land under two conditions: that Marbet continue his work, and that "everything I had be on wheels. I had to be ready to move at a moment's notice."

Indeed. Multnomah County Judge Michael Marcus's moldy mail van, in which Judge Marcus used to reside, sits settling into the ground in a way that suggests the van may one day (not unlike Kesey's bus *Furthur*) become one with the earth. 50 acres. It's been tough to retain a toe-hold. Ever since Marbet began protesting rare-earth metal producer Teledyne WaChang, the company has been sending helicopters over his land...

Inside, Lloyd's realm is a saw-milled space capsule insulated with books, books, books. Imagine an 1880 of the future. Often a buzz-killer with girlfriends. "That's always the problem with my relationships, they like to *visit*."

Marbet used to live nearby on the Clackamas River where he could, most any morning, run naked a mile up and down the beach...

Those were the days. "When I dropped acid," he says, "I saw it as a sacrament. So I sold acid. But I was a lousy dealer." Both his grandfathers were preachers. Raised in Binghamton, New York the son of a pharmaceutical salesman, "headed for the stratosphere of the American economy," Marbet grew up text-book middle-American. "My father was like the Reverend Mister Black. He was an enforcer." Upon high school graduation, Marbet was delivered to his local Navy recruiter by his dad, and ended up on a cargo ship delivering supplies to ports in Vietnam. "Mostly what we had on board was junk. Once we anchored off the mouth of the Mekong Delta when a battle was going on. Out of the fog and smoke came desperate soldiers, 'Do you have munitions?' 'No, all we've got is Kool Aid and Vicks Vapo Rub.'"

When his ship returned to port in San Francisco, Marbet jumped ashore and went AWOL. "I'd had enough war. I just walked away from the Navy." Back home in New York, Dad was not happy. "He disinherited me." No matter. Marbet helped form an SDS chapter, bought a VW bus, got his girlfriend pregnant and, seeking an abortion, headed for Colorado. "Along the way we kept meeting people who were going to Woodstock. When we got to Colorado we found out the abortionist had gone to Woodstock." The result: Marbet became the father of a beautiful daughter named Gathering, now a movie actress.

He came to Oregon more or less by accident and found Portland, "an arms-open place, never had I felt so welcome." Here, Marbet read Erik Erickson on Gandhi, then got the message that was to give the direction to his life when he picked up *The Perils of the Peaceful Atom, the Myth of Free Power* by Richard Curtis and Elizabeth Hogan. "That made it all clear. To me, nuclear power was bringing the war home… the American people were sold a concept, not a technology. Because a resolved technology did not exist in viable form."

"No sooner than I'd said if they turn on Trojan we should go to Canada, I turned the page and the next chapter was titled, 'Don't Bother Running.' I'd run from my father, run from Vietnam, I can't run from this. The world's a closed system."

In 1973 he saw a PGE "Boardman Nuclear Power Plant" ad in the paper about a hearing on licensing. "I went. They asked, 'Does anybody care to intervene?' Nobody raised a hand. I did. Their lawyer said, 'You're going to have to write a petition,' I said, 'Where's a piece of paper?'"

"Trojan had been a rollover. Bechtel was the contractor.[25] Human failure was not even a consideration. The designer was actually named Muhammad Ali; he didn't even design earthquake protection."

Lloyd took a bus to Boardman, ended up sleeping on the beach, went to the meeting, where the state attorney said, "You'll be making a big mistake."

Lloyd said to himself, "I can't do this…Then I saw the proceedings and realized, I can do this. I'd watched 'Perry Mason.'"

It wasn't as if the local power elite had come up with a bullet-proof plan. "They were going to put the nuke next to a bombing range, then they decided to move the whole shooting match to Pebble Springs (now a huge garbage dump)."

It was not long after that he heard about Kesey's upcoming "Bend in the River." At first, most of what he knew was that the conference was named after a movie and a book. But by the time he was named a delegate, Lloyd was inspired enough to bike 180 miles from Detroit Lake to Central Oregon Community College to pick up on the action.

Kesey was a fan of Oregon Governor Tom McCall, and when he chanced to meet the creator of McCall's odd day/even day gas plan, the national solution to Jimmy Carter's 1973 gas shortage (which left cars in my Portland neighborhood snaking halfway around the block behind gas pumps still gallons from running dry), Kesey could not have been more complimentary. "It was like meeting the inventor of the cockroach."

---

25 For those not acquainted with Big Brotherish construction behemoths: super secretive Bechtel is the largest construction consortium in America—famous as a progenitor of the Hoover Dam and for its connection with the bin Laden family, and it is a big force behind nuclear power.

McCall returned the favor a year later when he applauded "Bend in the River," Kesey's brainstorm for reinventing American government. "It's in the populist tradition in the finest sense."

Oregon was one of six states where an initiative petition could create law. Where a prescribed number of signatures could put an issue on the ballot and, defined by Kesey's great notion, perhaps the greatest one he ever had: Instead of having vital government-directed decisions brokered through the muddy, self-serving medium of elected politicians, why not have these decisions determined by ballot initiatives? If, for example, the government wanted to build a nuclear reactor in your neighborhood, why should the decision be left to local politicians who might be—in fact, likely would be—seduced by power company lobbyists with pockets as deep as the Marianas Trench?

Kesey got the idea at a November 1973 Billings, Montana land use conference where, as a guest panelist, he had informed conferees: "We can either sink or swim. We're at the level of 'earthquake consciousness.' There are those who say everything is falling in the sea anyway, so why not forget it? (But) we're not finished as far as I'm concerned."

There at the conference Kesey was asked by a pig farmer: "You one of those ecologists flew in here to talk about yourselves?" Kesey said yes, and then asked the farmer what he would do to solve problems, ecological and otherwise. "Put it on TV. Then let the folks at home vote on who won."

The Kesey brand was still riding high. In 1974 *Book World* listed *Cuckoo's Nest* as number three on college campuses behind *Slaughterhouse Five* and *Lord of the Rings*. But Kesey was on to more nine-to five issues—like the end of politicians—preaching a "second consciousness" divorced from "blind consumerism, violence and destruction of the land." The land was being "ripped off—just like men have ripped off women. We must begin to treat the earth like a good wife and she will treat us like a good husband."

"We're going through a great time, an incredible revolution. There is much good on one side, much bad on the other." He insisted people relearn the idea of yin and yang. "We have the best and worst of all possible worlds right here in this country. We have the potential for all kinds of ends, all kinds of beginnings. If we can't pull this out, no one can."

Forget novels, forget acid, forget even the actually already pretty much forgotten Movie, it was time to save the world. Not the old forgotten pie-in-the-sky psychedelic way, but by way of "electronic populism," "Bend in the River" pioneered the idea that politicians were useless middlemen, that people could use the democratic process to govern themselves directly. "People want to testify," Kesey said, "It's a religious thing almost. People want to jump up and testify."

Kesey was nothing if not optimistic, proclaiming, "The future is ours to mold like a piece of clay. We have a choice. Choosing is not judging. It's when we relinquish choice that we give it over to judgment... Choosing not to put all your marbles in a Winnebago. Choosing to go against the grain of our national madness. We know that, until we heal the whole community, everybody is subject to a kind of SLA (Symbionese Liberation Army) treatment."

Then down to cases. "Anytime somebody lights a cigarette and blows the smoke at you, they're violating your area. You stop them right there. You do not sanction it any longer. Once we realize that, we join together and the haggle is bearable.

"With the price of food on the rise and the country on the brink of ecological homicide, more people realize that everything may end, that this could be it. Our alternative is to get back to another way of life—our own farms, our own little gardens, our own participation in a balance of life and nature.

"If people would grow Victory Gardens again, that would be the ultimate consciousness, making our own produce, grow(ing) what we need for existence."

So, "Bend in the River." 1974. Kesey took to quoting the Master, "When Gandhi was asked (what he thought) about western civilization, the gentleman replied, 'I think it would be a fine idea.'"

Poets Marty Christensen and Walt Curtis, author of *The Mad Bomber's Notebook,* were named delegates. Kesey explained, "It's vital that poets participate. Poets know about affection and there can be no civilization without affection. It's affection that's on the line in Bend." (The Oregon town, not the Kesey campaign).

As touched on previously, Marty had met Kesey at a poetry reading across town at "Fool's Paradise" in Portland in 1972 where Marty competed with acts like Sam the Saw and the musical epiphanies of my pal, croaky-voiced Cork Hubbard, the world's tallest dwarf (think a shorter, younger and tubbier Bob Dylan)who'd later star in *Under the Rainbow* and do a wild turn in the Hunter Thompson bio-pic *Where the Buffalo Roam* but who, right then rocked the tavern with songs like "So Sorry I Came on Your Dress." Anyway, Kesey showed up at the tavern with Prankster second-in-command Ken Babbs. They set up an applause-o-meter in the back of the gloomy beer mill as Marty was reading from a portfolio of poems.

Of all the poets performing that night, Marty got the highest score on the Prankster applause-o-meter. Kesey was so impressed he named Marty head of the Portland delegation to "Bend in the River." By then, Kesey's full-blown plan for a national symposium designed to determine the hippie/utopian/Keseyian future of the Republic. Asked why there could not be more delegates, Kesey replied, "Because voting on the delegates is one of the most important things we are doing. We are choosing to choose rather than choosing not to choose and that means unkinking the choosing muscle. Going through the whole process. Having to stand up and speak. Having to vote. We are demystifying the democratic procedure...Besides; we want to keep the number of delegates at Bend to around 100 so we don't end up with a rock and roll show."

No matter. "All kinds of people are being elected delegates—farmers, housewives, city councilmen, longhairs. Human affection is being put on the line at Bend. I'm betting we can all stand each other's body odor, that we all like each other more than we dislike each other."

This would be accomplished at the intimate tactical level. "All the delegates will be living in dorms. By the conference's end—well, if you took all these people and boiled them in water, and if you drank the water, you'd get one of the greatest highs God has ever known."

But that was scarcely all. "Now, when all these people get together they'll see that the great gods that are supposed to be taking care of us all—those gods have fallen." The Rx? "What we must all have—a way of keeping in touch without staging a rock festival. We're finding the guys at the top can't run things. The future of Oregon must be decided by the community."

Delegates wrote up a ten-point "media referendum." When the Bend Women's Caucus asked the "full conference" to stand behind a call for free abortions, Kesey announced, "I'm not against women.

I'm defending the small. As a nation, we take the life of the small. Any woman who feels she wants an abortion because she can't take care of the child can give me the child."

Kesey's stand on abortion ran against the tide. "I feel abortion to be probably the worst worm in the revolutionary philosophy, a worm bound in time to suck the righteousness from the effort we are engaged in."

His wife Faye agreed, "Even if I were raped, I wouldn't get one."

Kesey wrapped the issue up with: "You don't plow under the corn because the seed was planted with a neighbor's shovel."

But Kesey's message, however reinforced by additional rape analogies, was otherwise pretty much eco uber alles. At a Portland recycling meeting May 9, 1974 at Couch Grade School, he resorted to Old Time Religion: "Please don't mess up the earth. The rape of the earth is like the rape of a woman."

Then, for the sake of perspective, time for a little combobulated Zen. Noting, "We get it together for a little while and then lose it all to a cosmopolitan hat and garment manufacturer who needs more juice to run more sewing machines we don't even know about," Ken descended to the cosmic essentials. "Let me define what I mean when I say we. There are five different we's. First we is the we that sits around the pitcher of beer. The second is the revolutionary we, wanting to take care of things. The third we is all of human kind. The fourth we, all the rocks and birds and stars and everything. The fifth we is the consciousness that knows the other four. This group tonight represents the second we, the we of Martin Buber's nation, the we that is neither collectivist nor individualist, but the we that moves between the two, helping humankind out of bad times. These are the people who take care of business in a community when it needs to be taken care of: the school nurse, the prison guard who tries to put a little humanity in his work. It's whoever decides that somebody's going to have to take up the slack."

One of the speakers at "Bend in the River" was the young and suddenly recognized Andrew Weil, whose out-of-nowhere bestselling *The Natural Mind* had rocketed to the top of *The New York Times* best seller list three years before as an Alice-falls-down-the holistic-rabbit hole day-for-night redefinition of drugs. Weil's premise began: "There are no bad drugs, only…" and took off from there: "I have never seen anyone have as much physical trouble giving up heroin as I have seen many people have giving up cigarettes...In a supportive setting, with proper suggestion, a heroin addict can withdraw without medication other than aspirin and have little more discomfort than that of a moderate cold...If heroin could be isolated from its content in our society; we would soon see that the drug per se is relatively innocuous from the purely medical point of view."

Weil went from there to the real belly laughs: "Let us be done with straight thinking for now; there is a bright alternative to consider." Which leads straight to Chapter 7: A Trip to The Moon. "Stoned thinking is the mirror image of straight thinking. When we step into non-ordinary reality even for a moment, we experience things directly, see inner contents rather than external forms, and suddenly find ourselves able to participate in changing things for the better."

Weil, perhaps more than anyone, brought a sort of expanded Kesey-think to the respectable middleclass.

Nothing that radical, really. Kesey praised what he termed the Magic Scepter of Democracy: "When a big log truck goes to pass you after jake-braking the back of your neck for twenty miles, give him the Magic Scepter of Democracy as he roars by."

Then off to the races. At an Astoria town meeting the big issue was the looming construction of an Amax Aluminum Plant. "The Media Referendum is a way of finding out if you really want the aluminum plant built," Kesey said.

"Too late for that," he was told by a "pessimistic student." "The aluminum plant has bought the land and cleared it and they've bought the power line right of ways from here to Bonneville Dam."

"Give them the Scepter of Democracy," Kesey said. "It's magical."

In the coastal town of Newport, Kesey railed against "the Venusians" ("They will do anything to suck up earth life") and what he called AGRA, which he described as his acronym for corporate farms. AGRA, Kesey claimed, was "locking laying hens in cages, feeding them amphetamines-loaded grain, eggs falling plop on conveyer belts, lights on all the time, don't know if it's day or night, they're laying two-three eggs every twenty-four hours, only last a couple months and they're burned out birds. AGRA runs in whole new chicken crews, old hulks sliced and sold for stew."

But AGRA chickens were the wrong issue for this shouting crowd. "They're all het up over selling logs to Japan and letting the Russians fish the bottom clean just off the coast."

So down the road, Kesey took a default position: "Over at the coast it was the Rooskies getting all the fish and the Japs the wood. Imagine a floating mill three-hundred miles off the Coast taking all the logs shipped out of Coos Bay and making fiberboard to sell back to Americans to build houses out of and then ask yourself, what ever happened to good old Doug Fir planks?

"Ah, our minds are gone, given away to Proctor and Gamble for so long there's nothing left. But it's not really our fault, because the energy that produces our mind rot is not human, it's a parasite, counting on us giving up our liberties a little at a time.

But! "We can change that. We can start right here, in a local community and we can recover our precious fluids if we spoke to one another freely."

The problem with Ken Kesey's potential political masterpiece was it had his signature all over it, especially as that signature related to Kesey's old nemesis: Money. Driving into Portland, Kesey said, "When you have to go through six women to get to a VP over at Weyerhauser, it's pretty apparent they're doing so bad we can't even begin to imagine what."

"They're too big, spend too much money. We're setting an economic precedent with BITR: the smaller your budget, the more righteous you can be."

Besides, if you were the Powers That Be, wouldn't having Ken Kesey as a new government power broker be like hiring Typhoid Mary to distribute serum for The Plague? Gloria Steinem, I.F. Stone, Elliot Richardson, Alvin Toffler, Carl Sagan, Russell Means, David Brower, Dick Gregory were all invited to the democracy-morphing shindig. But a more lowdown civilian crowd showed up. A lot of cowboy boots and shirts. Kesey appeared in burgundy double-knit slacks and a pink and burgundy flowered "Three Musketeer" shirt and "matching mauve leg wear." Paul Krassner was "a symphony in blue denim, complete with brightly colored patches, and hand embroidery!" Then there was the colorful politics. Kesey: "Life begins at conception and we haven't got the right to deny it." (But) If we get into abortion that's all that will come out of this council." Krassner "told us he was having a thousand condoms pinpricked. So that everyone could have the right to life…"

Then it was down to brass tacks. Kesey: "We need a community center which would combine a recreation center, daycare, beer tavern, a pizza and snack place for kids and families and flush toilets under one roof."

Kesey also aired it out on public support for "prisoner rehabilitation." "Well and good, mate, but as one old con to another it wasn't the public that gave Oregon's reasonably good rehab program a kick in the balls… What I learned from the time I did was it is the prisoners who rehabilitate the prisoners, all the other stuff is fried ice cream."

He concluded the BITR End manifesto: "Oregon's greatest resource is the concern, the unabashed care of its citizens for the well-being of our state's forests, waters (did you know Waw-re-gon means 'beautiful water?') fields and skies, and, above all, for each other. As long as this concerns exists, no force—not Nixon, not Japan, not Russia, not even the Venusians—will bring us down." Meanwhile. "I haven't given up on my work on acid." But as for us sheep? "Most kids today have given up. They just want to smoke dope and giggle."

PART FIVE:
THE SAVED

Ken Kesey walking with son Zane at the Kesey family farm,
Pleasant Hill, Oregon, June 5th, 1976

Chapter Thirty-three:
The District Sleeps Alone
Tonight

"Lovemaking is not a paranoid and threatening gesture that you have to hide from the world. It is tribalized. You are in the community. You do your thing; it is yours. Others may want to watch, learn, comment, even laugh."
— from the sign at the entry to the Sandstone Retreat

Heroin.

Dawn at the Portland Golf Club, down by the lake. Lost golf balls down there, worth up to 25 cents apiece if fished out, murky treasure orbs, like Easter eggs on the furry bottom. My old pal Big G Little O with his shotgun. Who says you can never go home again? A duck floating from the pale sky, orange triangle feet skidding lace over the mirror water before, kerblewy.

Dead duck. Big G, happy hunter/nervous junkie trying to kick (I thought he was just having a nervous breakdown) slashing into the mirrory murk here by the swamp trickle of Fanno Creek which fed the lake, bending over to fetch his bloody bird. Afternoons we'd spend at the womb-dark "Golden Garter Tavern," drinking 25 cent beers with all the other Raleigh Hills junkies, one of whom I remember, red-haired already ex-con Phil G., took me outside in the dim bright of dusk to show me where the veins on the back of his pudgy hands converged like the meeting of the Tigris and Euphrates rivers, and where a needle might find the best home it might ever have. I thanked God I could not stand shots. Mostly I hung out at the bar and drank Buds, underwritten by my pal Billy Wilson. The Marine Corps was compensating Vietnam vet Billy

$1,200 a month for losing his leg. A lot of money back in 1973 but, after what he'd been through, we'd earned it.

I was coming up in the world. At night I tended bar at a dance hall where Signe Anderson, the original vocalist of the Jefferson Airplane, sang jazz standards, her angelic voice humbling psychedelia, serenading the strippers from the topless-bottomless emporium across the street, staggering around in front of the bar in their dagger-heeled pumps like lost deer…Working behind the beer taps at the "American Museum," I discovered a new world of power. For—across the street from "Satan's Disco,"[26] this was the lap of bohemian anti-luxe. In which the young bartender becomes the authority figure—the 24 year-old father advises his 55 year-old son to go home—to the one that had his wife in it…

…At the "Veritable Quandary" a hot barfly said, given my OK symmetry and the fact she could have me gone before breakfast, did I want to go back to her apartment and check out her mood meter?

The Quandary was a little brick womb with a view, a Portland bar where you could get married for a night almost any night of the week. Ex boys and girls—students from Portland State, young real estate brokers, journalists, and stewardesses would, at about fifteen minutes before the witching hour, pair up. It made me wonder about alcohol, thanks to which the choices got pretty approximate, like whatever young woman you were sitting closest to at 12:55.

Too, I had worries about acid. It was clear by now that the illusion had been that an illusion was the Answer. Mania from hallucinatory heaven, blessed acid was supposed to rescue the Pepsi Generation from the lockstep grid of corporate consciousness to release a super sane super consciousness for a super man.

Instead we got a loaded gun impossible to aim. It had apparently

---

26 Owned by former baseball and basketball star Frank Peters, who had not yet run for Governor, not yet been thrown in jail for constructing a "downtown pot ranch," but who drove a red Cadillac convertible, rode a Harley Davidson with hand-stitched leather saddlebags whose pouches he'd tailored to hold on either side a block of giveaway government cheese, who was manager of the Portland Mavericks baseball team whose roster sported actor Kurt Russell and Jim Bouton, author of the greatest nonfiction book ever—*Ball Four*—and who, when one of his players, Reggie Thomas, put a .44 magnum to his—Frank's—head after not being named to the starting lineup [which Frank picked out of his hat], did not throw Reggie off the team but made him leadoff hitter, who was engaged to punk rock chanteuse Kate Fate who tried to shoot him through the door of his penthouse apartment when he failed to seal the deal [four slugs, but a no-hitter], and who I was convinced was, if not the inspiration for Randle McMurphy, then perhaps a better real life version of Randle McMurphy, a real Democrat.

made friends crazy. One of the best writers I knew had tripped his brains out, become homeless in New York City, and ended up drinking holy water from Catholic churches where voices told him that in order to escape the Venusians out to kill him he had to throw them off his scent by stripping naked and covering himself in dog shit. Thus undressed, he walked into the lobby of the Algonquin Hotel, was arrested and thrown in an insane asylum.

You are what you eat, and by the beginning of the 1970s, capitalism had devoured the revolution, in great big Levi's bellbottomed, RCA record, and new BMW bites. Suburbanurchins were inheriting the earth. Becoming, case in point, the pigs. Freaks were now cops. They'd tip-toe into the American Museum, baby faced and still new to their uniforms, less like real police than social workers who could kill you, literal boys in blue stoned on the tie-dyed idea you could *reason* with people. Plagued nightly by violent wino space aliens, my front teeth never not in peril, a pool cue cocked to my ear like Mickey Mantle eyeing the fence, I had to remind them how to deliver whack, whack, whack nine from the sky (No joke: we'd just had this black tornado of a kid go berserk because I wouldn't serve him a drink because he wasn't 21, punching people all over the place, including me, while Portland's crew cut hippie finest stood by the bar, hands on the butts of their holstered new revolvers trying to *talk* to him). Meanwhile Kesey's freak freely culture was being codified by the new Establishment. Us. Everybody got to toke, rock and sleep with everybody else.

When I told Ms. America that had I come home while she was staying in my room with her new hole-in-a-doughnut Random Oooooomster, I would have killed him and thrown her down the stairs just to hear the bones break, she said I must have lost my mind, that I meant everything to her and I should be happy to let her use my room, what was wrong with that? I wasn't there, was I? We were no longer each other's possessions. She wasn't doing anything wrong, just making love and, besides, she actually owned the bed and she'd changed the sheets, and I must be seriously sick and lost to say something hideous like that, it made no sense at all.

* * *

As Soldier One in the KISS Army my penthouse pauper embourgiosement was going pretty well. John Shirley had been the first to interview the new group on their debut schlep through Portland and I put them on the cover of OD as our new publication was sometimes known. Now on the phone though, a voice from the recent past, the yellow-haired Sprite. We were no longer As One. For one thing I was terrorized by her Catholic aversion to birth control and for another she was into 7th dimensional shit like this: She had a new boyfriend LVL, who was short, muscular and fresh-faced, a chimp-like version of the guys on The Brady Bunch. LVL for some reason hated my guts, the last time I'd seen him he leapt on my back and tried to strangle me but now, according to the Sprite, he needed my advice about a serious potentially relationship-killing sex problem, so if he called could I be cool for once, let bygones be bygones and lend a helping hand?

What kind of sex problem?

"It's super embarrassing. Could you just wait and let him tell you?"

Why not?

I was now a magazine editor. Mornings, I'd come to the eighth or seventh or sixth or whatever floor it was on offices downtown at *One Dollar Magazine*. A Portland monthly, founded on our prematurely balding 21 year-old jock publisher's BankAmerica card, brainchild of our six-three dental floss-thin highly talented and discriminating ("I like *some* of the Mona Lisa, but not all of the Mona Lisa") 22 year-old, suave, lady's man art director James Kiehle, who never met a kitten with a whip he didn't like.

Fun. Pretty much, I sold out to the Alpha Annies. For the End of Capitalist Pig Amerika was on life support and *One Dollar*—which sustained itself on ads for expensive stereo systems, high fashions and designer furniture none of our staff could remotely afford—was an obedient-to-the-buy product whore. A schizophrenic capitalist's tool all about paranoia, crime, getting loaded and experimental fiction, *One Dollar's* bare-walled offices were a $400 a month delapitorium Raymond Chandler might have loved, but our basic message was: *Buy more, think less.*

Within three issues the "editer" could spell editor and, as that man, I published stories including *Confessions of an American Glue Sniffer,* Walt Curtis's *Wino Consciousness,* the first work of writers like soon-to-be cyber-punk Jesus, John Shirley, and Mikal Gilmore, a track-runner-thin, extremely polite, peaceful genius whose artist brother Gary would soon achieve greater heights as a world famous killer, and, as a sort of magazine within the magazine homage/rip off of Paul Krassner, *Conspiracy Digest,* in which my pal, the World's Tallest Dwarf Corky Hubbard headlined articles such as HOW ARI ONASIS RIGGED WORLD WAR II and WIN A SHOPPING SPREE WITH PATTY HEARST, and trumpeted theories like: Mamie Eisenhower had not died of "old age" as contended by the "liberal press," but had, in fact, been "eliminated" by the CIA after it was discovered she'd served as a mole for the Soviet Secret Police for 31 years.

But the best part of the magazine were the visuals, for we also had Clyde Keller who, at nineteen, had been Bobby Kennedy's official family photographer. Many if not most professional photographers approach photography as a sort of minuet, a formalized overtly controlled dance to *snap.* Clyde did it the other way around, like a genius terrorist or Marx brother, he'd swoop in, be talking away, and click, click, click, his trigger finger would be working completely separate from the rest of the corporeal Clyde.[27]

Clyde also introduced us to Father. Post Soma, primordial downhome awe-shucks shamanism was on the wane, and its ancient younger brother Guru culture was on the march. Here in Oregon in the person of Father, a grinning fifty-ish white-robed maharishi manqué from Bombay or Fresno, whose ethereal essence, complete with ringed fingers and waterfall beard, and whose celestial Zen appeared to revolve around chicks and food, approached me with the idea of a Father article in mind (Father somehow "owned" a "gourmet" restaurant named "Father's" by the beach in Manzanita that was operated by, well, chicks)—to be fair we published two yin-yang articles, one titled FATHER IS GOD, the other NO, HE'S NOT.

My phone rang. It was LVL. "Truce," he said.

"Truce," I replied. "Zup?"

"You know the Sprite? What a hot little bod she's got and how when her motor gets running, it's Katie bar the door? Well, you got a minute? Cuz therein lies a tale."

What I heard next, on top of what Ms. America had visited upon

---

27 He doesn't like to be confined; Clyde could get claustrophobia in the Sahara (not to jinx his future, but God only knows what he'll do in a coffin).

me by way of the Random Ooooomster, the fucking Love Pirate and Annie Fucking Alpha's Free Love Pussy Power Uber Alles Holy Grail convinced me that my future as a novelist was doomed, that I had no inkling to the 1970s human heart and that the best I could do was fail to conjoin with as many Alices as possible as they fell down their rabbit holes—and stick to my new job: pimp for the system.

It only took my partners and me three years to drive our magazine into bankruptcy, but anyway, on the phone, the world's saddest song on the world's smallest violin. What inspired this call? The Sprite itchy for a reunion? LVL reminding me that the Sprite was, unsatisfied or not, his? LVL's problem? His inability not to, in his words, "detonate on contact" and if my advice: "Try to think of the most boring least sexy thing possible: Like the Super Bowl or your last New Year's Eve Party" helped, cool, but...

...One day, contemplating the story about Ken Kesey that I was about to write and that he was about to hate, I stepped from the elevator into the hall to discover a ransom note: WE HAVE KIDNAPPED YOUR FIRSTBORN SON AND IF YOU DO NOT MEET OUR DEMANDS WE WILL TURN HIM INTO GOD.

CHAPTER THIRTY-FOUR: VENUSIANS

"The first time that I ever saw Marty he was walking in the Portland rain with the hood of his jacket pulled over his head like a deep sea diver wearing a bell helmet.

Observing him from the safety of my car, which was stopped at a stop light, Marty looked as if he was seeing things that most of us would never see. And doing things that we would never do. And thinking things that I will never think. And he was saying things that we would never be able to say. He is psychically deep sea diving, and protecting himself from the elements while gathering images in his head, the hood meant to keep them inside-o-his head until he gets home and he can deal with them there in the solitude of his confines, near his printing press."

—Gus Van Sant

AT THE END OF A DRUNKEN BINGE
explosions of twilight
twinkle over the river
as sometimes my body shudders
while my hands keep shaking

loneliness whisks all my emotions
far back inside bewildering memories

I remember meeting dead green men
survivors of a dream I woke up in
and knew then that they were much
much more than mere hallucinations

afterwards I screamed for thirteen hours
in jail before being handcuffed to a bed

now I have returned to normal brain
and watch the sunset slash its vein
—Marty Christensen

As you may recall from the beginning of this text, Ken Kesey, after returning from a trip to Egypt with Paul Krassner and the Grateful Dead, took another, shorter trip, from Portland to his farm near Eugene, driving the hundred miles down the I-5 in his aging Pontiac convertible with the Portland poets wiry Walt Curtis and short, round, grizzled and quick Marty Christensen, and Marty's tall, lovely sad eyed wife Lorna. With them was a bottle of whisky.

You may also recall that the topic of conversation was whether or not the world was controlled by Venusians or the CIA. Kesey reported that Krassner felt the CIA and their henchmen, the military-industrial complex, were in control, but Kesey leaned more toward the Venusians. Marty was inclined to agree with Ken, if only on the grounds that "I think the CIA is not that smart. I don't think they can put it together." Perhaps because it was Kesey's bottle of whisky, Marty added, "I think the common man is probably on your side," before reversing himself. "I doubt ten percent of (the American people) believe the CIA is in control. But all of the evidence points out to me"—Marty suddenly spoke in headlines, "That they probably are!"

Kesey maybe also a little gassed, then took a centrist position, saying that while he felt the Venusians were real and that they were "the bad guys," the Venusians were not running amok because certain friendly "arcane forces have those otherworldly villains under their thumb. Because, in the first place, they are binaural."

Kesey's attentions had been sucked, lured, tugged or pushed back toward the otherworldly. Not the acid otherworldly, but another otherworldly. New gnosis. Tim Leary, champion of "the fifth freedom," the civil right to control the state of your own consciousness, had written Kesey prophesying a new age: "I believe H. I. (higher intelligence) has already sent complex signals to the planet earth, not in the form of laryngeal-manual symbols, but in scientific and mathematical messages. I suggest that the periodic table of elements, the DNA code, the obvious sequence of metamorphosis and evolutionary mutation, and mathematical systems are codes which can be deciphered and which communicate message...The message is that life is seeded in womb planets (like earth) and is designed to pass through larval terrestrial stages and then to metamorphose into interstellar existence...I believe the occult-guru-consciousness movement and the back-to-nature-take-care-of-your-animals-survival movement are boring...In my opinion, the more publicized remnants of the counter-culture of the 60s—rock stars, Hell's Angels, occultists, commune-hippies, mad bombers—have attracted attention away from the most hopeful and important legacy of the last decade...a new generation of turned-on young scientists. . .long-hair mathematicians, computer adepts. Bio-chemists, geneticists, particle physicists, astronomers..."

And poets. As they continued on the drive to Springfield, Kesey presented Walt Curtis, Marty and Marty's wife Lorna further ideas about the likelihood that our world is shot through with people who look like humans but who were actually born on the second planet from the Sun." On the way Marty, in the back seat of Kesey's Pontiac convertible, nursing the scotch, wondered: "Structures like the pyramids, or Stonehenge or whatever, are ways in which people could control the forces—Venusian forces—by the construction of those sites?"

Kesey said, "Uh, no."

Lanky "street poet" Walt Curtis, whose wavy graying hair sometimes appeared to be an explosion above his high forehead, said, "Then why did the Arabs build it there?"

Kesey said, "It (was) built to pass something on. When you're there in Egypt, they have it—see! They're in control of the past. Think what that means! When you know anything about hermetic philosophies—if you have control of the past, you have control of the future! They're just beginning to know what they have. Realizing that they have all the records—since the burning of the Alexandria library."

Marty said, "As strange as the burning of the Alexandria library was—there is a comment in Bernard Shaw's play on Caesar. Caesar comes into Alexandria and he sees the burning library. He says, 'Well, forget about it, I'm an author too. It's not that important.' What is that play—*Man and Superman?*"

Kesey said, "Must be."

"Which is as close as Bernard Shaw got to it, or Caesar. Because what—what did they figure? There was only one-one thousandths of the known writing of the world left after the fire? Which accounts for the fragments of Sappho, and so forth."

Kesey said, "Uh huh."

"And it was all in this one fucking building."

Kesey said, "Uh huh."

Marty, who turned pre-literate moments into poetry, asked, "Why would ninety-nine percent of the literature of the known world be in one fucking library?"

Kesey said, "Well. I can understand that. It's because there are certain people that care and take care of—"

Walt Curtis exclaimed, "Scribes!"

Kesey said, "It is the bureau of standards on this globe! It's located there. Nobody has fully understood what that means yet. It means that—it's like your balls are right between your legs!"

Walt agreed and Kesey continued, "You wouldn't find your balls in your armpit, or hanging from under your ear."

"But what does that mean?" Walt asked.

"Egypt is like your balls," Ken replied, "I mean, residing in Egypt is the DNA signal."

Walt said, "We're approaching the Albany plant."

Kesey, "The armpit of Oregon, as (Governor) McCall used to call it."

Marty said, "I think (Blank) was a Venusian. He came out from Chicago. He was an executive with the Kraft Corporation."

"Well," Kesey said, "this is the very sort of people Venusians like."

"Who knows anything about him?" Marty wondered, "I've heard he has a really shoddy past in Chicago. He's part owner of this monstrosity—the Albany paper mill. And on the Portland planning commission for years and years."

Kesey said, "That's what I call a Venusian, man. I'll tell you the way you can recognize them. Because they don't have auras. You look at 'em and you finally think, there's something really—something missing—I can't see it. He's got his nose, his ears, his eyes—"

Marty made the obvious connection, "Just like Jay Gatsby!"

"Look at this cloud! See, over this place." Kesey pointed to the mill. "This is not by accident!"

Meanwhile, New Noir. If Ken Kesey's former Stanford classmate Robert Stone's requiem for the wreckage of the 1960s, *Dog Soldiers,* was any indication, the novel might not be dead, but God, rest His soul, was coming home in a body bag. *Dog Soldiers* was the tale of brutally hapless heroin people, Vietnam vets, cons and junkies, who visit their variously queer, fatally nervous, heavily armed and strung-out selves upon the Mexican hide-a-way of a balding burly psychedelic mushroom and wine-by-the-pitcher enthusiast, ex-Love Generation deity Dieter—"a roshi who freaked out"—AKA Dr. Dope, who goes by Ken Kesey's lyric:

Of offering more than what I can deliver,
I have a bad habit it's true
But I have to offer more than what I can deliver,
to be able to deliver what I do.

And who explains his former profession this way: "I am not now—nor have I ever been—God. In any ordinary meaning of the word. I made certain statements for political reasons. In my opinion they were what the times demanded. If things had worked out everything would have been clear in the end."

In Dieter/Kesey's realm, neo-Zen would render thought and action one as the Way was revealed in void-pure clarity, but if the deliciously pessimistic *Dog Soldiers,* published in 1973, was any indication, absolutely nothing was clear in the end. Stone's novel was like a beautifully designed department store for every scuzzy failed aspect of the Love Generation's collapse into irrelevance or hell. And all Dieter gets for his troubles is a bullet in the head, delivered by a former disciple, a Vietnam vet who brings the war home on a magic carpet made of smack.

What was to become of us? Who was to blame? So long, California. Hello, Mars. Could Ms. America have really been that angry? Despite my clockwork unreliability and occasional toddler's temper, I'd never threatened her even vaguely and was, face facts, at best a C+ asshole.

I was in need of ballast and good thing I met my future ex-cousin,

Marty Christensen, "Auxiliary" Prankster Marty—who perhaps Kesey liked because, as a genuine nuthouse alum, Marty—who'd dropped acid as often as the sun has rays, but preferred the earthier sacrament, Budweiser—had lived the zero gravity life Kesey only dreamt about. Locked up for expressing too many "opinions" in front of a judge after a drunk and disorderly charge when he was in his early twenties, Marty—like the *Cuckoo's Nest* anti-hero Randle P. McMurphy—parlayed a soft spot for hospital food and Demerol into a "Ward Leader" position at the state mental institution in Salem. Marty's relationship with Kesey was in ways like that of the war vet and the army recruit. Kesey wrote about the insane, Marty had been insane, confined to the Oregon State Mental Institution—where *Cuckoo's Nest* was filmed.

And, if you were anybody who was anybody in Portland, Oregon, running around with Kesey was fine, but if you wanted to be shot to an unplottable future from the storied past, you ran with Marty and Walt. For, forget the long and now somewhat cobwebbed shadow of Ken Kesey, they were the future of hell in a hand basket. Marty, author of

MISS UNIVERSE

Pink & blue
hydrangea buds
imbued
enfolded by
the ocean
walk and shimmer

weirded out
her labia
caress themselves

3 of the judges
notice. 2 give
extra points.

and Walt were hosting indoor brawls, poetic smackdowns in local taverns in which they would trade poems and insults with other local poets like the Impossiblists, a da-da group of Yippie-like street freaks led by the very talented Mark Sargent. This poetry was not about peace, love or hippie heaven on earth, but cocks, monsters and visionary codfish.

Marty grew up under gray skies in the fishing village of Astoria, was smoking Marlboros by ten, surfed at that very age the roof of a house that was sliding down a hillside after a winter storm, and later played junior high school football. Tackle and guard mostly. He was a terror on the field, though at eighty-five pounds he had a tough row to hoe. In high school he got in trouble with a girl, and more trouble for beer drinking and reading James Joyce. Getting caught with *Lolita* was the knockout punch. Two weeks before graduation, Marty was called to see his school counselor, who told Marty, "They have plans for you."

"Who was 'they?'" Marty asked.

"They" were his schoolteacher mother and the Principal. The counselor, tears in his eyes, told Marty he had better make tracks.

That Monday his mother had wards from the state mental institution there at the house to take Marty away. But Marty had—three days before—signed up for the National Guard and was already on a bus to basic training.

As for the reedy author of *The Leper*, young Christian fundamentalist Walt Curtis was still in college at Portland State University when he met Kesey, courtesy his writing professor. "As a green Oregonian sick of the rain I visited Ed McClanahan and his family in sunny California. Ed took me to a Prankster party where I shared a joint with Neal Cassady who was dressed in brown coveralls like my mechanic dad used to wear. Disappointed, I was looking for Kerouac, my writer hero. A year later, on to visit Kesey at his house in La Honda, we were stopped by the cops. Blue lights flashing, Hell's Angels were roaring up to the compound, wooooie. My first taste of the rebel life style, I was convinced marijuana was going to drive me insane, but something else did."

By the time scarecrow thin, "street poet" Walt Curtis met Kesey the second time, Kesey—prompted by the allures and distractions of fame—had gone from golden boy to godhead. Instead of his fiction appearing in *The New Yorker,* his face could appear in *People* Magazine— which was more fun and less paperwork.

It had been seven years since the Summer of Love, five since Woodstock, Richard Nixon in deep shit, Quaaludes, disco and cable porn right out there on the horizon, Kesey's emeritus years already upon him, and on the ride south along the long ribbon of freeway asphalt from Portland to Eugene, tall, pretty, sad-eyed Lorna (publisher of Lorna Viken Books, her one author: Marty), in the back seat of Kesey's barge-like convertible Pontiac, said to the back of the Commander's curly head, "Oh, come on now. What do you mean it's not by accident?"

"It's not by accident!" Kesey exclaimed, "There's always a cloud there, when you drive by."

"But that's the way the land is set out here," Lorna said. As the bottle of whisky was still circulating inside the car.

"It's like there's a cloud over Weyerhauser," Kesey said. "I don't just mean by magic. I mean—"

Compact owl-eyed Marty, he of the high forehead and slightly pregnant-looking stomach, interjected, "Lil Abner!"

"Yeah," Kesey said, "It's like Lil Abner. Right. I mean that there is enough heat being separated off this place to actually have a weather change. So, it creates a thermal situation. It makes—uh, thunderheads."

Kesey said he had a friend who was a teacher at the University of Oregon who wrote his thesis about a theory the ancient Chinese had about dragons. "The coils of the dragon go around the earth, representing magnetic fields of flux. There's an old book called *The Light of Egypt,* written in 1890. The guy says, as the planet is forming, in its early hot stages, of gases, and rocks—that—first there's a ball of molten stuff spinning, and just because it's spinning, it creates its own magnetic force…Well, because of that, the lines of force that go from pole to pole—the elements begin to line up—inside the earth. The iron finally comes together. First, it's all molten, mixed up like this." The Commander moved his hands. "Finally, as it cools, the iron will line up. Klunk, klunk, klunk down…The earth finally has formed, and those magnetic lines are going through the earth, that earthly part of life is ready. And the heavenly part of life comes down and blends with it, and you end up with human life."

Walt Curtis said, "Ha! Ha! Ha! I love it."

Marty said, "I have to go to the bathroom."

Lorna laughed and Kesey said, "Okay. I'm going to get off this freeway."

"Pull into this supermarket," Walt said, "I'm a Venusian! You didn't know that. In disguise!"

Kesey said, "Okay, K-Marts and pissers. That's where the Logging Carnival is held." He pointed to a pond. He had turned off the freeway onto an old highway. Children were playing in the park next to the pond.

"Oregon. Man," Walt said, "What did you call it?"

"The citadel of the spirit," Marty said.

"Yeah," Walt agreed, "Oregon is the citadel of the spirit."

"Okay," Kesey said, "what I'd like to find is this pisser by this nice little restaurant. It's right up here. I know where it is. Close. It is this little old woman's one-shack hamburger place—if I can find it."

"Don't you worry about eating those beef cattle you raise?" Walt asked. "What are they thinking about out there in the barn at night, man?"

"While we were in Egypt," Kesey said, "Krassner and I traveled across the country and we debated the Venusians as opposed to the CIA. He believes the CIA military-industrial complex has a conspiracy."

Walt said, "That's his—"

"And I believe," Kesey said, "that it's the Venusians."

"It's a little far out," Marty said. "That doesn't mean it isn't true."

Kesey, beefy hand atop the Pontiac's steering wheel, said the Venusians "don't know something that we do, as humans. The human being is a very resourceful and resilient fucker! And I think it's because we have a sense of mercy which—"

"They don't have," Walt exclaimed, "the villains don't have!"

"Which they do not have," Kesey said.

"They are totally evil forces," Walt affirmed.

CHAPTER THIRTY-FIVE:
LAST SUPPER

"Stand in this spotlight, feel this eye pass over you. You are suddenly changed, lifted, elevated and alone. But, there's the scaly rub, right? Because, if you go around to the other end of that eye, and look through at the star shining there so elevated, you see that the adoring telescope has a cross hair built in it, and notches in the barrel filed for luminaries…Kennedy…King…Joplin…Hemingway."

—Ken Kesey

White walls, white bookshelves, white bar, white TV, white fur rugs, the whole San Francisco penthouse white, accented by a plexiglas coffee table and a maid who arrived every day promptly at 4 and kept the San Francisco penthouse "spotless" and then served Michael Douglas dinner.

Douglas was a young man of wealth and monochromatic taste, co-star of a successful primetime television cop show, *The Streets of San Francisco*, and the proud recipient of the film rights to *One Flew Over the Cuckoo's Nest*. "Dad finally gave up on it and handed the book to me as a present. He said, 'You want to produce a picture? Here's a great novel. See if you have more luck with it than I did.'"

The problem had not been with the play, but the player—the singer, not the song, Hollywood could not buy the fantasy of a man in his fifties playing a man in his twenties.

And there were other problems. "After I took it over from my father," Michael said, "I sent the project to all the studios. The answers were all the same. Nobody wants to see a movie about crazy people. 'Too depressing.' They didn't see the comedy that was inherent to the story."

But what young Douglas saw was the numbers. "5 million people have already seen the play and millions have read it (*Cuckoo*) around the world since it's been translated into 12 languages. Consequently, I believe we have a built-in audience. We were also fortunate to get Jack Nicholson for the lead. And Milos Forman to direct. With that combination, it's got to be a hit."

Kesey needed one. From Bend in the River there had been a trend downhill. *The Electric Koolaid Acid Test* brought fame but no fortune. There was to be a life-long return to the farm where, by 1973, the Revolution no longer revolving, Kesey would eagerly step away from his typewriter to run off to a shopping center to put on an impromptu magic show for kids. Would Dostoyevsky have done this? Fitzgerald? Barbara Cartland? What was left of all that the 1960s had promised?

So now Kesey found his "simple Christ parable" going into production with Jack as Jesus. It was left to Fantasy record producer Saul Zaentz to save the day. "Zaentz committed to a $1.5 million initial budget," Douglas revealed. "Then we decided we had to do it right, and Saul committed $1 million more. That took a lot of guts."

Douglas claimed Kesey was actually paid "twice" what Kesey claimed. $44,000. "In 1962 that was a fair amount of money for a novel that never made the best seller list."

After the Academy awards in which *Cuckoo's Nest* was nominated for nine Oscars and won five, including statues for Best Picture and Best Actor, Kesey was quoted by Bob Greene as saying he "felt pride and hurt at the same time" and that he didn't even want to see the movie after his rotten experience in its creation. He further lamented the fact that while the tale of Big Nurse and her sorry charges grossed between $40 million and $60 million, all he'd got out of the deal was a long gone $28,000, which he'd been paid 14 years previously. "That's the last money I've seen from it. Right now I'm broke. It's a beautiful day out here today. If I had $300 for fertilizer, I'd be out fertilizing my fields."

Initially, Kesey had been part of the production as a screenwriter, but after a month or two he began to feel he was no longer part of the evolving *Cuckoo* movie bandwagon, and was "dreaming" to think his script would be used. "I don't mind so much except that they were jerking me off for a long time, saying, 'yeah, yeah, great stuff but don't you think you ought to do this, ought to do that?

"Everybody was part of some fraternity house except me. They had parties, swung together, snorted coke together and I was over here by myself.

"And when they've got your book, it's like buying a doll house. When you buy a doll house you want to be able to arrange the furniture the way you want to and move the characters around. For a writer this is painful business to begin to see characters picked up and moved over here and there, people just moved around without any feeling."

Kesey claimed he did not even receive an invitation to the Academy Award ceremony and that, further, "It was made very clear to me that if I showed up, I was going to have a hard time getting in. I'm just not a part of their Hollywood fraternity." For the legendary frat boy BMOC this was a bitter come-down. Kesey watched the Academy Awards on TV while playing poker—which he lost. "No artist wants to be raped; no artist wants to be poor. I'm broke as hell. It should be one of the great days of my life, like my wedding. What I'm working on now is gnashing my teeth and railing at the sky."

When the producers called to inquire if he'd like to attend the premiere of *Cuckoo's Nest* in Oregon, Kesey said no thanks. "That's like calling me and saying, 'Hey, we're raping your daughter down here in the parking lot, would you like to watch?'" Kesey claimed he couldn't afford a ticket to go to the Eugene premiere of *Cuckoo* and regarding his lawsuit against the producers: "It would have been great if the subpoenas could have been slipped into the winning Best Picture envelope."

As far as he was concerned, *Cuckoo's Nest* had flown to the pot of gold at the end of the rainbow for others, but not for him, claiming, injury to insult, that he received money neither from paperback rights or the stage plays, victim of his own gee-whiz naivete. "I was just a kid when I was writing that book. I was twenty-two years-old. I didn't know what I was doing, I mean here was *Kirk Douglas* offering to buy the movie rights. I would have signed that contract at the bottom of a volcano."

Now the chickens had come home to roost—broke. "Once a year, every year, a little money comes in. Sometimes it's enough money to make it through the year, sometimes it isn't. I raise cattle and sheep here and grow blueberries too. I'm banking on the blueberries. I've mortgaged everything I own. I've had to borrow money on the land."

Though denying that he was "bitter," Kesey did allow, "Michael Douglas is a punk. I could swallow him with a glass of water." By his reckoning Douglas had simply been awarded a monster plum by his rich and powerful father, and as for producer Saul Zaentz. "I saw him up on that stage, and he was thanking everyone in the world who ever did anything for him, right up to the hall monitor in fifth grade who helped him up off the floor the time he fell down and broke a tooth."

Just about the only recognition Kesey got that night was from Milos Forman, who mentioned his name. Kesey complained that without *Cuckoo* the novel there obviously could have been no *Cuckoo* movie— nor any *Cuckoo* bonanza, awards, or hoopla. "If I didn't write that book, none of them would have been up there. You know what I heard from a friend? That after the Oscar ceremonies Jack Nicholson and Michael Douglas were standing outside the theater and signing autographs of *One Flew Over the Cuckoo's Nest.* Isn't that wonderful?"

* * *

Months later, over a table, crouched up out of his chair, fists balled and shaking, the lenses of his glasses—not quite coke bottle—magnifying his round eyes, Marty Christensen paused a moment, ran an unwashed hand through the thick comma of tan hair atop his high forehead, and with the passion of a Sepp Dietrich exhorting his doomed troops before the Battle of the Bulge, rallied to the defense of the man whom he identified as "the Commander."

"THEY CAN'T DO THIS TO KEN KESEY! THEY CAN'T GET AWAY WITH IT!"

What he was alluding to was the Milos Forman film of Kesey's *One Flew Over the Cuckoo's Nest,* about which the Commander, who did not cotton to the script, Jack Nicholson or his cut of the profits, was, as we have just observed, not happy. Ken's mom predicted, "This is going to be a biggie," and she was right. The Eugene premiere of *Cuckoo's Nest* sported a bomb threat which cleared the theater, though Ken himself declined attendance, requesting instead that Dean Brooks, head of the Oregon State mental institution where *Cuckoo* had been filmed, solicit audience members to "just send a dime out to Kesey at Pleasant Hill to help sue those sonsabitches." Brooks demurred, but by that time *Cuckoo's Nest* had been nominated for nine Academy Awards, and paperback sales had hit 4 million copies. Explaining, "When you're insulted, you must squawk," dimes or not, Kesey filed suit against the "producers, owners and distributors" of the film for $869,000. Claiming he'd been paid $18,000 for the movie rights and another $10,000 to write a screenplay version, Kesey demanded 2½% of the gross receipts promised by Douglas and Zaentz.

Marty, his face by this time pumped with blood and a livid orb, had captured the attention of not only everyone around the table but half the other people in the tavern as well. Orotund but forceful, booming, yet incisive, Marty's style was not celebrated everywhere. Recently, he'd been discharged from the "P, C & S Tavern" here in Portland for "beating on the walls."

"I was not beating on the walls," he insisted, "I was beating on the table. I asked the manager about that. I said: 'You know I wasn't beating on the wall. *So why did you choose that image?*'"

Images being Marty's stock in trade, the big trucks on the sleek freeway of his career, he was concerned about them, especially as they applied to himself. "I am not just some wall-to-wall wino," he confided, "I am one of the most fascinating men in the world."

Meanwhile, Ken Kesey had not written a major novel since *Sometimes a Great Notion* more than a decade before, and hippies were beginning to look like refugees from a future that never happened. When I first interviewed my ex-cousin Marty Christensen, Steve Jobs had just founded Apple, the Ramones had just released their first album, Malcolm McLaren was thinking up The Sex Pistols, and Marty'd just starred in a film, *Marty's Apartment,* produced by Norman Gould, best known previously for his docudrama, *Thirteen Stories for Marcia,* about a young woman who jumped off the Meier & Frank department store building in Portland.

"I like Norman because of his spectacular bad taste," Marty admitted. I asked him what *Marty's Apartment* was about and he replied that it was about his apartment. "I had all my stuff in there, my rubber boat and everything."

At that time Marty was having problems with his car, a circa 1960 Ford station wagon he had bought from Ken Babbs, an automobile that, along with Babbs, had been immortalized in an offhand way in Tom Wolfe's *Electric Kool Aid Acid* test, and Marty considered the Ford a valuable artifact.. The car problems had to do with the fact somebody tried to steal it, and left it with its ignition wires cut. Immobile, the Ford began to collect parking tickets which, because the title change had not gone through, began streaming to Babbs like letters to Santa Claus.

No sooner had Marty got the Ford going, however, than he had an accident, colliding with a Pontiac. "It was a triumph of early sixties craftsmanship over mid-seventies technology. I wiped the guy out."

Nevertheless, the Ford was in bad shape. Brush-painted white, its front end looked like it had been slugged with God's fist. There were five holes in the radiator, only four of which Marty'd managed to fix. Worried, pacing my apartment, he asked, "Now what do you want for the interview?"

"For starters, what kind of poet are you?"

"An abstract realist."

"What's that?"

"Lookit–type this down: Here are my views: I'm–comma–at this point–comma–interested primarily in the emerging climate away from provincialism in Portland–comma–which can lead to more interaction and collaboration between writers, painters and poets. There was–apparently–comma–a period in the late fifties and sixties when painting and poetry and poetry and music and so forth were more closely interactive than they have been recently. Marty Christensen wants to see that happen again."

He pulled at his beard, trying to think of more quotes. "I'm trying to think of a way to plug my show."

I asked him what he did for a living.

"I can't go into that."

"Why not?"

"It's a secret. Unfortunately, many of the most spectacular details of my life can never be made public."

I asked Marty if he was crazy.

"Not true," he replied.

Marty and Walt Curtis were both scheduled to read at Kesey's 1976 "Intrepid Trips Society for Aesthetic Revolutionary Training" (ITS ART) Festival in Eugene—also known as the First and Last Annual Poetic Hoo-Haw. Set to coincide with the 32nd anniversary of the D-Day landing on Normandy Beach. Kesey had also invited Norman Mailer, Erica Jong, Kenneth Rexroth, Tim Leary, Paul Krassner, Gurney Norman, William

Burroughs, Dick Gregory, Allen Ginsberg, Tomas Fuentes, Stewart Brand, Wendell Berry and Grace Paley.

As previously noted, Marty had replaced Norman Mailer on the bill (Kesey scratching out Mailer's name and scrawled in Marty's with a shrug, "Same thing") after Mailer became incensed about a purported anti-Semitic remark Kesey made about Mailer's son.

There were some other no-shows. Snipping that fellow poet Tomas Fuentes had been "stumbling drunk" at a previous poetry festival in Santa Barbara, Kenneth Rexroth complained "the arrangements for this affair seem to be most amorphous" and found himself dropped by Kesey "on the grounds of amorphisity."

The week before the festival Ken Babbs and Fuentes drove into Portland in Kesey's convertible to publicize the event. The Commander was to have made the trip, but was tied up getting ripped off for his share of the *Cuckoo* movie profits, claiming that the only money headed his way was "what's left after the producer buys his secretary's mom a Datsun," and remained in Eugene huddling with lawyers.

To say that the tall angular Babbs and the shorter more rotund Fuentes were artful tacticians but disastrous strategists of hype would probably be inaccurate. Arriving in town just before noon, Fuentes slid out of the car and asked where he could "take a leak." Babbs leaned against the car and filled balloons with helium from a tank propped up in the back seat. The balloons each had an Intrepid Trips logo printed on their thin rubber hides and the day before Kesey had launched one carrying a check for $1,000. It too was to publicize Kesey's upcoming Poetic Hoo-Haw and was last seen drifting in the general direction of Pullman, Washington.

Still I was impressed. Ken Babbs, Kesey's major-domo from the Prankster days, had given me a story, *How to Fix a Bicycle Tire,* equipped with a series of photos that illustrated how to do just that. It was unique—not only the droll subject and format—but in that it provided utility, backassward hilarity (the unspoken message: "you fucking stereo-playin' BMW-drivin' coke-snortin' yuppies ought get back to basics") and also had a touch of performance art, it was published to what I can only call explosive minor acclaim. As co-creator of the new bohemia, friendly unpretentious Babbs didn't quite appear the part. Tall, good-looking— the longhaired hippie shitkicker look sort of laminated on to what was otherwise the All American Boy, or ex-boy, another Wheaties-eatin', acid-droppin' beloved mother's son. Babbs looked above all American, not a from-the-mercantile America but the meadowed one…

* * *

Kesey still lived in a barn with his wife Faye and their kids. It was a big playhouse and looked like it hadn't been finished yet. A strip of theater seats provided part of the furnishings, paperback books lined the walls, the stairs were painted different colors and in the bathroom there was a bathtub that was less a bathtub than a big metal box with spouts and a drain.

The Revolution, what was left of it, was arriving at his doorstep. The outside of the barn-house wasn't painted—except for a big white star on the second story—and a few small windows near the peak of the roof were broken. If Kesey was as rich as he'd been accused of being, you wouldn't guess it from his estate.

His legendary bus, *Furthur*, sat out in the fields among his more recently legendary cows. Inside, the bus was pretty neat. The interior had been gutted, and stuffing was coming out along a split in the seam of the driver's seat. The paint was still the wild, fractured paisley, and I sat behind the wheel.

On the day before the Poetic Hoo-Haw Kesey threw a party for the poets at his house. People arrived from all over. Paul Krassner was there. William Burroughs was there. Steward Brand was there. Marty Christensen was there. All milling around dressed in work shirts, beat up leather jackets and cowboy boots, making Kesey's home look like the sudden site of a skinny loggers' convention. And clearly these bards weren't the spaghetti-waisted devotees of the fluffy sonnet, the penners of attenuated tubercular verse, a bunch of fops or blow brothers. These folks were the virile backbone of American letters, men and women who worked with a pen in one hand and a can of beer, bottle of whisky, pick-ax, gearshift knob or revolver in the other.

A robust and grinning Kesey, dressed in a herringbone greatcoat, Levis, khaki shirt and combat boots, wheeled off the road in his Pontiac convertible, splashing gravel up the driveway. He looked happy, this being the first time he'd sponsored a project since the sagging souffle that was the "Bend in the River" campaign two years before—he was also planning new issues of *Spit in the Ocean,* the last of which was to be edited by Tim Leary—whom Kesey would later define as "the point guard on the psychedelic dream team."

But Leary, just out of jail, had yet to show up—the word was that he had squealed on so many of his pals in prison that he had gone in hiding, fearing for his life.

The times they were a changin'. Not only had the Sex Pistols begun to berserk their way to anti-Jesushood, but Leary was parsing the gods. Writing for the conservative *National Review,* he pissed on Bob Dylan, concluding, "It's All Over Now Baby Blue," had "probably caused more biological and philosophical suicides than any poem in western history." Did Dylan, Leary wondered, "stand in picket lines? Get his head busted by Company police?" Or for that matter, "put his nervous system on the line in neuronaut exploration?"

A serious charge. "When an entire generation was on the move, swirling into unchartered neurogenetic territory, where was the young millionaire? Protected, dear boy, in the arms of producer Al Grossman, promoter Bill Graham, Golda Meir, Allen Ginsberg."

Golda Meir? "It is not an accident that the Weathermen, the most publicized group of Dylan groupies, a bewildered, fugitive band of terrorists now cut off from their culture and condemned to underground existence, took their name from a depressing Dylan song."

Kesey, trailing a wedge of buddies, factotums and coat-holders, moved in and out of his house and around his grounds setting up a stage, divvying up beers. Inside, Faye worked in a kitchen that was suddenly very crowded. Outside, at the edge of Kesey's pond, one of Kesey's sons took practice casts with a fly rod. He whipped his pole back and forth in the air and his line made long sliding S's against a dark green background of trees and scrub.

On the stairs in front of the house another guest. Actually, a visitor. A big guy with a big stomach. If it were on a woman you would guess her pregnant. He'd been talking about macho. Behind a wind of bad breath he proclaimed, "Hey man, don't look up in the clouds, you won't find macho up there."

William Burroughs and Kesey came out of the house, tracked by newsmen carrying cameras and microphones as long as baseball bats. Burroughs stopped to talk with people sucking on a joint. Burroughs took a puff, and made a remark about growing marijuana. The macho man, ricocheting sluggishly around the crowd, largely unnoticed, and clearly nursing a sotful of resolute meanness, loomed up to Burroughs, a man old enough to have been his grandfather, and bellowed, "You are full of shit," and then stalked back into Kesey's house, emerging a moment later, slowing on his exit just long enough on his walk down the driveway to stick his fingers into the mouth of Kesey's multi-colored macaw, a huge bird with a big beak that had a note tacked onto its perch that reads, "Be careful. I bite."

Stewart Brand, late of *The Whole Earth Catalogue,* sat on a tree trunk with Kesey, any hard feelings they may have had over Kesey's "Abdul and Ebenezer" manuscript shelved or forgotten. The story was first to have gone to Brand's *Co-Evolutionary Quarterly,* but ended up at *Esquire* instead, where Kesey had been paid purportedly about fifteen times what he could have got from Brand. Time-Life's John Riley wrote, "The perpetually cashless Kesey became miffed at Brand's refusal to lend an occasional $5 for a tank of gasoline."

Those were the days.

In the house, Paul Krassner, who was there with his daughter, picked at the remains of a pot roast someone had left in the dining room. Krassner and Kesey were close and, like Kesey, Krassner told stories, but continuously: "You know there's new information on Oswald's motive: Kennedy was messing around with his wife."

Marty grew restless, unhappy about the talent of one of the headline poets. He was standing right behind where Kesey was sitting, standing right behind the swirling blond hair atop the Commander's balding head when he announced, "You can't just stand up in front of twenty thousand people and scream into a microphone, 'Rimbaud was Jesus! The Nile flows North!' and call it poetry."

But the Commander, completing a joke whose punch line was "Six Pollacks," didn't seem to hear.

Here at the first "Kesey's Poetic Hoo-Haw" Kesey, as ever larger than life in tennis shoes, jeans and a shirt that may have started out as a potato sack, bounded up on stage, did a little broken field running in place, jumped up and down a few times and then led the audience in the calisthenics of hyper-ventilation. "Let's everybody stand up, breathe in and out fifteen times and see how you feel." How Cam Stauth, editor of *Eugene Magazine,* felt was unconscious. After breathing in and out the prescribed fifteen times he toppled over, and Krassner, who was talking to him, grew alarmed that he was having a seizure.

Late in the afternoon, following a troupe of exotic dancers, Marty read at last. But just before he was to go on, something bad happened. The Count, a local magician who did a drugstore version of Houdini's old routines, had preceded Marty on the bill. He was supposed to have been chained and handcuffed, locked to a concrete cinderblock and lowered into a huge pickle barrel full of water. Regrettably, the Count's tricks failed to blossom as planned. The Count (Bruce to his friends) couldn't get the god-damned handcuffs off. He didn't drown or anything but the terrible scene-stealing upshot was he was still thrashing around in the water, yelling, "Gimme the keys, gimme the keys!" while Marty was trying to get a little dramatic traction by way of screeching, 'I wanta do it over, I wanta do it over!' The Count succeeded in diluting the impact of Marty's reading considerably.

That evening inside Mac Court at the University the headliners went on. Kesey, ski glasses pushed up over his forehead, his scalp auraed under the stage lamps, read a children's story about a bear that eats sundry members of his forest community only to be outfoxed by a squirrel. William Burroughs read a piece that sounded like it might be for children except that it was about murder and dope, and Walt Curtis delivered an ode to his penis, titled "My Hard On."

Days after the Hoo-Haw Marty levitated up to my apartment for a final interview so he could get in a final plug for his book. As ever, courteous and helpful, he offered to take my place behind my typewriter and—indecisive Queequeg at the helm—immediately tapped out the following:

"Well Marty, how are you coming along with your trilogy, *The Paranoid's Revenge?"*

"I'm glad you asked that question, Mark. So few young writers are aware these days that I am bringing out a work of almost 30 years. The first volume, *My Flashlight was Attacked by Bats,* was released by Out of the

Ashes Press last year and the public's demand for my poems has been extraordinary. Thus: this summer I will be releasing an illustrated version of that now out of print classic.

"But, before that even, my agent will be releasing the second volume of my trilogy, *Dying in the Provinces.* This (actually one extended sequence of symbolic non-representational innuendo) has been so skillfully produced that the publisher wishes to remain anonymous, to be known under the nom-de-plume, Big Foot Press.

"Which brings me to book three, *The Dreams of Unknown Codfish.*" Marty typed. "Only yesterday, I sealed a verbal pact with Harold Plople, ruin expert in the extreme. Harold and I will be working until September, at which time the three books will be released in one combined deluxe volume of fifty pages and I will have assumed my rightful place in the universe."

Marty then slid away from my typewriter, bobbed up, lit a cigarette, and wondered aloud if I might prepare him "an ensemble" of bacon and eggs, then added, "Here's the formula for success: don't put anything in about me saying insulting things about my fellow poets, make sure everybody knows you and I aren't related, make me look big and Walt look small, and put Kesey in his place. You'll get yourself a Pulitzer."

CHAPTER THIRTY-SIX:
DYING IN THE PROVINCES

"I looked through all of these books the high school kids are reading. They're not getting Faulkner, they're not getting Hemingway, they're not getting Melville: they're getting me. I'm not a classic: I'm not a wart on a classic's butt yet. I'm working at it. I may make it as a classic, but I know I'm not in there with Moby Dick yet. You don't need to teach Cuckoo's Nest; there's nothing to be said about it. It teaches itself. It's a simple Christ allegory taking place in a nut house."

—Ken Kesey

"Fool's Paradise" ne' "Demetri's" had retained the dim majesty of the wino bar it was once was. In its former incarnation, the bar was a profitable enterprise. Also, a rowdy one. The chief bartender was a steamy Mexican hulk named Adolf who disliked all minorities, including Mexicans. Adolf had had a hard life. Bilingual, he'd been shot in the throat and now had a speech impediment in two languages.

Marty was to read there that night. Among the poems:

POOR FISH
upon the slimy boat
the ancient fisherman
paws coldly at his privates
as the lights flash on & off

while we lie here together
sucking madly through our gills

the scene
has happened now

and no one is the wiser
not even the blond dagger
of a lightbulb in the cold

Walt would read too. Writing in *The New York Press,* Bruce Benderson claimed that the "boys" in Walt's work "are impossible objects of desire, and tools of daring social provocation. They are pre-Stonewall commodified sex objects calculated to raise the ire of bourgeois Portlanders…as well as the embarrassed disapproval of the gay establishment everywhere."

Alter-Prankster Walt's problem was that he had a delinquent nestling between his legs. Consider this:

TO MY PRICK
I am looking at my prick.
Small odd thing it is.
Five inches or so, not much more.
A vein beating in it,
A vein connected to my heart.
Graceful, elegant instrument,
all alone my flesh.
Drunk, I unzip my pants,
look at my prick tenderly,
and zip them up again.
I don't know.

"Other people might hurt you.
I won't."

In truth, Walt's troubled sidekick—his wiener—appalled him, got him in trouble. Walt, alone in a world he never made, was rendered but a horrified hostage. For Walt's wiener wasn't much interested in the usual prom queens, movie starlets, buxom barmaids, no, Walt's tubular Tonto lusted for more forbidden fare.

Walt and I and Marty decided to have a meeting at Marty's house in the country to discuss good ways to make Walt and Marty more famous than Kesey. There were promising avenues—Marty had promised to reveal ("spectacular in its economy of language, unity of theme and relentless evocation of speed and technology"—Marty) a "Howl-level" new epic poem.

Walt's curly-haired, handsome pal George wanted to come along. When Walt arrived at George's house George got into a discussion in Greek with his girlfriend, presumably about whether or not it was a good idea for George to take off without her on a trip to Marty's. She was very young and had a round, pretty face. When Walt went out the door he said goodbye, and she screamed, "Fuck you!" not in Greek. George's car was parked by the side of the house and just as Walt and George were getting inside, George's kitchen window splashed apart, exploding into flying shards by a speeding dish. Walt said, "Oh my God."

The several mile trip to Marty's farmhouse in Scappoose was uneventful until the road became rutted with snow. George lost control of the car, and it whipped off the icy pavement into a ditch.

Kids in a four-wheel drive Jeep pulled it out.

Later that day, Marty Christensen greeted us with: "There's enough blood in one of my rats to fill a wine glass." He sat on his shining hardwood living room floor, Lou Reed intoning from the stereo, and Marty continued, "It's frightening. I've bought the largest rat traps they make and they still get sprung. At least one of them is a monster, possibly the size of a small dog.

"I've experimented with poison, but that's an art. You can't have them gobbling up the stuff and dying inside the house where their meaty corpses are free to rot inside some wall and stink up the place. No, the idea is to leave a hole in the wall so the little devils can get out. That's what they want to do after they've eaten the stuff and it starts to incinerate their insides. They want to get out and drink some water."

Meanwhile, was the quality of transcendental horseflesh going downhill?

"Of course I have written new material," Marty stood and floated to a table where his typewriter sat surrounded by a choppy sea of papers, books and folders. "Just today I composed this." He picked up a piece of translucent onion bond paper. "Appreciate, if you will, the unity of theme, the control of language and the steely selection of just the right words." He cleared his throat. "The title of my latest work is *Speedometer.*" A brow arced skyward as he recited, "'Speedometer, speedometer, speedometer, speedometer, speedometer, speedometer, speedometer, speedometer, speedometer, speedometer, speedometer, speedometer.' It goes on from there, but that's the gist."

* * *

With Budweisered Marty and Walt buzzing in and out here at the "Kingston Tavern," Ken Kesey announced to me, across a table decorated with empty beer glasses, that I, Mark Christensen, had "ruined poetry in Portland" and that "I oughta knock you back to the Ohio river."

Since I wasn't a poet and not even aware that there was an Ohio River, I was puzzled. Then Ken announced we'd arm wrestle for the supremacy of poetry in Portland. Since Ken didn't live in Portland and I wasn't a poet, this was unusual. Still. I had pipe-stem arms but, as a veteran of a billion pushups and chin-ups, think *pipe*—though it was a good thing too my cousin Jerry had taught me how to cheat. I slipped my hand into The Commander's, not palm to palm—a conjoining to render me a more likely loser—but thumbs hooked, so Kesey could get little traction, my forearm a bone hypotenuse to a triangle formed by his shorter meatier forearm and the table top. Cut to the action: Our elbows ice-skated over and over and over what looked like a clear frozen water surface of the table—Gym coat or whatever they slapped on wood—we struggled, our hands locked thumb to thumb, my otherwise fragile extension was by now a squiggling pipestem there on the beer-laked wood, so...a tie!

How had it come to this? Words are weakest in this realm. The easy answer would be strength through delirium. My twenty-seventh birthday had flown past like an exit sign on an Interstate, and to turn back time, I had embarked on an Emergency Fitness program lifting weights for hours every day, 200,000 pounds 24/7 day after day after day, supplementing pumps of iron with a "Run Til You're Done" program at a local high school track, running until the world found itself a pointillist Picasso and I'd list speeding crazy-legged off the cinder...and collapse face first on the grass. Better to sweat myself fatless I'd adopted the Beaverton High School Girls' fitness diet of one hardboiled egg and all the diet coke I could drink. Suffering, I had discovered, beat drugs.

Ken, tractionless, was pissed.

Sliding back into the booth to hear news of Ken's latest plans for conquering—in which I was included as an example of going nowhere—Marty, bright as a mushroom cloud, leaned across a table watery with spilled beer. Simultaneously stern, shocked and confidential, his eyes from behind their bottle lenses gone from their usually wide-as-a-baby bird's-round to stern, slim and eagle-ish, Marty suggested, "Mark is a young man of frightening limitations, Ken, but at least he is—" He leaned in closer, "*aware* of them."

So why didn't Kesey like me? My social skills had improved lots since the halcyon days of hassling Fat Shit Larry. At "Duh" I'd learned not to say zzzzzzzzzzzzzzt, zzzzzzzzzzzzzzt to nonlinear girlfriends, and as a bartender I was great with all the major fringe groups—lesbians, bikers, cops—The only people I didn't get along with were organizations, literati, academics and bosses.

Marty and Walt and their poems popped up every time I wrote about Kesey—maybe the Commander felt as if I'd staged Hamlet starring Rosencrantz and Guildenstern.

Anyway, Marty wanted to introduce me to "one of the three great minds in history." He also wanted to sell that great mind a painting. A "Marty"—as Marty's paintings were known. Marty's Martys weren't representational, but as far from formalism as right is from wrong. Marty made Jackson Pollack look like Norman Rockwell, and a Marty could go anywhere from $35 to $35,000.

Anyway, according to Marty one of his patrons was one of the three greatest minds in western cultural history. One was Captain Beefheart, the other, I believe, the ancient alchemist Paracelsus, and the final greatest of all minds was a young woman who, not incidentally, he worshipped, who'd written a novel, *Truck*. I got a *Truck* from Marty. Stripped of the mores and stays of conventional fiction, *Truck* flew through me like a waking bad dream, the best nightmare ever, the story of "Dutch" Gillis, a teenage girl often mistaken for a prepubescent boy, a luminous little monster-ette whose feral prowler's tale put me in a trance and who, small world, trolled as a creature of fiction the same unholy waters of Fanno Creek I had trolled—home to zooming bullheads and a 1,000 other 1,000,000 BC things. Now a Styx of literature spelled as if from the dying Devil's final fever dream. Kesey was about brilliant show, *Truck* was about transcendent secrets. Like the question of the age: What do women want? Here is the conclusion of a scene in which Dutch relishes a fantasy of her own gang-rape:

"They slap me when I fight and beat me, ripping at my hair if I bite the cocks in my mouth. When they have all come in me or on me I lie still on the moss and rest awhile. The flies wade happy in the scum and they all lie around me with their balls loose and pricks tiny and soft. We doze and wave at the flies and smile at each other gently. It's nice. We do it every day."

What could LSD have on that? The best novel ever. The author was Katherine Dunn.

* * *

So time to go meet her. But best to mellow out first. As we did on our way to "Dante's Inferno," a Portland nightclub stocked with black guys who had white girlfriends but which, who or God knows why, hosted Captain Beefheart for a weekend. Arriving just as Beefheart launched into Marty's favorite song, "China Pig," Marty was so shocked he upchucked at the door. Later, joining the Captain in his hotel room, Beefheart—who once didn't go to sleep for ten years—and Marty talked all night while I slept in a chair. Now, seeking ballast, stomach pregnant with a pitcher or two of Coors recalling in his perfectly tattered herringbone sport coat a gentleman farmer without a farm, Marty discovered at a liquor store by Katherine's red brick aerie the new Budweiser 40 Ouncer—later aka 40 Oz. of Freedom—a brown bottle big as a glass artillery shell, which Marty knighted: "a wonder of lumpen post-acid leisure tech, a superb delivery system" Or: "Swill, but a lot of it for 99 cents." Marty cadged three dollars from me and bought two, and soon, 40 oz. of Bud installed in situ just above our beltlines, Marty's compact fist was banging on Katherine's door.

* * *

A circus family created in a timeless but almost placeless America who had created themselves as their own attraction. Not a bad idea. Katherine said she got it at the Rose Gardens at Washington Park above the bohemian Northwest Portland neighborhood where both of us, Marty as well, lived, and where roses were bred toward infinite splendor and where Katherine had been inspired as, well, as a Mom fantasizing that her wise guidance to her beloved energetic son could be aided by perhaps a little helpful genetic mutation.

Though not famous yet, Katherine—who'd already had two novels published—was well known locally as, among other things, a genius bartender, like a young freak freely Miss Kitty from Gunsmoke who, like Miss Kitty who ran the gun-slinging waterhole the "Long Branch Saloon," tended bar at a local wateringhole, the kind of place populated with guys who call you brother and want to play eightball for five bucks.

Katherine was an expert at controlling crazies, she was very nice looking and psychotics liked her a lot and when, after too much down the hatch, one among them might find all his tethers unknot and screaming at the ceiling toward the moon, Katherine was known to utter incantations to leave him moments later, at worst, sobbing peacefully over a last $1.59 glass of rose...

One morning, coffee cup to coffee cup at a neighborhood cafe, she confided to me that, as a poor teenager in neighboring less well-endowed Tigard, she'd back-floated in protozoic Fanno Creek. The same Fanno creek that twined its feverish Faulknerian way through antiseptic Raleigh Hills, but upstream closer to the dark blue-collared headwaters, a rain and sewer-fed wandering embarrassment to nature alive with frogs, bullheads and a dirty galaxy of mosquitoes. Too poor to buy beer or drugs, she had floated Ophelia-like on her slender back in the mirror-still backwater— nothing but her delicate nostrils above the calm slime-carpeted waters, praying to get high on fever and the burning dreamy heat of delirium. Say what? Could that possibly be true?

CHAPTER THIRTY-SEVEN:
THE STORY OF H

"God is dead and I want his job."

—John Shirley

When the golf-shirted, pot-bellied lead singer of the Mentors, who defined their music as "secretary hump rock," pulled out a butcher knife and disemboweled himself mid-song, I knew psychedelia was over. For the acidless Mentors had finally delivered IT. A new day was dawning. Witness their warm-up act.

Black shirts, black coats, black pants, black boots and hair of every Crayola hue. Formica and the Bitches, nee' Randee of Randee and the Randees was restless. It was opening night at the "Revenge," Portland's premiere New Wave and/or No Wave dance hall, an abandoned brick tenement made dancehall by the import of booze and electricity. Formica was petulant and impatient to rock. Taller than most men, she had salt-white skin and led the Bitches on stage. All in black, the girls played "Louie, Louie" "for the coalminers." Formica, fourteen, was a delicious little ghoul with big eyes, coffin-white face and lips red, lush and weighted like the wax lips kids wear at Halloween.

So long, peace and love. On the dancefloor, everybody pogo-ed. Ideally pogo-ing was accomplished with hands and feet bound, as partners jumped up and down and tried to strangle each other in time to the music.

Their repertoire exhausted after three songs, the Bitches surrendered the stage to the author of *Confessions of an American Glue Sniffer* and local maximum co-leader of the new culture and lead singer of punk band King Bee. Known to the phone company as Mark Stanley, to his readers as Mark Sten, and to the rest of the populated universe as Stenula—when the mood struck he wore fangs—Stanley/Sten/Stenula—stood on stage, tall, skinny, hair a greasy duck-tailed black surf, Dr. Frankenstein's take on Ricky Nelson—and obliterated Chuck Berry. Then mascara-eyed Rozz, soon to become the first Love of Courtney Love's life, a duck-taped bull's eye plastered to his bare, snake thin chest, launched into

HUMAN FAILURE
Wish your mama had taken the pill!
Your daddy hates you and he always will!
Cuz you're HUMAN FAILURE,
HUMAN FAILURE!

before the Mentors did their set (turned out the pot-bellied lead singer had stuffed his golf shirt with chicken guts, but still) and finally John Shirley, future founder of cyber punk science fiction clawed himself bloody on stage while the "biker security" went crazy because somebody was squirting a hose over all the electrical equipment just to see what would happen and...

I'd published Shirley's first short story. He didn't know it yet, but he was about to become the founder of cyber-punk science fiction (William Gibson's *Neuromancer* is dedicated to him). I first met Shirley when he was nineteen, at a house in East Portland. Dressed in TV Indian Chief gear—war paint, feathers, buckskin, he slid toward me face first down a banister—and Shirley's tale was delivered to my ratty office by aspiring rock star John as a stack of papers, in no particular order, each bearing one scene. On our way to the typesetter we taped together situation, complication, crisis, climax and resolve to make a scroll resembling a failed roll of toilet paper.

Shirley represented a new utopian fiction that reached well beyond "simple Christ parables" and psychedelics for its staggering surrealities. Classic science fiction was all about the future of the future, Shirley's invention, cyber-punk—for all its admiring bows to sideways sex, drugs, mis-information and dystopia, was all about the future pissing on the present. And soon, in novels like *City Come a Walkin'* he'd revitalized fiction in a way Ken Kesey never dreamed of—not by writing iconic Kesey-like 'give me liberty or give me meth' blockbusters (though the lynchpin to the hugely successful 'cyber-punk' science fiction genre, *City Come a Walkin'* was, otherwise, a cult classic) but by using the novel as a bully pulpit to satirize Kesey's blessed Now as yesterday's papers and a waste of newsprint besides. Shirley's vision: Technological hippie utopian society was an eat it, digest it, poop it joke.

* * *

Acid was on its way out. Not user-friendly enough. I had become pals with Henry. The largest heroin dealer in Oregon history.

Henry lived in a purple house in an otherwise all-white neighborhood out by my parents in Raleigh Hills. He owned race cars, an airplane, a Ferrari, several Lincolns, a pit bull, a motorized skateboard and a Rolls Royce "with the steering wheel on the wrong side," a diamond ring with a three-carat center stone; "It has 240 diamonds in it," he confided, "the smallest ten points," and, known as Super Pimp, Super Man or Super Fly, he had a bevy of slender, sepia-colored, high-fashion girlfriends.

The drug culture, Henry-style, was going upscale.

Bon vivant, teetotaler, doper, Henry was no middle-class Prankster. One of nine kids, his mother did housework for rich white ladies and in rest homes. The Horiatio Alger of the Oregon underworld, "I became one of the most notorious car thieves in P.O." Which earned him enough money to buy a Cadillac to use as a pimpmobile. Sadly, his first punch, Bev, took Henry to the cleaners after he couldn't resist sampling the merchandise. "The first thing I did," he told me, "was forget all the rules. The number one rule is never let your little head rule your big head."

Henry took Bev to a hotel, played with her parts, fell asleep and Bev made off with his watch, ring, wallet and trousers. Henry ended up having to hotwire his pink Cadillac in a pair of bib overalls lent him by the motel's gracious manager.

His third whore, Yvonne, later became his wife. They got married a year after doing business together. Marital bliss, until one night Yvonne told him she wanted to earn some extra money. Though he thought it was a rotten idea, he gave his consent. "If a whore wants to whore, she's going to whore, no matter what, and I didn't want anyone pimping my wife besides me."

It didn't work out. "Her tricks would come by the house at night and

I would hide in another room until they finished. Sometimes I would listen through the door and peep through the keyhole and get plenty mad and jealous seeing another man be with my wife for $20 or $30."

But thanks to his heroin business, Henry was able to rescue dozens of young women from a life of prostitution. It was a young capitalist's dream. Everything was taken care of for him. He had a main woman who cut the dope and packaged it. He had a guy to deliver the dope to each of his 12 sales ladies for $25 a drop. The next thing he knew he was making $32,000 a week and all he had to do was keep those gals in cars, clothes, apartments and spending money.

"You show'em you care. You show 'em the advantage of selling dope. You tell 'em:' 'Don't take no knowledge to lay on your back for $20. You have female trouble before you're 25. You want to better yourself.'"

I got to know Henry after he wrote me a fan letter from jail where he'd been deposited after being ratted off by his white partner and set up by the police. "Stuck a bag a dope under the seat of my motorcycle. Then pulled me over. I never knew nothing about it. I don't ride around with no dope in my motorcycle. Cops think I'm crazy?" I'd been writing about the drug culture and Henry, who read my stuff in "One Dollar," wanted to set me straight: "You got a lot of the shit right, but you ain't got all the shit right." Acid days were over, brother, heroin was where the money was and money, not dreams or epiphany or Jesus was the future. Henry wrote that he was about to be sprung from the state penitentiary and that when he got released, we could hang out and he'd show me the secrets of the trade. "I'm gonna make you rich," he promised.

"I'm making $10,000 a week," thin and dapper Henry, surrounded in the clean, well-lit hip little restaurant by beautiful coffee-skinned girls who looked like Beyonce as quadruplets, told me. "You're a white boy; you'd make ten times that."

Selling heroin. Food for thought. It might be the time. Especially with Henry as my mentor. In books like *Dog Soldiers,* written by Kesey's friend Robert Stone, heroin dealers tended to be bad guys, sleazy, mean, and unreliable. But not Henry. He wasn't a bad guy, he wasn't a good guy either; Henry was a *great* guy. Just ask the Portland police. They loved him. As a boy, Henry had been the brightest black kid in a bunch of police-supported ghetto programs, and even a lot of the vice squad cops who busted him really regretted it.

For Henry was an idealist. He planned to plough heroin profits back into the community by way of a social service known as Wash House Unlimited, a combination of a vast laundromat, grade school sized daycare center and low cost high nutrition cafeteria where poor Portland black people could take care of life's basic needs at a low, low, low if not to say nonprofit price—because the whole operation would be financed off Henry's heroin sales. Which were going gangbusters. So well in fact that Henry offered one-day-a-week smack scholarship to his most deserving clientele. "On Sunday the best junkies geeze for free!"

He was also proud to be a heroin dealer—"a junkie's gonna geeze no matter what"—and considered himself a sort of methadone clinic just without the methadone. "You gotta let people get well."

"Get well" meant get high. Otherwise they'd get "sick."

So Dr. Henry. Not that you'd want to fuck with Henry. "One time," he told me, "a guy went to the playground where my stepson was at and put a knife to his throat and started demanding money and dope. My wife didn't have any dope, but she gave him $150."

"Did you call the cops?" I asked.

Henry laughed. "How'm I gonna do that? Call up and say, 'Chief Baker, this is Henry, so and so just attacked my son and stole my dope money. Go catch him.' No, I didn't call no cops. I just put up a $1,000 reward and a piece of dope.

"Later some guys catch the guy. They work him over with tire irons, and I drive by and they ask me: 'Do you want us to beat him within one inch of his life or two?' And I say, 'One.'"

* * *

1980. A watershed year. If John Updike's *The Coup* was any indication, the novel was no longer dead. Punk had killed its only begotten son, Sid Vicious, and the new rock gods were post-modern, their gospels delivered by the Blondies, Blues Brothers, David Byrnes and Bruce Springsteens of this world. Infinite riches the new fantasia. Reagan was President and greed was good. Brokers, setting their sales in the new freer trade winds…The Morning in America pirates were just getting their sea-legs on Wall Street. Like a lot of bigots, I despise most what I don't understand, and I hated the stock market. Brutal and crazy. Love, cheap if not quite free, was going the way of the Big Mac. Soon, instead of marriage or even relationships, we'd all be having McSex.

Pet Rocks, Post modernism, Pac Man and Power Lunches, here we come. In Los Angeles The Dead were being upstaged by the dying. At "The Whisky" in Hollywood a couple of the local antichrists were talking to a guy who thought he was Johnny Carson's coke dealer. All the guy's really important circuits were probably burned out years ago, but he could still finesse a linear point: "If it don't lead to stupor or ejaculation," he revealed, "I ain't interested."

The event tonight was yet another wake for Jim Morrison and the drinks were on the house. Two pooltable-sized television screens projected twin images of dead Jim writhing and howling on a stage, microphone to mouth. Cops took to the stage on screen. Doors fans were seen being cracked with long billy clubs. Cut to scenes of the National Democratic Convention in Chicago in 1968. More cops, more smacking. Cut to a close up of J. Edgar Hoover. Cut back to the Doors, gothic maestro Morrison moaning, "This is the end, my only friend, the end."

And it sort of was. Welcome to uptown LA, land of spandex and insanity. Where a snazzy hovel down the street in Beverly Hills could cost as much as a Peoria mini-mall and the best entertainment in town was free. Winos on roller skates, spike-heeled call girls from Mars hobbling delicately along Rodeo Drive, Gay Nazis for Ronald Reagan, you name it.

The decomposing rationale for acid (bad fun versus freak out ratio, for one) was providing fertilizer, so to speak, for a growing market of more linear, supersonic, flat-footed drugs. Like cocaine. A drug for a more literal age, cocaine sent you from zero to Mars in nothing flat. Which caused cute girls to lose their morals if not their minds even more effectively than the finest Orange Sunshine.

Herald the un-psychedelic world, given up to the bulldozer ecstasies of heroin and crack. Here at the Whisky, New Weird meets Old Weird. At least two geriatric Doors fans were in togas, and Tim Leary—or at least a Tim Leary hallucination—worked the crowd. Posing for pictures and whatnot. Morrison continued to devolve on the two TV screens.

Fifteen miles away, America's greatest stand-up comic, the freshly flambéed Richard Pryor, was doing the same thing—'80s style. He'd been charbroiled from the belly button up, was lying suspended on a protective mattress at the Sherman Oaks Burn Center in the San Fernando Valley and had been given a one in three chance of living. A pioneer on the frontiers of feral zonkitude, Pryor fell hapless victim to an astounding freak accident. A glass of rum blew up in his face. Honest to God.

Sure, you heard stories that he was using the cocaine derivative freebase. And that he caught on fire while cooking some up. Well, don't believe it. Puerto Rican rum did him in and that's a fact. Just ask his attorney. A hot ash from his cigarette was all it took, and bwaaamo!

The new acid. From out of nowhere three years previous, freebase now had about three million fans—or addicts—in the United States and here in Southern California it was not uncommon for rich entertainment people to inhale $250,000 worth a year.

The UCLA pharmacologist Ron Siegel told me the attraction to compulsive use was greater than heroin. "Unlike LSD where you observe the hallucinations, with freebase the hallucinations become a direct part of your reality…in an emergency room situation, it's relatively easy to deal with somebody who's taken too much LSD—you can handle their fears by talking them down. But a guy who is really messed up on freebase may take seven to ten days just to detox."

I was writing for *High Times* and Playboy's *OUI* magazine, where the Love Generation, at least the phallused half, had been fluffed, folded and if not embalmed, at least zombified. A Harman-Kardon stereo in hand was worth nirvana in the bush, we didn't want God we just wanted *stuff*, and the view from on high was that the baby boomer had devolved to a consumption machine.

AIDS, Rainbow Coalitions, bye-bye Revolution—everything from free love to race war had gone down the shitter.

Say hi to Post Modernism and its runty brother Retro—1950s flavored greaser punk shades that threw, in its blunt rudeness a perfect blow to disco. Tom McGuane, adopting the persona of Captain Berserko, drank and drugged himself sane, abandoning the elliptical hilarities that had animated his ozoned *92° in the Shade* for the woozy flat-footed reality *Panama*, and out here in the real West, Marty's beloved Lorna had not, in classic way, passed the acid test. In fact, after she dropped acid she became convinced Kesey was in league with Venusians to take over the world, tried to stab Marty and ended up in a mental institution in Santa Cruz. Marty walked eight miles from their house each way to see her every day.

* * *

I could fly. Mushrooms had just told me so. Here I was, not just thinking I could fly, but knowing I could fly. No more strychnine-laced acid; I'd gone holistic and attained the divine dream state. At the "Veritable Quandary," feeling like the Wright brothers at an airplane-less Kitty Hawk, I walked to the bar, weightless, afraid I would drift to the ceiling.

I got the mushrooms from Moon. Depressed that *Animal House* had been a smash and at the end there was nothing on the credit crawl that read:

> *Inspired by the mayhem of Moon*
> *Whose Beta House exploits made the*
> *Commander look like Ron Ziegler.*

He got them from a crazy guy who said we'd go nuts if we ate more than two. Having a mere lunatic tell Moon how to lose his mind was like an eighth grade student telling an eighth grade teacher how to teach an eighth grade class. Moon said "let's eat the whole bag." Next the Veritable Quandary became heaven. I'd never been so happy. Now I could fly. Just go across the street, climb the stairs six floors up in the parking garage where my old Porsche was parked and jump off. I'd be soaring high above the concrete in seconds, the law of gravity airily revoked.

I'd see what Adam saw; feel what Christ felt (What of the clubfoot, the pinhead, innocents elected to an impossible condition? Where was their Christ?) Moon had a new love, a hot tempered blond Amazon on the run from the mob. The former girlfriend of a Boston Mafioso, she'd witnessed the murder of another Mafioso and was, according to Moon, on a hit list, at the top of the Mafia top forty, number one with a bullet, a dead moll walking. So, to cheer her up, he decided to redo the floors of their apartment. Moon lived upstairs from my girlfriend and me and suggested I do my floors too, go halves with him on all the sanding equipment, and, to sweeten the deal, he offered the mushrooms.

Moon and I had spent the day in a petrochemical sauna, coating the floors with some kind of gasoline-based fiberglass glass which, in addition to the mushrooms, wafted us higher and higher. A whole bag was a lot, but you were either on the bus or off the bus, right?

Cut to the chase, I made a deal with the devil, Satan's Disco owner, Satan Himself: Lady's man Frank Peters, who also owned the Karova Milk Bar, where you and your posse—Lunk, Ronny Joe, Big G Little O, Billy Brizz, Loog and, etc. etc. could order a "Mescalino Shake" for a Special Mission to Mars, was running for Governor and wanted me to accompany him on his "Fight for Oregon" tour (the plan? We'd travel the state in his red Cadillac convertible, find the meanest bar in every town, where, to get everybody's attention, Frank would begin his speech, "You people are a bunch of assholes"—it was all about "name recognition"— and after we got stomped, we'd retire to one of Frank's statewide "love modules" where he had rodeo princesses and ex-cheerleaders stashed. When I told him I couldn't because I was getting married, Frank replied, "Then you can watch," advising me, "You can live the weird life or write the weird life but you can't do both."). He told me that if I would forgo "flying" from the sixth floor of the Veritable Quandary parking garage I could, all night, buy any drink I wanted at the VQ. So fly or drink, which? Thanks to Frank, I got to wake up alive and hungover instead of dead.

What had drugs done to me? Maybe I was running with the wrong crowd.

* * *

Geek Love. Delivered from Ken Kesey's unvarnished underdog West, but far more psychedelic in its wily unreality. Imagine: Twin goddesses sharing one set of gorgeous legs, a Y presence not an I presence in any room, delivered to this earth by the loving atrocities of their carnie artist parents. A tale told by a sainted dwarf who lived in a mythic America more real than my own. As ad hoc canary in the literary coalmine, I got the manuscript as it scrolled from Katherine's typewriter. She worried the novel was too weird. I thought it was (finally!) the new New Testament. So, thank God, did my literary agent. But who knew? As a writer I had learned well from Hunter Thompson who had learned well from Paul

Krassner. As a newspaper columnist I interviewed the mayor of Portland and reported he'd written the greatest lyric in rock history, "Roll over and let Jimi takeover," then I interviewed the Police Chief and reported he'd just written a book titled, *Cars I Want,* apparently just 300 pages of random used car ads but praised in *The New York Times* by John Leonard as "an existential post modern masterpiece." The mayor and police chief threatened to sue. Then I reported the staff of my newspaper had lured a horse up a freight elevator into our office and had the horse snort what the horse thought was cocaine but which was actually New Blue Cheer laundry detergent and the horse freaked, leapt out a window, broke three legs when it hit the sidewalk and had to be shot. The staff freaked (Susan Orlean among the only ones who stuck up for me) many threatening to go on strike unless I was fired.

Portland, 1982.

"Okay, OK. Shut up! Cool it. OK. Now, look. I mean it you guys. Show a little respect. You sir!" Under a poster of Che Guevara, Walt Curtis—what's left of his gray hair waving heavenward like smoke—put a slender arm out. "Drink your beer and shut your yap."

Smoked rivered the room.

Wiry, bright eyes and a beak for a nose, Walt wore a tattered plaid shirt and jeans that barely hung on his waist. "This poem stinks," he said, without telling anyone which poem it was. "This thing is obscene." He shook his head, as if dismissing the work of a drastically inferior bard. "How could I have possibly written such filth?" He looked at the piece of paper again, closing one eye. "I'm wasting my life, people." His spidery hand shot up in the air and then, as if seized by a life of its own, grabbed his chin and massaged his whole face. He shuffled through his papers again and began to read a poem he'd recently had published in *The Atlantic Monthly.*

"The girl with the green eyes," he began, his free hand out in front of him, an inverted claw.

"took me into her room of surprises.
There was a dish which had never been eaten
on.
A flower that would not wilt,
and a small jewel, like one of her eyes,
marble-like, rolling around in a tray.

We laughed profusely;
and the green curtains shimmered like the sea,
wavy.

I kissed her on the nose.
She embraced me like a martyr,
as a daughter would a father,
a cousin kissing her cousin.

As I began taking off her clothes,
green cherries, string beans and artichokes
spilled on the bed.

I kept thinking of the vegetable cabbage.
Her eyes began flashing signals
like the electric weather vane

Emerald for rain, white for fair weather."

Applause popped around the room.

"More," someone shouts.

"No, no, no, no," Walt waved a hand in front of his face. "The moon is too weird. Is there a moon?" He glanced behind him, out a window, then answered, "No." He took a swig of beer that rested on a stool beside the microphone. "Somebody else get up here!"

CHAPTER THIRTY-EIGHT:
LAST GO ROUND

"Author Ken Kesey and singer Taj Mahal have announced plans for a movie based on the Pendleton Round-Up. Kesey had written a script for the film in which Mahal has agreed to play a famous black cowboy...Racism will be an issue in 'Last Go-Round,' which will tell the true story of the first world championship bronc riding contest...They hope to film the movie at next year's roundup."

—Dick Cockle

Ken Kesey got into the biggest legal tangle of his middle-aged life by way of his old friend Hollywood. Guess how?

Beautiful, brainy women enjoyed a star billing in the Ken Kesey sex, drugs and rock and roll circus, but few were brainier or more beautiful than tall, willowy, dark-haired MiSchelle McMindes, who was from Pendleton by way of Nebraska and Los Angeles, and who had not yet posed for *Playboy* when she met Kesey and gave him the idea for a hit movie, a cowboys-screw-the-Indians Western set at the 1911 Pendleton Roundup. But—a face to launch a thousand ships, legs that went on forever, a winner of beauty pageants and college scholarships, idealistic MiSchelle was herself a star of her own movie, let's call it "The Producers II," a tragi-comedy whose plot was about to include quixotic Kesey as leading man.

MiSchelle, inspired by a unique account of racism, the dying West she found in Rick Steber's book *Rendezvous,* darkened Keze's barn door and announced that that tale would be a perfect vehicle for his return to "the movies." Let Kesey tell what is known in Hollywood, as the "back story": "It's about a rodeo that happens in Pendleton, Oregon, every September. It's removed from everything—there's no other town close—and this rodeo's been going on since 1911. I write a thing about the first rodeo from the point of view of one of the guys who was the third runner-up of the...rodeo riders. His name's Spain and he's from the south. The two older guys are a black guy named George Fletcher and an Indian named Jackson Sundown. The three of them were tied at the end of the three day rodeo, and then they have a very famous last go-round. And the horse that won is in the Pendleton Museum there, mounted. I don't mean he's got somebody on him, I mean he's dead and stuffed with stuff."

After that, it gets complicated.

At the time they met, MiSchelle was only 26, but already a young woman with a knack and enthusiasm for doing a lot of different things. She'd already knocked around the movie business in Hollywood and by the early eighties was living the quasi-cowgirl life in Pendleton, Oregon, employed as a social worker but keeping her eyes out for something a little more effervescent.

Situated in the top right hand corner of Oregon, Pendleton is a charming reminder of the Wild West—cattle and wheat country—the kind of arid backwater where the Marlboro Man might hang his hat, but not a lot of action otherwise. So MiSchelle counted herself lucky to meet former Prankster Mike Hagen, whose mother had been the local beauty queen, and who was largely resting on his laurels as a semi-famous dropout and "first hippie."

Hagen told MiSchelle the story of Spain, Fletcher and Sundown. She got further particulars reading *Rendezvous*. Steber, who grew up in central Oregon cowboy country went on to launch his own publishing company, Bonanza, the flagship of which was his beautiful and ambitious four-color leather jacketed volume of Oregon history, *Rendezvous,* that included the story of Fletcher and Sundown.

MiSchelle concluded that what she had in her hands was Butch Cassidy and the Sundance Kid as a Rainbow Coalition. The ultimate wild west movie, reflecting profound racial themes as a classic action story— and it was not too long after she met Mike Hagen that she suggested the story might be presented to Hagen's legendary pal Kesey as the Next Movie.

Not long after that MiSchelle and Mike were side by side in Hagen's Ford Mustang driving the 325 miles to Kesey's barn-home in Springfield. Forty-nine year-old Kesey needed a hit and, on January 8, 1984 Kesey was offered a check for $5,000 to write a "first draft" of "Last Go Round."

"I didn't allow Mike (Hagen) to give him the check until after we had the agreement that stated the corporation on it, what he was writing," MiSchelle testified in depositions. "Ken is a, you know, a kind of rebellious sort. You don't push too hard. I remember Mike saying, 'Let's just go. He's agreed; he's said yes, he's an honorable man. He said he would do it. We got it. Let's go. So at this point I was ready to go back a third time, but my partner was, you know, basically pulling me out of the place."

"I told him (Ken) what needed to be in it—I had been advised, and then he went to his computer, a brand new computer at the time, and typed it up. We were at his house, we were in his office, his writing loft" and, cut to the chase: after receiving $5,000 "seed money," Kesey wrote the following letter, directed at—among others—his former Prankster partner Mike Hagen.

To Whom It May Concern,
I have agreed to write a screenplay about bygone rodeo greats Jackson Sundown and Nigger George Fletcher, concerning their historic confrontation at the Pendleton Round Up in 1916. The name of the production company that I am writing for is SUNDOWN FLETCHER INC. and the people I am dealing with are Mike Hagen and MiSchelle McMindes.

Years later, MiSchelle recalled, "When Ken agreed and took our check we flew into action." Kesey was about to initiate a mess from which he was unable to extract himself, even from the grave.

Redemption, validation, whatever you want to call it, perhaps it was all destined to happen. The movie of *Cuckoo's Nest* had hijacked the book. Kesey didn't like it that—forget 7 million copies sold in 66 printings, after the stardust settled paperback copies bore the face of Jack Nicholson. "How would you like it if your best book was plastered over with a picture of this five-foot six inch wimp?" A sore subject.

To rewind. Whether Kesey had been too lost, loaded or lazy, he had not, for a long time, produced much that really mattered. "When I wrote that book I'd never known a single Indian. It's strange, like magic. You have to be prepared. You have to stay nimble, because it might happen again. I can go back into that back room night after night and sit at the typewriter and nothing will come. I can't push the buttons or pull the levers to make it happen. I could do every drug imaginable and that still wouldn't pull those levers that make for creative release. It is something bigger, more mysterious, a far more abstract force that dictates that. If it happens a third time then I've got to be prepared."

So began the story of George Fletcher and "The Last Go Round." MiSchelle subsequently paid Kesey $43,000 (put up by her "pee-pee doctor" urologist boyfriend) to write a script she termed "awful."[28] In a note MiSchelle recently wrote to me, she stated in part: "Kesey was selfish and dishonest. He verbally promised many things when he needed people for something, but in the end basically accepted everybody's help—including his 'best' friends—with literary and video projects and then kept all the $ and credit. There was no free love from Kesey (except maybe for his lawyers). He was litigious and everybody paid."

I then was told by John Tillman, a former Rhodes Scholar given the chore of "rescuing" Kesey's script, that, "It was so bad it was impossible to rewrite."

The legal wrangling over "Last Go Round" has been great. An adjudication made by weight of the facts. All ten pounds of them. And though this number was arrived at by way of a bathroom scale, ten pounds of court documents recording the fight for the rights for what many have seen fit to call a dead-on-arrival screenplay is a lot, and therein lies a tale…

Graduating from Pepperdine University in Los Angeles, where she roomed with Angela Lansbury's daughter, MiSchelle moved to Oregon following her marriage to a young Pendleton psychologist. After the marriage collapsed, she then set herself up as a private-investigator doing mostly child abuse and workman's comp work. She'd read *Cuckoo's Nest* and *The Electric Kool-Aid Acid Test*—but before she had even met Kesey she'd been fund-raising, and had hired attorneys to represent her interests in the fledgling "Last Go Round" project.

When she first visited Kesey, she brought her research work, and photos of Fletcher, Sundown and Spain. She had already secured a $30,000 line of credit from her Pendleton urologist boyfriend.

MiSchelle testified that Kesey had been frank about his concerns

---

28 Though attractive to Kesey's arch enemy Jack Nicholson who was evidently eager to be executive producer—until the wheels fell off the deal after Jack allegedly went berserk in a traffic jam and smashed the head of a golf club through the windshield of a car which got in his way.

re. the movie business, telling MiSchelle that during *Cuckoo's Nest* "he had been treated like 'a three-legged coyote.' He felt bad they asked him to write the screenplay and then they rejected it and said it wasn't good enough or what they wanted."

For her part: "Mike (Hagen) and I never considered ourselves great movie producers. We felt just like the developers of this...I had been told by Mike on the way down there that Ken was notorious about refusing to sign contracts and being difficult in business agreements, that he was very suspicious of any kind of attorneys, business arrangements, anything like that...but the substance when we walked out of there as far as verbal agreements and written agreements was that Ken Kesey was on board, he was very excited and was very positive...almost childlike, he was so excited about this story...there was a lot of talking going on that day (January 8, 1984), it was nonstop...I knew at a minimum that he said he was writing it for the corporation, to mention our names and to get something in writing from Ken Kesey before money exchanged hands, before we gave him the check for $5,000. (Ken) said he needed $5,000 for the first draft and $5,000 for the second draft."

Asked if $10,000 was all Kesey was to receive, MiSchelle replied, "That's all that he asked for," but that "Mike and I always felt there would be other compensation." Kesey voiced his reservations, noting: "I've been burned before."

Next, 2,500 promotional brochures that went out to a whole world of potential investors...Hagen was friends with Jim Henson's wife, producer BJ Rack, who had optioned and sold a lot of properties, and she was "interested and helpful." But "Ken was struggling," MiSchelle claimed. "I remember he had a hard time with the screenplay format. He didn't even know how to set it up and he didn't know what a screenplay format would look like."

But that was not the real problem. "We had verbal agreements and then no verbal agreement," MiSchelle recalled, "and, I don't know, rest in peace and bless his soul, I liked Ken, but you never knew which Ken you were going to meet. One meeting he was like 'Yes, we're going to do this and, MiSchelle, I'm going to set you up a meeting with so and so, we're going to do this.' And then the next meeting he would just be very difficult and almost so negative on everything and saying that nothing would happen...And then a little time would pass and he would call up or something and say, 'MiSchelle, you know, let's talk about this now. You know, maybe we can do this.' And so then I began to realize what I was dealing with. Or, you know, I don't think I really understood, but it was that '*Whoa*.' The first meetings with him were so encouraging (but) I don't know if that's the person that's going to show up at a meeting or, you know, to bring investors in. I felt that we had—we had a problem."

Further agreements were "dismissed by Ken" Kesey wanted "more cash up front."

"He had had some choice words for me at different times," MiSchelle recalled, "At certain times he loved me because I was working hard."MiSchelle was anxious to go fishing, to test the waters among Pendleton's landed gentry who she knew were "excited about a Northwest story." Kesey wanted business cards made from a real deck of cards, so MiSchelle had their business cards made from real playing cards that had cowboys on them…

During depositions, Kesey's lawyer asked, "Did Sundown and Fletcher provide any health benefits for Ken Kesey or Irbie Smith?"

"No," MiSchelle admitted.

"No dental coverage, I take it?"

"No."

"There wasn't any kind of training program for Ken Kesey, I take it?"

A puzzling question, to which MiSchelle answered, "Nothing formal."

"Did you provide any vacation days?"

"No."

"No sick days?"

"You're enjoying this, aren't you?"

"No."

"I asked Ken in a phone conversation," MiSchelle, frustrated, explained. 'Okay, just give me the $10,000 back' and he just, didn't really answer me…and, of course, he never gave it back. A lot of directors and producers were calling him at home, and he was getting full of himself and 'This is going to be my deal. I'm going to go ahead and do this.'"

MiSchelle got a first draft of the screenplay. The second draft was not delivered until there was a big promotional event at the Pendleton

Roundup. "Willie Nelson's people were there, Taj Mahal, Ken and his whole family came down and stayed all week"

Then: "We had the tragic event of the death of Ken's son Jed."

Big SUVs and pickups in the parking lot and inside, in the gymnasium, kid wrestlers, whose parents, dressed in jeans and sweatshirts and flannel, looked like people who actually made things. Larry's Topliff's lanky well-muscled son, was making short, if interrupted, work of a boy whose best effort was to grab on and hold, ride out Larry's teenaged boy as if he were a storm, and between rounds, Larry's son stepped off the mat. He leaned over Larry's wheelchair and his arms scooted back and forth over his dad's shoulders, "The guy's all slither, slither, slither, Dad."

A big suburban high school in Milwaukie, Oregon. Under a cold blue March sky, old fashioned Sales America: Miles of car lots, a gauntlet of gleaming grills, car lot after car lot, Ford, Chevrolet, Kia, Toyota and BMW compete with local venues like "Street of Deals" and the "Used Car Warehouse."

Larry Topliff was coach out here, zipping across the gymnasium floor in his electric wheelchair, the father of three sons, boys who all became wrestlers like their dad, who was in that dilapidated van the University of Oregon wrestling team was riding in, a van his attorney called "a borrowed chicken wagon." It had been loaned to the university by Willamette Poultry and had no seat belts, bald tires and doors which all popped open on impact.

Topliff was then still a teenaged wrestler on the U of O team. Born in Portland, he'd been a competitive swimmer in grade school, but hated swimming practice, and fell immediately in love with wrestling in sixth grade when encouraged by a teacher to try out for a middle school team. He began wrestling in the 70-pound class and was competing at about double that by the time he met Ken Kesey's son Jed at the University of Oregon, where Jed was then a light middleweight sophomore wrestler.

The team had been wrestling in Pendleton, and Jed one of the only wrestlers who lost his match that night. Topliff recalled, "The next morning we got up and it had been snowing and the roads were icy and the driver, Dean Dixon, was inexperienced driving in icy conditions. There were twelve of us on the bus. Ten wrestlers and two kids to run the cameras. Dixon was driving too fast, hit ice, hit a guardrail, the guardrail was too low, so rather than bouncing us back, it caught the front bumper, the backend fishtailed around and went up and over the guardrail and the van rolled down the embankment 190 feet. One kid was lying in back on top of our gear, on impact he was thrown out and landed on his feet and stood watching as the van rolled down the embankment with wrestlers being ejected along the way. By the time the van stopped rolling, everybody had been ejected. He flagged a car down, but, at that time, there were no cell phones. It took 45 minutes for the first ambulance to get there and it was two hours before anyone got to a hospital."

Jed died in the hospital shortly thereafter. Kesey recalled, "After we had been at the hospital two days and nights we were informed that Jed was brain dead. We needed to sign a release so they could harvest his organs. Xeroxed forms were spread out on a cold Formica countertop for our signatures. It was the hardest thing I ever did. Nothing before that moment and nothing imagined after would ever be that hard. It was midnight and dirty snow was swirling in the parking lot...Along with all us wrestling families there were other couples who had journeyed to the hospital to offer their support. They had all experienced the same agony and signed similar releases. Their silent embraces gave us a solace that even our immediate families couldn't quite match. They understood. We were all members of a very elite order none of us wanted to join. A nurse told us later that they used 12 things out of Jed...an even dozen."

Kesey created a mountaintop monument to his son: "I had this flash, and I knew if we were going to meet somewhere Jed would know to meet me up here on Mt. Pisgah."

After Jed's funeral, Kesey suggested athletic buses should be equipped with CB radios, medical kits and, if needed, studded snow tires: "The front line is out there on the highways. It's not in Grenada or Beirut. We lose more children on the highways than in 100 border skirmishes around the world, and the parents' anguish is the same."

Grieving, Kesey solicited his in-law director and producer Irby Smith to help with his "Last Go Round" screenplay. Smith had recently co-produced "Young Guns" and its sequel, as well as the now classic "City Slickers." Together Kesey and Smith wrote the second draft of the screenplay and Smith was awarded $3,000 for his efforts. A month later Kesey was paid $5,000 by Prankster Mike Hagen and MiSchelle McMindes. According to a "time line" attached to a suit against the

Kesey Estate, "Much interest in the screenplay ensues from Hollywood, but all potential producers and directors have expressed that there are many changes they would require of the story. Everyone has different ideas and no one will seriously make an offer."

Mischelle testified that when Jed died everything stopped and that a fair amount of time passed before Kesey called and said he was ready to work again. Kesey got back to writing and the script "completely changed. He put medical sequences in there because of his experiences with his son in the hospital, and those were all things he wrote after— after Jed's death."

MiSchelle recalled that, while she attempted to remain stoplight clear and straight forward, she could never really understand what was on Kesey's mind. "Ken at times would be direct, and he—one of the lines he always said to me and Mike, was 'If you can't make a deal on a bar napkin, you can't make a deal.' You know, 'A deals a deal, and just calm down, honey, don't worry. A deal's a deal.'"

She asked Kesey to return the money. "He never did." Then she found herself back on board the rollercoaster. One day all was congenial, the next day not. "But no, he never said clearly to me, 'You don't own the copyright.'" There was now always the specter of Jed's death. "I was very sensitive to that…He was very depressed. It was a very hard time." But, according to MiSchelle, Kesey's essential song remained the same: "I don't sign anything. We have a deal."

Kesey wanted 2½ percent of the producer's net and MiSchelle recalled, "Crazy numbers were tabled at this time, really crazy numbers, creative control, and you know all kinds of crazy terms." Nothing she could agree to. "I was more than happy to pay Ken more money, but I wanted…to keep the original deal intact and have us all move together forward."

Kesey told MiSchelle that he might cut a deal with one of the many producers and directors who were contacting him personally, and she was afraid she was about to be left on the sidewalk. So she made a real effort to create terms her famous writer would be amenable to, so that she, Mike Hagen and Kesey could present themselves as inseparable Siamese triplets to a studio, and a movie with all their names on it could be made "so we could eat popcorn."

And then? MiSchelle recalled receiving dozens of offers…perhaps a hundred or more and that Faye Kesey wanted "cash," that the Kesey's needed money. Likely money was out there: Burt Reynolds, who was part Indian, was interested, he wanted to play the Indian, Hal Ashby was calling Kesey, though Ashby did not like the first draft, Lucas Films was interested but, "If Ken wouldn't sign a contract, we were all—it was dead."

By October 2, MiSchelle, unable to deal with Kesey's multi-faceted psyche, was "ready to punt. It was all these back and forth changes and rearranges and 'we love you, we want you to go meet with these investors...'" During depositions Kesey's attorney inquired, "Wasn't it Ken's right not to sign an agreement if he didn't want to make a deal with you?"

"It's America," MiSchelle replied, "He can do what he wants. But he had already agreed with me and Mike...he accepted those funds, he would write the screenplay for the corporation. To us that was a deal, that was an agreement...I spent a lot of hours and days and weeks with him...He was a very intelligent man. He was very cagey and radical and a rebel, but he understood. He understood exactly what we were talking about."

MiSchelle had a meeting, minus Kesey, with Faye: "It got shrill, it got real shrill...I was being tough about our investment. It was an investment on behalf of some other people's part, and it was an effort to make me back down. Faye said 'What you gave Ken (was) a gift.' That's what started it. She said, 'You gave Ken, that was just a gift.' And I was very clear, 'No...I would not say that it was a gift.' This was an effort to say we were just kidding around. You know, this wasn't a business deal. We've only spent, you know, at that point probably $25,000 of the investment money, venture capital money. And I was absolutely clear in that meeting as I am today, no, this is a business arrangement. Sundown & Fletcher owned the screen rights...Ken was so happy to take our $10,000 to write this story. It was just our little story about our little cowboys from our home town. All of the sudden it was his story, his idea. You know, he fell in love with the story.

But without a percentage agreement from Ken, no deal could be made. Thus nothing, so to speak, kept happening. For months, years, finally decades. MiSchelle concluded: "We had been kicked in the teeth so many times while we were earnestly spending money and a lot of energy and a lot of time…And then when we'd get very close to a really good deal, what we felt was a very good deal for Ken and, of course, for us, it would blow up…This project, I had pitched this, you know, to a dozen people. But no, not as a person in charge. I was young, I was very young."

CHAPTER THIRTY-NINE:
A LONG TIME GONE

"He hates being an addict. He fights it as much as he can, and I know he knows he's losing. He has a self-hatred deeper than any man I've ever known. He looks in the mirror and sees a guy who is fat, ugly and forty-five. He only sees the self he chooses to see. This is not anything he is enjoying. This is not a joke. He's sick."
—Graham Nash

Autumn 1985. Dusk at David Crosby's. His brown clapboard house was perched high on a hill above Mill Valley, near San Francisco, at the end of a mouse's maze of skinny avenues and asphalt switchbacks. As the sibilant squawk of an alto sax floated from the thick tangle of woods below the house, Jan Dance, Crosby's girlfriend, came down to the pool. She was very thin and her skin nearly translucent. Several of her teeth were missing, and a long red comma of ruptured skin curled down her cheek. She served us Cokes in paper cups, then slipped back inside the house.

I was there with Crosby's friend, photographer Henry Diltz. We drank the cokes. Twenty minutes later, David Crosby came out the back door, acoustic guitar in hand. Big and bear-like, a ski hat pulled low over his eyes, he sat down beside the pool and played a new song. It was lovely, complicated.

"I gotta come up with a lot more like this," he said when he finished playing the song. "Capital Records rejected my last album. Said it wasn't enough like Devo or Elvis Costello or something. Stupid jerks. I spent damn near every last cent I had buying back my contract. I gotta make a statement. I can't hack this. I'm such an easy target. I've obviously had terrible problems with drugs. But I'm not a vegetable or some vacant-eyed lump of flesh in a corner, with disarrayed clothes covered in blood and spit. I'm a human being with a mind, a spirit, a soul and a heart. It's when—"

Suddenly, we heard the startling sound of a woman wailing coming from the house. Crosby got up, strode around the pool.

"It's Jan," he said. "She's just real upset now all the time." Crosby took the steps to his back door three at a time. "Things have been real bad for us lately, man."

Surprising, at least at first glance. For with Jim Morrison, Jimi Hendrix and Janis Joplin dead, Brian Wilson crazy, and Dylan—at least temporarily—a Jesus freak, David Crosby should have been the driving force in the late American super group. But the stories were terrible: that Atlantic Records had dropped Crosby, Stills and Nash, that their voices were so far gone that ghost vocalists had to be employed backstage to counterfeit their famous harmonies, that David Crosby was freebasing $600,000 of cocaine a year and that the Hell's Angels had assumed ownership of his Marin County house to cover his drug debts; and finally that Crosby would be arrested and jailed by the Texas police the minute he set foot in the state on their upcoming nationwide tour—this in the wake of his cocaine and weapons convictions two years previous.

For a lot of West Coast kids like me, David Crosby, far more than Ken Kesey, represented the beginning and end of whatever the 1960s sex, drugs and rock and roll revolution thought itself all about. Crosby's dad had been a medium large shot in the movie business, Crosby grew up at the ocean in southern California and was nothing if not the prototype for the West Coast suburbanurchin. Both the most rebellious and thoughtful of Rock Gods, he had the wide-psyched ability to remain unfailingly polite while giving the universe the finger. And what a musician. First architect, before the Beatles or Rolling Stones, of a whole new sound.When I was barely a teenager the Byrds' weightless guitars swept from my father's stereo to announce a new kingdom, a super Oz where your every wish might soon come true. Singer, sailor, drinker, a loadie spiraling fatally out of control, Crosby had once stood for absolute freedom, but now he was a prisoner on his own death row.

During the past several years, he had been tracked by police and press and plagued by coke busts, an assault and battery suit, arrests for illegal guns and knives, you name it. Said to be living like a wino and "rock's favorite threat to society," Crosby was portrayed in the media as a fanatically unhappy man too zonked to engineer a successful overdose, his life a Mobius strip of trials and tribulations substantial enough to earn him a place in the Bible.

He also was at the center of one of the greatest franchises in rock music. Less grubby than the Grateful Dead, less fun than the Beach Boys but a lot more fun than the Doors, CSN provided the soundtrack for a generation at war with authority. But, between the time Stephen Stills confessed to the crowd of 400,000 at Woodstock that "We're scared shitless" and Richard Nixon bombed Cambodia, CSN began a long history of family feuding. The ever increasing inventory of elixirs didn't help. "For awhile," a friend recalled, "the drugs were there to make the music better. Finally, though, the music was there to make the drugs better."

"I'm not ashamed," Crosby once said, "of being stoned…Everyone's been on my case so long, saying I'm so smashed, so stoned, strung out. But I was stoned for every bit of music I've ever played. Every record. Every performance…If they can match the music, let them criticize it. Anybody who can't ain't got no fuckin' right to tell me nothin' about getting high…I want to get high."

I had been assigned by *Rolling Stone* to write what Editor Jann Wenner considered the most important story of the year: the death's door devolution of one of the greatest talents in contemporary music, a plummet propelled by drugs whose gravities were in ways as immense as any sun. Why I'd been picked, I'll never know, having just botched the story of Bruce Springsteen's wedding in Portland to a young model who happened to live next door to one of my mother's best friends. The marriage was to be Normandy Invasion-level top secret but the model's mom blabbed to my mom's best friend and, cut to the chase: I promised RS I'd climb up on my mom's friend's roof for the intimate bird's eye view of the nuptials. Sadly, hit by the worst flu ever, I was left delirious (and scoopless) on the big wedding day.

But next thing I knew, I was somehow with Crosby's PR agent, the bearish, fantastic Wayne Russo. Russo, who went on to become a software giant, was what PR guys claim to be and rarely are: a really decent human being. Wayne loved Crosby like a brother. But Wayne was unique in PR. For example, one day he called and said he'd just fired himself from his own firm and that he needed me to help him break into his old office and steal all his computer equipment back. We did. Then Wayne revealed his master plan: I was not to go soft on David, this would be anti-PR. As means of making Crosby see that he was practically already dead, Russo's suggestion: paint the starkest portrait possible. Then he put me on tour with the band.

I have to say it was not a pleasant task. Crosby had been a hero to me since I was fourteen and in person he did not disappoint. He was a humble and wonderful guy, completely vulnerable and completely fucked up by drugs. In Texas, sitting with him in "The Lab," his tour bus, he told me, "I'm like a guy who does everything right nine days in a row, then stumbles on the tenth day. That's all everybody wants to talk about. The tenth day. It's not fair, it's just not fair."

"The Lab's" décor could have best been described as Attempted Holiday Inn. Formica. Dim fabrics. His entourage included his bus driver and…that was about it. No family. Few friends. While Graham Nash reminded me of the genial tour director and host, and still bantered with anyone who would listen about everything from Shakespeare to his tax problems, Crosby kept to himself. In "The Lab." Alone.

Staph infection had raised hell with his skin, and in the half light he looked like an eighteenth century pirate sorely in need of vitamin C.

"Look, man," he said, "I've never hurt anybody in my life. I don't do bad stuff to people. But I've had my name dragged through the dirt. Those two girls who brought that assault and battery charge? I'm a gentleman. I've never hit a girl in my life. Not once. They filed a civil suit to make money. They saw their chance to make big bucks."

Crosby swallowed. "I'm not violent or dangerous. All I ever wanted to do was make people happy…I've been a good boy, man. I went through such a long period of time in jail, kicking. Getting clean…It's an immense psychochemical readjustment, okay? I've been getting high for twenty years. Constantly. And I stopped. The readjustment was turbulent. Like being in the center of a cyclone. I was very crazy.

"Jail is hell on wheels, man. Guys made it hard on me. Imagined I was rich. Imagined I was a star. They think a star is real. They don't know that it's nothing. It was really bad. I cried myself to sleep every night, man."

Which, I thought at the time had led him to change his tune on freebasing. "Don't do it," he told me. "It's a blind alley, a definite dead end. I think reefer is the only thing that doesn't fuck you up. I've seen too much pain, too much suffering. Too much death. Just look at the friends I've lost. Cass, Jimi, Janis. I'm decent. I don't want anybody to think I'm just some outlaw rebel giving America the finger."

Minutes later he began to weep.

So what the fuck was going on inside the house? When Crosby reappeared, it was already night, and with no explanation other than "Jan's a little upset," he said he was up for some dinner. He decided to drive into town in a big, new Lincoln Continental he's rented. On the way, he checked his mail.

'Dear David,' he said, mocking a recent missive, 'Jesus told me to write you…Myself," he continues, "I talk to God. I call God Ernie. Less pretentious. 'Ernie,' I say, 'Why?'"

He sped through the narrow, twisting roads into Mill Valley, pulled into a parking lot, spotting a diagonal spot stamped COMPACTS ONLY and whipped the Lincoln right in, front tires bumping up over the curb. Its snout stuck three feet across the sidewalk. "Just another VW, officer," he said, getting out of the car.

Crosby led us into D'Angelo's. "This is a fantastic place,' he said, stepping into the large, airy restaurant. Waiters constellated around our table. He ordered a steak, a salad and several kinds of pasta. Then he pulled a walkie-talkie from his herringbone jacket and called Jan. "Hi, listen, we're at D'Angelo's," he said, "You want me to bring back something? Veal Parmesan? Antipasto?…Anybody call?…Linda from Sausalito? Never heard of her. Love you. Bye."

Then Crosby said, "The other day I read that Graham told this guy I'm going to die. How could he have said that? He's my best friend. He said I was just going to die." Crosby's voice wobbled. "How could he have said that? So cold. I would never have said something like that about Graham in a million years, man. It was so crude, so out of hand.

"What does Graham think, that I'm so stupid he's going to shock me into some perception I haven't already attained? You think I haven't thought about this every minute of every day? There's not a damn thing he's going to teach me about this I don't already know! I know more about freebase than anybody! You think you plan to become an addict? It sneaks up on you. Oh, I'll just get a little high. I've kicked cigarettes, heroin, booze, everything. But this is the most horrible drug in the universe. It stays with you. I was in jail four months. Want to know how long I stayed clean when I got out? Two days. It never lets you alone. All I want to do is be clean, man. But I'm scared I'm gonna crave it forever."

Crosby sat there, breathing noisily in and out, as if exhausted. Then, an epiphany: "Hey, John Coltrane was a junkie. And who could make better music than him? I'm gonna beat it, I am."

The food arrived and he passed the plates around. "I love fish," he said. "Last time I sailed to Hawaii, we had lines trailing out. Three days out of the islands we caught three mahi-mahi."

A waiter appeared. "Cheese for the pasta, David?"

"Just for the fettuccine. Whack it on there. Lots." He knifed his steak in half. "This is not quite medium. Just a couple minutes more, please... What a trip, beating the windwards—motoring the windwards lots of times-Mexico to Hawaii. 3,000 miles in the trades."

Crosby talked about going to Tahiti. "Sexy, wonderful people. All they want to do is get smashed and fuck. That's their whole program Oooooooh, let's get drunk! Make shooner, baby! Fuck the white boys. Get the bloodlines all mixed up. Paradise. Crosby, Stills and who? Whaaaat ees you name? Trade winds at ten knots. Baby's breath, man. No circular storms. No typhoons. So rich with life. You'd have to be blind, deaf and dumb and have a lot of *enemies* to starve there. Ocean's not fished out. So clean and sparkly..."

Crosby picked up his walkie-talkie and called Jan again. "I love you" he proclaimed. "I love your skinny little ass. I wanta grab ya! Sounds like a good idea, huh? Well, I'm gonna come home and stuff ya. All right, sweetie."

His steak returned. "Money is fun, but it'll trash you out," he said. "I've got guys who invested in me, yeah. Saved me from the IRS. I give'em what I can. That's it. Sometimes things get hard. Jan was crying last night. Called it eyelash soup. But there are good things, too—"

Crosby then fell asleep, instantly. His eyes closed. They looked as if they were about to slide off the side of his head. He began to snore.

"Gimme something hard and heavy," Crosby told the clerk at the Mill Valley 7-Eleven. The clerk handed him a hammer.

Crosby had just bought forty dollars worth of cat food, soda pop and ice cream and discovered he'd locked his keys inside the Lincoln. Henry Diltz's flight was the last one for the night and only an hour away.

"Maybe we should call somebody," Henry said.

"At this hour?" asked Crosby.

"But…"

"You don't want to miss your flight, do you?" Crosby raised the hammer, his arm came down in an arc. Wham. The Lincoln's driver's side window was history. Little diamonds of smashed glass everywhere. Then he carefully cleaned out the car and swept the parking lot.

"Don't worry," he said, "I'll pay for it. It'll just get stuck on my bill like everything else."

CHAPTER FORTY:
DROWNING IN THE WISHING WELL

"Did you ever read The Spear of Destiny? It's by a guy named Trevor Ravenscroft—a fantastic name for an English writer. It's the spear of the Roman centurion who pierced Christ's heart at the moment of his death. In Christian symbolism, that's the heavy moment, the moment of decision because the rap is Christ's blood was spilled to wipe out the sins of all people. That's what spilled the blood, so that's a tool of great power. All kinds of people had it—Charlemagne, the first Christian emperor of Rome—what was his name? Constantine—then a whole bunch of German kings and princes. It was in the Vienna Museum and when Hitler flashed on it—the book is essentially about Hitler's occult side, the guys who turned Hitler on to Mescaline. His first mescaline trip, he saw the spear and decided he had to have it, because...whoever has this thing has the power of absolute good or absolute evil."

—Jerry Garcia

Hunter Thompson was the punch line to the joke the Love Generation had become, and when Thompson paid a visit to Kesey's farm, Kesey remarked, re: The Hell's Angels. "It even reached the point where I gave up on them. They just wouldn't be nice." Kesey also reminded Thompson, "The crosshairs of fame move around and you can sure feel it when they're on you."

"I know what you mean," Hunter agreed, and referring to his battle to have the quote, "I don't advocate the use of drugs, alcohol and violence—but they've always worked for me," removed from the poster advertising *Where the Buffalo Roam*, "Things like that create the Billy the Kid syndrome. People come gunning for you. They come up to you and say, Hi, I'm Sam Smith from Kansas. Want to fight?"

He'd been selling himself in soundbites. That diva Thompson wasn't otherwise as unproductively and uselessly unhinged as, say, Britney Spears, made no difference. Because in our time an even comatose Britney Spears is a money machine and in his, Thompson wasn't. Hunter: "Why would I save anything if I'm not going to be around to spend it? The problem is, I keep outliving my money supply."

The athletic, theatric and solipsistic similarities between Kesey and Thompson are fascinating. To Kesey, drugs were a new sacrament, to Thompson, the anti Kesey, they represented a wonderfully dangerous toy. The anti-Kesey, Thompson's hilarious psychedelic atheism was renunciation of Kesey's acid religiosity; the psychedelic revolution was an exciting fraud. Blowing your mind as a career move? Thompson broke the mold, from 1973 to 1981 busy, busy, busy getting almost nothing published. All energy went into throwing an eight-year-long party for himself.

Never mind conjuring Great American Novels, thanks to magic elixirs, for most of the great white psychedelic literary hopes, it had become difficult to get *anything* done. While a few, like Richard Brautigan, found resolve of sorts (he blew his brains out), for Kesey the muse had become now almost always out of reach, recalling the old story of the carrot dangling from the fishing pole held by the rider on the donkey's back.

Perhaps Kesey's problems with the *Last Go Round* script had to do with the fact that he had more irons in the fire than a steel mill. Not the least of which was the grass-roots revolution. His plan: "We can put this crop in your field and in five years," Kesey proclaimed, "you'll be turning out hemp that will be the answer to the world's building problems." He revealed that he and his brother Chuck had taken stalks of hemp, squished them in cheese presses and " made beams as hard as any you can find. They'll take a nail just like a wood beam. The only difference is they have those pithy centers, so they are light."

Kesey further claimed the ability to grow hemp stalks to eighteen feet and, abracadabra, "Imagine what starts happening if you get the Luther Burbank of grass who starts to grow it up. You'll be able to harvest five foot-high grass off the Willamette valley in 20 years that won't get you high at all. But nobody will care."

Next, a little perspective. In 1983, speaking out in favor of the decriminalization and taxation of pot sales in Oregon, Kesey said, "I'm not scared of my kids becoming weed heads. They've been smoking dope since they were this high. I'm scared of them buying dope. And the connections they make. Just like my folks told me, dope leads to harder drugs. It's on these channels that coke and smack are eventually traveling. We can pull the rug out from under the criminals by passing this law."

This was after the state revealed marijuana sales had surpassed logging as Oregon number one cash crop. $500 million a year was going up in smoke. "We're not here today as dope smokers," Kesey assured his audience, "we don't need this law passed to be able to smoke dope, because we know we can get all the dope we want to smoke anyway. We know that. I've never had any lack of dope in the last twenty years. It comes and comes. I'm trying to lance something that has built up under the surface of this state that could poison and kill us."

Kesey concluded by saying that he did not like being a criminal, that he didn't care for criminals and that "I don't like the leak crime has caused in Oregon. I mean, if there are $500 million moving around under the surface of this state, that money is passing back and forth and there's no day care centers being built off that money. There's no chuck holes being fixed with that money. That money is untouched. And if you check it out. . .you'll see that at the end of the line are some big, bad guys. And with $500 million in illegal funds moving around, if we don't begin to attract the Mafia from Las Vegas, then they're not the Mafia I've grown to love and respect."

Here in a state Kesey called "the citadel of the spirit," manger to the modern American environmental movement, the whole "Never Give an Inch" thing, "Louie, Louie," and "The Father of the Counterculture." A state home to *Animal House*, Nike and America's James Joyce, Matt Groening, creator of *The Simpsons*, who here in Oregon owned the zeitgeist now?

Undifferentiated psychedelic psychosis, we hardly knew ye. Acid and Ken Kesey had nothing on Bhagwan Shree Rajneesh. An Indian neo-Prankster extraordinaire who'd swooped into Oregon to hijack the zeitgeist with biblical vengeance—"If Jesus had a little intelligence and rationality he would not have gone (to Jerusalem and the cross)," Bhagwan declared. "But, there was no need (for him) to declare (that he was) the Messiah and Son of God…those messiahs are basically insane. If anyone is responsible for the crucifixion, he himself is responsible. He asked for it. And no Jewish or contemporary source says there was a resurrection. Only the New Testament. It is fictitious. There was no resurrection." But no worries. "You can be a Christ: Why be a Christian? …Let me be your death and resurrection."

Rewind to Summer 1983. See the new future: Rajneesh Chandra Mohan, aka Bhagwan Shree Rajneesh aka just plain God to his friends (Though if Bhagwan—who claimed to "own nothing"—were God he'd be a God who did not own Heaven, but leased it instead) was breaking a year and a half long vow of silence to announce the coming end of the world. His bully pulpit: Paradise aka "The Big Muddy Ranch" aka the middle of nowhere. Morning in America. Ronald Reagan was President, the Soviet Union—though it didn't know it yet—headed for the trash heap of history, and here at the Ranch thousands of Rajneeshees were "worshiping" twelve hours a day dawn to dusk. "Worshiping" was Rajneeshee for "work." Bhagwan's apostles had pumped $100 million into the property and planned to earn $25 to $30 million a year for the next five years. "The Big Muddy," a hundred miles or so down the road from Kesey's farm, was soon to be home to hundreds of thousands of purple-robed "sannysins." Meanwhile, the author of Oregon's "cult bill," Joanne Boies declared, "Rajneesh is the fifth one on the Devil's chain of command…(The Rajneeshees) are going to kill all the people that are Christians."

So there I was. Dawn, the sun a bleeding flash on the desert horizon, media people everywhere, because here in sex utopia, big news: "Man is now living in his most critical moment and it is a crisis of immense dimensions. Either he will die or a new man will be born."

Imagine Krishnamurti with a big mouth and a bottomless credit card (Headline in a local newspaper: IS OREGON BIG ENOUGH FOR BOTH KESEY AND BHAGWAN?). Kesey-like in charisma, but more flamboyant, more outrageous, more utopian, a more prolific writer— Rajneeshees claimed Bhagwan had penned an estimated 33 million words showcased in 350 books, oversaw a publishing empire said to gross hundreds of thousands of dollars a month and was one hell of a lot richer. Even more precocious than Ken, Bhagwan claimed to have attained "enlightenment" at age 7. He espoused "dynamic meditation."

Sannysins would jump up and down yelling 'Hoo! Hoo! Hoo!'' and/ or spend three hours a day for a week crying, then three hours a day for a week laughing and finally three hours a day for a week in silence. Bhagwan had taken Kesey's concept of the "group mind," to the nth degree.

For with his flowing robes, waterfall beard, laser-eyed gaze and 106 Rolls Royces BSR was nothing if not a guru's guru, and as the "Swami of Sex" whose motto was, "Be a joke unto yourself," and who forecast "floods which have never been known since the time of Noah, along with earthquakes, volcanic eruptions, and everything else that is possible through nature…There will be wars which are bound to end in nuclear explosions…Tokyo, New York, San Francisco, Los Angeles, Bombay, etc…all these cities are going to disappear."

Leaving nothing but this, the biggest commune in America. A 126-square-mile spread, an area twice the size of the city of San Francisco, home to the new countercultural action, it made Kesey's former farm commune look like a Girl Scout slumber party. Bhagwan's freaky legion was composed mostly of bright, middle class libertines who followed, like the Pranksters, what amounted to a Reader's Digest condensed version of the Ten Commandments. And in ways the Rajneeshees were like the toga-ed children of the original bus-bound Pranksters, sons and daughters who out-outnumbered, out-media-ed and out-crazied their psychedelic ancestors.

Anyway, the end of the world. Bhagwan's PR "Twinkies," attractive young women who spoke the language of love and apocalypse and dressed in the height of post-apocalyptic fashion—purple leg warmers, pumpkin-colored sweaters over burnt sienna blouses—handled both TV film crews and apocalypse with the same efficient, cheery geisha/ Dallas Cowboy cheerleader style that they'd used to handle rumors that Bhagwan was planning a mass suicide here at the ranch that would make Jonestown look like a picnic, and that the Rajneeshees were building missile silos on the ranch to house their own H-bomb-tipped ICBMs.

These folks weren't a bunch of hippies in Birkenstocks out pitching pup tents or the kind of wobble-noggined zombies who wore galoshes and togas and sold chrysanthemums at airports. These people were pros. Days before, I had left Rajneesh "city" and attempted to check out the missile sites, said to be hidden behind the tall, tan mountains but had been turned back at a roadblock by Rajneeshees cradling Uzi-submachine guns. By this time an estimated six million Americans belonged to cults ranging from the Love Family to the Church of Scientology, but this was a whole new twist, a "religious community" complete with a gambling casino, a disco, a shopping mall, a 145-room luxury hotel, more Rolls Royces per capita than any other place in the world including Beverly Hills and Kuwait, and enough gourmet bars and restaurants to start a new Sausalito. Paradise for rich vegetable eaters.

Unmindful of the End, construction continued apace. Under a rising sun, heavy equipment moved out from sheltered bivouac areas. Heavy, heavy equipment: dump trucks, road graders, back-hoes and immense front loaders each as big as a house. On vegetation-carpeted hills where only sagebrush grew before, the Rajneeshees had the technology and the warm bodies to plant an acre an hour, grow 60 different crops and raise hundreds of cattle for sale. They even had their own airline, Air Rajneesh. Parked beside their airstrip along Nirvana Way sat three DC-3s, a commuter turboprop and a Convair once owned by Howard Hughes. Meanwhile, though, the natives were getting…restless.

Someone flew over the commune and dropped leaflets announcing "hunting season" on commune members. Purportedly from the "Oregon State Department of Fish and Wildlife" the statement read, "there will be an open season on Rajneesh, known locally as the "Red Rats" or "red vermin."

'These Red Rats may be a little rough to dress out and if gut shot, probably not worth the effort.

"IT WILL BE UNLAWFUL TO
* Hunt in a party of over 700
* Use more than 50 attack dogs in one group
* Use less than a .25 caliber rifle or double .00 buckshot (they are thick-skinned).
* Possess a road-killed Red Rat. It is OK to hit one, but don't pick the bastard up."

Rajneeshpurim Mayor Krishna Dava took it all in stride. "We have machine guns and whatever else it takes. And they're not here for hunting deer, I can tell you that. If I were the folks out there, I'd take out my frustrations elsewhere. Because we're ready for anything."

By then, Kesey had, in a manner of speaking, gone to the mattresses.

In 1983 Kesey told *The Saturday Review:* "We got into acid. We felt like we were dealing with the end of time. I felt that writing was one for the future and that suddenly we were cut off from the future." Yet there was hope. Outer space: "It is a very American feeling. It has to do with our destiny as a nation. Our destiny is off the planet. We know what space is—every American knows that if he really wants to get away from it all, all he has to do is drive for an hour and a half and he'll be in an empty space with no one else around. That is the frontier consciousness that is part of our country."

Perhaps. In an *Esquire* profile titled *Ken Kesey Kisses No Ass,* Chip Brown described Oregon as looking like Ireland without the history. As a native, I'd say it looks more like the Ruhr Valley without Krupp. Anyway, Kesey told Brown, concerning his brother Chuck's creamery being 86'd from Springfield. "They don't want it there anymore—nobody wants to see a factory downtown. They think if they make it all pretty, people will spend money. Turn away from what the town was built on and that's the quickest way to cut your own throat. It's like Eugene trying not to be a logging town."

He had a new and excellent anthology out. "I feel very feminine about *Demon Box.* It's like putting my child out there, something I've given birth to." It was a very personal book, in which Kesey confessed, "The air is thick with broken promises coming home to roost, flapping and clacking their beaks and circling down to give me the same as Prometheus got... worse! Because I sailed up to those forbidden heights—more times than he had—as many times as I could manage the means, but instead of a flagon of fire all I brought back was an empty cocktail glass...and I broke that."

What was the problem? "You don't stop writing, you just stop publishing...All writers continue to write, but at a point, nobody likes to publish. It's demeaning, demoralizing. It's like taking your baby and having somebody say, 'let's change the eyes a little."

On New York: "I'm frightened there and uncomfortable, and I don't make correct decisions. For me to go there for a book project is like taking my cows to New York instead of having a buyer come look them over in my field." Yet had he not allowed *Demon Box* to be published,

"Then someone would have brought it out after I died as a sociological study of a failed writer…It's not the best stuff I've written. But it gives me a box—a box to put my gonzo in. A gonzo is our persona of the way we write. Mailer is a good example: his gonzo often upstages his characters. Writers can get trapped by their gonzo. Not Shakespeare. You don't get a sense of Shakespeare on stage, only his characters come through…It frees me to do the Alaska book, I don't have to be Kesey to do the Alaska book."

Old fashioned family values: In a 1986 *Esquire* article, "Blows to the Spirit, How the American Male Has Taken it on the Chin," Kesey waxed sociological: "you know, some people say syphilis came from screwing sheep and pigs, and there are some who say AIDS may have come from monkeys. So when the Scriptures, not just the Judeo-Christian Scripture, but lots of Scripture say 'don't screw animals,' it's not because God doesn't want us screwing animals, he's telling us if we're going to screw animals, we're going to get things from them…It seems to me it's one's job to put sperm in a place that's designed for it. You don't put crankcase oil in your power-steering system. And when God says, 'Do not put crankcase oil in your power-steering system,' he's not saying, 'If you do you'll go to hell,' he's saying, 'If you do, you'll blow the seals out of your power steering.'"

Made sense. Meanwhile, my ex-cousin Marty had bought a little house in Portland complete in the backyard with Marty's Black Hole of the Gods, dug by Satan or a neighbor, a bottomless shaft sunk miraculously, endlessly to the center of the earth, an earth revealed in its blacker than black to be not molten core but, more biblically, the color of Nothing.

One of the last times Walt Curtis had been to Ken Kesey's house, he'd driven out with Marty and Lorna and, after drinking a lot, crashed in Kesey's sons' bedroom, and listened to Neal Cassady's "bus tapes," and when Walt went to use the bathroom, he saw THE STATEMENT, which he says is still pasted up there in the john today. It read I SHALL STRUGGLE. AND I SHALL WIN. FOR I AM SUPREME AMONG BEINGS OF THE UNIVERSE.

To Walt it was all a matter of perspective. "I like the mad side of a writer. Writers are not sane, they were not born to be sane. You don't get god's gift, Jesus Christ didn't get god's gift, Kesey didn't get god's gift,

I didn't get god's gift, nobody gets god's gift—you are challenged and tortured and twisted—then you are mad and crazy, you don't get god's gift, you have to pay for god's gift.

"We were at the farm, we were in the backyard by the barn. You gotta go down there. The barn is magnificent. We were out there, I had poets Carl Henne and Leanne Grable. There was the boat by the backyard pond, grounded, called *Deeper*, then the bus *Furthur*."

At Kesey's, as everywhere else, Walt found that the devil was in the details. "Hairballs. Kesey mentioned the bull frogs, they're southern ones, gigantic, they love the pond. Beautiful green and blue dragonflies skim the surface, a bullfrog sings like Caruso, a great blue heron sweeps down to the pond as we lounge in chairs. Somebody says the heron is the writer's bird, Ken agrees but says he doesn't let him fish there too long because he'll kill the bull frogs."

"They're a large and impressive animal, about the size of a man. I say, 'I got spooked by one on the Clackamas river when I was lying down.'"

"Ken said, 'My brother Chuck got hit on the side of the head by one, could have put his eye out.'"

Out in his barn, with a copy of the book *Spear of Destiny* in hand, Kesey told Walt, "For a thousand years or more—there has been this group of Nazi-like Aryan controllers. And they've had a secret clique."

Carl Henne asked, "You mean they've been a cabal?"

"Yes," Kesey replied, "they've been a cabal to control the hearts and minds of us humans on planet earth."

Kesey opened the paperback copy of *The Spear of Destiny*. As Walt recalls, "And for Chrissakes, there is a photo of a spear which pierced the side of Jesus. Supposedly."

CHAPTER FORTY-ONE:
KISS NO ASS

"Reporters come up here expecting me and all my friends to be eaten by drugs and living out of garbage cans. And we're family people. We put all our kids through college and we're strong in the community. My wife teaches Sunday school. We're Norman Rockwell...corny 'America the Beautiful' people."

—Ken Kesey

Winter 1984. A Bell helicopter hovered against the brown desert hills—darting this way and that like a fish in an aquarium— then bolted across the sky, its rotors beating *thwapthwapthwapthwap* across the cold blue. The muzzle of a machine gun or assault rifle sticking out one side, it swept across the thousands of red-garbed people gathered along Nirvana Way. Then below, a big station wagon appeared. Inside, two men in purple. Mounted on a gun rack behind their heads, an M-16.

The red people, Bhagwan sannyasins—young women, old men, old women, young men—started to go bananas. For at the end of Nirvana Way was another car. A Rolls Royce. Inside sat Bhagwan Shree Rajneesh. He was at the wheel. Dark skin, big almond eyes. That waterfall beard and a gray robe. One look and you knew: Perfect Master. Straight from central casting. His Holiness drove slowly. A man in purple walked behind, cradling an Uzi, hand firm around the pistol grip, his eyes ticked this way and that, trigger finger tapping at the stock.

People were now beating on guitars and singing a song that sounded like "Hava Nagilah" sung by the Lovin' Spoonful, drunk. They warbled, *"Oh Bhagwan, my sweetest, sweetest love. The love you give me, I give it back to you!"* Half were jumping up and down as if they were on pogo sticks. Bhagwan continued to drive very slowly, keeping time with his hands, which ratcheted up and down behind the windshield. Beside him on the passenger side, a young blonde nurse. She accompanied him everywhere. The sound crescendoed in waves as the Rolls Royce moved down the loving gauntlet of thousands. "Oh Bhagwan, my sweetest, sweetest love. The love that you give to me, I give it back to you!" Some people laughing, others crying, tears zigzagging down their cheeks

But all was not well in the Promised Land. The Rashneeshees had moved straight into the heart of Marlboro Country. A desert rangeland where the cowboys and Indians were *still* shooting at each other and where folks were inclined to view people like John Denver and Donnie Osmond as degenerate hippies.

The commune had taken on a fortress mentality, encouraged by Bhagwan's fear of AIDS. After somebody set off two handmade bombs inside the Portland Rajneesh Hotel—blowing up one side of the building—commune members began arming themselves with Uzis and Galil assault rifles, CAR-15s, Mini-14s, 357 magnum revolvers and 12 gauge shotguns. Word had it that Bhagwan was purchasing tanks and helicopter gunships. Intoned Oregon state representative Wayne Fawbush. "They are a bunch of people who have gambled and who are in the process of losing…what I see is the prospect of violence out there."

Rajneeshpurim Mayor Swami Krisna Deva was equally to the point: "What I see here today is the beginning of civil war."

* * *

Maybe you can't go home again. In 1993 Kesey said, "The old bus, when she got back from Woodstock, her heart was broken. She said, 'This isn't what I got in the business for—carousing with hippies.' The people from The Smithsonian were out a few weeks ago. They're the most nervous, strange people in the world and you can see why: It's necrophilia. I asked 'em. 'If you had a chance to go out with Madonna or to take a big sack of Marilyn Monroe's rotting remains to a restaurant with you—which would you take? And they said, 'Oh Marilyn's Monroe's rotten remains!'

The Smithsonian people nosed around all over the farm and finally,discovered an old acid test placard in one corner of the barn under spider webs and covered with sow bugs. Kesey was informed, "We're going to send a fine arts collector out here to get it," and next he was getting all sorts of phone calls and shortly thereafter, "There was the hugest truck I've ever seen out in front of the barn."

Whose purpose was to pick up the acid test sign and drive it all the way back to Washington, DC. Kesey asked, "Why didn't you just have one guy pick it up?"and was told they couldn't, "because of the Teamsters."

"So a huge truck had to drive this little sign across country so they could put it next to Archie Bunker's armchair. No wonder the country is crazy."

Ken's Rx? He'd been working on it for several years: Cultural history as replica. Because, face it, the bus was just a *symbol*. Modest maximalist Keze had been at work all the way back to the fall of 1990, painting the "new and improved *Furthur,*" an International bus he planned to fob off on the Smithsonian in place of the original, now settling into the weeds at his farm.

A last prank. On posterity. Kesey's commitment to cartoon reality remained in mint condition. He was proudly showing off a new old bus of indeterminate genitalia, a bus born in 1947 scripted with a likeness of Michelangelo's Sistine Chapel Adam reaching out to touch "not God but the flukes of a whale." Kesey told writer David Loftus: "Before we had the whale, we had him touching Godzilla. That didn't work, so we tried Donald Duck. He didn't work either, so now we have Adam and Humphrey." The whale. "Pogo, the comic strip possum, floats above the door in a balloon. The Cowardly lion, the Scarecrow, the Tin Woodman, and Toto follow the Yellow Brick road. The Silver Surfer glides along the left rear corner. Diatoms drift into fish and lizards, then into an Egyptian pyramid in a sort of capsule account of evolution."

Kesey's friend Ed McClanahan had been told by a "spokesparty" with the Smithsonian that, "Mr. Kesey is running around Oregon in something he calls the original bus, invoking the Smithsonian name without our permission. We are not interested in reproductions, facsimiles, simulations, or counterfeits of any description whatsoever."

To which, Kesey replied, "Are we dealing with the body or are we dealing with the spirit? Because that is what the bus is, a spirit, not a bucket of nuts and bolts. Giving this bus to the Smithsonian would be like putting your balls in a golden chest and sending them to the Queen.

It would be a nice thing to do, but it would be a mistake."

The "new" original bus was to be the centerpiece of Kesey's latest book tour, and, when MClanahan asked his pal if this could be viewed as "just a hustle," Kesey was quick to provide perspective. "That's like saying I put on the Acid Tests to promote Tom Wolfe's book." Then, having put the Smithsonian in its place, he upped the ante. "On these book tours, publishers want to kiss the bookstore owners' asses, and they want the writers to be their lips. I'll never sell enough books on this tour to make any money. But the bus isn't a thing, it's an event, it doesn't work until it's full of people, and music, and begins to warble and reverberate. It wouldn't be right to turn it into a relic or artifact."

Well…In 1997 Kesey fobbed off his 1947 bus on the Rock and Roll Hall of Fame, where it was parked between John Lennon's Rolls Royce and Janis Joplin's Porsche. A shameless Kesey declared, "I kind of feel bad about it because it's going to be so much more beautiful than the other rock and roll cars." Not long after in 1998, he was interviewed by Nick Hasted of *The Independent* who wrote: "His face looks suddenly noble and serious; his eyes are revealed as piercingly, beautifully blue." Kesey declared he no longer had any aspirations as Great American Novelist. "I'm not gonna bark after that dog any more. There's plenty of books. I don't want to be Stephen King, and just do that because I can. A lot of my writer friends were hard-ass solid revolutionaries, but somehow they got off on the mezzanine, and they started writing fiction and novels. I see the internet as what's happening outside. This is the new way to speak, the way the shaman always would. I think it's very righteous, because it's mechanical, nothing else. It's not insidious. It's not a thing that's going to drain our minds."

Beauty was in the eye. Of Tom Wolfe, Kesey had kind words: "It's hard for people to understand how good he was. He didn't have a tape recorder and he didn't take notes. His eyes are wide open and he doesn't blink."[29]

Kesey recalled how after the bus and acid trips were over, Tom Wolfe came to visit at the farm. "We were up at my brother's farm, Spaceheater House, and we were moving this statue up onto the wall, and (my brother Chuck) had painted it with pigment. He had not used the right stuff,

---

29 Though on another occasion he was not so generous. "He (Wolfe) had all the notes and all our tapes, so it was accurate. But his was an East Coast take on the West Coast, and the East Coast is always 30 years behind."

so the paint had never dried. Wolfe was out there, and he had his note pad, and me and (Grateful Dead Roadie-in-chief) Ramrod were trying to move this thing up on the wall, and obviously we needed help. And there was only three of us, and Wolfe was out there, and he was dressed the way he always dresses in his blue suit, and we finally says, 'God damn it, Tom, give us a hand.' So he puts his note pad down, and he went to put it up there, and he got this huge swatch of red on the side of his coat, of oil pigment. We stood there, in this moment of realization, and I said, 'You just can't expect to fool around with it without getting it on you.' And that's the last time I ever saw Wolfe."

Of what was once known as the Establishment, less kind words: "If our government had its wishes, it would have Baptists coast to coast, all the same. Our job is to keep alive Buddhists, and Satanists and witches, and Hell's Angels, and scorpions and rattlesnakes and the blues—all the stuff the government would like to take away because they're an irritant." And what would that be? "The Constitution is written on hemp. Now we're eroding our Constitution to pursue this war on drugs. The issue is not whether we buy drugs, but who we buy them from. They want us buying from them." Kesey was not a fan of legal drugs (well, you gotta draw the line somewhere). He'd had a bad personal experience with Halcyon. "It was the biggest selling drug on the world for awhile, you'd have been a hell of a lot better off with a slug of whisky. We know it's bad for ya, but we know in what way it's bad for ya."

Of fellow literary lions Mailer, Stone and Jerzy Kosinski, all of whom appeared together in tuxedos at the PEN/Faulkner Awards, he dismissed them, shaking his head, "We sold out. You wouldn't have seen Woody Guthrie there. Faulkner would have stayed home and said, 'I've got another two days to drink.' We betrayed the mission of the writer, which is to always defend the small. The large can hire public relations people. To be caught kissing up to the government…"

He did not have optimistic words for himself and his. "The truth is we're losers. You make enough fuss and you attract the real forces down on you. And then you have to hide. We're always gonna be in the minority, and we're always gonna lose. We've always lost, all through history. We're the divine losers. And I keep inviting all these young, smart people: 'Come with us. Lose with us. Lose beautifully. We're not meant to win.'"

No. Kesey operated from a higher realm (in the Portland Downtowner 1992): "I received my working orders high on acid. The Lord came down and told me what to do and I've been doing it steady. I haven't received any orders countermanding those...What is true is, kiss no ass. No matter how big, how white, how righteous, how Republican, God himself or Gloria Steinem. Kiss no ass. That is the theme of my books." Asked (in 1992) if he'd quit the revolution, Kesey replied, "Shoot, how do you get loose from it? Nobody quits the mob. The '60s are still going on. We were arrested and treated poorly, but look what came out of it. Greenpeace. All the holistic consciousness. The whole feminist movement. The civil rights movement. Just because we didn't get it all accomplished in that decade doesn't mean we stopped and became something else in the next decade. You have a task and you work on it until it is either done or you can't work on it any longer. Everybody I know who was working on it then is still working on it just as hard as they can."

He was looking for a new audience. "There's an energy I haven't seen out there in 25 years. They're tired of being jacked off. They know the stuff they put under their arms ain't gonna get 'em the girl." It was make or break. "If we don't get hold of the MTV world, the MTV people are going to corrupt our world beyond hope."

The answer? "We've got to do the same kind of thing Shakespeare did, go around in front of the audience and confront the audience and grab 'em by the eyeballs."

So why not reinvent himself as a Native American shaman? "When Lulusku comes out on stage, he's *ugly* and he *shouts*." While writing *Sailor Song*, Kesey thought that he might rise anew by way of ancient Indian oral tradition practiced by a 400 pound Lulika Indian shaman, who came on stage dressed in "shaman's robes" and wearing masks, "I am hoping this can become a new art form." One to rise from the ancient oral tradition of Indian storytelling. "There's no electricity, only fire."

Freshly stressed from writing *Sailor Song*, Kesey told *The Galveston Daily News*: "Novel writing is a corrosive, inhospitable pastime. It's not like writing little haikus, little epiphanies. A novel really exposes you. If you fall down with a novel, you fall down real hard...During the writing I felt like I was dating Emily Bronte...This is a real old-fashioned form. But it is sort of the Vatican of the art. Every once in a while you've got to get a blessing from the Pope."

But it was living life that was most important. Kesey: "We raise cows, bring in the hay, raise chickens, bring in the eggs, grow tomatoes. It's wonderful! People say, 'Why don't you hire somebody to mow the hay and fix the fences?' I say, 'That's like marrying Marilyn Monroe and paying somebody to sleep with her.' If you're really in love with your land, you don't want to hire somebody to sleep with it." The payoff? "It's a nuisance, but it beats jogging and sure as hell beats one of those things you pedal in your room to nowhere."

In a 1994 unpublished review by Lawrence Gerald, Kesey returned to favored themes flavored by the new occult. "We've been on a war economy since the '50s. If that thing begins to collapse the system starts to panic. You know who Colin Wilson is? Author of *The Mind Parasites*. It's sci-fi. A chilling book, man."

Were there real Mind Parasites?

Oh yeah. "The same old guys, the military industrial thing. You ought to read something that'll make the hairs on your neck stand up. *The Spear of Destiny*. A scary piece of business about Hitler and what brought all that cult stuff into obsession." No matter that the paranoia jamboree that was *The Spear of Destiny* could not have passed the laugh test at a witch's convention; even this did not cool Kesey's ardor for ethereal claptrap.

"I think there are demons and I think we're battling them and they have minions that work for them. You can recognize them and get to know them. All the guys doing bad shit are generally working for those demons. The demons catch sight of us and come to get us." Also: "The Mind Parasite God doesn't want the Grateful Dead."

CHAPTER FORTY-TWO:
END GAME

"He was the guru; he was the master."

—Walt Curtis

A magic trick in Philadelphia, down in the bar at the Latham Hotel, described by Kesey's companion writer Ellen O'Brien as having air as "dark and cool as ice tea."

O'Brien, describing Kesey as "a pink-skinned balding bear" who, at 60, "has the bluest eyes to be seen outside the face of Paul Newman." Kesey told O'Brien that all over, from Michigan to Poland, he drew crowds of up to 2,000, "there to see me not as an author but as an avatar of the 60s," that, "Kids all over the world want a part of the 60s." and she listened, earlier, as Kesey waxed eloquent.

On the artist and his art: "All the great writers have a touch of magic. I really don't care about 'Freudian' novels. I don't really care that much about other people's psychological problems—I go to the movies to see 'Star Wars.' (but) When you finish reading a thing you ought to feel more human, not less human. Even in *Hamlet*. Everybody's dead, but somehow you're uplifted."

On the harmless and still enlightening viability of the old war horse: "I've seen a lot of people get in trouble with drugs, but not LSD...If they'd just sprayed Waco (the site of the FBI slaughter of the David Koresh cultists, the Branch Dravidians) with LSD...it couldn't have been worse. When I say that to people, they laugh."

On perhaps the reason why: "I don't know if times have changed, or kids have changed, or drugs have changed. But they don't seem to get the sense of holy illumination." This after Kesey revealed, "All my friends are no longer taking big doses of anything," at which point O'Brien observed, "A sign of common-culture adulthood rears its head before a thoughtful Kesey concluded, 'We're all so involved in other things, we don't have time to get way-out. That's a younger person's job,' and O'Brien amended , "Instantly, the sign disappears."

On The Answer: "The cure for a bad attitude and other serious evils," Kesey told O'Brien, was "the cure of the 60s gospels. Love. Peace. And, yes, drugs." To wit, "All of the stuff that started in the 60s, it isn't over. Feminism, environmentalism, civil rights...are changes in consciousness that started there. I've told people before, the 60s aren't over until the fat lady gets high."

So how was this message to best be delivered, Ms. O'Brien asked. Kesey replied, "You Christ trip them. The I Ching says, "the best way to fight evil is to make energetic progress in the good."

Then on to the magic trick down in the hotel's basement bar where Kesey ordered a gin and tonic, took a card from a deck of cards, snapped a swizzle stick into two, borrowed a barfly's wedding ring, set one half of the broken swizzle stick on the card, and bent the card slightly. O'Brien watched as the swizzle stick began to levitate above the curved card and was wowed when Kesey took the borrowed wedding ring and appeared to pass the plastic stick now hovering above the playing card right through the O of that wedding ring.

Later, in a sweatlodge-hot Unitarian Church packed to the holy gunwales with a young crowd who lined the wall in back and sat in the aisles, Kesey revealed, "My real interest is not in revolution or politics, or television or in drugs. My real interest is in warriors. I believe that's what we are." Ellen O'Brien, sitting near the back of the church, ended her story, which had appeared in the "Accent on Seniors" section of her newspaper, this way: "From that distance, his voice sounds old, and tired, although still merry. From that distance, he looks his age."

* * *

When Jerry Garcia went to a better place in 1995, dying of a heart attack at 53 in a drug rehabilitation center, Kesey had kind words. "Hey, Jerry—what's happening? I caught your funeral. Weird. Big Steve was good. And Grisman. Sweet sounds. But what really stood out—stands out—is the thundering silence, the lack, the absence of that golden Garcia lead line, of that familiar lick with the up-twist at the end, that merry snake twining through the woodpile, flickering in and out of the loosely staked chords…a wiggling mystery, bright and slick as fire… suddenly gone…

"Nobody ever heard you use that microphone as a pulpit. No anti-war rants, no hymns to peace. No odes to the trees and All Things Organic. No ego-deaths or born-againnesses. No devils denounced or gurus glorified…No baying of belief."

The man who had provided Kesey his "religion" had pretty much been beaten to death by drugs. Yet, editing his disappoints and regrets (thumbs down to heroin and, no matter how much of it might be flying through his veins, few good words for the speed that, with booze, would eventually kill him), Kesey remained unrepentant, declaring "The frontiers we broke into in the 60s are still largely unexplored" and that, "When we first broke into that forbidden box in the other dimension, we knew that we had discovered something as surprising and powerful as the New World Columbus came stumbling onto."

Rebel and patriot, Kesey found himself in late middle age as a sort of philosopher king without portfolio of the radical center. He spoke to real freedoms. "Nowhere else in history has there been a flag that stands for the right to burn itself. This is the fractal of the flag. It stands for the right to destroy itself." And, in ways, he seemed to have found himself content as a once-upon-a-time door opener for a better libertarian if not levitating present.

After he made Walt Curtis's *Mala Noche,* film director Gus Van Sant and Kesey became friends and later found themselves together at musician Mason Williams' house watching old bus footage.

Van Sant recalled, "As we watched a sequence of the bus getting bogged down in a swamp, Ken grew weepy, and lifted a hand to dry his eyes. I said it must be moving, watching some of that old footage. He said it wasn't the personal memories that made him tear up, but that 'we lost the battle…we weren't playing to lose, we were playing to win. We knew we were playing a big game, and that's what makes me sad. . .we lost the big game.'"

Jeff Forester, a talented young writer and, part of the student ensemble at the University of Oregon which created Kesey's "team" novel *Caverns*, had been star-struck, describing Kesey's exit from his white 1972 Cadillac convertible at the University: "Kesey strode across the lawn like an American superhero, white pants, white driving cap, red socks, white moccasins, a sky-blue T-shirt stretched across his broad chest. His smile began in eyes as blue as that day's hopeful skies and spread like pond ripples across his face."

But toward the end, like, say, the last two decades, Kesey had relied less on acid than revelation's lesser light: bargain basement shots of whisky at the Vet's Club in Eugene. So again, why did he stop writing great books? According to Forrester, "He always attributed it to aging, but that wasn't it, because a lot of people write great stuff late in life. It was a lifestyle thing. A novel is such a long, complicated thing that you can't smoke pot and keep it all sitting in your head.

"Ken drank himself to death. Even after he found out he had hepatitis C, he kept drinking. He had diabetes. But he kept drinking, and he just wasn't gonna stop. We'd once asked him, 'Did drugs ruin you?' He said, 'No, I know what's done me harm, and it's not LSD or marijuana, it's too many vodka martinis.' So he was self-aware, unlike most addicts."

And of his own legacy? "It was quite obvious," Kesey said, "that while it was going on, we were changing history." To the suggestion consciousness might be raised through meditation rather than acid, Kesey objected, "People who talk like that are really saying, 'I'm scared to take it.' Sure, you might reach the same level but it'll be slow. Stick by stick. There have been drugs for thousands of years, but psychedelics are not like that. There is nothing else like them. The experiences pertain only to you, to your situation...yet they are heralded in by some kind of higher being."

CHAPTER FORTY-THREE: STAIRWAY TO HEAVEN

"When the fog cleared, Kesey held his face in his hands, his elbows on his knees, his sky-blue eyes pooled with tears. My heart sank. 'I just don't care about novels anymore,' he said. Even laughing gas could not take the edge off. Allison put her hand on his shoulder. I mumbled, 'It's cool. Don't finish the damn book.' Kesey was silent for a long time. Tears fell down his cheeks and dropped to the floor."

—Jeff Forrester

In 1996 Tim Leary and Ken Kesey were reunited when they appeared together with Bobby Seale at Leary's alma mater, the University of Alabama, where Leary declared to the crowd, "The war on drugs is the war against pro-choice. The war on drugs is a war to make Americans respect authority."

Dr. Leary was dying. So might he not best rest in peace in outer space? Leary considered having his ashes blasted into orbit. Or, perhaps more advantageously, given his doubts about the Other Side, the possibility of having his freshly dead head severed from his body and cryogenically frozen to await reattachment courtesy future technology. Noting, "I have been very involved in the high tech of dying," he posted his typical daily bread on the internet: 44 cigarettes, 3 cups of coffee, 2 glasses of wine, a beer, a reefer, Tylenol PM, two morphine pills, 12 balloons of nitrous oxide, and three "Leary Biscuits"—cheese-soaked pot on a Ritz. This while "actively exploring" the possibilities of dying live on the net, committing suicide.

Kesey, too, was beginning his tap on heaven's door. In 1997 he awoke from a nap and discovered he was unable to use his right arm. This while another drug, speed, was eating his liver, and Kesey's "never give an inch" dedication to acid was delivered via slightly short-circuited locution: "There's 27,000 people a year killed here in alcohol-related deaths. You don't see any big thing about alcohol being evil. There's how many people smoking and dying of it? How many of all of these? And yet nobody's been killed. Why is it people think that it's so evil? What is it about it that scares people so? Even the guy who invented it. What is it? Because they're afraid that there's more to reality than they have confronted. That there are doors that they're afraid to go in and they don't want us to go in either, because if we go in we might learn something they don't know, and that makes us a little bit out of their control."

Before his final trip to the hospital, Kesey spent a "last afternoon" at the farm. According to his son Zane: "He was doing really well and he came home. It was a beautiful day and he just walked around, then he lay down on his back on the porch and looked up at the sky for awhile. It was like he was saying goodbye."

* * *

Father figure/Santa Claus/Great White Loadie, dead of a slow motion overdose at 66. In a note posted on his web site, Kesey spoke from the great beyond: "Now, all you people over there, get the news spread around that they're going to do a memorial service for me at the McDonald Theater in downtown Eugene at noon. And if you can't get inside we're going to put speakers out on the sidewalks so everyone can hear all the hoopla bound to be spreading out the theater like moths on the wing."

"Meanwhile, I've got lots of forms to fill out and they're looking for a bigger halo but durned if I'm going to play that harp. I'm holding out for the thunder machine. See you around—Kesey."

The service included everything from a Prayer from the Book of Isaiah to "a benediction in the form of a Grateful Dead song, "And We Bid You Goodnight."

But good news: genius survives. As you may recall my ex-cousin Marty Christensen[30] author of:

---

30 His older sister Marilyn married my beloved eye surgeon cousin Jerry, who as a medical student helped raise me after my mother died. Jerry and Marilyn had a rough go of it and after she threatened to shoot him, Jerry decided to split the sheets.

AT SUNDOWN
Our gazes meet and fructify
like raw eggs, broken open,
just beginning to dry up. Colors
splash the moonless landscape
then leave us completely in the dark.

read at the 2003 Kesey "wake" gathered at the Bagdad Theater in East Portland, where surviving Pranksters celebrated the author of four novels, several short story collections and a lifestyle that largely defined post-war American culture. Shortly thereafter, as you may also recall, Marty got up one morning, had a few beers and, crossing a street, was struck by a car, bounced off its windshield, and was hurtled skyward to the asphalt. Six concussions, a broken neck, shoulders and four ribs, a steel rod in his leg, a month in the hospital. But then, after a few more beers, he was up and running, and, thank God, remains small, handsome, grizzled, quick, retaining the riches to rags élan of a broke billionaire, an oligarch down on his luck. Though he's getting old, and I worry. He orders a $10.00 Manifest Destiny Burger at the "Twilight Room," on me. An Everest of hamburger patty, cheese, avocado, tomato, pickles, lettuce, another hamburger patty, so tall that, taking his first big bite, his head is lost behind an avalanche of lettuce and tomato. The pretty neo-hippie waitress at the Twilight Room likes Marty a lot. He's very charming and funny, sort of like a magic alter-dad. But Marty, pushing 65, still mixes it up with the rest of the world. The other night I got a call from his nephew, Kurt, who looks after Marty as if he were Marty's son. Kurt is young, fit and civilized, but couldn't keep the lid on his uncle. "We got 86'd from four bars," he said, "and refused service at two."

Times change. In Portland my bartending alma mater "The American Museum," occasional watering hole for Marty and Walt in the days of their youth, is now "Dante's Ground Zero." A sign out front advertises "KAROKE FROM HELL."

Anti-psychotic drugs have loosened Marty's teeth, and some have fallen out. The Devil's Bottomless Hole to Nowhere in his backyard looks more mortal now, less a spectacular hole to China or nowhere than just homely and ungodded. Marty has written his will. In blank verse. It is six pages long. He wants to make sure that wonderful Lorna gets all his stuff, his tapes, his rubber boat, his money, if he ever dies.

CHAPTER FORTY-FOUR:
LAST RITE

"Everyone I've seen die has died of being alone. They go off and do it by themselves. When it happens, whenever the heart breaks like that, when Brautigan goes off and it's a whole month before they find him, that's sad. William Holden who was the same way, and that's sad.. So let's keep track of each other. That's it, really. Let's just keep better track of each other."

—Ken Kesey

Paul Krassner, who knew Kesey for 36 years, remembers his friend in white suit, white hat, white tie, white shirt, white shoes—probably white socks and white underwear driving a white convertible in Mexico with Krassner riding along to Mexico when they got a flat tire. Kesey changed it without getting a spot of grime or grease on his white self. Krassner drove across country with Ken and Faye, slept in a graveyard one night, Kesey sprinkling pot seeds on the graves…

"I still have a conversation with him, he appears in my dreams. After he died one of his grandkids said, 'Now who is going to be there to teach us how to hypnotize the chickens?'"

What becomes a legend most? Fame? Fortune? A lasting legacy? Living legend can be a killer career move. If, say—for reasons even you do not remotely understand—you have enjoyed stunning literary success in your twenties eclipsing even the likes of young Ernest Hemingway and Norman Mailer, but if, say, that literary success is for some reason not enough, you may find yourself concluding: books are just books. There had to be something more (well, the Movie). Celebrity was okay. For awhile. But Culture Jesus is as Culture Jesus does, and what did it all come down to other than, really, a waking dreamscape? Obsessed by magic and metaphysics, Kesey was a young man for whom the sky did not even begin to be the limit, who saw LSD as literally a stairway to heaven. But elixirs giveth and elixirs taketh away, and by 1975 the zeitgeist had passed him by. By then more venerated than emulated, he no longer had the culture by the balls.

By then his flock had moved on, too impatient to create a Keseyesque psychedelic utopia. Far less a creative than a consumer class, Baby Boomer acidheads were the audience, not the auteurs, the buyers not the sellers. Though as a shepherd Kesey was only as important as his sheep, to the end a walking, talking, hawking billboard for hallucinogenic drugs. It has been said an age is over when it has exhausted its illusions, but could he have imagined the Revolution, the great, awful dregs of it at least, would come to such whimpering, lethal ruin? Jimi Hendrix, Janis Joplin, Brian Jones, if you count the rock star dead from drugs it probably numbers less than a platoon, but if you count the fans who went out the same way, it makes the beaches of Iwo Jima seem unbloodied by comparison. And what is left of the drug culture?

Younger than the Mafia, paler than the Crips.

Meet the scary new street freaks. When Oregon's own big burley Sam Cochoran nearly beat to death a blind man with his own cane, he had no idea he would become Poster Thug for a growing nationwide web of young crime families whose freak flag flies under banners including the Sick Boys, Nihilistic Gutter Punks, The Scum Fucks, No Sanity Left Kids, Denver Drunk Punks, the Harvard Pitt Rats—and Fat Bitch Killers. The latter were christened after a group whose dozen members spent hours torturing and finally burning alive a teenage mentally disabled black girl member who "broke" their rules.

Born from the Kesey dreamscape, street kid culture was originally driven by kids seeking truth, love or God and whatever's at the end of the psychedelic rainbow. Now, most new "street kids" have no such dreams. They know they are at the end of the road. And, protected from laws and normal constraints, maybe it's not such a bad place.

And here a hundred miles down the road in Kesey's home town Eugene, host to college professors, anarchists, Nike and loggers, sculptor Pete Helzer has created a statue of the psychedelic bard, book in metal hand, offering presumably sage counsel to three bronze school children in front of the McDonald Theater where Kesey did magic tricks on stage as a boy and where thousands of people attended his wake.

While even a "non boss" of a humble new 20,000,000 member international bohemian subculture may be less likely to be guided by stellar principles, idealism and vision than the old warhorses, regulation, subjugation and manipulation, it is hard to imagine such a municipal display erected on behalf of a guy who spent half his adult life encouraging the world to get high. But in our time, writers pimp as ventriloquists or their dummies for ideas greater than their own. No longer is it likely that a super bright college jock go from ham-fisted potato eater to culture Christ. Kesey parlayed an unholy trinity of language, drugs and hunger for an anti-authoritarian god to a briefly glorious Yellow Brick Road to nowhere.

Posterity did not give Ken a standing "O," at least not from all quarters. James Campion defined the bus trip as "formulaic mania" in which Kesey "captured the pointless rebellion of youth with hallucinogenic stupidity."

Prozac Nation doesn't drop a lot of acid, and it remains in critical but stable condition. LSD didn't take forever to shed its cleric's clothes. By the time Kesey was laid to rest in his tie-dyed coffin, acid was simply a gizmo, something between a metaphysical cheeseburger and an exciting, psychotic e-ticket to dreamland or simply, as Graham Greene once said of his more commercial novels, an "entertainment."

Yet Kesey kept the faith: come one, come all to the very end. To Nancy Reagan's "Just say no," the great Truth Teller countered, "Just say thanks," crowing the aforementioned: "It's not over until the fat lady gets high."

While it's unlikely Ken Kesey's grandchildren are spending afternoons toking up and playing granddad's Beatles albums backwards, and we've seen the bankruptcy of guru-culture (Dr. Phil is the best we have, a man who has taken the reformative skills of a first rate high school football coach and squandered them getting rich and famous), ask yourself: Rescued from hippie heaven by the horrors of Manson and AIDS—would we not have been doomed to an earthly fantasia? In a world where you could just screw *everybody*.

What's the legacy? Walt Curtis says, "There was something about the man that I really trusted at a sort of primordial existential Alan Watts kind of level, Jesus Christ kind of level, Jesus Christ acid freak kind of level. I wrote 'When I looked into those sky blue eyes, I felt the jolt of eternity. Ken Kesey was a warrior of the spirit.'"

Perhaps. At a time in his life, long after the flash and glow of *Cuckoo's Nest,* when he spent all night every night sitting awake in front of his typewriter waiting if not begging for the muse, Kesey had wondered, "It's 'why me?' what is it about me, my family, my father, this part of the country that caused me to be the one who wrote *Cuckoo's Nest?* It is not something I set out to do. It's as though all the angels got together and said, 'Here's a message that America desperately needs. Now let's pick him to do it.'"

Epilogue: Flashbacks

"What's the job of a writer in contemporary America right now? I'm not sure. But here's an example. We started off with what not to do.

You're going to be walking along on the street one of these days and suddenly there's going to be a light over there. You're going to look across the street, and on the corner over there, God is going to be standing right there and you're going to know it's God because he's going to have huge curly hair that sticks through his halo like Jesus, and he's got little slitty eyes like Buddha, and he's got a lot of swords in his belt like Mohammed.

And he's saying.

'Come to me.

'O, come to me, I will have muses say in your ear you will be the greatest writer ever; you will be better than Shakespeare.

'Come to me, they will have melon breasts and little blackberry nipples.

'Come to me, all you have to do is sing my praises

Your job is to say

'Fuck you, God!

Fuck you! Fuck you! Fuck you!'

Because nobody else is going to say it. Our politicians aren't going to say it. Nobody but the writer is going to say it. There's time in history when it's time to praise God, now is not the time.

Now is the time to say

'Fuck you and the Old Testament you rode in on!

'I don't care who your daddy was

'Fuck you!'

And get back to your job of writing."

—Ken Kesey

Woodstock without Kesey sounds like sugar absent sweet and would rival the Via Dolorosa without Jesus Christ, yet there was no Kesey at Woodstock. He didn't make it. After throwing a hissy fit over which prankster womenfolk could or couldn't ride with him on the revivified bus to New York, he ended up stuck, busless, snowed in on a mountain top in Colorado as the storied event of the decade unfolded without him.

Realpolitik 101: Was it Adolf Hitler who said, leaders don't make movements, movements make leaders? Handsome Mister Upside-down America wearing the flag by way of a cowboy hat and red, white and blue shirt. Rock jawed great writer, near great athlete, magician/musician/two fisted lady killer, a balding man near the dawn of middle age when he anointed himself First Flower Child, Kesey was nothing if not the new All American boy.

Hemingway saw that the future of art was celebrity, that Americans wanted not great writers but great men.

The novelist as protagonist. Kesey, whose ambitions ran less to the page than the stage, took Hemingway jock heroics one step further: Americans wanted not just a Man but a Superman, sub species Psychedelic or, scratch that: Messiah. Just as Christ had earned his street cred as a celestial not so much by His revolutionary guarantee of a salvation by compassion as by his dirty walk on the Via Dolarosa, blue eyed Kesey's blue ribbon provenance as an American authentic was guaranteed not in his vita as a genius, but in his street cred as a maniac of the people.

Still. Kesey may have been the greatest jack of all trades of all time. Try to write a great novel. It would be easier to truck farm the moon. Then go try and write another one. I never understood *Cuckoo's Nest* as a crow bar to pry open the psychedelic doors of perception—for me the greatest service psychedelics provided Cuckoo was to make its narrator, the Indian—Chief Bromden—just that, nuts. A full-blown hallucinating schizophrenic. But Randle McMurphy on acid? However effectively and even presciently rebellious, he was a thoroughbred citizen of whatever the hell happened before 1963, not after it. Kesey invented himself less as acid messiah than as Neo Wild West woodsman/cowboy/outlaw hero, an image that was to reflect or channel a new uber-myth via the greatest pharmaceutical abracadabra ever. LSD was an all American gadget to hyper-accelerate collision with God. In the post-knowledge, post-information realm, reality was just the candy wrapper. There was nothing in 1965 science to explain the self. Ken Kesey, Tim Leary and the guys could say: your realm, reality, is obsolete, mine is the new realm, metaphysical paradise, which the scientific witch doctors know nothing about. Ultimate virgin territory. Unassigned, untouched and unbelievable. The true Wild West, in which the purpled mountain majesties were whatever you said they were.

* * *

Flashback 1964. OO7 and Dr. No, the little black dress and Jayne Mansfield losing her exquisite platinum blonde head above her creamy howitzer shell breasts; zip guns and Ricky Nelson singing Lonesome Town. There was a Disneyland of sadness, sex and doom out there. Everybody headed to Supermarket U before blasting off for the moon.

But change was gonna come. Beats out, hippies in: naïf pessimism versus naïf optimism. The beats dour loner loser elitists, the hippies manic populists. The wildly conformist post war years—apogee of the sick joke and science fiction--a golden age of basic black, the sound of one hand clapping, the white negro, saxophone solos —for the beats everything was already over. For the hippies everything had just begun.

Time flies. People forget. Today say "1967" to the average random Ooooomster on the street and he or she is likely to reply: isn't that the year Led Zeppelin went down on the Hindenburg? But flashback: Had pie in the sky ever had it so good? LSD represented, if little else, unanchored amateurism at its levitated best. The lift of a driving dream, and so far as heaven went, I was already measuring the drapes. All I knew was I was hurtling toward the Beginning or the End, it didn't really matter which, and as a Catholic boy waiting for Kesey, Tim Leary and the guys to put some 6th dimensional bones on my psyche, I dreamed I'd one day be whooshed to paradise, which to my tennybopper techno-war mind under command of Sergeant Rock and the Combat Happy Joes of Easy Company meant a heaven with a scorched earth policy.

No rules, no clocks, no worries, no real idea that drugs could kill you. The 1960s were cartoon Eden. Yet from the beginning, our innovations didn't work out so hot. Pussy power feminism soon proved the Edsel of ecstasies, screwed partly by herpes and AIDS but even before young attractive women who tried to use their young attractiveness to fuck guys into submission found out they usually just got fucked instead. Stuck back in Oregon with my sorry band of serial monogamists, I got, nevertheless super lucky, struck by lightning twice. Though all I ever asked of a girl was that she be gorgeous, athletic, brilliant, honest, hard working and funny, what a miracle I'd met Ms. America II: an even more angelic face, smile to light an even larger city, a lid on her id, born whole as Helena with the ability to design the interior of homes like nobody's business.

I married Ms. America II in Judge Robert "Iceman" Jones's chambers during the recess of the trial of an ax murderer from Mars, a young man, either believing himself from the Red Planet or believing the guy who he killed was from the Red Planet, buried an ax into the forehead of the latter. By that time I was freak-freelied out.

* * *

Flashback 1980. Somehow I was picked to pick up Hunter Thompson and squire him around town after he gave a "speech" at the University of Oregon. In my mind, Hunter was the small guy I saw in Doonesbury. No. Not quite. Subtract 50 points off his IQ, the Hunter I saw on stage was a guy I'd see every other night at the American Museum Bar & Grill. Big and fatless, swollen forearms pumped full of heartache and pain, Hunter had, according to *Rolling Stone Magazine,* insisted on driving the RS writer's rent-a-car and had, forthwith, trashed it—ramming the rental car into other cars and—

—I had a '67 Mustang convertible I didn't want that to happen to. A former "suicide frog," its tires packed with kilos of pot my pals had driven across the border from Tijuana to Chula Vista. Though laminated with Bondo from TJ body shops, I had plans to return it to Detroit virginity and—The Hunter Thompson reeling balletically around the stage at the U of O was no gnomish Doonesbury apparition, but a healthy, real, big man, less zombie wastrel than one kick-ass NFL running back gone, in a Crazy Guggenheim/Twyla Tharp kind of way, nuts. The Darwinian implications of "the show must go on" demand these folk return from super maniacal to Clark Kent form long enough to be paid, fed and shipped to their next gig or the arms of Morpheus. But Dr. T? His talk, titled "Bad Craziness"—was free and we all got our money's worth. Though was Dr. T. as loaded as advertised? His drunken stumbling was as gracefully sure-footed as vintage OJ picking his way through a defensive secondary and—cut to the chase; I split and moved to Los Angeles.

But first a side trip to Hawaii to visit the unhinged door of perception that was Fred Exley's, author of the greatest nut house novel ever, *A Fan's Notes*. For Exley was the real thing, a hellbound horror story driven to the depths by the bad gravities of the American consumer dream, as able to describe the joyride down as Dante. Lanai was a Hawaiian island that was little more than pineapples and Budweiser. But Fred made it happen, believe me. At the old white Lanai Hotel, Fred spent money as if it were just paper—a truly subversive and subverted—by booze—man who'd been fucked over and fucked up. But, boy, could Fred throw a one-man party.

His latest book, *Pages From a Cold Island,* had just been panned in *The New York Times* and Fred got on the phone to the reviewer and panned the panner. The guy freaked. A writer didn't call a critic and criticize the reviewer's criticism of the writer's book. It wasn't done, but chortling, froggy-voiced Fred, his bulky sad face roped with cigarette smoke, playing to a peanut gallery of giggling tourist college girls, had no problem doing just that.

Back in the City of Angles, I met Tim Leary, seated with him at a *Playboy* roast for Milton Berle. Tim was as down to earth as a dirt clod, funny, and LA was OK. Shiny cars, shiny girls, though the smart money said the only ones in town with any brains were David Lynch, Steve Bochco, Madonna and Pat Riley's barber. Through *Playboy*, I met Ed Dwyer, founding editor of *High Times*. Ed, who resembled a young, worried Paul McCartney, who had written the program for Woodstock, and was an excellent mentor, once told me, "Mark, the good news is, your ego's too big. The bad news is, it isn't nearly big enough for Hollywood."

We wrote a screenplay about the baby boom's own Acid Christ, Michael Brody. While it hadn't turned out so hot for Michael— he'd committed suicide and Ed had snorted his ashes—Brody was a phenomenon. While here on earth, as it was in heaven, our Jesus, Scarsdale-style, like Christ Himself, sheep-cum-shepherd-cum-savior Michael Brody had pulled himself up by the sandal straps of his own staggering implausibility to announce himself to the world in the biggest way. His medium even more profound than the Lord's: TV. Whereas Christ had to accommodate Himself to the cross, handsome

Baby Boomer Brody had been awarded center stage on the Ed Sullivan Show—previous host to Elvis, the Beatles and the Rolling Stones. Brody sat before the audience, plunked out a song titled "I Love the World as It Falls on My Veins."

His message: "You want love, you'll get love." The overnight heir to "$25 million," he tipped a taxi driver almost $1,000, gave a newsboy $100, and walked this mortal coil with his shoes padded with $100 bills. His good news: He was huddling with Billy Graham, Richard Nixon and Soviet Premier Leonid Brezhnev. "I gave away $80,000 today. If you want my death you can have that too. I'm ready to die for you. If that's what you want."

Next? He announced he was worth not his previously announced $25 million, but $100 billion and… "Wait a minute. That was yesterday. Maybe I'm worth a trillion today." But it wasn't just the money. "I have cures for all diseases. I have a cure for cancer." Plus: "I will give $10 billion in aid to North Vietnam to retreat from the South. If they do this I will give them $20 billion more in aid and go over there and personally help them build their country."

Too good to be true? Bohemian asterisk Brody sold himself to 60 Minutes as a "hippie zillionaire" by passing out $100 bills to everybody he saw—including Ed Bradley. After Brody promised to build a recording studio for producer Bunny Jones, she rhapsodized, "He's like an angel from God. I want to get him together with the Beatles and together they'll rescue the world."

* * *

What's to become of us, who is to blame? Laguna Beach 2010. What would bull goose loony Randle McMurphy (or Hank Stamper for that matter) think of this? Trophy wives, trophy grandmas, trophy toddlers and teeny boppers, a platinum- haired lady legion in every gourmet grocery store. Fit women who jog to their plastic surgeons. Balding, deeply middle-aged gay guys who look, in their straight-man golf shirts and Bermuda shorts like flighty ex-Presidents. Only the long-haired gray ghosts of the Brotherhood of Eternal Love remain here in a 21st Century USA in which the President is just the guard at the castle gate and in which Chrysler is more communist than the Kremlin, and where the Wal-Mart /Microsoft Combine has become more bread and circus friendly, but even more corporate and, all those skinheads with their shrapnel piercings and mural tats notwithstanding, the counterculture has fallen into the hands of white cracker Tea Partiers and rightwing racist grandmas.

So what went sideways? No matter if we cured cancer or mowed lawns for a living, my generation's gift to the world was to eat it, to take the codified buy-more-think-less consumerism pioneered by our First Yuppie parents to ravenous extremes. Otherwise? What did the Love Children give to art/architecture/music? I like Jeff Koons and *Dude Looks Like a Lady* as much as anybody, but where's our Picasso? Our Keith Richards? And who once said that Bruce Springsteen is not a rock star but *about* a rock star? Is it an accident our most significant film maker, Steven Spielberg's best works, *Saving Private Ryan*, *The Pacific*, and *Schindler's List* focus not on his own but on his father's generation? Baby Boom sports heroes and movie stars fly by in a blur. Rambo, Kareem, Mark Spitz and some other guy. Yes, we've got our monsters of the midway, Bill Gates and…Steve Jobs? We're not even that good at evil. Why no Baby Boomer Pol Pot, or a freak freely Saddam Hussein? And as visionaries? Baby Boomer clerk minds evicted us from the moon and shut the door to Mars.

Maybe Kesey was right: literature is art's new buggy whip. For where's the 2010 freak freely and/or Gen X. Y or Z Hemingway, Steinbeck, Bellow or Updike? The few who have enjoyed both critical and book after book commercial success have failed to deify themselves ala Ken Kesey. Not for want of trying.

Flashback 1988. Gone now even the scraps of the psychedelic dream, the utopian NEXT swallowed by the dystopic NOW. But wasn't it possible that the driving dream of a living dreamland could somehow rise from its own ashes? My own private Randle Patrick McMurphy, the man who I once took for Kesey's original RPM inspiration—lady killer, social lion, candidate for Governor of Oregon, captain of the American Athletic Association World Champion basketball team and the big brother I never had Frank Peters had been recently sprung from the Oregon State pen for pot dealing (where he became the warden's personal lieutenant) and came to California to visit. He brought his young clean-cut preppie pal jail bird buddy, Bobby. We met in a wood cave of a single's bar. Frank, looking fresh as a 47 year-old daisy in the dim, ordered drinks all around and said: "Mark, ask Bobby what he was in for."

I bit. "Okay, Bobby, what?"

Bobby, his choir boy's face lit devilishly by a red shaded table lamp, replied, "Coke dealing and murder."

Frank said, "Mark, ask Bobby how it came down."

"Okay," I asked, "how?"

Bobby said. "Some asshole burned me for a pound of coke. I put a gun to his head and said, 'Get down on your knees and blow me.' When he did, I pulled the trigger."

For me that was the end.

#   #   #

MC: June 2010

ACKNOWLEDGMENTS

Acid Christ was born from my publisher's idea of a "participatory biography." Unlike a conventional biography which keeps its subject at arm's length and attempts at every level to be fair and balanced, a "participatory biography" would be the tale of how a major modern cultural figure, in this case Ken Kesey, effected the life of the author personally and subjectively. I believe this to be the best new format idea ever and I'd like to thank both Doug Holm and Paul Krassner for recommending that I audition the prototype. And, my thanks to Lance Kramer and Zack Soderberg, my excellent research assistants, who helped to compile and edit the source material that provided the raw material for this book.

I'd like to thank Walt Curtis—who I consider along with my ex-cousin Marty Christensen to be the most woefully under-recognized poets in America—for providing literally piles of Kesey background material. As co-chair of the Oregon Cultural Heritage Commission, Walt also organized the Ken Kesey symposium and memorial Hoo-Haw where Kesey's college roommate Boyd Harris told the story of Kesey's sojourn to Hollywood.

Publisher's Acknowledgments

The Publisher wishes to thank the following for granting permission to reprint excerpted material used in this book:

Alcatraz Corner Music: "I Feel Like I'm Fixin' To Die Rag." Words and Music by Joe MacDonald © 1965 renewed 1993 Alkatraz Corner Music Co.

The American Scholar. "The God in the Flowerpot" by Mary Ethel Barnard, from *The American Scholar,* Volume 32., No. 2, Spring 1963. Copyright © 1963 by the author

Farrar, Straus & Giroux, LLC. Excerpts from *THE ELECTRIC KOOL-AID ACID TEST* by Tom Wolfe. Copyright © 1968, renewed 1996 Tom Wolfe. Reprinted by permission of Farrar, Straus & Giroux, Inc.

Grove/Atlantic, Inc., excerpts from *STORMING HEAVEN: LSD AND THE AMERICAN DREAM* by Jay Stevens, Copyright © 1987 by Jay Stevens, used by permission of Grove/Atlantic, Inc.; and *ACID DREAMS: THE CIA, LSD & THE SIXTIES REBELLION* by Martin A. Lee and Bruce Shlain. Copyright © 1985 by Martin A. Lee and Bruce Shlain, used by permission of Grove/Atlantic, Inc.

Hachette Book Group, excerpts from *LIVING WITH THE DEAD* by David Dalton. Copyright 1996 David Dalton. By permission of LITTLE, BROWN & CO.

Hal Leonard Corporation:
"Soft Parade"
Words and Music by Jim Morrison.
Copyright © 1969 The Doors Music Co.
Copyright Renewed
All Rights Reserved Used by permission.
Reprinted by permission of Hal Leonard Corporation.

SELECTED BIBLIOGRAPHY

Abbie Hoffman, American Rebel by Marty Jezer. Rutgers University Press. 1993

Acid Dreams: The Complete Social History of LSD, the CIA, the Sixties and Beyond by Martin A. Lee and Bruce Shlain. Grove Press. 1985

The Age of American Unreason by Susan Jacoby. Pantheon Books. 2005

The Age of Great Dreams: America in the 1960s by David Farber. Hill and Wang. 1994

Altered States of America: Outlaws and Icons, Hitmakers and Hitmen by Richard Stratton. Nation Books. 2005

Amazing Dope Tales by Stephen Gaskin. Ronin Publishing Company. 1999

Anti-Intellectualism in American Life by Richard Hofstadter. Alfred A. Knopf. 1962, 1963

Aquarius Revisited: Seven Who Created the Counterculture That Changed America by Peter O. Whitmer. MacMillan Publishing. 1987

The Art of Grit: Ken Kesey's Fiction by M. Gilbert Porter. University of Missouri Press. 1982

Beyond the Waste Land: The American Novel in the Nineteen-Sixties by Raymond M. Olderman. Yale University Press. 1973

Bill Graham Presents: My Life Inside Rock and Out by Bill Graham and Robert Greenfield. Perseus Book Group. 1992

Boomer Nation: The Largest and Richest Generation Ever and How It Changed America by Steve Gillon. Free Press. 2004

Breaking Open the Head: A Psychedelic Journey into the Heart of Contemporary Shamanism by Daniel Pinchbeck. Broadway Books. 2002

Can't Find My Way Home: America in the Great Stoned Age by Martin Torgoff. Simon & Schuster. 2004

Castaneda's Journey: The Power and the Allegory by Richard de Mille. Capra Press. 1976

Chemical Psychoses: LSD and Related Drugs by Leo. E. Hollister. Charles C. Thomas Publisher. 1968

City of Words: American Fiction 1950-1970 by Tony Tanner. Harper & Row. 1971

Confessions of a Raving Unconfined Nut: Misadventures in the Counterculture by Paul Krassner. Simon & Schuster. 1993

Conversations with Malcolm Cowley Edited by Thomas Daniel Young. University Press of Mississippi. 1986

Conversations with Tom Wolfe Edited by Dorothy Scura. University Press of Mississippi. 1990

Dark Star: An Oral Biography of Jerry Garcia by Robert Greenfield. Broadway Books. 1996

Demon Box by Ken Kesey. Penguin Books. 1986

Do It: Scenarios of the Revolution by Jerry Rubin. Ballantine Books. 1970

Dog Soldiers by Robert Stone. Houghton Mifflin. 1972, 1973

The Dream Life: Movies, Media, and the Mythology of the Sixties by J. Hoberman. The New Press. 2003

The Ecstatic Adventure Edited by Ralph Metzner. MacMillan. 1968

The Eternal Adam and the New World Garden by David W. Noble. Grosset & Dunlap. 1968

Everything You Always Wanted to Know About Sex—But Were Afraid to Ask by David Reuben. Bantam Books. 1970

Fear and Loathing in America: The Gonzo Letters, Volume II Edited by Douglas Brinkley. 2000

Fear and Loathing: The Strange and Terrible Saga of Hunter S. Thompson by Paul Perry. Thunder's Mouth Press. 1992

From Walt to Woodstock: How Disney Created the Counterculture by Douglas Brody. University of Texas Press. 2004

Garcia: An American Life by Blair Jackson. Penguin Books. 1999

Garcia: A Signpost to a New Space by Jerry Garcia, Charles Reich and Jann Wenner. Da Capo Press. 1972

Genesis West 5: Celebrating Ken Kesey Edited by Gordon Lish. 1963

Gonzo: The Life of Hunter S. Thompson by Jann S. Wenner and Corey Seymour. Little, Brown. 2007

The Grateful Dead Interview Book by David Gans. Da Capo Press. 2002

The Haight Ashbury: A History by Charles Perry. Wenner Books. 2005

The Hero With a Thousand Faces by Joseph Campbell. Barnes & Noble. 1949

The Hippies by Burton H. Wolfe. Signet Books. 1968

The Hippie Papers Edited by Jerry Hopkins. Signet Books. 1968

The Hog Farm and Friends by Wavy Gravy. Links Books. 1974

I and Thou by Martin Buber. Simon & Schuster. 1970 edition

Insanity as Redemption in Contemporary American Fiction by Barbara Tepa Lupack. 1995

The Irresponsible Self: On Laughter and the Novel by James Wood. Farrar, Straus and Giroux. 2005

Kesey's Jail Journal by Ken Kesey. Viking. 2003

Ken Kesey by Bruce Carnes. Boise State University Writers Series. 1974

Ken Kesey by Barry H. Leeds. Frederick Ungar Publishing Company. 1981

Ken Kesey by Stephen L. Tanner. Twayne Publishers. 1983

Kesey edited by Michael Strelow. Northwest Review Books. 1977

The Kitchen Readings: Untold Stories of Hunter S. Thompson by Michael Cleverly and Bob Braudis. Harper Perennial. 2008

Land of Promise: The Story of the Northwest Territory by Walter Havighurst. MacMillan. 1946

Last Go Round by Ken Kesey with Ken Babbs. Penquin Books. 1994

The Lives of Norman Mailer: A Biography by Carl Rollyson. Paragon House. 1991

Living With the Dead by Rock Scully with David Dalton. Little, Brown. 1996

Made Love, Got War by Norman Solomon. PoliPointPress. 2007

Make Love, Not War. The Sexual Revolution: An Unfettered History by David Allyn. Routledge. 2001

Mindfuckers Edited by David Felton. Straight Arrow Books. 1972

The Mind Parasites by Colin Wilson.Oneiric Press. 1967

Monday Night Class by Stephen Gaskin. Book Publishing Company. 2005

The Movement and the Sixties: Protest in America From Greensboro to Wounded Knee by Terry H. Anderson. Oxford University Press. 1995

My Flashlight Was Attacked By Bats by Marty Christensen. Lorna Viken Books. 1975

On the Bus: The Complete Guide to the Legendary Trip of Ken Kesey and the Merry Pranksters and the Birth of the Counterculture by Paul Perry. Thunder's Mouth Press. 1990

One Flew Over the Cuckoo's Nest by Ken Kesey. Viking Press. 1962

Outlaw Journalist: The Life and Times of Hunter S. Thompson by William McKeen. W. W. Norton and Company. 2008

Paul Krassner's Impolite Interviews by Paul Krassner. Seven Stories Press. 1999

The Politics of Ecstasy by Timothy Leary. Ronin Publishing. 1998

A Prophetic Minority by Jack Newfield. Signet Books. 1966

The Psychedelic Reader Edited by Timothy Leary, Ralph Metzner and Gunther M. Weil. Carol Publishing Group. 1997

Psychedelic trips for the Mind Edited by Paul Krassner. High Times Books. 2001

Revolution for the Hell of It by Abbie Hoffman.Thunder's Mouth Press. 1968

Rick Griffin by Gordon McClelland. Last Gasp. 2002

The Road of Excess: A History of Writers on Drugs by Marcus Boon. Harvard University Press. 2002

Sailor Song by Ken Kesey. Penguin Books. 1992

The Sensuous Woman by "J." Lyle Stuart. 1969

A Separate Reality: Further Conversations with Don Juan by Carlos Castaneda. 1971

Sexing the Millennium by Linda Grant. Harper Collins Publishers. 1993

Shamanism: Archaic Techneques of Ecstasy by Mircea Eliade. Princeton University Press. 1964

The Secret Histories, an Anthology: Hidden Truths that Challenged the Past and Changed the World Edited by John S. Friedman. Picador. 2005

The Sixties: Years of Hope, Days of Rage by Todd Gitlin. Bantam Books. 1987

Soma, Divine Mushroom of Immortality by R. Gordon Wasson. Harcourt, Brace, Jovanovich (no publication date listed)

Sometimes a Great Notion by Ken Kesey. Penguin Books. 1964

Songs of the Doomed by Hunter S. Thompson. Simon & Schuster. 1990

Spit in the Ocean: All About Ken Kesey Edited by Ed McClanahan. Penguin Books. 2003

Steal This Dream: Abbie Hoffman and the Countercultural Revolution in America by Larry Sloman. Doubleday. 1999

Storming Heaven: LSD and the American Dream by Jay Stevens. Grove Press. 1987

Story of O by Pauline Reage. Ballantine Books. 1954, 1965

The Teachings of Don Juan: A Yaqui Way of Knowledge by Carlos Castaneda. Washington Square Press. 1968

Timothy Leary, a Biography by Robert Greenfield. Harcourt. 2006

Timothy Leary: Outside Looking In Edited by Robert Forte. Park Street Press. 1999

Turn On, Tune In, Drop Out by Timothy Leary. Ronin Publishing Company. 1999

Tripping, a Memoir by B. H. Friedman. Provincetown Arts Press. 2006

Understanding Media: The Extensions of Man by Marshall McLuhan. Signet Books. 1968

Wallace Stegner: His Life and Work by Jackson J. Benson. Penguin Books. 1996

When the Going Gets Weird: The Twisted Life and Times of Hunter S. Thompson by Peter O. Whitmer. POW Books. 1993

Who's Afraid of Tom Wolfe? By Marc Weingarten. Aurum Press Limited. 2005

The Worlds of Herman Kahn: The Intuitive Science of Thermonuclear War by Sharon Ghamari-Tabrizi. Harvard University Press. 2005

Your Brain is God by Timothy Leary. Ronin Publishing Company.

ENDNOTES: SOURCES AND ATTRIBUTIONS

Note on abbreviations: For the sake of brevity the following names and book titles have been initialized.
Ken Kesey/KK; Marty Christensen/MC; Walt Curtis/WC; Timothy Leary/TL; Paul Krassner/PK; Tom Wolfe/TW; Burton H. Wolfe/BHW; Wallace Stegner/WS; Malcolm Cowley/MCow.

One Flew Over the Cuckoo's Nest/OFOCN; Sometimes A Great Notion: SAGN; Electric Kool-Aid Acid Test/EKAAT; Spit in The Ocean/SITO; Kesey's Garage Sale/KGS

Prologue: Neon Renaissance Man
i.   "When you've got something like we've got you can't just sit on it and possess it, you've got to move off it and give it to other people. It only works if you bring other people into it."— KK quoted in Tom Wolfe's *Electric Kool-Aid Acid Test,* p.172

iv.   Footnote 1. And man of the people too...Paul Krassner to Mark Christensen

v.   Footnote 2. Leary once announced, "I declare that the Beatles are mutants...ever produced" from *SHOUT: The Beatles and Their Generation* by Philip Norman/ (c) 2005 Fireside Books/ Simon & Schuster, Inc.

vii.   "We're in the same business. You break people's bones, I break people's heads." Ken Kesey to Hell's Angels quoted in Warren Hinkle's article, "A Social History of the Hippies" in *Ramparts,* March, 1967

PART ONE: THE SHEPHERDS

Chapter One: Requiem for A Heavyweight
p.11   Once upon a time a young man of American background thought he had discovered the great Secret...the answer to 'What Makes It All Go?'"—from the prologue to Ken Kesey's unproduced screenplay *Over the Border* from *Kesey's Garage Sale,* p. 33, Viking/Compass Copyright (c) 1973

p.11   "The Shaman" by Marty Christensen, reprinted by permission of Marty Christensen (Note: This poem and all others by Marty Christensen are taken from his collection, "My Flashlight Was Attacked by Bats" Lorna Vikken Books)

p.13   "Lasting Hate" by Marty Christensen, reprinted by permission of Marty Christensen

p.16   "I never knew...sense of possibility." Robert Stone eulogy at the Ken Kesey Memorial at New York's 92nd Street Y (Feb. 11, 2002) that was later reprinted as "The Boys' Octet" in *Spit in the Ocean, #7: All About Kesey,* p.200 (Penguin Books, 2003)

p.17   Footnote 3, Kesey on Kesey: "I'm a power junkie, I love power. For one thing, I think it's not corrupting like some people think; it is purifying. People who think they have power, yet do not, are corrupted. People who really have power are humbled by it." from *Aquarius Revisited* by Peter Whitmer, MacMillan Press (1987)

pp.18-19 Ken Kesey to Marty Christensen, Lorna Viken and Walt Curtis, from taped recording of conversation by Walt Curtis. Used by permission of Walt Curtis.

p.19   "Of offering more than I can deliver...what I do." Ken Kesey as quoted by Robert Stone in his eulogy, Ken Kesey Memorial at New York's 92nd Street Y (Feb. 11, 2002) that was later reprinted as "The Boys' Octet" in *Spit in the Ocean, #7: All About Kesey,* p.200 (Penguin Books, 2003)

pp.19-20 "I've used cornstarch...like a nursery."from "Kesey's Last Prank" by Paul Krassner, from *Spit in the Ocean #7: All About Kesey,* p. 15. Copyright (c) 2003, Penguin Books USA. Reprinted by permission of Paul Krassner

Chapter Two: Natural Man
p.23   "Though my mama came from Arkansas and my daddy came from Texas, and ...Being an Okie is a low-rent, aggravating drag, but it does learn you some essentials." KK from "Ken

Kesey's Oregon" in *Vis a Vis* magazine, March 1989

p.24   Of the trip Kesey recalled, "All the long, sweltering August afternoon we rolled…But you could tell he was having some misgivings himself." KK from "Ken Kesey's Oregon" in *Vis a Vis* magazine, March 1989

p.24   "As I stood filling my mouth with this wild bounty, I watched the light come up…hope itself to the new day." Ibid.

p.24   "Following as if in a parade being led by a drum major…until they threw up." Jim Kesey (Internet)

p.27   "What the hell you looking here for, Daisy Mae?" Which inspired Kesey to admit: "I achieved some kind of *satori*…that's what I want for my books." From *Esquire*, September 1992 interview

p.27   His idea of story came from his bootlegger grandma. "It was over 50 years ago before there was television," from "Suppressed" interview with Kesey, for *High Times*

pp. 27-28 "The vein lies under the topsoil…Why not let him stalk?" p. 166, Bloom's *Critical Interpretations* by Harold Bloom (c) 2008, University of California Press

p. 28   "When asked…reply was quick: magic." see Robert Faggen Interview with Ken Kesey from the Paris Review, "The Art of Fiction: 136," Copyright © 1994, The Paris Review and Robert Faggen

p.29   Kesey recalled, "My dad was a mighty (University of) Oregon fan, and every fall was full of Duck talk from "Ken Kesey's Oregon" in *Vis a Vis* Magazine, March 1989

p. 29   "My senior year we got a new coach…for college football" Ibid.

p.30   In fact, the term Merry Pranksters likely came from a Disney movie, "The Liberty Story," from *Walt to Woodstock: How Disney Created the Counterculture* by Douglas Brode, p. 49. Copyright © 2004 University of Texas Press

Chapter Three: Adams and Eves

p.33   "…It was as though the walls of our house dissolved…that lay behind the ancient Mysteries?" from *Soma: Divine Mushroom of Immortality* by R. Gordon Wasson, Copyright © 1972, Harcourt, Brace, Jovanovich

p.34   Huston Smith, whose *The World's Religions* remains, after three decades, the standard collegiate text, writes, "In the pantheon the Aryans brought with them when they swept into Afghanistan…'We have drunk Soma and become immortal.'" From *The World's Religions* by Huston Smith, 50th Anniversary edition Copyright © 2009, HarperOne

p.34   Wasson who, in his introduction concludes, "In a word, my belief is that Soma is the… from the Introduction to Soma: Divine Mushroom of Immortality by R. Gordon Wasson, Copyright © 1972, Harcourt, Brace, Jovanovich

p.34   Consider the serpent's promise from the Old Testament, "Ye shall not surely die…and ye shall be as gods." The Book of Genesis, Chapter 3: Verses 4-5 from the Authorized King James Edition of the Holy Bible

p.35   The poet Mary Ethel Barnard, "looking at the matter, coldly, unintoxicated and unentranced…in great expanded vistas?" from *"The God in the Flowerpot,"* published in *The American Scholar,* Volume 32, No. 2, Spring 1963 Copyright © the author.

p.35   "At the session of the Societe Mycologique de France held on October 6, 1910," according to Wasson…" in a colloquy with Eve." from *Soma: Divine Mushroom of Immortality* by R. Gordon Wasson © Copyright 1972, Harcourt Brace Jovanovich

p.35   Wasson recalled, "From 1955 on I was in intermittent correspondence with Aldous Huxley…reaching for the moon." Ibid.

p.36   He concludes, "Ponce de Leon early in the 16th Century…the towering Siberian birch." Ibid.

Chapter Four: BMOC

p.39   "One's parents remembered the sloughing common order, War & Depression…The Flash—but of course!" from *The Electric Kool-Aid Acid Test* by Tom Wolfe, p.39 of the Picador Edition. Copyright (c) 1968, renewed 1996 by Tom Wolfe. Reprinted by permission of Farrar, Straus, LLC

pp.39-40 Kesey: "The guys on the wrestling team used to say, 'You write? You act?… I learn about the sort of man he is." From *Genesis West* Interview with Ken Kesey

p.39   Footnote 7. "Wrestling is the sport of reason…but it's correct." from Genesis West

Interview with Ken Kesey

p.40 "At U of O, I got some other thoughts...career in honor." Ibid.

p.41 As literary critic and author of *Understanding the Beats,* Edward Halsey Foster wrote, "men were supposed to be logical, efficient, and coolheaded, organizing their lives according to their employers' needs." From *Understanding the Beats,* Copyright © 1992 University of South Carolina Press

pp.41-43 Kesey didn't smoke or do drugs and told Boyd, "I think they're lying to us about marijuana, if I ever get a chance, I'm going to do it...but it was a great trick." From Boyd Harris eulogy for Ken Kesey at Kesey Memorial in Portland, OR.

p.43 Kesey took off for Los Angeles and Boyd went down to visit him shortly thereafter... ditto

p.45 "He was a one man entertainment center," Portland lawyer Brian Booth recalls (to Mark Christensen)

p.46 "It was no big deal that he was married," Herman says, nor that Kesey wasn't a big partier... but not every term" (to Mark Christensen)

pp.46-47 Kesey later recalled, "I had this record of Ferlinghetti, Rexroth and Ginsberg reading beat poetry...and the human mind" Ken Kesey interview with *Digital Interviews*

p.47 Kesey's junior year at the U of O his instructor in a screenplay writing class informed Kesey, "You need to learn something about story. I'm transferring you to J. B. Hall's fiction class." As Kesey later recalled, Hall "strode over in his white shoes and stabbed a paragraph in the middle of my textbook...and eventually got me in the door." from "Earthshoes" by Ken Kesey, p143-144 reprinted in S*pit in the Ocean # 7,* Copyright © 2003 Penguin USA

Chapter Five: The Good Book

p.49 "Me, a stoodunt, gets asked by my buddy, a sighcologiz, dos I wanna go over to... visions swirling indescribable between us." —Ken Kesey, from Kesey's *Garage Sale* ('Who Flew Over What?") Copyright © 1973 Viking/Compass Editions, p. 7

p.50 McMurtry recalled a half dozen fellow great novelists: "Like stoats in a henhouse, we were poised to rend and tear...when it stopped." From the anthology *The Company They Kept: Writers and Unforgettable Friendships,* Chapter 25: Larry McMurtry on Ken Kesey p. 254, published by New York Review Books, Robert Silvers, ed. Copyright © 2006 *New York Review Books*

p.50 Kingston Trio, whose early hit "Coplas" gave America a hint, "Tell your parents not to muddy the water around us, [porque] they may have to drink it soon." From "Coplas" by The Kingston Trio, Words and Music Copyright © 1961 The Kingston Trio

p.51 Discovered accidently by Swiss chemist Albert Hofmann just before World War II (Hofmann took the first "hit" from *Acid Dreams : The CIA, LSD and The Sixties Rebellion,* p32-33 by Martin A. Lee and Bruce Shlain (see Acknowledgments for copyright information)

p.51 Creatively. Take MKULTRA's Operation Midnight Climax, in which CIA agents had San Francisco...from *Acid Dreams : The CIA, LSD and The Sixties Rebellion,* p32-33 by Martin A. Lee and Bruce Shlain (see Acknowledgments for copyright information)

p.51 Psychedelia may owe its life to CIA super-spook Al Hubbard, "the Johnny Appleseed of Acid," Ibid, pp44-45

p.52 "Everywhere in Kesey," controversial literary critic Leslie Fiedler wrote much later, "the influence of comics...to write or even draw it." from "The Higher Sentimentality" by Leslie Feidler, p. 253, *The New Leslie Fiedler Reader* Copyright © 1999 Prometheus Books

p.53 "I had a neighbor," Kesey recalled, "a psychologist booked to do the experiments (one Tuesday, he chickened out." Paul Krassner's Impolite Interviews Seven Stories Press (1999), also *Aquarius Revisited* page 202

p.53 "The government said we've discovered this nice room, we need somebody to go in and look it over...chicken wire inside the glass." Ibid.

p.53 One night Kesey, who had keys to Hollister's offices, came in and "went into his room, into his desk, and took out a lot of stuff...were absolutely permanent."

p.54 Kesey "saw it all...I saw the looks on these people's faces...and realized that Freud was full of shit...and yet the dream was perverted." in *Aquarius Revisited,* p. 202

p.54 Footnote 9: Transcendental lunacy provoked comic turns. Blasted out of his tracks on a "double-ought capsule of pure mescaline" as an orderly, Kesey recalled arguing "so fervently with the big knotty pine door across the office from me that I actually chalked a broad yellow line across the floor between us and told the door, 'You stay on your side, you goggle-eyed son of a bitch, and I'll stay on mine.'" p. 91, *Can't Find My Way Home: America in the Great Stoned Age, 1945-2000*, Simon & Schuster Inc. Copyright (c) 2004 by Mark Trogoff

Chapter Six: Unholy Grail

p.55　"It's all God's flesh. LSD is always a sacrament, whether you are a silly thirteen year old girl popping a sugar cube on your boyfriend's motorcycle...or even a psychiatrist giving LSD to an unsuspecting patient to do a scientific study." —Tim Leary from *Acid Dreams: The CIA, LSD and The Sixties Rebellion*, p.225 by Martin A. Lee and Bruce Shlain (see Acknowledgments for copyright information)

p.55　"When I was doing those experiments at the Vets hospital...our ability to create, to imagine." Ken Kesey to Todd Brendan Fahey, phone interview, "the Far Gone Interview," Sept. 13, 1992

p.55　"I grabbed that handle, legally too I might add, almost patriotically, in fact..." from Introduction to *One Flew Over the Cuckoo's Nest* (Penguin Ed.) 2002, vii, (c) 2002 Ken Kesey LLC

p.55　"I felt I was doing as American a thing as Neil Armstrong...that's just titillation" KK in the Gainesville Sun, Feb. 18th, 1990, p. 30

p.55-56 Ken Kesey wrote regarding Cuckoo in utero, "Those faces were still there, still painfully naked...I just held the pen and waited for the magic to happen." KK Introduction to the 2002 Penguin edition of *One Flew Over the Cuckoo's Nest*, viii

p.56　It looked like "the sort of punch Satan would serve," recalled Malcolm Cowley, from "Ken Kesey at Stanford" in *Northwest Review Book Series: KESEY*, Copyright © 2001 University of Oregon Press

p.56　Footnote 10: Lit up by government acid, the natives were getting restless. "It had been happening...whole different, larger, stranger circle." Laird Grant, from *Dark Star: An Oral Biography of Gerry Garcia*, written by Robert Greenfield. Copyright © 1996 by Robert Greenfield

p.56　"The first drug trips were, for most of us, shell-shattering ordeals...We were alive and life was us." from p. 175, *Kesey's Garage Sale* Copyright © 1973 Viking/Compass Paperback Editions

p.57　"It was "the kind of writing that can be done...With nothing that will go bad afterwards." From *Green Hills of Africa* by Ernest Hemingway, p. 26 Scribner Classics hardbound edition. Reprinted with the permission of Scribner, a division of Simon & Schuster, Inc. Copyright 1935 by Charles Scribner's Sons. Copyright renewed © 1963 by Mary Hemingway.

p.57　"Sometimes it's hard to tell if Hemingway...he never crossed anybody except himself." from "Hemingway" p. 181, *Kesey's Garage Sale* Copyright © 1973 Viking/Compass Paperback Edtions

p.57　"There's something about seeing reality with a new light shining on it...that opened it." KK quote found in "Natural Hallucinogens and Your Mind" by Matt Waterman, April 2009 (Internet)

p.58　"We," Kesey later reflected ("we" meaning he), "had read a certain amount of Oriental literature...a lot of people are lost." from the Far Gone Interview by Todd Brendon Fahey Nov. 14, 2001

p.58　"There once was a blonde from Nahant...You finish this damn thing, I can't." Limerick by Wallace Stegner from *Wallace Stegner: A Biography* by Jackson Benson, Copyright © 1997, Penguin Books

p.58　Dick Scowcroft allowed, "Neither Wally nor I thought he had particularly important talent..." ibid, p. 131

p.58　"a person of more force than mind...a fairly big raw talent." *Wallace Stegner and the American West* by Philip L. Fradkin, p.60. Copyright © 2008 Alfred Knopf, Inc.

p.58　"He was better than a teacher. He was like Vince Lombardi...we drew the line between us right there." from "The Prankster Moves On" by John Daniel, reprinted in *SITO #7*, p.135 as told by Kesey to John Daniel

p.59　Footnote 11: Later Cowley added, "The faults of this novel...are obvious...enormous vitality."MCow from *The Portable Malcolm Cowley*, p.508 Copyright © Viking Penguin, 1990.

p.58-59 Malcolm Cowley wrote of his student Kesey: "He hasn't ever...would HAVE to be published." from *The Portable Malcolm Cowley*, Copyright © Viking Penguin, 1990.

p.59   "The book was full of powerful scenes…is never lost." MCow. from *The Portable Malcolm Cowley*, p. 508. Copyright © Viking Penguin, 1990

p.59   Cowley knew why. "His first drafts…the readers in mind."from p. 3 from "Ken Kesey at Stanford" (M.Cow) in *Northwest Review Book Series: KESEY*, Copyright © 2001 University of Oregon Press

p.59   "Kesey had his own crazy visions…Chief Broom(sic)." MCow from *The Portable Malcolm Cowley*, Copyright © Viking Penguin, 1990.

p.59   Describing Kesey as "an Oregon roughneck," Cowley went on to say, "He's tough, sentimental…many books." from *The Portable Malcolm Cowley*, p.508. Copyright © Viking Penguin, 1990

Chapter Seven: Big Mother and the Whores

p.61   "A man like McMurphy secretly admires…then slams it in your face." from *Classic Cult Fiction* by Thomas Reed Whissen, p. 164, Copyright © 1992, Greenwood Press

pp.61-62 "They're out there. Black boys in white suits up…I can catch them." from *One Flew over the Cuckoo's Nest*, p.1, Copyright © 1962 by Ken Kesey. Reprinted by permission of Sterling Lord, Literistic. Copyright Kesey LLC.

p.61   Malcolm Cowley, in retrospect, came to this conclusion: "Artists who succeed are strong characters…do scandalous and even scoundrelly things." MCow from *The Portable Malcolm Cowley*, p.536 Copyright © Viking Penguin, 1990

p.62   "Her face is smooth, calculated, precision made…bitter she is about it." from *One Flew over the Cuckoo's Nest*, p. 11. Copyright © 1962 by Ken Kesey. Reprinted by permission of Sterling Lord, Literistic. Copyright Kesey LLC.

pp.62-63 "The actors…capture that nuthouse feeling so completely…I had written it for him." KK

p.63   Howard Taubman concluded, "How can a thread of compassion…villainy?" Theater critic Howard Taubman, review of Broadway production "One Flew Over the Cuckoo's Nest" for *The New York Times*

p.63   Kesey began by saying, "The answering of one's critics has always struck me…it is in real life." KK letter to editor in response of negative review of the play

p.65   As novelist Gurney Norman claimed "when Chief Broom throws the control panel through the insane asylum window…that was the first shot of the revolution." From Ed McClanahan interview with KET's Guy Mendes: "Ed McClanahan/"A Conversation"

p.65   "We need that Vaseline,…kiss of water on the green tile." from *OFOCN* Copyright © 1962 by Ken Kesey. P. 15 Reprinted by permission of Sterling Lord, Literistic. Copyright Kesey LLC.

pp.65-66 It's been said that *Cuckoo's Nest* owed much of its success to the drive provided by "the great binaries of sane and insane, male and female, free and captive," from *Classic Cult Fiction* Thomas Reed Whissen, p. 164, Copyright © 1992, Greenwood Press

p.65   Ken Kesey's advice in the 1990s to his students at the University of Oregon was to first find a locale: "What place? The road to Canterbury…been a little squeaky." *The New York Times*, December 31st, 1989

p.66   "McMurphy comes perilously close…who vast numbers imitate." from *Classic Cult Fiction* Thomas Reed Whissen, p. 164, Copyright © 1992, Greenwood Press

p.66   "Kesey seems to envision a post-cataclysmic utopia of some kind…the new Christ… McMurphy." From Ken Kesey (Boise State University Western Writer's Series, No. 12) by Bruce Carnes, Copyright 1974, Boise State University Press

p.66   "*Cuckoo's Nest* deserves to be recognized as the preeminent literary paradigm of redemption secularly conceived."—from *Religion in Contemporary Fiction* by George N. Boyd, Assistant Professor of Religion Trinity University. Copyright © 1973 Trinity University Press

p.66   "You are strapped to a table, shaped, ironically, like a cross, with a crown of electric sparks in place of thorns…as if you thought yourself to be a God!" from OFOCN Copyright © 1962 by Ken Kesey. Reprinted by permission of Sterling Lord, Literistic. Copyright Kesey LLC

p.67   "He let himself cry out…when he finally doesn't care anymore about anything but himself and his dying" from OFOCN Copyright © 1962 by Ken Kesey. Reprinted by permission of Sterling Lord, Literistic. Copyright Kesey LLC

p.67   —"with a loud cry, Jesus breathed his last" Mark 15:37—"And when Jesus had cried out again in a loud voice, he gave up his spirit." and Matthew 27:50 (The Holy Bible: King

James Version)

p.67　　"The only people for me are the mad ones…spiders across the stars in the sky." from p. 8 of *On the Road* by Jack Kerouac, Copyright © 1958 Jack Kerouac, granted by permission of Penguin Group USA

p.67　　"a cartoon world, where the figures are flat and outlined in black, jerking through some kind of goofy story that might be real funny if it weren't for the cartoon figures being real guys." from OFOCN Copyright © 1962 by Ken Kesey. Reprinted by permission of Sterling Lord, Literistic. Copyright Kesey

p.68　　"There was me, that is Alex, and my three droogs, Pete, Georgie and…a bit of the old ultraviolence."from *A Clockwork Orange* by Anthony Burgess, p. 1. Copyright © 1963, W.W. Norton & Co., Inc.

p.67-69　"There was only one catch and that was Catch-22…"It's the best there is," Doc Daneeka agreed." From *Catch-22* by Joseph Heller, p.52. Reprinted with the permission of Simon & Schuster, Inc. Copyright © 1955, 1961 by Joseph Heller. Copyright renewed © 1969 by Joseph Heller

p.68　　As Kesey would later write, "Suddenly there was a bunch of us high…where you stood in eternity." KK in *Spit in the Ocean: VII: All About Kesey,* p. 141, *Earthshoes* by Ken Kesey

p.69　　Footnote 13: Years later, when reviewing the film version of *Cuckoo* in *The New Yorker,* Pauline Kael wrote, "the novel preceded the university turmoil…Americans." From *5001 Nights at the Movies* by Pauline Kael., p.594. Copyright ©1982, 1984, 1991 Pauline Kael

PART TWO: THE SHEEP

Chapter Eight: Holy Land

p.73　　"American history is totally involved…for that escape." KK in The Seattle Times, June 6th, 1993, "The Ends of the Earth: How the Northwest Came to Be Just a Little Off-Center" by Curt Hopkins

p.75　　"Kesey, 26…has used his empathy…who enforce them." From *Time* Magazine, February 16, 1962

Chapter Nine: Notion

p.83　　"When I first was getting to know him,…That's what I'm writing this book for, to find out whose arm it is." From *Famous People I have Known* by Ed McClanahan, Copyright © 1985 University of Kentucky Press

pp.84-85　"What Kesey and others discovered at the time…this was gibberish to (Wallace) Stegner."from *Wallace Stegner and the American West* by Philip Fradkin. Copyright © 2008, Alfred Knopf/Random House, LLC.

p.85　　"Sometimes I get a great notion to jump into the river and drown." From the song "Good Night, Irene" by Huddie Ledbetter, transcribed by Alan Lomax

p.85　　"The River…water flowing out to sea." From Ken Kesey's notes on "Sometimes A Great Notion" at the University of Oregon archives, reprinted in *The Northwest Review Book Series: Kesey,* p.53. Copyright © 2001 University of Oregon Press

p.85　　"The job of the writer," Kesey once said, "is to kiss no ass, no matter how big and holy and white and tempting and powerful." *Esquire,* November 1986

p.85　　Footnote 16: Kesey: "I want to find out which side of me really is…in the novel are each one of the ways I am." from *Storming Heaven: LSD and the American Dream* by Jay Stevens, p.232. Copyright © 1987 by Jay Stevens. Used by permission of Grove/Atlantic, Inc.

p.85-86　"The river flows out to the sea…The rains tear building(sic) away." From Ken Kesey's notes on "Sometimes A Great Notion" at the University of Oregon archives, reprinted in The Northwest Review Book Series: Kesey, p.53-54. Copyright © 2001 University of Oregon Press

p.86　　"I was staying up 20 to 30 hours at a run…was going to be at writing." KK from *Digital Interviews*

p.86　　"We made it up out of the sea, stormed around the land for a time, now the sea is bent on reclaiming us…to nothingness, to nothing." From Ken Kesey's notes on "Sometimes A Great Notion" at the University of Oregon archives, reprinted in *The Northwest Review Book Series: Kesey,* p.53-54. Copyright © 2001 University of Oregon Press p.86   "More me, the author, into a different dimension. Godlike, able to float across the land and into the minds." KK (see above)

p.86   "Big Brother believes: You fight, you struggle, you don't give up, you don't let down, you don't accept death." From Ken Kesey's notes on "Sometimes A Great Notion" at the University of Oregon archives, reprinted in *The Northwest Review Book Series: Kesey*, p.56. Copyright © 2001 University of Oregon Press

p.86   "But me...Like Bromden tells the story of McMurphy." (University of Oregon archives)

p.86   "his conflict...screw his mother." (University of Oregon Archives)

p.86   "I have lived alone...Blanching limp and white." (University of Oregon Archives)

p.87   "When he lost his two fingers in the donkey drum...four inches of the arm."from *Sometimes A Great Notion* by Ken Kesey, p.162. Permission for use granted by Penguin USA. Copyright © 1964, renewed 1992 Kesey LLC

p.89   Orville Prescott of *The New York Times* sniffed: "His monstrous book is...I have had to read in many years." From *New York Times* review titled "Tiresome Literary Disaster" as quoted from EKAAT/TW., p. 103 Picador Editions.

Chapter Ten: Theater of Sheep

p.91   "For Kesey, redemptive self-sacrifice is heroic,...takes up his own cross." from *Religion in Contemporary Fiction* by George N. Boyd, Assistant Professor of Religion Trinity University. Copyright © 1973 Trinity University Press

p.92   Glenn O'Brien in Interview with Paige Powell: Paige Powell: "If Warhol had a wife, it would have been the quirky associate publisher of Interview, a favorite date and a power behind the scenes..." *Interview*, June-July 2008

Chapter Eleven: I Am A Camera

p.97   "There was no question of his limitless energy...shooting lions in Arusha." from *PRIME GREEN: Remembering the Sixties* by Robert Stone, p. 94 Copyright (c) 2007 Ecco Press

p.97   "*Sometimes a Great Notion* has Shakespearean themes played out against a raw, burly Oregon backdrop...unchallenged, unsurpassed." From *Northwest Passages: A Literary Anthology of the Pacific Northwest from Coyote Tales to Roadside Attractions*, Bruce Barcott, ed. Copyright © 1994 Sasquatch Books

p.97   "*Notion* to my mind, is a great piece of work...you've got to have youth to do that." KK article by John Marshall, *Seattle-Post* November 16, 2001

p.97   "Like Day-Glo Johnny Appleseeds," Forester wrote, "Kesey and the Pranksters planted a wonderful psychedelic garden." Jeff Forester was co-writer with Kesey of *Caverns*, a collaborative novel published by Viking Penguin

p.98   "Before I took drugs,...suddenly I saw it. I saw it all." p. 105 from *Acid Dreams: The CIA, LSD and The Sixties Rebellion,* by Martin A. Lee and Bruce Shlain (see Acknowledgments for copyright information)

p.99   "Hello operator," he said, "This is God. G-O-D. I want to talk to Kerouac in Long Island."AG from *Timothy Leary: A Biography* by Robert Greenfield, p.129, Copyright © 2006 Harcourt Books, Inc.

p.101   "It was like tying yourself to the railroad track and seeing how big the train is, which is rather big." TW from *Conversations with Tom Wolfe,* page 132. Copyright © 1990, University Press of Mississippi

p.101   On the lam, Kesey declared, "If society wants me to be an outlaw,...all times need outlaws." KK to Burton Wolfe

p.102   "He is standing up with his arms folded...he is more muscular." from *The Electric Kool-Aid Acid Test* by Tom Wolfe, p.7 of the Picador Edition. Copyright (c) 1968, renewed 1996 Tom Wolfe. Reprinted by permission of Farrar, Straus & Giroux,LLC

p.102   "hairy, ape-chested, bulging biceps and triceps...back like a doll's wig." From *The Hippies* by Burton H. Wolfe,p.30. Copyright © 1968 Burton H. Wolfe

p.102   Anointed a "legitimate religious leader" by the media...EKAAT by Tom Wolfe

p.102   Footnote 16: Kesey: "...yes, if Southern Comfort is over-cloying honeysuckle... Faulkner is my admitted favorite." from *Kesey's Garage Sale*, p.183, by Ken Kesey, Copyright, (c) 1973 Viking/Compass Paperback editions

p.103   "I think," Robert Stone later observed, "he believed...labor that went into the creating of art." from "The Boys Octet," reprinted in *Spit in the Ocean # 7: All About Kesey*, p. 200,

Copyright (c) Penguin Books, 2003

p.104 "Oh, we were the All American Dream," Jay Thelin recalled...After my first LSD experience, I knew there was more to it than that." From *The Hippies* by Burton H. Wolfe,p.26. Copyright © 1968 Burton H. Wolfe

p.104 "Suddenly I saw all the bullshit in the whole educational...dropping out meant to conduct a revolution against the system." Ron Thelin to BHW in *The Hippies* by Burton H. Wolfe,p.26. Copyright © 1968 Burton H. Wolfe

p.104 "This was the avatar," Kesey said of the great speedy Beat, "Cassady. One of the great failures of all time...influenced by him." From "The Grateful Dead News," Robert Greenfield ed.

p.105 According to Dr. Leary: "There will probably be a dean of LSD... to qualify for an introduction to LSD 101." TL from *Timothy Leary: A Biography* by Robert Greenfield, p. 280. Copyright © 2006 by Robert Greenfield and Houghton Mifflin Harcourt, Inc.

p.105 "Everyone should start their own nation. Write their own declaration of Evolution." TL Ibid.

p.105 McLuhan had advised: "You call yourself a philosopher, a reformer...The new and approved accelerated brain." Ibid, p. 282

p.106 "Lysergic acid hits the spot/Forty billion neurons, that's a lot." Ibid, p. 282

Chapter Twelve: Auteur

p.107 "The Merry Pranksters never verbalized about the Other World...in the past or the future." from *Storming Heaven: LSD and the American Dream* by Jay Stevens, p.232. Copyright © 1987 by Jay Stevens. Used by permission of Grove/Atlantic, Inc.

p.109 Of Babbs, Ken Kesey later assessed: "He looked like a gleef, a Midwestern term for somebody who's not quite an oaf but is on his way there." KK Interview with Nick Hasted, "The Independent," Sunday, August 8th, 1999, "How We Met: Ken Kesey and Ken Babbs"

p.112 Allen Ginsberg concluded, "Neal Cassady drove Jack Kerouac to Mexico in a prophetic automobile...roads of an awakening nation." Allen Ginsberg from *Ginsberg: A Biography* by Barry Miles, Copyright © 1994 Viking Press.

p.112 "I saw that Cassady did everything a novel does, except he did it better because he was living it and not writing about it." KK p. 296, *Neal Cassady: The Fast Life of A Beat Hero* by David Sandinson and Graham Vickers (c) 2006, Chicago Review Press

p.112 "There's something about Cassady that keeps this nation moving and meeting itself. He's an avatar of the bohemian yesterday." KK from *Popular Paranoia: A Steamshovel Press Anthology* by Ken Thomas, p. 223 quoted from AP, July 28, 1999

p.113 "Like all the other candidates for beatitude,...the slash of oncoming sealed beams was his spots." From "The Day After Superman Died" by Ken Kesey from *Demon Box,* pg. 76. Copyright © 1987 Penguin Books

Chapter Thirteen: Blows Against the Empire

p.115 "Kesey was already talking about how writing...Furthur!" from EKAAT/TW. Copyright © 1968, renewed 1996 Tom Wolfe. Reprinted by permission of Farrar, Straus and Giroux LLC.

p.115 Kesey would conclude that the bus "was a metaphor that's instantly comprehensible...just like Cowboy Neal." to Jeff Barnard, Associated Press April 24, 2000.

p.116 "I never felt the slightest hesitation...stick around." from *New York* Magazine Feb 14, 1972

p.116 "the yoga of a man driven to the cliff...moments of a life with no retreat." *A Long Strange Trip: The Inside History of the Grateful Dead* By Dennis McNally, p. 109, Copyright © 2002 Broadway Books/Random House, Inc.

pp.116-117 "What was it that had brought a man so high of promise to so low a state in so short a time? Well, the answers can be found in just one short word, my friends, in just one all-well-used syllable: Dope!" from EKAAT/TW p.5 Copyright © 1968, renewed 1996 Tom Wolfe. Reprinted by permission of Farrar, Straus and Giroux LLC.

p.117 he'd "rather be a lightning rod than a seismograph." EKAAT/TW p.8 Copyright © 1968, renewed 1996 Tom Wolfe. Reprinted by permission of Farrar, Straus and Giroux LLC.

p.117 "We're the people who planted the seeds. Whether it's artistically valid or not, we have to cultivate the crop." KK to Jeff Barnard, AP Interview, April 24, 2000

p.117 identified Ken Kesey as "hero...an eternal binge." from *The Hippies,* p.27, Copyright ©

1968 by Burton H. Wolfe

p.117-118   Chloe Scott testifies, "I've been on better Mexican buses...motifs and décor of the trip."from *The Further Inquiry* by Ken Kesey, Published by Viking Press. Copyright © 1990 Ken Kesey and Kesey LLC

p.118   "Gradually the Prankster attitude began...naïve faith in causality." From EKAAT/ TW,p.142 Copyright © 1968, renewed 1996 Tom Wolfe. Reprinted by permission of Farrar, Straus and Giroux LLC

p.118   Footnote 19: "The painted psychedelic bus is an American icon like Thoreau's Walden Pond or the Statue of Liberty. It is a modern Ark of the Covenant, rusting in a cow pasture"—Walt Curtis, writing for the Oregon Cultural Heritage Commission website OregonCulturalHeritage.com

Chapter Fourteen: Days of Heaven

p.121   from *The Proud Highway,* p. 512 by Hunter S. Thompson, Copyright © 1997 by Hunter S. Thompson. Used by permission of Villard Books, a division of Random House, Inc.

p.121   "I'm trying Kesey's book...fuck 'em." HST from *The Proud Highway,* p.653 by Hunter S. Thompson, Copyright © 1997 by Hunter S. Thompson. Used by permission of Villard Books, a division of Random House, Inc.

p.122   "The hordes snarling down the road...but this was incredible." HST from "Walking with the King," p. 80 of *Spit in the Ocean #7: All About Kesey,* Copyright © 2003 Penguin USA

p.123   "You had no sense of there being any light...We out-eviled them." KK

p.123   Jerry Garcia remembered, "We were younger than the Pranksters...Our music scared them." Ibid

p.124   "Garcia was as well read as anybody I'd ever met. He understood Martin Buber's *I and Thou*...My mind is moving him!" KK in *Dark Star: An Oral Biography of Gerry Garcia* by Robert Greenfield, p. 76

p.124   "You can read *I and Thou* for two hours...things." from Kesey's Garage Sale, p.180, Copyright © 1973 Viking/Compass Editions

p.124   "like a really crack terrorist group...that people were playing to." KK from *Dark Star: An Oral Biography of Gerry Garcia,* Robert Greenfield, ed, p.78. Copyright © 2009, Plexus Publishing

p.125   In 1968, shortly after publication of *The Electric Kool-Aid Acid Test,* he told Lawrence Dietz of *New York Magazine:* "I thought, gee, this guy's...can come out in some way.'" TW in *New York Magazine*

p.125   "Following a profound new experience,...interpreted." TW in EKAAT, p.128 Copyright © 1968, renewed 1996 Tom Wolfe. Reprinted by permission of Farrar, Straus and Giroux LLC.

p.126   from *City of Words* British literary critic Tony Tanner wrote "Kesey's...a super-victim." From *City of Words: American Fiction 1950-1970,* Copyright © 1971 Harper & Row

PART THREE: THE SAVANT

Chapter Fifteen: Krassner Agonistes

pp.129-141: All references to Paul Krassner's material whether published or as told to author by Paul Krassner are used by permission of Paul Krassner. See Acknowledgments.

Chapter Sixteen: Utopian Thought in the Western World

p.143   "It's bad on the nerves to see a tough-ass in quicksand,...nobody knows the difference anyway?" from *Proud Highway* p. 512 by Hunter S. Thompson, Copyright © 1997 by Hunter S. Thompson. Used by permission of Villard Books, a division of Random House, Inc.

pp.143-144   The Grateful Dead, who were everything to Ken Kesey: "They weren't just playing what was on the music sheets...in touch with the invisible." KK from Video Short following Documentary by Pete Shapiro, "Tie-Died; Rock n. Roll's Most Deadicated Fans"

p.145   Listen to him speak about his future and fate in 1965: "First, let me make it understood I am not a writer...couldn't continue my work." p. 94-95 from *The Road Story and the Rebel: Moving through Film, Fiction and Television* by Katie Mills Copyright © 2006, University of Southern Illinois Press

p.147   Jay Stevens...believes that minus "that cocky little boho" Owsley the Acid Tests...from

Storming Heaven: LSD and the American Dream by Jay Stevens, copyright ©197 by Jay Stevens. Used by permission of Grove/Atlantic, Inc.

p.147   "And, Jesus, boy," Owsley later recalled, " that was sort of like getting strapped onto a rocket sled...it by playing around." Bruce Eisner, "Interview with an Alchemist" August 28, 2004 *Bruce Eisner Interviews*

p.147   Owsley told writer David Gans, "Kesey was the kind of guy...at another level." From *Conversations with the Dead*, p. 299. Copyright © 2002 Da Capo Press

p.147-148 "None of these people in Kesey's scene...and he kind of laughed at me." Owsley "Interview with an Alchemist" August 28, 2004 *Bruce Eisner Interviews*

p.148   Owsley was quoted in *Rolling Stone*: "For most people the proper...or where it would've gone?" RS Interview with Owsley

Chapter Seventeen: Holy Mayhem Inc.

p.149   "The man in the space suit is the prince of disorder...bossdom for one second." from *Living With the Dead* by David Dalton, p. 32. Copyright © 1996.By permission of Little, Brown & Co.

p.149   Lee Quarnstrom provides an aerial view: "We were, in Kesey's own words, exploring inner space...without going crazy." from "The Bust at Ken Kesey's Place" by Lee Quarnstrom *The Realist*: Issue 139

p.150   "Go back to your cuckoo pad. You should have stayed in the nest instead of flying over it, you big cuckoo!" see EKAAT/TW p. 152

p.150   "You can write it and put my name on it. Write anything you want." Lee Quarnstrom from "The Bust at Ken Kesey's Place" by Lee Quarnstrom *The Realist*: Issue 139

pp.150-151 Krassner said, "I was MC-ing...10,000 years." PK to author

p.151   Good fun according to Jerry Garcia: "The Acid Test was the prototype...cross interference and weirdness." Gerry Garcia from *Dark Star: An Oral Biography of Gerry Garcia*, Robert Greenfiled, ed., Copyright © 2009 Plexus Publishing

p.152   "The man has all the usual stigmata of the bohemian...to smile diplomatically." KK from p. 368-369, *The Portable Sixties Reader* by Ann Charters. Copyright (c) 2003 Penguin Books

p.152   Kesey waxed reasonably: "The general tone of things...(A. C. outlets will be provided.)" from "The Acid Test Files" internet

p.153   Then, according to Grateful Dead manager Rock Scully, "One of the cops pulls out his gun...Peace!'"from *Living With the Dead* by David Dalton, p. 31. Copyright © 1996. By permission of Little, Brown & Co.

p.153   According to Scully, Graham "won't let Kesey in. He's not on the list!...elicited from the astonished Kesey, "It's my show, asshole." "Says fucking who?" Ibid, p. 32

p.153   Footnote 19: Re: The Trips Festival, Graham had a bone to pick with Kesey from the beginning: "I remember the Merry Pranksters were there and they were pretty spaced out... How can you know that?" from Bill Graham Presents: My Life Inside Rock and Out by Bill Graham and Robert Greenfield, p.136 Copyright © 1992 Bill Graham

pp.153-154 Bill Graham recalled the fracas differently...see p. 136-137 from *Bill Graham Presents: My Life Inside Rock and Out* by Bill Graham and Robert Greenfield, p. 136 Copyright © 1992 Bill Graham

p.154   "The first full rock dance concerts...nobody would give a damn." From *The Hippies* by Burton H. Wolfe, p.43. Copyright © 1968 Burton H. Wolfe

pp.154-155 "It was a peaceful, relaxing time in Mexico...cow." From *The Hippies*/BHW, p. 33

p.155   "I thought Jed was zapped out for good...a superhuman job." From *The Hippies*/BHW, p. 201

Chapter Eighteen: The Jail Interviews

p.157   "Oh trials, trials. Man, they're a horrible experience...will spread to other institutions." From *The Hippies*/BHW, p. 201

p.158   "There was always grass in jail," Kesey recalled, "and speed...that are influencing our lives." KK to BHW in *The Hippies*, p. 202

pp.158-159 "You know, I have a theory about all this...because of their position in the straight society." KK to BHW in *The Hippies*, pp. 197-198

p.159   "Our boss is an old white-haired fart known as Bushie," he wrote...And don't cut on the push, cut on the pull.' KK from *Kesey's Jail Journal*, p. 40. Copyright 2003, Kesey LLC

p.159   "Jail didn't hurt at all. I liked it…movie ours is invalid." KK from "GoodReads"(Internet)

p.159   "There are too many things to be done…The millennium started some months ago." BHW in *The Hippies*, pp. 198

p.159   "Well, like take McMurphy. He was just there, like antimatter…minds are blown." KK to BHW in *The Hippies,* pp. 199, copyright © 1968 Burton H. Wolfe

pp.160-161   "The movement is growing and will last a long time…and they will be that way forever."

p.161   "We used to be equals. Now it's Kesey's trip. We go to his place. We take his acid. We do what he wants."Neal Cassady From *The Holy Goof* by William Plummer (Thunder's Mouth Press) Copyright © 1981 William Plummer

p.161   "More and more," William Plummer wrote in *The Holy Goof,*…" to change the world." From *The Holy Goof* by William Plummer (Thunder's Mouth Press) Copyright © 1981 William Plummer

Chapter Nineteen: Sea Change

p.163   "What the Kesey thing depended on was who you were when you were there…It was magic, far-out beautiful magic." Jerry Garcia from *Jerry Garcia from Conversations with the Dead: The Grateful Dead Interview Book* by David Gans, , Copyright © 2002 Da Capo Press

p.164   "They'll have to take LSD,"…The whole world will have to turn on." KK to BHW from *The Hippies,* p. 202, copyright © 1968 Burton H. Wolfe

Chapter Twenty: The Rise and Fall and Rise Again of the High Ideal

p.169   "A new man was born smoking pot while besieging the Pentagon,…as he destroys the old." From *Do It: Scenarios of the Revolution* by Jerry Rubin, Copyright © 1970 Touchstone Books

p.170   "Each person will become his own Buddha…most powerful aphrodisiac ever discovered by man" Tim Leary from *Playboy Interview,* September 1966

Chapter Twenty-One: Fantasy Island

p.181   Tim—"a specific cure for homosexuality…" from *Playboy Interview,* September 1966

p.182   "neopagans, neochristians, agnostics, witches…diviners and occultists" TL from *Playboy Interview*

p.182   He discovers, "all forms, all structures…God-heart-penis light." TL from *Playboy Interview,* September 1966

p.183   "After several billion years…I was stunned with guilt." Ib.cit

p.184   (Of the October 1966 performance in The Reincarnation of Jesus Christ as Timothy Leary, Abbie Hoffman's wife Anita recalled…Shameless!") from Abbie Hoffman *Tim Leary: Outside Looking In* Parker Street Press

p.185   "Late terrestrial species architecture…from tidal wave and avalanche." TL from *The Ghosts of Tim Leary and Hunter S. Thompson* by Joe Bageant in The Beast June 2007

p.185   In 1961 Wilson Van Dusen wrote in *LSD and the Enlightenment of Zen,* "It has been called satori in Japanese Zen…universal experience." TL

p.185   "Take it from me—it was no illusion," Tim Lott of the *London Independent*…tap the drug's full potential." Obituary of Albert Hofman

p.187   According to Brotherhood alum Bob Stubby Tierney, "There was nothing in the world…We really had power." from *Dazed and Confused,* November 2006, p 121

p.188   For Kahn, who "war-gamed" apocalypse after taking LSD, all was context: "War is…degree and standards" from *Tar Sands* by Andrew Nikiforuk, Greystone Press 2006.

Chapter Twenty-Two: High Crimes

p.189   "Consider the basic metaphor of the 'shepherd' and the 'sheep'…who the fuck are you?" TL from *Timothy Leary: A Biography* by Robert Greenfield.

p.190   Dr. Leary handicapped the race: "There is, of course, a high church and a low church. Watts is high-church Anglican"). TL from *Timothy Leary: A Biography* by Robert Greenfield.

p.191   "Every brother should have what he needs to do his thing…It's all free because it's yours!" from *The Realist* (1967) Copyright © Paul Krassner. Granted by permission of Paul Krassner

Chapter Twenty-Three: The Abuses of Enchantment

p. 193   "The utopian sentiments of these hippies was not to be put down lightly…traditional forms of leadership." From Ramparts article, "the Social History of the Hippie Movement" by Warren Hinckle, March 1967

p.194 "world controlled by a stupid thug from Texas...the White Hope of the west." HST from *The Proud Highway,* Copyright © 1997 by Hunter S. Thompson. Used by permission of Villard Books, a division of Random House, Inc.

pp.194-195 Sara H. quotes from interview with Mark Christensen

Chapter Twenty-Four: .000001 and Much, Much More

p.197 "...the other end of the rainbow was Haight-Ashbury...without being hassled."from *Acid Dreams: The CIA, LSD and the Sixties Rebellion* by Martin A. Lee and Bruce Shlain. Copyright © 1985 by Martin A. Lee and Bruce Shlain

pp.197-198 "It was interesting for me to find Negroes and some of my beatnik friends... time washing your soul."from *The Hippies,* p.56. Copyright © 1968 Burton H. Wolfe

p.198 Inside the envelope was a triangle of Swiss cheese and a note from Kesey: "All we can really offer is shelter, lunch and infamy. Even so, you are my No. 1 draft choice." from the Oregon Cultural Heritage Commission website on the origin of "Spit in the Ocean," written by Walt Curtis. OregonCulturalHeritage.com

p.199 "Our Syxx-eyed Jacky Butts...His slogan: 'It's thee water makes thee wette.'" from Introduction to *"Spit in the Ocean, #1"* Copyright Kesey LLC

pp.199-200 Writing for the Oregon Cultural Heritage Commission, Walt allowed, "I realize it's too soon to evaluate...the road of its own volition."

pp.200-205 from interview conducted by Mark Christensen with Tom McGovern and Walt Curtis

Chapter Twenty-Five: Manchild in the Promised Land

p.207 "School sucks. The white honkie structure that has been handed down to us on a plastic platter is meaningless to us!...of the universe." White Panther Manifesto

p.207 "I think it's time we graduated out of acid!...Des Moines is taking it." from *The Village Voice,* October 27th, 1966, Vol. XII, No. 2

p.208 Take this from the Berkeley Barb: "In unity we shall shower the country with waves of ecstasy of purification!...rhythm and dancing." from The Berkeley Barb

p.208 Tim Coffin got down to particulars: "Dope not drugs—alcohol is a drug, pot is DOPE;!... we all have to make our choices." From *The Great Speckled Bird*

p.210 "Where but the moment before," London had written, "was only the wide desolation and invincible roar, is now a man, erect, full-statured!...His heels are winged, and in them is the swiftness of the sea!..." Jack London from *The House of Pride and Other Tales of Hawaii 1912*

p.214 "Listen! Wake up! You are God!!...You'll be reborn!" TL from *The High Priest,* Copyright © 1995 Ronin Publishing.

Chapter Twenty-Six: Heaven on Earth

p.215 "!...the summer of love!...rocketing towards them. From Scott Hulet, *Longboard Magazine*

p.221 from "I Feel Like I'm Fixin' To Die Rag" Words and Music by Joe MacDonald. © 1965, renewed 1993 Alcatraz Corner Music. Permission to reprint lyrics granted by Alcatraz Corner Music.

Chapter Twenty-Seven: Burbank Babylon

p.229 "The cybernetic age entails a change!...acceptance of a new age." From *Play Power: Exploring the International Underground* by Richard Neville © 1970 Jonathan Cape, Ltd. p.233

p.229 Tim Leary's important advice: "When you turn on, remember, you are not a naughty boy getting high for kicks." TL from *Start Your Own Religion* by Tim Leary, Ronin Publishing, 2005

pp.229-230 "To turn on, you need a sacrament. A sacrament is a visible external thing which turns the keys to the inner doors. Today the sacrament is LSD. New sacraments are coming along." "You must start your own religion!...Mythic context." TL from *The Politics of Ecstasy* by Tim Leary, Ronin Publishing, 1998

p.230 "You will find it absolutely necessary to leave the city!...a god in the Garden of Eden." TL from *Turn On, Tune In, Drop Out,* Ronin Publishing, 1999 (6th ed.)

p.231 "When I was back there in seminary school,!...You CAN NOT petition the Lord with prayer!" from "The Soft Parade" words and lyrics by Jim Morrison and the Doors, © 1969, renewed 1995. Permission granted by Hal Leonard Publishers, LLC.

PART FOUR: SHEEP, THE SEQUEL

Chapter Twenty-Eight: Working on My Fantasy
p.237 "The escalation of the war so completely dovetails!...it took a political form" from *The 60's: Day of Hope, Days of Rage* by Todd Gitlin © Copyright 1987, Bantam Books
pp.237-239 Conversations with Jean Whitman, Interview with Mark Christensen
pp.240-243 Quotes from Jean and Bobby Miller, from interviews with Mark Christensen
p.245 The quest for the Apocalyptic...bring her sweet release." From *Soul on Ice* by Eldridge Cleaver © 1971 Eldridge Cleaver, renewed 1999, Delta Books
p.245 Ken Kesey told his pal Ed McClanahan, "It's a cop trip, and it's a big mistake. They shouldn't be trying to out-asshole...be the good guys." From *Famous People I Have Known* by Ed McClanahan, p. 82. University of Kentucky Press, 1985
p.245 "But this is not a commonplace shirt," Ed wrote...my Saturday-night-at-the-Fillmore shirt." Ibid.
p.247 Faye Kesey in *Rolling Stone:* "Her image is water gushing forth...blocking its progress." in *Rolling Stone Interview,* March 7, 1970
p.247 "His voice is soft and gentle...Hagen position, working on my fantasy." in *Rolling Stone* Interview, March 7, 1970

Chapter Thirty: The Revolution Has Happened
p.249 "Kirk, what's happening with Cuckoo's Nest?" letter to Kirk Douglas, producer of film version of "One Flew Over the Cuckoo's Nest"
p.249 "I was supposed to have deep intellectual discussions with Kesey...jails we had in common." Dale Wasserman p.287 from *The Impossible Musical* by Dale Wasserman, p.70, "Beautiful. Outasight...It's giving me a complex."
p.250 "They've not only gone back to the book, making a lot of changes in the Wasserman script,...caught thirty trout by noon."
p.250 "I have had to go through two crappy arbitration procedures which took a couple of years...I think the timing is right now and I'm ready to go." Letter from Kirk Douglas to Kesey, July 30, 1970
p.250 "What must be done, he feels, is to involve the audience...the film is being spliced together." Kirk Douglas to KK. Ibid.
p.251 Personally" Kurland found no "visualization that would be more empathic to the audience...in the minds of the audience." Kurland letter to KK
p.251 "The thing about writing is that writers never seem to get any better than their first book... and I worry that I won't." Kesey, Interview with Mary Jane Fenex and Matthew Rick
p.251 "I talked with Norman Mailer about it,...is *Cuckoo's Nest* the best I will ever be?" Meanwhile..."I'm not through with my work on acid, and nobody I know is either." (see above)
p.251 "The revolution has happened...All that incredible education is teaching them there is no way out." Kesey to Robert Strand, *The Los Angeles Times,* December 14, 1971
p.252-253 "I moved to San Francisco in February 1971,"..."It was a most auspicious beginning." From *Kesey's Last Prank* by Paul Krassner, p. 14 of *Spit In The Ocean #7: All About Kesey,* © 2003 Penguin Books. Originally published in "High Times," February 2002, reprinted by permission of Paul Krassner

Chapter Thirty: The Dream Museum
p.255 "This book and the mindset it speaks...for a handful of dust" from *Introduction to Kesey's Garage Sale* by Arthur Miller, Copyright © 1973 by Arthur Miller
p.263 "To shoot a genocidal robot policeman...stay high and wage revolutionary war." TL to *Rolling Stone* editor Robert Greenfield, "Tim Leary: Or, Bomb for Buddha," *Rolling Stone,* December 2, 1970
p.263 "Don't misunderstand me, Doctor; I wish in no way to cool your fervor...creation, not more headlines." Ken Kesey, "An Open Letter to Timothy Leary," *The Marijuana Review* 1, no 6 (January-June, 1971)
p.264 "We don't believe Ken Kesey...white racist ethic to me." TL to *Rolling Stone* editor Robert Greenfield, "Tim Leary: Or, Bomb for Buddha," *Rolling Stone,* December 2, 1970
p.264 "Read the writings of Huey P. Newton...That's what the Panthers are." TL from *Timothy*

Leary: A Biography, p. 414, Copyright © 2006, Harcourt Books, Inc.

p.264   "It's inevitable. Their system is based on guns…white light of the Buddha." TL Ibid.

p.264   "My advice to the Weathermen…to free John Sinclair" TL, ibid pp. 414-415

p.264   "Something's wrong with Leary's brain…his mind has been blown by acid." Ibid, p. 419

p.265   I've just met a Marxist/Leninist named Kim Il Sung…I'll never stop saying Kim Il Sung" from *The Los Angeles Times,* Zachary Lazar, October 19th, 2008

p.265   "As for this 'don't trust anyone over 30 shit,'…'drop the zero." From James Kunen, author of *The Strawberry Statement*

p.267   Berkeley Barb declaring, "A new sex-pot church will attempt…truly Venereal religion." From the *Berkely Barb,* November 1971

p.267   "Proper love today is uninhibited…wild, delicious things." From *The Sensuous Woman* by J. Footnote 24, 267: "When a man enters a woman,…that takes muscle" Ibid.

p.268   "In the hagiography of the Bod Biz…true and total awareness." From Jane Howard, *A Different Woman,* Plume 1982

p.268   "who can and must relate to their sexual drives…are human beings." From *The Harrad Experiment* by Robert Rimmer, Prometheus Books, 1990 (25th Anniversary Edition)

Chapter Thirty-One: California Girls

p.271   "Every woman has built into her cells…and appropriate at the time." —Tim Leary, *The Politics of Ecstasy*

Chapter Thirty-Two: Scepter of Democracy

p.294   'House organs proliferate espousing…Even corruption gets recycled." —Kesey's *Bend in the River* "Official Policy"

pp.296-298 Conversation with Lloyd Marbet with author Mark Christensen

p.300   "We're going through a great time, an incredible revolution…no one can." KK in Kesey's *Bend in the River* "Official Policy"

p.300   "The future is ours to mold like a piece of clay…need for existence." KK in Kesey's *Bend in the River* "Official Policy"

p.301   "Because voting on the delegates is one of the most important things we are doing…The future of Oregon must be decided by the community." KK

p.302   Kesey announced, "I'm not against women. I'm defending the small…from the effort we are engaged in." KK

p.302   "You don't plow under the corn because the seed was planted with a neighbor's shovel." KK from *Kesey's Garage Sale,* p. 219, "An Impolite Interview with Ken Kesey" conducted by Paul Krassner © 1973 Kesey LLC

p.306   "We get it together for a little while…to have to take up the slack." KK in Kesey's *Bend in the River* "Official Policy"

p.303   Weil's premise began: "There are no bad drugs, only…point of view." From Andrew Weil, *The Natural Mind* by Andrew Weil, Chapter 7, p.129, Copyright © 1998 Houghton Mifflin Co.

PART FIVE: THE SAVED

Chapter Thirty-Three: The District Sleeps Alone Tonight

p.313   "Lovemaking is not a paranoid…even laugh." From *Thy Neighbor's Wife* by Gay Talese

Chapter Thirty-Four: Venusians

p.325   p.299 "Stand in this spotlight, feel this eye pass over you. You are suddenly changed, lifted, elevated and alone. But, there's the scaly rub, right? Because, if you go around to the other end of that eye, and look through at the star shining there so elevated, you see that the adoring telescope has a cross hair built in it, and notches in the barrel filed for luminaries… Kennedy…King…Joplin…Hemingway." *Demon Box,* p.304-305, © Copyright Viking Penguin, Inc. and Kesey LLC 1986 pp.322-326 Conversation between Marty Christensen and author Mark Christensen reprinted courtesy of permission of Marty Christensen

p.331   claiming that the only money headed his way was "what's left after the producer buys his secretary's mom a Datsun," KK from the *Oregon Times* Magazine, July 1976

p.333   Writing for the conservative *National Review,* he pissed on Bob Dylan, concluding, "It's

All Over Now Baby Blue,"… line in neuronaut exploration?" TL from *Timothy Leary: A Biography* by Robert Greenfield, page 522

p.333 "When an entire generation…Bill Graham, Gold Meir, Allen Ginsberg," Ibid.

p.333 "It is not an accident that the Weathermen…took their name from a depressing Dylan song," Ibid.

p.334 Time, Inc.'s John Riley wrote, "The perpetually cashless Kesey became miffed at Brand's refusal to lend an occasional $5 for a tank of gasoline." John Riley, *People* Magazine, March 22, 1976

Chapter Thirty-Five: Last Supper

p.327 "The first time that I ever saw Marty…near his printing press." Gus Van Sant in his Introduction to Marty Christensen's poetry collection, "My Flashlight was Attacked by Bats"

pp.328-335 from conversation held between Ken Kesey, Walt Curtis, Marty Christensen, and Lorna Viken, February 1975. Recorded by Walt Curtis. Permission granted for use by Walt Curtis

Chapter Thirty-Six: Dying in the Provinces

p.337 "I looked through all of these books the high school kids are reading…Christ allegory taking place in a nut house."Ken Kesey from "Earth Shoes" *Co-Evolution Quarterly* Spring 1976, reprinted in S*pit In The Ocean #7: All About Kesey*, Copyright © 2003 Kesey LLC

p.337 "Poor Fish" permission granted by Marty Christensen

p.338 "To My Prick" permission granted by Walt Curtis

p.342 "They slap me when I fight and beat me…We do it every day." From *TRUCK* by Katherine Dunn, p. 48 Copyright © 1971 by Katherine Dunn, used by permission of the author.

Chapter Thirty-Seven: The Story of H

p.354 "The Girl with the Green Eyes" permission granted by Walt Curtis

Chapter Thirty-Eight: Last Go Round

p.357 "Author Ken Kesey and singer Taj Mahal…at next year's roundup." Dick Cockle, *The Portland Oregonian,* September 14th, 1984

pp.357-367 from interviews conducted with MiSchelle McMindes and court transcripts

Chapter Forty: Drowning in the Wishing Well

p.377 "Did you ever read The Spear of Destiny?…whoever has this thing has the power of absolute good or absolute evil." Jerry Garcia from *Conversations with the Dead: The Grateful Dead Interview Book* by David Gans, p. 74, Copyright © 2002 Da Capo Press.

p.377 Kesey remarked, re: The Hell's Angels. "It even reached the point where I gave up on them. They just wouldn't be nice…feel it when they're on you." KK to Hunter Thompson from *Fear and Loathing: The Strange and Terrible Saga of Hunter S. Thompson* by Paul Perry and Ralph Steadman,p. 243. Copyright © 1997, Thunder's Mouth Press

p.377 "I know what you mean,… Want to fight?" HT Ibid. p.244

p.383 "We got into acid. We felt like we were dealing with the end of time…that is part of our country." Kesey from the *Saturday Review* Interview, 1983 from *Can't Find My Way Home* by Martin Torgoff, p. 95 Simon & Schuster Paperbacks, 2004

p.383 "They don't want it there anymore—nobody wants to see a factory downtown…logging town." from "Ken Kesey Kisses No Ass" Interview with *Chip Brown Esquire* Magazine, September 1992

p.383 "I feel very feminine about *Demon Box*…" Kesey to Chip Brown from "Kesey Kisses No Ass"

p.383 "The air is thick with broken promises…and I broke that." from *Demon Box*, p. 369, by Ken Kesey, Copyright (c) 1986 Viking Press and Kesey LLC

p.384 "You know, some people say syphilis came…'If you do, you'll blow the seals out of your power steering.'" from "Blows to the Spirit; Where and How the American Male Has Taken it On the Chin" Dialogue between Robert Stone and Ken Kesey. From *Esquire* Magazine, June 1986

p.385 "I like the mad side of a writer…then the bus *Furthur*." Walt Curtis to Mark Christensen

p.385 "Hairballs. Kesey mentioned the bull frogs,…because he'll kill the bull frogs." WC to Mark Christensen p.385 "For a thousand years or more...pierced the side of Jesus. Supposedly." Ken Kesey in conversation with Walt Curtis, as told to Mark Christensen

Chapter Forty-One: Kiss No Ass

p.387 "Reporters come up here expecting me...corny 'America the Beautiful' people" Ken Kesey quoted in The Oregonian (Jeff Baker obituary of KK) November 11, 2001

p.389 In 1993 Kesey said, "The old bus, when she got back from Woodstock, her heart was broken...No wonder the country is crazy."

p.390 Kesey's friend Ed McClanahan had been told by a "spokesparty" with the Smithsonian that, "Mr. Kesey is running around Oregon...It would be a nice thing to do, but it would be a mistake." from *Famous People I Have Known* by Ed McLanahan, p. 169. University of Kentucky Press

p.390 A shameless Kesey declared, "I kind of feel bad about it because it's going to be so much more beautiful than the other rock and roll cars." from Associated Press, quoted from Spokane Spokesman-Review, April 22, 1997

p.390 "His face looks suddenly noble and serious; his eyes are revealed as piercingly, beautifully blue." Nick Hasted from *The Independent*, August 19, 1998

p.390 "I'm not gonna bark after that dog any more. There's plenty of books. I don't want to be Stephen King, and just do that because I can....going to drain our minds." to Nick Hasted (see above)

p.390 "It's hard for people to understand how good he was...and he doesn't blink." about Tom Wolfe in interview with David Loftus

p.391 from Footnote "He (Wolfe) had all the notes and all our tapes, so it was accurate...the East Coast is always 30 years behind." (see above)

p.391 "We were up at my brother's farm, Spaceheater...And that's the last time I ever saw Wolfe." from *Kesey's Garage Sale,* Copyright © 1973 Ken Kesey

p.391 "If our government had its wishes, it would have Baptists coast to coast, all the same...We know it's bad for ya, but we know in what way it's bad for ya." interview with D. Loftus

p.392 "We sold out...We're not meant to win." interview with David Loftus

p.392 "I received my working orders high on acid...working on it just as hard as they can." to David Loftus, 1992

p.392 "There's an energy I haven't seen out there in 25 years...our world beyond hope." interview with David Loftus

p.393 "Novel writing is a corrosive, inhospitable pastime...get a blessing from the Pope." from *The Galveston Daily News*

p.393 "We raise cows...you pedal in your room to nowhere."

Chapter Forty-Two: End Game

p.395 On the artist and his art: "All the great writers have a touch of magic...Everybody's dead, but somehow you're uplifted." KK from interview with Ellen O'Brien article, "Accent on Seniors," *Philadelphia Inquirer*

pp.396-397 Additional quotes from same interview

p.397 Kesey had kind words. "Hey, Jerry—what's happening? I caught your funeral...gurus glorified." KK from "Departures: Three Heavies Take Their Leave"/*Spit In The Ocean #7,* p.63, Copyright © 2003 Penguin Books.

p.397 "The frontiers we...came stumbling onto."

p.397 ""Nowhere else in history...to destroy itself."

p.396-398 Van Sant recalled, "As we watched a sequence of the bus getting bogged down...we lost the big game."" KK as quoted by Gus Van Sant in the Foreward to *Spit In The Ocean #7,* "Shazam!" p. xviii, Copyright © 2003 Penguin Books

p.398 Jeff Forester quotes as told to Mark Christensen

p.398 "It was quite obvious," Kesey said, "that while it was going on, we were changing history by some higher being" KK to Joseph A. Lieberman in *The Eugene Weekly*

Chapter Forty-Three: Stairway to Heaven

p.399 "When the fog cleared, Kesey held his face in his hands,...dropped to the floor." Jeff Forester, "Sparks Fly Upward: Remembering Ken Kesey," *San Francisco Chronicle*, November 30, 2001 p.400 "The war on drugs is the war against pro-choice. The war on drugs is a war to make Americans respect authority." TL , *The Politics of Pharmacology* (Ronin Press)

p.400 "I have been very involved in the high tech of dying." TL, *Aquarius Revisited,* by Peter Whitmer page xvi. Copyright © 1987 MacMillan Press.

p.400 "There's 27,000 people a year killed here in alcohol-related deaths…a little bit out of their control" KK in BBC documentary, "LSD: The Beyond Within"

p.400 "He was doing really well…he was saying goodbye." Zane Kesey

p.401 "At Sundown" permission granted by Marty Christensen

Chapter Forty-Four: Last Rites

p.403 "Everyone I've seen die has died of being alone…keep better track of each other." KK in *The Los Angeles Times,* October 5, 1986

p.404 "I still have a conversation with him, he appears in my dreams. After he died one of his grandkids said, 'Now who is going to teach us how to hypnotize the chickens?'" PK from "Kesey's Last Prank," p. 17 from *Spit in the Ocean #7* reprinted with permission from Paul Krassner.

p.406 Walt Curtis says, "There was something about the man that I really trusted…a warrior of the spirit." WC to Mark Christensen

p.406 "It's 'why me?' what is it about me,…him to do it." KK in *Aquarius Revisited* by Peter Whitmer, p. 441. Copyright © 1987 MacMillan Press.

Epilogue: Flashbacks

p.407 "What's the job of a writer in contemporary America right now?…" Ken Kesey from Video Reality Club Presentation October 24, 1989

Photo Credits: ACID CHRIST

All black & white photographs that appear in this book are by Clyde Keller, Copyright © 2009 Clyde Keller Productions

Front Cover: Ken Kesey in Performance, the night of the Hoo-Haw Arts Festival, June 6th, 1976

Part One: Ken Kesey takes the stage at the Hoo-Haw Arts Festival, June 6th, 1976

Part Two: Kesey turns the camera on the press as a young, bemused Bill Murray (left, with mike) looks on, June 5th, 1976

Part Three: Walt Curtis (foreground) and Paul Krassner in the Kesey barn, on the eve of the Hoo-Haw Arts Festival, 1976

Part Four: William Burroughs (left) and Marty Christensen outside the Kesey Barn, June 5th, 1976

Part Five: Ken Kesey walking with son Zane at the Kesey family farm, Pleasant Hill, Oregon, June, 1976

INDEX

Note: Page numbers followed by "n" refer to footnotes.
Page numbers in italics refer to illustrations.